W9-DCV-681

A Certain World

Robert B. Love
Oxford
Jy 27, 89 (Sept 11, 89)
3508

A Certain World

A Commonplace Book

❧

W. H. AUDEN

3508

faber and faber

First published in Great Britain in 1971
by Faber and Faber Limited
3 Queen Square London WC1
First published in Faber Paperbacks in 1982
Printed in Great Britain by
Fakenham Press Limited, Fakenham, Norfolk
All rights reserved

©1970 by W. H. Auden
Pages 427–431 constitute an
extension of this copyright page

CONDITIONS OF SALE

This book is sold subject to the condition that it shall not, by way of trade or
otherwise, be lent, resold, hired out or otherwise circulated without the
publisher's prior consent in any form of binding or cover other than that in
which it is published and without a similar condition including this condition
being imposed on the subsequent purchaser

British Library Cataloguing in Publication Data

Auden, W. H.
A certain world.
1. Literature—History and criticism
I. Title
809   PN523

ISBN 0-571-11940-9

For Geoffrey Grigson

Foreword

Biographies of writers, whether written by others or themselves, are always superfluous and usually in bad taste. A writer is a maker, not a man of action. To be sure, some, in a sense all, of his works are transmutations of his personal experiences, but no knowledge of the raw ingredients will explain the peculiar flavor of the verbal dishes he invites the public to taste: his private life is, or should be, of no concern to anybody except himself, his family and his friends.

I realize, however, that this compilation is a sort of autobiography. As Chesterton wrote:

> There is at the back of every artist's mind something like a pattern or a type of architecture. The original quality in any man of imagination is imagery. It is a thing like the landscape of his dreams; the sort of world he would like to make or in which he would wish to wander; the strange flora and fauna of his own secret planet; the sort of thing he likes to think about. This general atmosphere, and pattern or structure of growth, governs all his creations, however varied.

Here, then, is a map of my planet. Certain features are, deliberately or necessarily, missing. There are, for example, hardly any references to music, which is very important to me. Aside from purely technical analysis, nothing can be *said* about music, except when it is bad; when it is good, one can only listen and be grateful.

Then, much as we should all like to, none of us can preserve our personal planet as an unsullied Eden. According to our time and place, unpleasant facts from the world we all have in common keep intruding, matters about which either we are compelled, against our will, to think or we feel it our duty to think, though in such matters nobody can tell another what his duty is. The bulk of this book will, I hope, make pleasant reading, but there are some entries which will, I trust, disturb a reader as much as they disturb me.

I have tried to keep my own reflections (the unsigned entries) to a minimum, and let others, more learned, intelligent, imaginative, and witty than I, speak for me.

W. H. A.

A Certain World

Accidie

❧

Our sixth contending is with that which the Greeks called ἀκηδία and which we may describe as tedium or perturbation of heart. It is akin to dejection and especially felt by wandering monks and solitaries, a persistent and obnoxious enemy to such as dwell in the desert, disturbing the monk especially about midday, like a fever mounting at a regular time, and bringing its highest tide of inflammation at definite accustomed hours to the sick soul. And so some of the Fathers declare it to be the demon of noontide which is spoken of in the Ninety-first Psalm.

When this besieges the unhappy mind, it begets aversion from the place, boredom with one's cell, and scorn and contempt for one's brethren, whether they be dwelling with one or some way off, as careless and unspiritually minded persons. Also, towards any work that may be done within the enclosure of our own lair, we become listless and inert. It will not suffer us to stay in our cell, or to attend to our reading: we lament that in all this while, living in the same spot, we have made no progress, we sigh and complain that bereft of sympathetic fellowship we have no spiritual fruit; and bewail ourselves as empty of all spiritual profit, abiding vacant and useless in this place; and we that could guide others and be of value to multitudes have edified no man, enriched no man with our precept and example. We praise other and far distant monasteries, describing them as more helpful to one's progress, more congenial to one's soul's health. . . . Towards eleven o'clock or midday it induces such lassitude of body and craving for food as one might feel after the exhaustion of a long journey and hard toil, or the postponing of a meal throughout a two or three days' fast. Finally one gazes anxiously here and there, and sighs that no brother of any description is to be seen approaching: one is for ever in and out of one's cell, gazing at the sun as though it were tarrying to its setting: one's mind is an irrational confusion, like the earth befogged in a mist, one is slothful and vacant in every spiritual activity, and no remedy, it seems, can be found for this state of siege than a visit from some brother, or the solace of sleep.

The Desert Fathers
(trans. Helen Waddell)

Acronyms

The Oxford English Dictionary does not recognize this term for a typical modern horror. As the author of the following poem says:

Anyone who reads the newspapers these days has to have a basic vocabulary of spare-part words like UNO and NATO (though the French, with characteristic awkwardness, of course, spell them backwards—ONU, OTAN), plus their specialized cousins like UNESCO, WHO, and GATT.

The massive congestion of linguistic traffic by these spare-part vehicles called acronyms is an entirely modern development, a product of our technological age that the developing nations have readily adopted, even though they are still short of more tangible forms of communication like telephones.

Intercom in Nasakom

"Euratom!" cried the Oiccu, sly and nasa,
"I'll wftu in the iscus with my gatt."
"No! No!" the Eldo pleaded, pale with asa.
"My unctad strictly nato on comsat."

The Oiccu gave a wacy little intuc,
He raft and waved his anzac oldefo.
"Bea imf!" he eec, a smirk upon his aituc,
And smote the Eldo on his ganefo.

The Eldo drew his udi from its cern,
He tact his unicet with fearless fao.
The Oiccu swerved but could not comintern;
He fell afpro, and dying moaned, "Icao!"

The moon came up above the gasbiindo,
The air no longer vip with intercom.
A creeping icftu stirred the maphilindo
And kami was restored to Nasakom.

"O kappi gum!" the fifa sang in cento,
"O cantat till the neddy unficyp."
The laser song re-echoed through the seato,
As the Eldo radar home to unmogip.

TOWYN MASON

Aging

❧

I was both the youngest child and the youngest grandchild in my family. Being a fairly bright boy, I was generally the youngest in my school class. The result of this was that, until quite recently, I have always assumed that, in any gathering, I was the youngest person present. It was not that I imagined myself to be younger in years than I actually was, a fatal delusion in a writer: I simply thought of others as older. It is only in the last two or three years that I have begun to notice, to my surprise, that most of the people I see on the streets are younger than I. For the first time, too, though still in good health, I am almost able to believe that I shall die.

After a certain age, the more one becomes oneself, the more obvious one's family traits become.

M. PROUST

. . . As the time of rest, or of departure, approaches me, not only do many of the evils I had heard of, and prepared for, present themselves in more grievous shapes than I had expected; but one which I had scarcely ever heard of, torments me increasingly every hour.

I had understood it to be in the order of things that the aged should lament their vanishing life as an instrument they had never used, now to be taken from them; but not as an instrument, only then perfectly tempered and sharpened, and snatched out of their hands at the instant they could have done some real service with it. Whereas, my own feeling, now, is that everything which has hitherto happened to me, or been done by me, whether well or ill, has been fitting me to take greater fortune more prudently, and do better work more thoroughly. And just when I seem to be coming out of school—very sorry to have been such a foolish boy, yet having taken a prize or two, and expecting to enter now upon some more serious business than cricket,—I am dismissed by the Master I hoped to serve, with a—'That's all I want of you, sir.'

RUSKIN

The young man is deliberately odd and prides himself on it; the old man is unintentionally so, and it mortifies him.

Nothing is more beautiful than cheerfulness in an old face.

J. P. RICHTER

Old age lives minutes slowly, hours quickly; childhood chews hours and swallows minutes.

MALCOLM DE CHAZAL

It does not become a man of years to follow the fashion, either in his thinking or his dress.

GOETHE

After the age of eighty, all contemporaries are friends.

MME. DE NINO

Twenty Years Ago

O, the rain, the weary, dreary rain,
  How it plashes on the window sill!
Night, I guess too, must be on the wane,
  Strass and Gass around are grown so still,
Here I sit, with coffee in my cup—
  Ah, 'twas rarely I beheld it flow
In the taverns where I used to sup
  Twenty golden years ago.

Twenty years ago, alas!—but stay,
  On my life, 'tis half-past twelve o'clock!
After all, the hours do slip away—
  Come, here goes to burn another block!
For the night, or morn, is wet and cold,
  And my fire is dwindling rather low:—
I had fire enough, when young and bold,
  Twenty golden years ago!

Dear! I don't feel well at all, somehow:
  Few in Weimar dream how bad I am;
Floods of tears grow common with me now,
  High-Dutch floods that Reason cannot dam.
Doctors think I'll neither live nor thrive
  If I mope at home so—I don't know—
Am I living *now?* I *was* alive
  Twenty golden years ago.

Wifeless, friendless, flagonless, alone,
  Not quite bookless, though, unless I chuse,
Left with nought to do, except to groan,
  Not a soul to woo, except the Muse—
O! this, this is hard for *me* to bear,
  Me, who whilome lived so much *en haut*,
Me, who broke all hearts like chinaware
  Twenty golden years ago.

. . . . . .

Tick-tick, tick-tick!—Not a sound save Time's,
  And the windgust, as it drives the rain—
Tortured torturer of reluctant rhymes,
  Go to bed, and rest thine aching brain!
Sleep! no more the dupe of hopes or schemes;
  Soon thou sleepest where the thistles blow—
Curious anticlimax to thy dreams
  Twenty golden years ago.

J. C. MANGAN

Venus and John Gower

Halvinge of scorn, sche seide thus:
"Thou wost wel that I am Venus,
Which al only my lustes seche;
And wel I wot, thogh thou beseche
My love, lustes ben ther none,
Whiche I may take in thy persone;
For loves lust and lockes hore
In chambre acorden nevermore,
And thogh thou feigne a yong corage,
It scheweth wel be the visage
That olde grisel is no fole;
Ther ben ful manye yeeres stole
With thee and with suche othre mo,
That outward feignen youthe so
And ben withinne of pore assay
'Min herte wolde and I ne may'
Is noght beloved nowadayes;
Er thou make eny such assayes
To love, and faile upon the fet,
Betre is to make a beau retret;
For thogh thou mightest love atteigne,
Yit were it bot an idel peine,
Whan that thou art noght sufficant
To holde love his covenant.

Forthy tak hom thin herte ayein,
That thou travaile noght in vein,
Whereof my Court may be deceived.
I wot and have it wel conceived,
How that thy will is good ynough;
Bot more behoveth to the plough,
Wherof thee lacketh, as I trowe:
So sitte it wel that thou beknowe
Thy fieble astat, er thou beginne
Thing wher thou might non ende winne.
What bargain scholde a man assaye,
Whan that him lacketh forto paye?
My sone, if thou be wel bethoght,
This toucheth thee; foryet it noght:
The thing is torned into was;
That which was whilom grene gras,
Is welked hey at time now.
Forthy my conseil is that thou
Remembre wel how thou art old."

  Whan Venus hath hir tale told,
And I bethoght was al aboute,
Tho wiste I wel without doute
That ther was no recoverir;
And as a man the blase of fir
With water quencheth, so ferd I;
A cold me caughte sodeinly,
For sorwe that min herte made,
My dedly face pale and fade
Becam, and swoune I fell to grounde. . . .

  Bot Venus wente noghte therfore,
Ne Genius, whiche thilke time
Abiden bothe faste by me
And sche which may the hertes binde
In loves cause and ek unbinde,
Er I out of my trance aros,
Venus, which hield a boiste clos,

And wolde noght I scholde deye,
Tok out—more cold than eny keye—
An oignement, and in such point
Sche hath my wounded herte enoignt,
My temples and my reins also.
And forth withal sche tok me tho
A wonder mirour forto holde,
In whiche sche bad me to beholde
And taken hiede of that I sighe;
Wherinne anon min hertes yghe
I caste, and sigh my colour fade,
Min yghen dimme and al unglade,
My chiekes thinne, and al my face
With elde I mighte se deface,
So riveled and so wo-besein,
That ther was nothing full ne plein;
I sigh also min heres hore.
My will was tho to se no more. . . .

Venus behield me than and lough,
And axeth as it were in game,
What love was: and I for schame
Ne wiste what I scholde answere;
And natheles I gan to swere
That be my trouthe I knew him noght;
So ferr it was out of my thoght,
Right as it hadde nevere be.
"My goode sone," thou quod sche,
"Now at this time I lieve it wel,
So goth the fortune of my whiel;
Forthy my conseil is thou leve."

"Ma dame," I seide, "be your leve,
Ye witen wel, and so wot I,
That I am unbehovely
Your Court fro this day forth to serve:
And for I may no thonk deserve,

And also for I am refused,
I preye you to ben excused
And natheles as for the laste,
Whil that my wittes with me laste,
Touchende my confession
I axe an absolucioun
Of Genius, er that I go."
The prest anon was redy tho,
And seide, "Sone, as of thy schrifte
Thou hast ful pardoun and foryifte;
Foryet it thou, and so wol I."
"Min holy fader, grant mercy,"
Quod I to him, and to the queene
I fell on knes upon the grene,
And tok my leve forto wende.
Bot sche, that wolde make an ende,
As therto which I was most able,
A peire of bedes blak as sable
Sche tok and heng my necke aboute;
Upon the gaudes al withoute
Was write of gold, *Por Reposer*.
"Lo," thus sche seide, "John Gower,
Now thou art ate laste cast,
This have I for thin ese cast,
That thou no more of love sieche.
Bot my will is that thou besieche
And prey hierafter for thee pes,
And that thou make a plein reles
To love, which taketh litel hiede
Of olde men upon the nede,
Whan that the lustes ben aweye:
Forthy to thee nis bot o weye,
In which let reson be thy guide;
For he may sone himself misguide
That seth noght the peril tofore.
My sone, be wel war therfore,
And kep the sentence of my lore,
And tarye thou my Court no more. . . .

For in the lawe of my comune
We be noght schape to comune,
Thyselfe and I, nevere after this.
Now have I said al that ther is
Of love as for thy final ende:
Adieu, for I mot fro thee wende."
And with that word al sodeinly,
Enclosed in a sterred sky,
Venus, which is the queene of love,
Was take into hire place above,
More wist I noght where sche becam.
And thus my leve of hire I nam,
And forth withal the same tide
Hire prest, which wolde noght abide,
Or be me lief or be me loth,
Out of my sighte forth he goth,
And I was left withouten helpe.
So wiste I noght whereof to yelpe,
Bot only that I hadde lore
My time, and was sory therfore,
And thus bewhaped in my thoght.
Whan al was turned into noght,
I stod amased for a while,
And in myself I gan to smile
Thenkende upon the bedes blake,
And how they weren me betake,
For that I schulde bidde and preye.
And whanne I sigh no othre weye,
Bot only that I was refused,
Unto the lif which I hadde used
I thoghte never torne ayein:
And in this wise, soth to sein,
Homward a softe pas I wente.

JOHN GOWER

Algebra

❦

Algebra reverses the relative importance of the factors in ordinary language. It is essentially a written language, and it endeavors to exemplify in its written structures the patterns which it is its purpose to convey. The pattern of the marks on paper is a particular instance of the pattern to be conveyed to thought. The algebraic method is our best approach to the expression of necessity, by reason of its reduction of accident to the ghostlike character of the real variable.

A. N. WHITEHEAD

Strictly speaking, the nought ought to be eliminated from algebra.

Algebra and money are essentially levellers; the first intellectually, the second effectively.

SIMONE WEIL

David Hartley offered a vest-pocket edition of his moral and religious philosophy in the formula $W = F^2/L$, where W is the love of the world, F is the fear of God, and L is the love of God. It is necessary to add only this. Hartley said that as one grows older L increases and indeed becomes infinite. It follows then that W, the love of the world, decreases and approaches zero.

Alps, The

❦

September 22, 1816

Left Thoun in a boat which carried us the length of the lake in three hours. The lake small; but the banks fine. Rocks down to the water's edge. Landed at Newhause; passed Interlachen; entered upon a range of scenes beyond all description or previous conception. Passed a rock; inscription—2 brothers—one murdered the other; just the place for it. After a variety of windings came to an enormous rock. Girl with fruit—very pretty; blue eyes, good teeth, very fair: long but good features—reminded me rather of Fanny. Bought some of her pears, and patted her upon the cheek; the expression of her face very mild, but good, and not at all coquettish. Arrived at the foot of the Mountain (the *Yung frau,* i.e., the Maiden); Glaciers; torrents; one of these torrents *nine hundred* feet in height of visible descent. Lodge at the Curate's. Set out to see the Valley; heard an Avalanche fall, like thunder; saw Glacier—enormous. Storm came on, thunder, lightning, hail; all in perfection and beautiful. I was on horseback; Guide wanted to carry my cane; I was going to give it him, when I recollected that it was a Swordstick, and I thought the lightning might be attracted toward him; kept it myself; a good deal encumbered with it, and my cloak, as it was too heavy for a whip, and the horse was stupid, and stood still with every other peal. Got in, not very wet; the Cloak being staunch. Hobhouse wet through; H. took refuge in cottage; sent man, umbrella, and cloak (from the Curate's when I arrived) after him. Swiss Curate's house very good indeed—much better than most English Vicarages. It is immediately opposite the torrent I spoke of. The torrent is in shape curving over the rock, like the *tail* of a white horse streaming in the wind, such as it might be conceived would be that of the "*pale*" horse" on which *Death* is mounted in the Apocalypse. It is neither mist nor water, but a something between both; its immense height (nine hundred feet) gives it a wave, a curve, a spreading here, a condensation there, wonderful and indescribable. Think, upon the whole, that this day has been better than any of this present excursion.

September 23

Before ascending the mountain, went to the torrent (7 in the morning) again; the Sun upon it forming a *rainbow* of the lower part of all colors, but principally purple and gold; the bow moving as you move; I never saw anything like this; it is only in the Sunshine. Ascended the Wengen Mountain; at noon reached a valley on the summit; left the horses, took off my coat, and went to the summit, 7000 feet (English feet) above the level of the *sea*, and about 5000 above the valley we left in the morning. On one side, our view comprised the *Yung frau* with all her glaciers; then the *Dent d'Argent,* shining like truth; then the Little Giant (the Kleiner Eigher), and last, but not least, the Wetterhorn. The height of Jungfrau is 13,000 feet above the sea, 11,000 above the valley; she is the highest of this range. Heard the Avalanches falling every five minutes nearly—as if God was pelting the Devil down from Heaven with snowballs. From where we stood, on the Wengen Alp, we had all these in view on one side: on the other, the clouds rose from the opposite valley, curling up perpendicular precipices like the foam of the Ocean of Hell, during a Springtide—it was white and sulphury, and immeasurably deep in appearance. The side we ascended was (of course) not of so precipitous a nature; but on arriving at the summit, we looked down the other side upon a boiling sea of cloud, dashing against the crags on which we stood (these crags on one side quite perpendicular). Stayed a quarter of an hour; began to descend; quite clear from cloud on that side of the mountain. In passing the masses of snow, I made a snowball and pelted H. with it.

Got down to our horses again, ate something; remounted; heard the Avalanches still; came to a morass; H. dismounted; H. got over well: I tried to pass my horse over; the horse sank up to the chin, and of course he and I were in the mud together; bemired all over but not hurt; laughed and rode on. Arrived at the Grindenwald; dined, mounted again, and rode to the higher Glacier—, twilight but distinct—very fine Glacier, like a *frozen hurricane*. Starlight, beautiful, but the devil of a path! Never mind, got safe in; a little lightning; but the whole of the day as fine in point of weather as the day on which Paradise was made. Passed *whole woods of withered pines, all withered;* trunks stripped and barkless, branches lifeless; done by a single winter— their appearance reminded me of me and my family.

LORD BYRON

There are many spots among the inferior ridges of the Alps, such as the Col de Ferret, the Col d'Anterne, and the associated ranges of the Buet, which, though commanding prospects of great nobleness, are themselves very nearly types of all that is most painful to the human mind. Vast wastes of mountain ground, covered here and there with dull grey grass or moss, but breaking continually into black banks of shattered slate, all glistening and sodden with slow tricklings of clogged, incapable streams; the snow water oozing through them in a cold sweat, and spreading itself in creeping stains among their dust; ever and anon a shaking here and there, and a handful or two of their particles or flakes trembling down, one sees not why, into more total dissolution; leaving a few jagged teeth, like the edges of knives eaten away by vinegar, projecting through the half-dislodged mass from the inner rock, keen enough to cut the hand or foot that rests on them, yet crumbling as they wound, and soon sinking again into the smooth, slippery, glutinous heap, looking like a beach of black scales of dead fish, cast ashore from a poisonous sea; and sloping away into foul ravines, branched down immeasurable slopes of barrenness, where the winds howl and wander continually, and the snow lies in wasted and sorrowful fields, covered with sooty dust, that collects in streaks and stains at the bottom of all its thawing ripples.

RUSKIN

Anagrams

Almost any name with a good distribution of alphabetic letters can be turned into either a flattering or an unflattering anagram of itself. Thus the full name of the author of this book, DMITRI ALFRED BORGMANN, lends itself to the flattering anagram, GRAND

MIND, MORTAL FIBRE!, as well as the negative anagram, DAMN
MAD BORING TRIFLER!

D. A. BORGMANN

WHY SHUN A NUDE TAG?

In 1610 Galileo published his observations of the planet Saturn
in the form of an anagram:

> SMAISMRMILMEPOETALEVMIBVNENVGTTAVIRAS

The solution:

> ALTISSIMVM PLANETAM TERGEMINVM OBSERVAVI

(I have observed that the farthest planet is a triplet.)

In 1656, using a much stronger telescope, Christian Huygens
corrected this observation, and he, too, published his correction
in the form of an anagram:

AAAAAAA CCCCC D EEEEE G H IIIIIII LLLL MM NNNNNNNNN OOOO
Q RR S TTTTT UUUUU

The solution:

ANNULO CINGITUR, TENUI, PLANO, NUSQUAM COHAERENTE, AD
ECLIPTICAM INCLINATO. (A thin ring, plane, without adherence,
inclined to the ecliptic.)

To read a mystical significance into anagrams is asking for
trouble. When Lady Eleanor Davis (1590–1652) discovered
that the letters of her maiden name, ELEANOR AUDLEY, could
make the anagram REVEALE O DANIEL, she became convinced
that she possessed the gift of prophecy, and from then on there
was no stopping her. Her two husbands tried; one dropped
dead, the other went mad. In 1628 she prophesied that the
Duke of Buckingham would die in August; he did. Em-
boldened by her success, she then foretold that King Charles the
First would come to a bad end like Belshazzar. This was too
much, and she was arrested. At her trial she was momentarily
disconcerted when one of the judges, taking her married name,
DAME ELEANOR DAVIS, produced the anagram NEVER SO MAD A
LADIE, but not for long. Her two persecutors, Archbishop Laud
and King Charles, both ended on the scaffold, and she hailed

Cromwell as the deliverer of his people. By this time, however, her crossword skill seems to have deteriorated. O. CROMWELL: what could that mean but HOWL ROME? It was the last and also the worst of her anagrams, for she had added an *H* and forgotten the *C* and one *L*.

Anesthesia

Anesthesia may be characterized by the fact that a variety of medical problems requiring *immediate solution* meet very dramatically at the anesthesiologist's end of the table; (general physiology, neurology, cardiology, etc., etc.). These multiple disciplines converge suddenly, occupying, as it were, the same space at the same time. This *simultaneity* constitutes a definite, specific trait of anesthesia, its distinctive stamp. How to deal with it is not only a technical challenge and a demand on scientific knowledge but also a philosophical problem: time acquires a new meaning, which must be explored.

Another inherent trait of anesthesia which again, and in an even more pointed way, brings up the problem of time, is its *reversibility*. The abolition of the defense reflexes and all possible complications such as apnea, tachycardia, bradycardia or anoxia are expected to disappear without leaving any traces. This means that reversibility is a conditio sine qua non. But what is reversibility, philosophically speaking, if not a negation of time? "What has happened—can it unhappen?" (Kierkegaard). Generalized and applied to the whole of human life, reversibility can mean only one thing: the complete overcoming and negation of time and history. . . .

Whatever its ultimate aim and reason, administration of anesthesia means intoxicating the patient. Anesthesia, in fact, is always evil, and the art is of chosing between lesser and greater evil, not between good and evil. This puts anesthesia on a par with other crucial problems of our contemporary life.

What first strikes the student of anesthesia and what is, later, ignored or taken for granted, is his complete, unmitigated loneliness. We may, of course, consider that the people in the operating room are working on the patient as a team. However, this must be further defined: the surgeon has an assistant, even two or three if need be; the scrub nurse has a second scrub nurse and a circulating nurse and a bell to ring for help with; they are all working in the same operating field and in apparent communion! Only the anesthesiologist is on his own. The surgeon may ask him whether everything is going well, the exceptionally kind circulating nurse may fetch him a larger airway, but those are minor, external contacts. Intellectually and spiritually the anesthesiologist is alone, facing that lesser evil.

The pathologist is in the lab with the specimen. He may know that cancer begins long before the cells show "atypical deviations," but discussions of this kind do not enter into his day's work. He prepares the slides in a friendly atmosphere, can make a telephone call to a colleague, and give an answer such as "frozen section not clear," "suspicious" (whatever that means) or "we need a paraffin preparation"; he can even send the slide by special delivery to Illinois or Massachusetts, can correspond, deliberate, and then come up with the answer: "I don't know what it is, I once had a similar case, the patient died, apparently from a lymphosarcoma. . . ."

The anesthetist, for obvious reasons, cannot do his work in such a fashion. He must always deliver the goods, here and now, by himself, in the presence of the impatient, often hostile, surgeon, and regardless of whether it "looks suspicious" or not, or whether he has already had such a case or not.

Considering that the time element does not exist for him in the usual sense, the anesthetist really cannot be assisted from without. Least of all in so-called private, i.e. commercial, institutions, where there are only competitors around. It is like in a Greek tragedy where the hero struggles against fate; or like a world series game with the pitcher throwing the ball while the classic chorus, the stadium audience, roars mercilessly: "Let's go, let's go —what's the matter!" This is also the voice of the surgeon—for the contemporary surgeon who races from one hospital to another, from a hernia to a pilonidal cyst and on to a stomach, cannot afford to lose ten minutes for induction and preparation of his case, or so it seems to him. He cannot understand why one induction takes five minutes and the next perhaps five times as long.

If this surgeon were asked how he would like the ideal anesthesiologist to behave, he would probably answer somewhat along these lines: "As a matter of fact I prefer a nurse anesthetist. But if I have to work with an anesthesiologist he ought not to be seen or heard and, in general, not be noticeable."

It is, indeed, ideal if the anesthetist's performance does not attract anybody's attention. In the easy, good-risk cases this is often achieved. But it so happens that sometimes, like the surgeon who cannot find the common duct because of anatomical anomalies, the anesthesiologist, too, encounters difficulties. Of course, he does the best he can—with the anatomical and physiological material furnished by the patient. If the cards you are dealt include aces and kings you easily win the rubber; if there are no honors you go down. In the latter case, the art consists in losing as little as possible.

After an easy, uneventful case, the surgeon may compliment the anesthesiologist; after a difficult case with ups and downs, in which the patient was still pulled through, the surgeon complains. And yet it is in the latter instance that the anesthetist demonstrates to the full his experience, judgment, knowledge and skill. So it is in retreat that a general demonstrates his talents and endurance. But the general has help—subordinates, assistants, chiefs of staff—while the anesthesiologist is alone: between him and the failing patient there is no one (perhaps only a prayer). . . .

It is the nature of anesthesia to strip the patient biologically and to put him through different antecedent stages of evolution. First, in the classic case, the spinal cord is affected, and reflexes are exaggerated before they are cut down; then, the cortex is irritated (hallucinations) prior to being completely switched off (unconsciousness); finally, cardiac and respiratory centers are approached. Thus the patient reverses as it were his phylogenetic stages—from human back to vertebrate and ameba. During this process, he may manifest himself in primitive forms, resembling in succession an anthropoid, a rodent, a fish, a mollusc, a vegetation. This is when racial, constitutional, genetic factors come to the fore, checked only, perhaps, by acquired and firmly established cultural and educational patterns. Lacking these, we have before us on the operating table what is, in great part, a result of physiological and phylogenetic factors. This crude material reacts differently in varying races, nations, and social stratas. . . .

While the patient is undergoing changes due to narcosis, the surgeon and the anesthesiologist too may demonstrate new, surprising aspects: under situations of specific stress this occurs frequently! The anesthesiologist suddenly discloses his other, underlying, constitution; the same may be true for the surgeon: the great contemporary hero, the bully, the primadonna, suddenly loses his head and calls for a doctor in the house. There is in surgical procedure the moment of truth exactly as in the corridas. An anesthesiologist or a surgeon who has once lost a child on the operating table can be recognized, like the previously gored toreador. During the preliminaries he does everything as he used to, as custom and accepted technique ordain. But at the decisive moment, when the "kill" must be performed, the man is frightened, frozen, paralyzed, and the arena understands: he is through, he must quit or he will be killed. And he either quits or gets killed. So it is with the toreador.

The case of the anesthetist or the surgeon is different: next morning you see them again. At this stage of the game they never voluntarily quit. As it is usually not the physician who expires in the operating room, they continue for several years their inadequate and disturbing activity. We all have seen such "wounded" specialists: they manifest an exaggerated reaction during a sudden complication—something similar to combat fatigue.

The patient in his turn, when brought into the operating room, may control himself in a civilized way, with dignity, or go completely to pieces, in panic and hysteria, despite premedication.

Thus, in the operating room we can always distinguish the worthy man from the pseudo-hero, the bully, the hum-bug. This holds true—in differing degrees and for different reasons—for patient, surgeon and anesthesiologist.

BASILE YANOVSKY

Angelology

❧

Surely, one of the oddest pastimes of the human mind. I owe the following information to Gustav Davidson's *A Dictionary of Angels*.

According to the fourteenth-century cabalists, the total number of angels is 301,655,722.

Angels of the Months (January–December): Gabriel, Barchiel, Malchidiel, Asmodel, Ambriel or Amriel, Muriel, Verchiel, Hamaliel, Zuriel or Uriel, Barbiel, Adnachiel or Advachiel, Hanael or Anael.

Angels of the Seasons (Winter–Autumn): Farlas, Telvi, Casmaran, Andarcel.

Angels of the Week (Sunday–Saturday): Michael, Gabriel, Samael, Raphael, Sachiel, Anael, Cassiel.

Angels of the Elements: Fire: Seraph or Nathaniel. Air: Cherub. Water: Tharsis or Tharsus. Earth: Ariel.

Miscellaneous: Wild beasts: Thegri. Tame beasts: Behemiel. Birds: Arael. Fish: Gagiel. Wild fowl: Trgiaob. Water insects: Shakziel.

Anglo-Saxon Poetry

❧

In the small extant corpus of Anglo-Saxon poetry, there is nothing as good as the best poems in the Elder Edda, but it was my first introduction to the "barbaric" poetry of the North, and I was immediately fascinated both by its metric and its rhetorical devices, so different from the post-Chaucerian poetry with which I was familiar.

The following example is more lyrical than is typical of Anglo-Saxon verse, but it is one of my favorites.

Deor

Wayland knew the wanderer's fate:
that single-willed earl suffered agonies,
sorrow and longing the sole companions
of his ice-cold exile. Anxieties bit
when Nithhad put a knife to his hamstrings,
laid cunning bonds on a better man.
   That changed; this may too.

Beadohild mourned her murdered brothers:
but her own plight pained her more
—her womb grew great with child.
When she knew that, she could never hold
steady before her wit what was to happen.
   That has gone; this may too.

All have heard of Hild's ravishing:
the Geat's lust was ungovernable,
their bitter love banished sleep.
   That passed over; this may too.

Thirty winters Theodric ruled
the Maering city: and many knew it.
   That went by; this may too.

We all know that Eormanric
had a wolf's wit. Wide Gothland
lay in the grasp of that grim king,
and through it many sat, by sorrows environed,
foreseeing only sorrow; sighed for the downfall
and thorough overthrow of the thrall-maker.
   That blew by; this may too.

When each gladness has gone, gathering sorrow
may cloud the brain; and in his breast a man
can not then see how his sorrows shall end.
But he may think how throughout this world

it is the way of God, who is wise, to deal
to the most part of men much favour
and a flourishing fame; to a few the sorrow-share.

Of myself in this regard I shall say this only:
that in the hall of the Heodenings I held long the makarship,
lived dear to my prince, Deor my name;
many winters I held this happy place
and my lord was kind. Then came Heorrenda,
whose lays were skilful; the lord of fighting-men
settled on him the estate bestowed once on me.

That has gone; this may too.

(trans. Michael Alexander)

A few years ago I was amazed to find that the standard verse
line of northern poetry, consisting of two half lines, separated
by a strong caesura and linked by alliteration, also occurs in
Somali poetry. In it, however, every line of a poem must contain
the same alliterative sound. In the original of the following
poem, the alliterating consonant in every line is *k*, e.g.:

Sida *k*oorta yucub oo La suray   *k*orommo buubaal ah
Ama geel *k*a reeb ah oo nirgaha   Laga *k*achaynaayo

The Poet's Lament on the Death of His Wife

Like the yu'ub wood bell tied to gelded camels that are
    running away,
Or like camels which are being separated from their young,
Or like people journeying while moving camp,
Or like a well which has broken its sides or a river which has
    overflowed its banks,
Or like an old woman whose only son was killed,
Or like the poor, dividing the scraps for their frugal meal,
Or like the bees entering their hive, or food cracking in the
    frying,
Yesterday my lamentations drove sleep from all the camps.
Have I been bereft in my house and shelter?

Has the envy of others been miraculously fulfilled?
Have I been deprived of the fried meat and reserves for lean
   times which were so plentiful for me?
Have I to-day been taken from the chessboard?
Have I been borne on a saddle to a distant and desolate place?
Have I broken my shin, a bone which cannot be mended?

RAAGE UGAAS
(trans. B. W. Andrzejewski and I. M. Lewis)

Arborvitae

With honeysuckle, over-sweet, festooned;
With bitter ivy bound;
Terraced with funguses unsound;
Deformed with many a boss
And closèd scar, o'ercushioned deep with moss;
Bunched all about with pagan mistletoe;
And thick with nests of the hoarse bird
That talks, but understands not his own word;
Stands, and so stood a thousand years ago,
A single tree.
Thunder has done its worst among its twigs,
Where the great crest yet blackens, never pruned,
But in its heart, alway
Ready to push new verdurous boughs, whene'er
The rotting saplings near it fall and leave it air,
Is all antiquity and no decay.
Rich, though rejected by the forest pigs,
Its fruit, beneath whose rough compelling rind
Those that will it break find
Heart-succouring savor of each several meat,
And kernelled drink of brain-renewing power,
With bitter condiment and sour,
And sweet economy of sweet,

And odors that remind
Of haunts of childhood and a different day.
Beside this tree,
Praising no Gods nor blaming, sans a wish,
Sits, Tartar-like, the Time's civility,
And eats its dead-dog off a golden dish.

COVENTRY PATMORE

Articles, the Thirty-Nine

Scene from a play, acted at Oxford, called "Matriculation"

(*Boy discovered at a table, with the Thirty-Nine Articles before him.—Enter the Rt. Rev. Doctor Philpots.*)

DOCTOR P.

THERE, my lad, lie the Articles—(*boy begins to count them*) just thirty-nine—
No occasion to count—you've now only to sign.
At Cambridge where folks are less High-church than we,
The whole Nine-and-Thirty are lumped into Three.
Let's run o'er the items;—there's Justification,
Predestination and Supererogation,—
Not forgetting Salvation and Creed Athanasian,
Till we reach, at last, Queen Bess's Ratification.
That's sufficient—now, sign—having read quite enough,
You "believe in the full and true meaning thereof."
 (*Boy stares*)
Oh, a mere form of words, to make things smooth and brief,—
A commodious and short make-believe of belief,
Which our Church has drawn up, in a form thus articular,
To keep out, in general, all who're particular.
But what's the boy doing? what! reading all through,
And my luncheon fast cooling!—this never will do.

BOY (*poring over the Articles*):
Here are points which—pray, Doctor, what's "Grace of Congruity"?

DOCTOR P. (*sharply*):
You'll find out, young sir, when you've more ingenuity.
At present, by signing, you pledge yourself merely,
Whate'er it may be, to believe it sincerely.
Both in *dining* and *signing* we take the same plan—
First, swallow all down, then digest—as we can.

BOY (*still reading*):
I've to gulp, I see, St. Athanasius's Creed,
Which, I'm told, is a very tough morsel indeed;
As he damns—

DOCTOR P. (*aside*):
        Ay, and so would *I*, willingly, too,
All confounded particular young boobies, like you.
This comes of Reforming! all's o'er with our land,
When people won't stand what they can't *under*stand;
Nor perceive that our ever-revered Thirty-Nine
Were made, not for men to *believe*, but to *sign*.

(*Exit Doctor P. in a passion*)

THOMAS MOORE

Bands, Brass

❦

When I was young, brass-band concerts were a regular attraction in the public parks of cities. Am I mistaken in thinking that they have become rarities? All I know is that this poem fills me with nostalgia.

Park Concert

Astounding the bucolic grass,
The bandsmen sweat in golds and reds

And put their zeal into the brass.
A glorious flustered major heads

Their sort of stationary charge.
Their lips are pursed, their cheeks get pink;
The instruments are very large
Through which they render Humperdinck.

The sailors and the parlourmaids
Both vote the music jolly good,
But do not worry if it fades
As they stroll deeper in the wood,

Where twenty French horns wouldn't stir
A leaf. The intrepid band try not
To mind the applause (as though it were
A testing fusillade of shot),

Polish their mouthpieces and cough,
Then throw their shoulders back to play
A Pomeranian march. They're off!
And Sousa scares the tits away.

JAMES MICHIE

Baroque

Of all architectural styles, Baroque is the most this-worldly,
a visible hymn to earthly pomp and power. At the same time,
by its excessive theatricality, it reveals, perhaps unintentionally,
the essential "camp" of all worldly greatness. It is, therefore, the
ideal style for princely palaces. But as ecclesiastical architecture
it simply will not do, for nothing could be further removed
from the Christian view of God and Man. The same is true

of the baroque literature, of *Paradise Lost,* or Bossuet's sermons, or the following example, which I found in Friedrich Heer's *The Intellectual History of Europe.*

In his *Délices de l'Esprit,* Desmarets has given us a perfect statement of this baroque view of the world. Man's inner life was, Desmarets wrote, a palace, and the great house of the Duc de Richelieu would seem to have been the model for it. In it, the hero, Philedon, was received in the apartment of Faith, visited the loge of humility and the prison of nothingness (*cachet du Néant*). Next he saw the balcony of hope, the thirty-three caverns of obedience, the grotto of patience, the halls of prayer, of meditation and of union with God. There was even a marine museum in Desmaret's heavenly palace in which various vehicles for missionary journeys were displayed. The staff of the palace consisted of Mary, the patriarchs, prophets and the Christian virtues who received and guided the visitors. An exceedingly ingenious system of mechanical staircases, on which Philedon ascended when he wanted to rise, led the way to different floors. The great architect, master mechanic, magician and mystic ruler of the palace was Christ himself. From the "great salon of God's love," the walls glittering with marble, gold and precious stones, Philedon passed through several arcades into the "chamber of love of the extension of the Faith" (*chambre de l'amour de l'extension de la Foi*).

Desmarets published the book in 1654, and went on to realise these "delights" as the leader of the secret police of State and Church.

FRIEDRICH HEER

When westward, like the sun, you took your way,
And from benighted Britain bore the day,
Blue Triton gave the signal from the shore,
The ready Nereids heard, and swam before,
To smooth the seas; a soft Etesian gale
But just inspir'd, and gently swell'd the sail;
Portunus took his turn, whose ample hand
Heav'd up the lighten'd keel, and sunk the sand,

And steer'd the sacred vessel safe to land.
The land, if not restrain'd, had met your way,
Projected out a neck, and jutted to the sea.
Hibernia, prostrate at your feet, ador'd,
In you the pledge of her expected lord,
Due to her isle; a venerable name;
His father and his grandsire known to fame;
Aw'd by that house, accustom'd to command,
The sturdy kerns in due subjection stand,
Nor fear the reins in any foreign hand.

At your approach, they crowded to the port;
And scarcely landed, you create a court:
As Ormond's Harbinger, to you they run;
For Venus is the promise of the sun.

The waste of civil wars, their towns destroy'd,
Pales unhonor'd, Ceres unemployed,
Were all forgot; and one triumphant day
Wip'd all the tears of three campaigns away.
Blood, rapines, massacres, were cheaply bought,
So mighty recompense your beauty brought.

As when the dove returning bore the mark
Of earth restor'd to the long-lab'ring ark,
The relics of mankind, secure of rest,
Op'd ev'ry window to receive the guest,
And the fair bearer of the message bless'd;
So, when you came, with loud repeated cries,
The nation took an omen from your eyes,
And God advanc'd his rainbow in the skies,
To sign inviolable Peace restor'd;
The saints, with solemn shouts, proclaim'd the new accord.

JOHN DRYDEN

Bath, The Cold

As cultural habits go, short-lived. I don't know precisely when it was first introduced (1840?), but I know more or less when it came to an end. When I was young, not only was every boy at a boarding school compelled to take a cold bath every morning, a rule based on the entirely erroneous theory that cold water subdued the carnal passions, but also most adult males of the upper and middle classes took one of their own free will. I believe I belong to the first generation which resolved, once we left school and got to the university, that we would never take a cold bath in our lives again. Today, inquiries lead me to think that there are few schools now where cold baths are obligatory, and I am sure no adult ever takes one except during a heat wave. Upon my sufferings in early youth, Ogden Nash has said the last word:

I test my bath before I sit,
And I am always moved to wonderment
That what chills the finger not a bit
Is so frigid upon the fundament.

Beauty, Feminine

Shee was brighter of her blee
   then was the bright sonn:
Her rudd redder than the rose
   that on the rise hangeth:
Meekly smiling with her mouth,
   and merry in her lookes.
Ever laughing for love,

as she like would.
And as shee came by the bankes,
    the boughes eche one
They louted to that ladye,
    and layd forth their branches;
Blossomes, and burgens
    breathed full sweete;
Flowers flourished in the frith,
    where shee forth stepped;
And the grasse, that was gray,
    greened belive.

                                    ANON.

Perfectioni Hymnus

What should I call this creature,
    Which now is grown unto maturity?
How should I blaze this feature
    As firm and constant as Eternity?
Call it Perfection? Fie!
    'Tis perfecter than brightest names can light it:
Call it Heaven's mirror? Aye.
    Alas, best attributes can never right it.
Beauty's resistless thunder?
    All nomination is too straight of sense:
Deep contemplation's wonder?
    That appellation give this excellence.
Within all best confined
    (Now feebler Genius end thy slighter rhyming)
No suburbs, all is *Mind*,
    As far from spots, as possible defining.

                                JOHN MARSTON

He saw coming from her bee-hives
Many centuries of beauty
In a few years of age.

                            GÓNGORA
                    (trans. Gerald Brenan)

Virginal exquisite queen, of long gentle thinking,
the colour of breaking day on a deserted sea.

CYNDDELW
(trans. Glwn Williams)

Behaviorism

Of course, Behaviorism "works." So does torture. Give me a
no-nonsense, down-to-earth behaviorist, a few drugs, and simple
electrical appliances, and in six months I will have him reciting
the Athanasian Creed in public.

Some phobias persist as habits long after the emotional conflict or
trauma which gave origin to them has disappeared. One case, for
example, was that of a professional man who suffered from an intense fear of thunderstorms. Since thunderstorms are not uncommon in Britain, he was often in a state of considerable tension,
fearing that he would incur the ridicule of his colleagues if he
suddenly felt obliged to seek refuge from thunder by hiding
under the table or retiring to a lavatory. His symptom took origin from a traumatic experience in early childhood in which he
had nearly been struck by a flash of lightning which was accompanied by a deafening clap of thunder. In other respects, a more
or less superficial enquiry indicated that this man was both happy
and successful. This isolated phobia of thunderstorms had little
obvious connection with the rest of his character structure; but,
like a diseased appendix, was a pathological appendage of which
he would have been thankful to be rid, and the removal of which
was likely to cause small disturbance to the rest of his personality.
In such a case, a behavior therapist would probably expose the
patient gradually to increasing intensities of the noise of thunder
and electrical flashes; at first, perhaps, combining this with sedation or other methods of extinguishing responses. When the pa-

tient had become sufficiently accustomed to reacting without fear to artificial thunder and lightning in the laboratory, it would be hoped that he could finally be exposed to a real thunderstorm and discover that his response of fear had been abolished.

If behavior therapy had been available at the time that this patient was seen, the author would undoubtedly have advised it: but such cases, unfortunately, are the exception rather than the rule in psychiatric practice. The majority of phobias do not spring from isolated traumatic incidents, but are intimately connected with the patient's style of life and his whole development from childhood onwards.

ANTHONY STORR

Belief

⚜

To all human experience, with the possible exception of physical pain, the maxim *Credo ut intelligam* applies. It is impossible for a man to separate a fact of experience from his interpretation of it, an interpretation which, except in the case of the insane, is not peculiar to himself but has been learned from others.

It is true, as Pascal says, that "to believe, to doubt, and to deny well are to the man what the race is to the horse," but only in that order. We must believe before we can doubt, and doubt before we can deny. And, with the exception of autistic children, we all do begin by believing what we are told.

Man is what he believes.

A. CHEKHOV

If there were a verb meaning "to believe falsely," it would not have any significant first person, present indicative.

LUDWIG WITTGENSTEIN

"By their fruits you shall know them" is a test which is, no doubt, true in the long run. In the short run, however, it seems ineffective. Out of erroneous beliefs, men have done the most absurd and wicked things, but how are they to recognise that their behavior is absurd and wicked until they have replaced their beliefs by truer ones?

Some like to understand what they believe in. Others like to believe in what they understand.

STANISLAUS LEC

He who believes in nothing still needs a girl to believe in him.

EUGEN ROSENSTOCK-HUESSY

There is a great difference between *still* believing something and believing it *again*.

G. C. LICHTENBERG

Doubts, unlike denials, should always be humorous.

It is fatal to repress doubt; it turns the doubter into a humorless bigot.

To deny A is to put A behind bars.

PAUL VALÉRY

Birds

Surcharged with discontent,
　　To Sylvane's bower I went
To ease my heavy grief-oppressed heart,
　　And try what comfort winged creatures
Could yield unto my inward troubled smart,
　　By modulating their delightful measures

To my ears pleasing ever.
Of strains so sweet, sweet birds deprive us never.

The thrush did pipe full clear,
    And eke with merry cheer
The linnet lifted up her pleasant voice.
    The goldfinch chirped and the pie did chatter,
The blackbird whistled and bade me rejoice,
    The stockdove mumured with solemn flatter.
        The little daw, ka-ka he cried;
            The hic-quale he beside
Tickled his part in a parti-coloured coat.
    The jay did blow his hautboy gallantly.
The wren did treble many a pretty note.
    The woodpecker did hammer melody.
        The kite, tiw-whiw, full oft
            Cried, soaring up aloft,
        And down again returned presently.
To whom the herald of cornutus sung cuckoo
Ever, whilst poor Margery cried: "Who
        Did ring nights 'larum bell?"
            Withal all did do well.
            O might I hear them ever.
Of strains so sweet, sweet birds deprive us never.

        Then Hesperus on high
        Brought cloudy night in sky,
When lo, the thicket-keeping company
        Of feathered singers left their madrigals,
Sonnets and elegies, and presently
        Shut them within their mossy severals,
And I came home and vowed to love them ever.
Of strains so sweet, sweet birds deprive us never.

                            ANON.
                    (set by John Bartlet)

When I awoke, dimly aware of some commotion and outcry in
the clearing, the light was slanting down through the pines in

such a way that the glade was lit like some vast cathedral. I could see the dust motes of wood pollen in the long shaft of light, and there on the extended branch sat an enormous raven with a red and squirming nestling in its beak.

The sound that awoke me was the outraged cries of the nestling's parents, who flew helplessly in circles about the clearing. The sleek black monster was indifferent to them. He gulped, whetted his beak on the dead branch a moment and sat still. Up to that point the little tragedy had followed the usual pattern. But suddenly, out of all that area of woodland, a soft sound of complaint began to rise. Into the glade fluttered small birds of half a dozen varieties drawn by the anguished cries of the tiny parents.

No one dared to attack the raven. But they cried there in some instinctive common misery, the bereaved and the unbereaved. The glade filled with their soft rustling and their cries. They fluttered as though to point their wings at the murderer. There was a dim intangible ethic he had violated, that they knew. He was a bird of death.

And he, the murderer, the black bird at the heart of life, sat on there, glistening in the common light, formidable, unperturbed, untouchable.

The sighing died. It was then I saw the judgment. It was the judgment of life against death. I will never see it again so forcefully presented. I will never hear it again in notes so tragically prolonged. For in the midst of protest, they forgot the violence. There, in that clearing, the crystal note of a song sparrow lifted hesitantly in the hush. And, finally, after painful fluttering, another took the song, and then another, the song passing from one bird to another, doubtfully at first, as though some evil thing was being slowly forgotten. Till suddenly they took heart and sang from many throats joyously together as birds are known to sing. They sang because life is sweet and sunlight beautiful. They sang under the brooding shadow of the raven. In simple truth they had forgotten the raven, for they were the singers of life, and not of death.

LOREN EISELEY

Bishops

It is an idle but entertaining pastime to imagine an alternative career to that which one has actually chosen, but in which one believes one possesses the talent and temperament which could have made one successful.

In my own case, I like to fancy that, had I taken Anglican Holy Orders, I might by now be a bishop, politically liberal I hope, theologically and liturgically conservative I know. I should like to believe that I would be long-suffering with those of my clergy who held different views, but I rather fear that I might be as intolerant as the dean of whom Sydney Smith said, "He deserves to be preached to death by wild curates."

In literature, bishops are usually presented as either unsympathetic or slightly comic characters, a price they pay for their worldly eminence and their odd clothes. A comic presentation is, in their case, particularly easy because they can be referred to, not by their own names, but by the place-names of their sees.

Frequently did Lord John meet the destroying Bishops; much did he commend their daily heap of ruins; sweetly did they smile on each other, and much charming talk there was of meteorology and catarrh and the particular cathedral they were pulling down at the time; till one fine morning the Home Secretary, with a voice more bland, and a look more ardently affectionate, than that which the masculine mouse bestows on his nibbling female, informed them that the Government meant to take all the Church property into their own hands, to pay the rates out of it, and deliver the residue to the rightful possessors. Such an effect, they say, was never before produced by a *coup de théâtre*. The Commission was separated in an instant: London clenched his fist; Canterbury was hurried out by his chaplains and put into a warm bed; a solemn vacancy spread itself over the face of Gloucester; Lincoln was taken out in strong hysterics.

SYDNEY SMITH

Black

◆§§◆

In my opinion, the most heroic living white American is Mr. John Howard Griffin. He comes from an old Texas family, is a Roman Catholic and a musicologist. There is now, it seems, a substance which, when injected into the body, so darkens the pigmentation of the skin that a white man can pass for a Negro. The effect, however, is temporary, so that, when the injections are discontinued, he regains his natural color. These injections Mr. Griffin took, and in his book *Black Like Me* he has described his experiences in the Deep South as a pseudo-Negro. When the book came out his parents were forced to leave their home town, and Mr. Griffin himself, while traveling in Mississippi, was hauled out of his car and beaten over the kidneys with chains, so that his health is now permanently impaired. Here are three extracts.

Behind the custard stand stood an old unpainted privy leaning badly to one side. I returned to the dispensing window of the stand.

"Yes, sir," the white man said congenially. "You want something else?"

"Where's the nearest rest room I could use?" I asked.

He brushed his white, brimless cook's cap back and rubbed his forefinger against his sweaty forehead. "Let's see. You can go on up there to the bridge and then cut down the road to the left . . . and just follow that road. You'll come to a little settlement —there's some stores and gas stations there."

"How far is it?" I asked, pretending to be in greater discomfort than I actually was.

"Not far—thirteen, maybe fourteen blocks." . . .

"Isn't there anyplace closer?" I said, determined to see if he would not offer me the use of the dilapidated outhouse, which certainly no human could degrade more than time and the elements had.

His seamed face showed the concern and sympathy of one human being for another in a predicament every man understands. "I can't think of any . . .", he said slowly.

I glanced around the side toward the outhouse. "Any chance of me running in there for a minute?"

"Nope," he said—clipped, final, soft, as though he regretted it but could never permit such a thing. "I'm sorry." . . .

By dark I was away from the beach area and out in the country. Strangely, I began getting rides. Men would pass you in daylight but pick you up after dark.

I must have had a dozen rides that evening. They blear into a nightmare, the one scarcely distinguishable from the other.

It quickly became obvious why they picked me up. All but two picked me up the way they would pick up a pornographic photograph or book—except that this was verbal pornography. With a Negro, they assumed they need give no semblance of self-respect or respectability. The visual element entered into it. In a car at night visibility is reduced. A man will reveal himself in the dark, which gives an illusion of anonymity more than he will in the bright light. Some were shamelessly open, some shamelessly subtle. All showed morbid curiosity about the sexual life of the Negro, and all had, at base, the same stereotyped image of the Negro as an inexhaustible sex-machine with oversized genitals and a vast store of experiences, immensely varied. . . .

. . . Each time one of them let me out of his car, I hoped the next would spare me his pantings. I remained mute and pleaded my exhaustion and lack of sleep.

"I'm so tired, I just can't think," I would say.

Like men who had promised themselves pleasure, they would not be denied. It became a strange sort of hounding as they nudged my skull for my sexual reminiscences.

"Well, did you ever do such-and-such?"

"I don't know . . ." I moaned.

"What's the matter—haven't you got any manhood? My old man told me you wasn't a man till you'd done such-and-such."

Or the older ones, hardened, cynical in their lechery. "Now, don't try to kid me. I wasn't born yesterday. You know you've done such-and-such, just like I have. Hell, it's good that way. Tell me, did you ever get a white woman?"

"Do you think I'm crazy?" . . .

"I didn't ask if you was crazy," he said. "I asked if you ever had one—or ever wanted one." Then, conniving, sweet-toned, "There's plenty white women would like to have a good buck Negro."

"A Negro'd be asking for the rope to get himself mixed up with white women."

"You're just telling me that, but I'll bet inside you think differently . . ."

"This is sure beautiful country through here. What's the main crop?"

"*Don't* you? You can tell me. Hell, I don't care."

"No, sir," I sighed.

"You're lying in your teeth and you know it."

Silence. Soon after, almost abruptly he halted the car and said, "Okay, this is as far as I go." He spoke as though he resented my uncooperative attitude, my refusal to give him this strange verbal sexual pleasure.

I thanked him for the ride and stepped down onto the highway. He drove on in the same direction. . . .

The policeman nodded affably to me and I knew then that I had successfully passed back into white society, that I was once more a first-class citizen, that all doors into cafés, rest rooms, libraries, movies, concerts, schools and churches were suddenly open to me. After so long I could not adjust to it. A sense of exultant liberation flooded through me. I crossed over to a restaurant and entered. I took a seat beside white men at the counter and the waitress smiled at me. It was a miracle. . . .

I ate the white meal, drank the white water, received the white smiles and wondered how it could be. What sense could a man make of it?

I left the café and walked to the elegant Whitney Hotel. A Negro rushed to take my knapsacks. He gave me the smiles, the "yes, sir—yes, sir."

I felt like saying, "You're not fooling me," but now I was back on the other side of the wall. There was no longer communication between us, no longer the glance that said everything.

JOHN HOWARD GRIFFIN

Book Reviews, Imaginary

⟨➤⟩

Brittle Galaxy. By Barbara Sporte.

A colorful and courageous attempt to put the point of view of the artist misunderstood in a world of wars and rumors of wars. Dalton Sparleigh is the eternal figure of the hero who is the center of his world, and regards his own personality as the most important thing in life. 1,578 pages of undiluted enthrallment.

Groaning Carcase. By Frederick Duddle.

A very delicate and tactfully written plea for old horses, against a background of country-house life. It is fiction made more compelling than fact by one who seems to be right inside the horse's mind.

Splendid Sorrow. By Walter Fallow.

Was Ernst Hörenwurst, adventurer and rake, the Margrave Friedrich Meiningen of Hohefurstenau-Lebensbletter? Mr. Fallow, in his new historical romance, has no hesitation in leaving the question unanswered.

Tricks with Cheese. By "Cheesophile" (of *Cheese World*).

The author appears to be able to make everything, from a model of the Palace of Justice in Brussels to a bust of his aunt, out of cheese. A good book for the fireside.

Fain Had I Thus Loved. By Freda Trowte.

Miss Trowte has been called by the *Outcry* the Anatole France of Herefordshire. There is an indescribable quality of something evocative yet elusively incomprehensible about her work. The character of Nydda is burningly etched by as corrosive a pen as is now being wielded anywhere.

No Second Churning. By Arthur Clawes.

An almost unbearably vital study of a gas-inspector who puts gas-inspecting before love. Awarded the Prix de Seattle, this book should enhance the author's growing reputation as an interpreter of life's passionate bypaths.

Pursuant To What Shame. By Goola Drain.

All those who enjoyed Miss Drain's romantic handling of a love-story in *Better Thine Endeavor* and *Immediate Beasts* will welcome this trenchant tale of an irresponsible girl who poisons her uncle. A famous tennis player said, before he had even seen the book, "In my opinion Miss Drain is unique and unchallengeable. Her command of words is a delight."

J. B. MORTON

Bores

Who on earth invented the silly convention that it is boring or impolite to talk shop? Nothing is more interesting to listen to, especially if the shop is not one's own.

We are almost always bored by just those whom we must not find boring.

LA ROCHEFOUCAULD

What is more enchanting than the voices of young people when you can't hear what they say?

L. P. SMITH

The most intolerable people are provincial celebrities.

A. CHEKHOV

'Twas when fleet Snowball's head was waxen gray,
A luckless leveret met him on his way,—
Who knows not Snowball—he whose race renowned
Is still victorious on each coursing ground?
Swaffham, Newmarket, and the Roman Camp
Have seen them victors o'er each meaner stamp.—
In vain the youngling sought with doubling wile
The hedge, the hill, the thicket, or the stile.
Experience sage the lack of speed supplied,
And in the gap he sought, the victim died.
So was I once, in thy fair street, Saint James,
Through walking cavaliers, and car-borne dames,
Descried, pursued, turned o'er again and o'er,
Coursed, coted, mouthed by an unfeeling bore.

WALTER SCOTT

Calvin

᠂ᢗᢲᢧᢅ

. . . It ought to be easier for us than for the nineteenth century
to understand his attraction. He was a man born to be the idol of
revolutionary intellectuals; an unhesitating doctrinaire, ruthless
and efficient in putting his doctrine into practice. Though bred
as a lawyer, he found the time before he was thirty to produce
the first text of the *Institutio* (1536) and never made any serious
modification of its theory. By 1537 he was already at Geneva and
the citizens were being paraded before him in bodies of ten to
swear to a system of doctrine. Sumptuary legislation and the ban-
ishment of the dissentient Caroli made it plain that here was the
man of the new order who really meant business. . . . The
moral severity of his rule laid the foundations of the meaning
which the word 'puritan' has since acquired. But this severity did

not mean that his theology was, in the last resort, more ascetic than that of Rome. It sprang from his refusal to allow the Roman distinction between the life of 'religion' and the life of the world, between the Counsels and the Commandments. Calvin's picture of the fully Christian life was less hostile to pleasure and to the body than Fisher's; but then Calvin demanded that every man should be made to live the fully Christian life. In academic jargon, he lowered the honours standard and abolished the pass degree.

Modern parallels are always to some extent misleading. Yet . . . it may be useful to compare the influence of Calvin on that age with the influence of Marx on our own; or even of Marx and Lenin in one, for Calvin had both expounded the new system in theory and set it going in practice. This will at least serve to eliminate the absurd idea that Elizabethan Calvinists were some-how grotesque, elderly people, standing outside the main forward current of life. In their own day they were, of course, the very latest thing. Unless we can imagine the freshness, the audacity, and (soon) the fashionableness of Calvinism, we shall get our whole picture wrong. It was the creed of progressives, even of revolutionaries. It appealed strongly to those tempers that would have been Marxist in the nineteen-thirties. The fierce young don, the learned lady, the courtier with intellectual leanings, were likely to be Calvinists. When hard rocks of Predestination out-crop in the flowery soil of the *Arcadia* or the *Faerie Queene*, we are apt to think them anomalous, but we are wrong. The Calvin-ism is as modish as the shepherds and goddesses. . . . Youth is the taunt commonly brought against the puritan leaders by their op-ponents: youth and cocksureness. As we recognize the type we begin, perhaps, to wonder less that such a work as the *Institutio* should have been so eagerly welcomed. In it Calvin goes on from the original Protestant experience to build a system, to extrapo-late, to raise all the dark questions and give without flinching the dark answers. It is, however, a masterpiece of literary form; and we may suspect that those who read it with most approval were troubled by the fate of predestined vessels of wrath just about as much as young Marxists in our own age are troubled by the ap-proaching liquidation of the *bourgeoisie*. Had the word 'sentimentality' been known to them, Elizabethan Calvinists would certainly have used it of any who attacked the *Institutio* as morally repulsive.

C. S. LEWIS

Camps, Concentration

‿❧

. . . The decision to remain alive or die is probably a supreme example of self-determination. Therefore the SS attitude toward suicide may be mentioned.

The stated principle was: the more prisoners to commit suicide, the better. But even there, the decision must not be the prisoner's. An SS man might provoke a prisoner to commit suicide by running against the electrically charged wire fence, and that was all right. But for those who took the initiative in killing themselves, the SS issued (in Dachau in 1933) a special order: prisoners who attempted suicide but did not succeed were to receive twenty-five lashes and prolonged solitary confinement. Supposedly this was to punish them for their failure to do away with themselves; but I am convinced it was much more to punish them for the act of self-determination. . . .

The layers of courtesy and kindness which made even negative attitudes sufferable outside the camp were nearly always absent. There was rarely a "No, thank you" either in tone or words; responses were always in their harshest forms. One heard nothing but, "Idiot!" "Go to hell!" "Shit!" or worse; and no provoking was needed to get this in answer to a neutral question. Men lay in wait for any opening to spit out their pent-up frustration and anger. Also, the chance to express vehemence was an added relief. . . . Even hurting someone's feelings was a satisfaction. It proved there was still somebody or something one mattered to, had an effect on, even if it was a painful effect. But in the process one came a step closer to the SS way of meeting life and its problems. . . .

Slowly most prisoners accepted terms of verbal aggression that definitely did not originate in their previous vocabulary, but were taken over from the very different vocabulary of the SS. . . . From copying SS verbal aggressions to copying their form of bodily aggression was one more step, but it took several years to reach that. It was not unusual, when prisoners were in charge of others, to find old prisoners (and not only former criminals) behaving worse than the SS. Sometimes they were trying to find favor with the guards, but more often it was because they considered it the best way to treat prisoners in the camp.

Old prisoners tended to identify with the SS not only in their goals and values, but even in appearance. They tried to arrogate to themselves old pieces of SS uniforms, and when that was not possible they tried to sew and mend their prison garb until it resembled the uniforms. . . . When asked why they did it, they said it was because they wanted to look smart. To them looking smart meant to look like their enemies.

Old prisoners felt great satisfaction if, during the twice daily counting of prisoners, they really had stood well at attention or given a snappy salute. They prided themselves on being as tough, or tougher, than the SS. In their identification they went so far as to copy SS leisure time activities. One of the games played by the guards was to find out who could stand being hit the longest without uttering a complaint. This game was copied by old prisoners, as if they were not hit often enough without repeating the experience as a game. . . .

Prisoners who came to believe the repeated statements of the guards—that there was no hope for them, and they would never leave the camp except as a corpse—who came to feel that their environment was one over which they could exercise no influence whatsoever, these prisoners were, in a literal sense, walking corpses. In the camp they were called "moslems" (*Muselmänner*). . . . It began when they stopped acting on their own. And that was the moment when other prisoners recognized what was happening and separated themselves from these now "marked" men, because any further association with them could lead only to one's own destruction. At this point such men still obeyed orders, but only blindly or automatically; no longer selectively or with any inner reservation or any hatred at being so abused. They still looked about, or at least moved their eyes around. The looking stopped much later, though even then they still moved their bodies when ordered, but never did anything on their own any more. Typically, this stopping of action began when they no longer lifted their legs as they walked, but only shuffled them. When finally even the looking about on their own stopped, they soon died. . . .

As long as they still asked for food, followed someone to get it, stretched out a hand for it and ate what was given eagerly, they could still, with great effort, have been returned to "normal" prisoner status, deteriorated as they were. In the next stage of disintegration, receiving food unexpectedly still led to a momentary lighting up of the face and a grateful hangdog look, though hardly any verbal response. But when they no longer reached out for it spontaneously, no longer responded with thanks, an effort to smile, or a look at the giver, they were nearly always beyond help. Later they took food, sometimes ate it, sometimes not, but no longer had a feeling response. In the last, just before the terminal stage, they no longer ate it. . . .

To survive as a man, not a walking corpse, as a debased and degraded but still human being, one had first and foremost to remain informed and aware of what made up one's personal point of no return beyond which one would never, under any circumstances, give in to the oppressor, even if it meant risking and losing one's life. It meant being aware that if one survived at the price of overreaching this point one would be holding on to a life that had lost all meaning. It would mean surviving—not with lowered self-respect, but without any. . . .

Second in importance was keeping oneself informed of how one felt about complying when the ultimate decision as to where to stand firm was not called into question. . . . One had to comply with debasing and amoral commands if one wished to survive; but one had to remain cognizant that one's reason for complying was "to remain alive and unchanged as a person." Therefore, one had to decide, for any given action, whether it was truly necessary for one's safety or that of others, and whether committing it was good, neutral or bad. This keeping informed and aware of one's actions—though it could not alter the required act, save in extremities—this minimal distance from one's own behavior, and the freedom to feel differently about it depending on its character, this too was what permitted the prisoner to remain a human being. . . .

Prisoners who understood this fully came to know that this, and only this, formed the crucial difference between retaining one's humanity (and often life itself) and accepting death as a human being (or perhaps physical death): whether one retained the freedom to choose autonomously one's attitude to extreme conditions even when they seemed totally beyond one's ability to influence them.

BRUNO BETTELHEIM

Affliction stamps the soul to its very depths with the scorn, the disgust and even the self-hatred and sense of guilt that crime logically should produce but actually does not.

SIMONE WEIL

A Commandant Reminisces

Even those petty incidents that others might not notice I found hard to forget. In Auschwitz I truly had no reason to complain that I was bored.

If I was deeply affected by some incident, I found it impossible to go back to my home and family. I would mount my horse and ride, until I had chased the terrible picture away. Often, at night, I would walk through the stables and seek relief among my beloved animals.

It would often happen, when at home, that my thoughts suddenly turned to incidents that had occurred during the extermination. I then had to go out. I could no longer bear to be in my homely family circle. When I saw my children happily playing, or observed my wife's delight over our youngest, the thought would often come to me: how long will our happiness last? My wife could never understand these gloomy moods of mine, and ascribed them to some annoyance connected with my work.

When at night I stood out there beside the transports or by the gas-chambers or the fires, I was often compelled to think of my wife and children, without, however, allowing myself to connect them closely with all that was happening.

It was the same with the married men who worked in the crematoriums or at the fire pits.

When they saw the women and children going into the gas chambers, their thoughts instinctively turned to their own families.

I was no longer happy in Auschwitz once the mass exterminations had begun.

I had become dissatisfied with myself. To this must be added that I was worried because of anxiety about my principal task, the never-ending work, and the untrustworthiness of my colleagues.

Then the refusal to understand, or even to listen to me, on the part of my superiors. It was in truth not a happy or desirable state of affairs. Yet everyone in Auschwitz believed that the commandant lived a wonderful life.

My family, to be sure, were well provided for in Auschwitz. Every wish that my wife or children expressed was granted them. The children could lead a free and untrammeled life. My wife's garden was a paradise of flowers. The prisoners never missed an opportunity for doing some little act of kindness to my wife or children and thus attracting their attention.

No former prisoner can ever say that he was in any way or at any time badly treated in our house. My wife's greatest pleasure would have been to give a present to every prisoner who was in any way connected with our household.

The children were perpetually begging me for cigarettes for the prisoners. They were particularly fond of the ones who worked in the garden.

My whole family displayed an intense love of agriculture and particularly for animals of all sorts. Every Sunday I had to walk them across the fields, and visit the stables, and we might never miss the kennels where the dogs were kept. Our two horses and the foal were especially beloved.

The children always kept animals in the garden, creatures the prisoners were forever bringing them. Tortoises, martens, cats, lizards: there was always something new and interesting to be seen there. In summer they splashed in the wading pool in the garden, or in the Sola. But their greatest joy was when Daddy bathed with them. He had, however, so little time for all these childish pleasures. Today I deeply regret that I did not devote more time to my family. I always felt that I had to be on duty the whole time. This exaggerated sense of duty has always made life more difficult for me than it need have been. Again and again my wife reproached me and said: "You must think not only of the service always, but of your family too."

Yet what did my wife know about all that lay so heavily on my mind? She has never been told.

When, on Pohl's suggestion, Auschwitz was divided up, he gave me the choice of being commandant of Sachsenhausen or head of DK.

It was something quite exceptional for Pohl to allow any officer a choice of jobs. He gave me twenty-four hours in which to decide. It was really a kindly gesture in good will, a recompence, as he saw it, for the task I had been given at Auschwitz.

At first I felt unhappy at the prospect of uprooting myself, for I had become deeply involved with Auschwitz as a result of all the difficulties and troubles and the many heavy tasks that had been assigned to me there.

But then I was glad to be free from it all.

RUDOLF HOESS

Castration Complex

As a child, one of my favorite books was an English translation of Dr. Hoffmann's *Struwelpeter,* and my favorite poem in the book was "The Story of Little Suck-a-Thumb."

One day, Mamma said: "Conrad dear,
I must go out and leave you here.
But mind now, Conrad, what I say,
Don't suck your thumb while I'm away.
The great tall tailor always comes
To little boys that suck their thumbs;
And ere they dream what he's about,
He takes his great sharp scissors out
And cuts their thumbs clean off—and then,
You know, they never grow again.

Mamma had scarcely turn'd her back,
The thumb was in, Alack! Alack!

The door flew open, in he ran,
The great, long, red-legged scissor-man.
Oh! children, see! the tailor's come
And caught out little Suck-a-Thumb.
Snip! Snap! Snip! the scissors go;
And Conrad cries out—Oh! Oh! Oh!
Snip! Snap! Snip! They go so fast,
That both his thumbs are off at last.

Mamma comes home; there Conrad stands,
And looks quite sad, and shows his hands;
"Ah!" said Mamma, "I knew he'd come
To naughty little Suck-a-Thumb."

Reading this poem today, I say to myself, "Of course, it's not about thumb-sucking at all, but about masturbation, which is punished by castration." But if so, why did I enjoy the poem as a child? Why was I not frightened? In so far as it did arouse fear, it was a wholly pleasing fictional fear. It so happened that I was a nail-biter, but I knew perfectly well that Suck-a-Thumb's fate would not be mine, because the scissor-man was a figure in a poem, not a real person.

Very different is the fear aroused in me by spiders, crabs, and octopi, which are, I suspect, symbols to me for the castrating *Vagina Dentata*.

Cats

The Monk and His Pet Cat

I and my white pangur
Have each his special art:
His mind is set on hunting mice,
Mine is upon my special craft.

I love to rest—better than any fame!—
With close study at my little book;
White Pangur does not envy me:
He loves his childish play.

When in our house we two are all alone—
A tale without tedium!
We have sport never-ending!
Something to exercise our wit.

At times by feats of derring-do
A mouse sticks in his net,
While into my net there drops
A difficult problem of hard meaning.

He points his full shining eye
Against the fence of the wall:
I point my clear though feeble eye
Against the keenness of science.

He rejoices with quick leaps
When in his sharp claw sticks a mouse:
I too rejoice when I have grasped
A problem difficult and dearly loved.

Though we are thus at all times,
Neither hinders the other,
Each of us pleased with his own art
Amuses himself alone.

He is a master of the work
Which every day he does:
While I am at my own work
To bring difficulty to clearness.

Anon. Irish
(trans. Kuno Meyer)

Peter

Strong and slippery, built for the midnight grass-party confronted
by four cats,

he sleeps his time away—the detached first claw on the foreleg,
which corresponds

to the thumb, retracted to its tip; the small tuft of fronds
or katydid-legs above each eye, still numbering the unit in
each group;

the shadbones regularly set about the mouth, to droop
or rise

in unison like the porcupine's quills—motionless. He lets himself
be flat-

tened out by gravity, as it were a piece of seaweed tamed and
weakened by

exposure to the sun; compelled when extended, to lie
stationary. Sleep is the result of his delusion that one must
do as
well as one can for oneself; sleep—epitome of what is to

him as to the average person, the end of life. Demonstrate on him
how
the lady caught the dangerous southern snake, placing a forked
stick on either
side of its innocuous neck; one need not try to stir
him up; his prune-shaped head and alligator eyes are not a
party to the
joke. Lifted and handled, he may be dangled like an eel or
set

up on the forearm like a mouse; his eyes bisected by pupils of a
pin's
width, are flickeringly exhibited, then covered up. May be? I
should say
might have been; when he has been got the better of in a
dream—as in a fight with nature or with cats—we all know
it. Profound sleep is
not with him a fixed illusion. Springing about with frog-
like ac-

curacy, emitting jerky cries when taken in the hand, he is himself
again; to sit caged by the rungs of a domestic chair would be
unprofit-
able—human. What is the good of hypocrisy? It
is permissible to choose one's employment, to abandon the
wire nail, the
roly-poly, when it shows signs of being no longer a pleas-

ure, to score the adjacent magazine with a double line of strokes.
He can
talk, but insolently says nothing. What of it? When one is
frank, one's very

presence is a compliment. It is clear that he can see
the virtue of naturalness, that he is one of those who do not
regard
the published fact as a surrender. As for the disposition

invariably to affront, an animal with claws wants to have to use
them; that eel-like extension of trunk into tail is not an accident. To
leap, to lengthen out, divide the air—to purloin, to pursue.
To tell the hen: fly over the fence, go in the wrong way in
your perturba-
tion—this is life; to do less would be nothing but dishonesty.

MARIANNE MOORE

The Long Cat

A short-haired black cat always looks longer than any other cat.
But this particular one, Babou, nicknamed the Long-cat, really
did measure, stretched right out flat, well over a yard. I used to
measure him sometimes.

"He's stopped growing longer," I said one day to my mother.
"Isn't it a pity?"

"Why a pity? He's too long as it is. I can't understand why
you want everything to grow bigger. It's bad to grow too much,
very bad indeed!"

It's true that it always worried her when she thought her children were growing too fast, and she had good cause to be anxious
about my elder half-brother, who went on growing until he was
twenty-four.

"But I'd love to grow a bit taller."

"D'you mean you'd like to be like that Brisedoux girl, five-
feet-seven tall at twelve years old? A midget can always make
herself liked. But what can you do with a gigantic beauty? Who
would want to marry her?"

"Couldn't Babou get married then?"

"Oh, a cat's a cat. Babou's only too long when he really wants
to be. Are we even sure he's black? He's probably white in
snowy weather, dark blue at night, and red when he goes to steal

strawberries. He's very light when he lies on your knees, and very heavy when I carry him into the kitchen in the evenings to prevent him from sleeping on my bed. I think he's too much of a vegetarian to be a real cat."

For the Long-cat really did steal strawberries, picking out the ripest of the variety called Docteur-Morere which are so sweet, and of the Hautboys which taste faintly of nuts. According to the season he would also go for the tender tips of the asparagus, and when it came to melons his choice was not so much for cantaloups as for the kind called Noir-des-Carmes whose rind, marbled light and dark like the skin of a salamander, he knew how to rip open. In all this he was not exceptional. I once had a she-cat who used to crunch rings of raw onion, provided they were the sweet onions of the South. There are cats who set great store by oysters, snails, and clams. . . .

By virtue of his serpent-like build, the Long-cat excelled in strange leaps in which he nearly twisted himself into a figure of eight. In full sunlight his winter coat, which was longer and more satiny than in summer, revealed the waterings and markings of his far-off tabby ancestor. A tom will remain playful until he is quite old; but even in play his face never loses the gravity that is stamped on it. The Long-cat's expression softened only when he looked at my mother. Then his white whiskers would bristle powerfully, while into his eyes crept the smile of an innocent little boy. He used to follow her when she went to pick violets along the wall that separated M. de Fourolles' garden from ours. The close-set border provided every day a big bunch which mother let fade, either pinned to her bodice or in an empty glass, because violets in water lose all their scent. Step by step the Long-cat followed his stooping mistress, sometimes imitating with his paw the gesture of her hand groping among the leaves, and imitating her discoveries also. "Ha, ha!" he would cry, "me too!" and thereupon show his prize: a bombadier beetle, a pink worm, or a shrivelled cockchafer.

COLETTE
(trans. Enid McLeod)

Chamber Music

❧

Of the audience at a chamber-music concert, an Oxford Don once remarked, "They look like the sort of people who go to the English Church abroad."

Chamber music is essentially an intimate affair, to be played in private houses by friends for friends. In the anonymous atmosphere of a public concert hall, it becomes "arty."

Chamber Music

FIRST VIOLIN

I, in love with the beauty of this world, endow it with my own beauty. The world has no abyss. Streaming out, my heart spends itself. I am only song: I sound.

SECOND VIOLIN

For me, beside your more ethereal being, it is forbidden to have an I. Not the world—but more firmly and substantially: the earth has taught me. There it is growing dark. Let me accompany you, sister!

VIOLA

My grey hair makes it my duty to name the abyss for you. As you two childlike kindred spirits skim along, even the quarrel about nothing becomes attractive. But I suffer.

CELLO

I know in my heart of hearts, that all is fate, the finely done and the unrelieved. I am true to the whole: enjoy life and repent! I do not warn. I weep with you. I console.

JOSEF WEINHEBER
(trans. Patrick Bridgewater)

Chef, Life of a

◆§§◆

CARÊME, Marie-Antoine: Like Theseus and Romulus, like all founders of empires, Carême was a sort of lost child. He was born in Paris in 1784, in a woodyard where his father was employed. There were fifteen children, and the father did not know how to feed them all.

One day, when Marie-Antoine was eleven years old, his father took him to the town gate for dinner. Then, leaving him in the middle of the street, he said to him: "Go, little one. There are good trades in this world. Let the rest of us languish in the misery in which we are doomed to die. This is a time when fortunes are made by those who have the wit, and that you have. Tonight or tomorrow, find a good house that may open its doors to you. Go with what God has given you and what I may add to that." And the good man gave him his blessing.

From that time on, Marie-Antoine never again saw his father and mother, who died young, nor his brothers and sisters, who were scattered over the world.

Night fell. The boy saw a lighted window and knocked on it. It was a cookshop whose proprietor's name has not been preserved in history. He took the boy and put him to work next day.

At sixteen, he quit this dingy tavern and went to work as an assistant to a restaurateur. His progress was rapid, and he already knew what he wanted to be. He went to work for Bailly, a famous pastrycook on the Rue Vivienne, who excelled in cream tarts and catered to the Prince de Talleyrand. From that moment he saw his future clearly. He had discovered his vocation.

"At seventeen," he says in his *Mémoires*, "I was chief pastrycook at Bailly's. He was a good master and took an interest in me. He gave me time off to study designs from prints. He put me in charge of preparing several set pieces for the table of the First Consul. I used my designs and my nights in his service, and he repaid me with kindness. In his establishment I began to innovate.

The illustrious pastrycook Avice was then flourishing. His work aroused my enthusiasm, and knowledge of his methods gave me courage. I sought to follow without imitating him. I learned to execute every trick of the trade, and made unique, extraordinary pieces by myself. But to get there, young people, how many sleepless nights! I could not work on my designs and calculations until after nine or ten o'clock, and I worked three quarters of the night.

"I left M. Bailly with tears in my eyes and went to work for the successor of M. Gendron. I made it a condition that if I had the opportunity to make an 'extra' I could have someone replace me. A few months later, I left the great pastryshops behind altogether, and devoted myself to preparing great dinners. It was enough to do. I rose higher and higher and earned a lot of money. Others became jealous of me, a poor child of labor, and I have often been the butt of attacks from little pastrycooks who will have far to climb to where I am now."

During the prodigality of the Directoire, Carême refined cooking into the delicate luxury and exquisite sensuality of the Empire. The Talleyrand household was served with wisdom and grandeur, Carême says. It gave an example to others and kept them in mind of his basic principles.

The culinary director in this household was Bouché, or Bouchésèche, who came from the Condé household, famous for its fine fare. So Talleyrand's cuisine was simply a continuation of the cuisine of the Condé household. Carême dedicated his *Pâtissier royal* to Bouché. It was there that he made the acquaintance of Laguipière, the Emperor's cook, who died in the retreat from Moscow. Until that time, Carême had followed his art. After Laguipière, he learned to improvise. But practice did not satisfy him any longer. He wanted to go more profoundly into theory, to copy designs, to read and analyze scientific works and follow through with studies parallel to his profession. He wrote and illustrated a *History of the Roman Table*, but, unfortunately, both manuscript and drawings have been lost. Carême was a poet. He placed his art on the same level as all the others. And he was right to do so.

"From behind my stoves," he says, "I contemplated the cuisines of India, China, Egypt, Greece, Turkey, Italy, Germany, and Switzerland. I felt the unworthy methods of routine crumble under my blows."

Carême had grown up under the Empire, and you can imagine his distress when he saw it crash. He had to be forced to execute the gigantic royal banquet in the Plaine des Vertus in 1814. The following year the Prince Regent called him to Brighton as his chef. He stayed with the English Regent two years. Every morning he prepared his menu with His Highness, who was a blasé gourmand. During these discussions he went through a course in gastronomic hygiene that, if printed, would be one of the classic books of cookery.

Bored with the gray skies of England, Carême returned to Paris but went back when the Prince Regent became King. From London he went to St. Petersburg as one of the Emperor Alexander's chefs, then to Vienna to direct a few great dinners for the Austrian Emperor. He returned to London with Lord Stuart, the English ambassador, but soon quit to return to Paris to write and publish. He was constantly torn from his study of theory by calls from monarchs and congresses. His work shortened his life. "The charcoal is killing us," he said, "but what does it matter? The fewer the years, the greater the glory." He died before reaching the age of fifty, on January 12, 1833.

ALEXANDRE DUMAS
(trans. Louis Colman)

Chiasmus

Ev'ry Swain shall pay his Duty
    Grateful every Nymph shall prove;
And as these Excell in Beauty,
    Those shall be Renown'd for Love

JOHN DRYDEN

Childhood

Gradually I came to know where I was, and I tried to express my wants to those who could gratify them, yet could not, because my wants were inside me, and they were outside, nor had they any power of getting into my soul. And so I made movements and sounds, signs like my wants, the few I could, the best I could; for they were not really like my meaning. And when I was not obeyed, because people did not understand me, or because they would not do me harm, I was angry, because elders did not submit to me, because freemen would not slave for me, and I avenged myself on them by tears.

ST. AUGUSTINE

De Puero Balbutiente

Methinks 'tis pretty sport to hear a child,
Rocking a word in mouth yet undefiled;
The tender racquet rudely plays the sound,
Which, weakly bandied, cannot back rebound;
And the soft air the softer roof doth kiss,
With a sweet dying and a pretty miss,
Which hears no answer yet from the white rank
Of teeth, not risen from their coral bank.
The alphabet is searched for letters soft,
To try a word before it can be wrought,
And when it slideth forth, it goes as nice
As when a man does walk upon the ice.

THOMAS BASTARD

To think that physical comfort makes for human relations is an error we make because the absence of all comfort interferes with good relations. But we base it on the correct observation that when a parent takes pleasure in going out of his way to provide comfort for his child, the child takes it as a proof that he is loveable and deserves care and respect. This feeling enables him to trust—we can trust our well-being to persons who find us so important. Out of such trust in their intentions toward us, and our importance to them, develop first fleeting and then permanent relations.

This is where a society of plenty can make it harder for a child to relate. If comfort for the child can only be gained, by the parent, with a certain amount of trouble, he will very likely feel pleasure when he offers it to his child. It is this, the parent's pleasure, that gives the child a sense of worth and sets going the process of relating. (Of course, there are many pitfalls, such as when the parent feels his effort is too great, and creates guilt in the child as the comfort is offered.) But if comfort is so readily available that the parent feels no particular pleasure in being able to provide it, then the child cannot develop self-esteem around the giving and receiving of comfort.

Many children, four to six years of age, communicate mainly in terms of their favorite shows and relate much better to the TV screen than to their parents. Some of them seem unable to respond any more to the simple and direct language of their parents because it sounds unimpressive compared to the suave diction and emotionally loaded idiom of TV professionals. . . . Children who have been taught, or conditioned, to listen passively most of the day to the warm verbal communications coming from the TV screen, to the deep emotional appeal of the so-called TV personality, are often unable to respond to real persons because they arouse so much less feeling than the skilled actor. Worse, they lose the ability to learn from reality because life experiences are more complicated than the ones they see on the screen, and there is no one who comes in at the end to explain it all. . . . Conditioned to being given explanations, the "TV Child" has not learned to puzzle for one on his own; he gets discouraged when he cannot grasp the meaning of what happens to him and is thrown back once more to find comfort in predictable stories on the screen. . . . This being seduced into passivity and discouraged about facing life actively, on one's own, is the real danger of TV, much more than the often asinine or gruesome content of the shows.

BRUNO BETTELHEIM

It is not that the child lives in a world of imagination, but that the child within us survives and starts into life only at rare moments of recollection, which makes us believe, and it is not true, that, as children, we were imaginative.

CESARE PAVESE

Buildings as Drawn by Girls and by Boys

The girl's scene is a house *interior*, represented either as a configuration of furniture without any surrounding walls or by a simple *enclosure* built with blocks. In the girl's scene, people and animals are mostly *within* such an interior or enclosure, and they are primarily people or animals in a *static* (sitting or standing) position. Girls' enclosures consist of low walls, i.e., only one block high, except for an occasional *elaborate doorway*. These interiors of houses with or without walls were, for the most part, expressly *peaceful*. Often, a little girl was playing the piano. In a number of cases, the interior was *intruded* by animals or dangerous men. Yet the idea of an intruding creature did not necessarily lead to the defensive erection of walls or the closing of doors. Rather, the majority of these intrusions have an element of humor and pleasurable excitement.

Boys' scenes are either houses with elaborate walls or façades with *protrusions* such as cones or cylinders representing ornaments or cannons. There are *high towers*, and there are entirely exterior scenes. In boys' constructions more people and animals are *outside* enclosures or buildings, and there are more automotive objects and animals *moving* along streets and intersections. There are elaborate automotive *accidents*, but there is also traffic channelled or arrested by the policeman. While *high structures* are prevalent in the configurations of the boys, there is also much play with the danger of *collapse* or downfall; *ruins* were exclusively boys' constructions.

ERIK ERIKSON

My parents were—in a sort—visible powers of nature to me, no more loved than the sun and the moon: only I should have been annoyed and puzzled if either of them had gone out . . . still less did I love God; not that I had any quarrel with Him, or fear of Him; but simply found, what people told me was His service, disagreeable; and what people told me was His book, not entertaining. I had no companions to quarrel with, either; nobody to assist, and nobody to thank. Not a servant was ever allowed to do anything for me, but what it was their duty to do; and why should I have to be grateful to the cook for cooking, or the gardener for gardening,—when the one dared not give me a baked potato without asking leave, and the other would not let my ants' nests alone, because they made the walks untidy.

My times of happiness had always been when *nobody* was thinking of me; and the main discomfort and drawback to all proceedings and designs, the attention and interference of the public—represented by my mother and the gardener. The garden was no waste place for me, because I did not suppose myself an object of interest either to the ants or the butterflies; and the only qualification of the entire delight of my evening walk at Champagnole or St. Laurent was the sense that my father and mother *were* thinking of me, and would be frightened if I was five minutes late for tea.

RUSKIN

Childhood

III

In the woods there is a bird, his song stops you and makes you
    blush.
There is a clock that never strikes.
There is a hollow with a nest full of white beasts.

There is a little carriage left in the copse, or which runs down
the lane with ribbons on it.
There is a troupe of little actors in costume, glimpsed on
the road through the edge of the woods.
There is, lastly, when you are hungry and thirsty, someone
who chases you away.

IV

I am the saint, praying on the terrace—as the peaceful beasts
gaze down to the sea of Palestine.
I am the scholar in the dark armchair. Branches and rain
hurl themselves at the library windows.
I am the traveller on the high road through the stunted
woods; the roar of the sluices drowns my steps. For a
long time I watch the melancholy golden wash of the
sunset.
I might be the child left on the jetty washed out to sea,
the little farm boy following the lane whose crest
touches the sky.
The paths are rough. The hillocks are covered with broom.
The air is motionless. How far away the birds and
springs are! It can only be the end of the world, ahead.

And if, having surprised him at unclean compassions, his
mother took fright, the deep signs of the child's affection would throw themselves, in defence, upon her astonishment. Everything was all right. She had received that blue gaze—which lies!

ARTHUR RIMBAUD
(trans. Oliver Bernard,
slightly modified by W.H.A.)

Aha, Wanton is my name!
I can many a quaynte game.
Lo, my toppe I dryve in same,
Se, it torneth rounde!
I can with my scorge-stycke
My felowe upon the heed hytte,

And lyghtly from hym make a skyppe;
And blere on hym my tonge.
If brother or syster do me chyde
I wyll scratche and also byte.
I can crye, and also kyke,
And mock them all berewe.
If fader or mother wyll me smyte,
I wyll wrynge with my lyppe;
And lyghtly from hym make a skyppe;
And call my dame shrewe.
Aha, a newe game have I founde:
Se this gynne it renneth rounde;
And here another have I founde,
And yet mo can I fynde.
I can mowe on a man;
And make a lesynge well I can,
And mayntayne it ryght well than.
This connynge came me of kynde.
Ye, syrs, I can well gelde a snayle;
And catche a coew by the tayle;
This is a fayre connynge!
I can daunce, and also skyppe;
I can playe at the chery pytte;
And I can wystell you a fytte,
Syres, in a whylowe ryne.
Ye, syrs, and every daye
Whan I to scole shall take the waye
Some good mannes gardyn I wyll assaye,
Perys and plommes to plucke.
I can spye a sparowes nest.
I wyll not go to scole but whan me lest,
For there begynneth a sory fest
Whan the mayster sholde lyfte my docke.
But syrs, what I was seven yere of age,
I was sent to the Worlde to take wage.
And this seven yere I have been his page
And kept his commaundment . . .

ANON.

From infancy through childhood's giddy maze,
Froward at school, and fretful in his plays,
The puny tyrant burns to subjugate
The free republic of the whip-gig state.
If one, his equal in athletic frame,
Or, more provoking still, of nobler name,
Dare step across his arbitrary views,
An Iliad, only not in verse, ensues:
The little Greeks look trembling at the scales,
Till the best tongue, or heaviest hand prevails.

W. COWPER

False Security

. . . I ran to the ironwork gateway of number seven
Secure at last on the lamplit fringe of Heaven.
Oh who can say how subtle and safe one feels
Shod in one's children's sandals from Daniel Neal's,
Clad in one's party clothes made of stuff from Heal's?
And who can still one's thrill at the candle shine
On cakes and ices and jelly and blackcurrant wine,
And the warm little feel of my hostess's hand in mine?
Can I forget my delight at the conjuring show?
And wasn't I proud that I was the last to go?
Too overexcited and pleased with myself to know
That the words I heard my hostess's mother employ
To a guest departing, would ever diminish my joy,
I WONDER WHERE JULIA FOUND THAT STRANGE, RATHER COM-
MON LITTLE BOY?

JOHN BETJEMAN

The Gate

We sat, two children, warm against the wall
Outside the towering stronghold of our fathers
That frowned its stern security down upon us.
We could not enter there. That fortress, life,
Our safe protection, was too gross and strong

For our unpractised palates. Yet our guardians
Cherished our innocence with gentle hands,
(They, who had long since lost their innocence,)
And in grave play put on a childish mask
Over their tell-tale faces, as in shame
For the fine food that plumped their lusty bodies
And made them strange as gods. We sat that day
With the great parapet behind us, safe
As every day, yet outcast, safe and outcast
As castaways thrown upon an empty shore.
Before us lay our well-worn scene, a hillock
So small and smooth and green, it seemed intended
For us alone and childhood, a still pond
That opened upon no sight a quiet eye,
A little stream that tinkled down the slope.
But suddenly all seemed old
And dull and shrunken, shut within itself
In a sullen dream. We were outside, alone.
And then behind us the huge gate swung open.

EDWIN MUIR

A child of seven is excited by being told that Tommy opened a door and saw a dragon. But a child of three is excited by being told that Tommy opened a door. Boys like romantic tales; but babies like realistic tales—because they find them romantic. In fact, a baby is about the only person, I should think, to whom a modern realistic novel could be read without boring him.

The child does not know that men are not only bad from good motives, but also often good from bad motives. Therefore the child has a hearty, healthy, unspoiled, and unsatiable appetite for mere morality, for the mere difference between a good little girl and a bad little girl.

In turning the pages of one of the papers my eye catches the following sentence: "By the light of modern science and thought, we are in a position to see that each normal human being in some way repeats historically the life of the human race." This is a very typical modern assertion; that is, it is an assertion for which there is not and never has been a single spot or speck of proof. We know precious little about what the life of the human race has been; and none of our scientific conjectures about it bear the remotest resemblance to the actual growth of a child. According to this theory, a baby begins by chipping flints and rubbing sticks together to find fire. One so often sees babies doing this. About the age of five the child, before the delighted eyes of his parents, founds a village community. By the time he is eleven it has become a small city state, replica of ancient Athens. Encouraged by this, the boy proceeds, and before he is fourteen has founded the Roman Empire. But now his parents have a serious set-back. Having watched him so far, not only with pleasure, but with a very natural surprise, they must strengthen themselves to endure the spectacle of decay. They have now to watch their child going through the decline of the Western Empire and the Dark Ages. They see the invasion of the Huns and that of the Norsemen chasing each other across his expressive face. He seems a little happier after he has "repeated" the Battle of Chalons and the unsuccessful Siege of Paris; and by the time he comes to the twelfth century, his boyish face is as bright as it was of old when he was "repeating" Pericles or Camillus. I have no space to follow this remarkable demonstration of how history repeats itself in the youth; how he grows dismal at twenty-three to represent the end of Medievalism, brightens because the Renaissance is coming, darkens again with the disputes of the later Reformation, broadens placidly through the thirties as the rational eighteenth century, till at last, about forty-three, he gives a great yell and begins to burn the house down, as a symbol of the French Revolution. Such (we shall all agree) is the ordinary development of a boy.

G. K. CHESTERTON

In every man there lies hidden a child between five and eight years old, the age at which naïveté comes to an end. It is this child whom one must detect in that intimidating man with his long beard, bristling eyebrows, heavy moustache, and weighty look—a captain. Even he conceals, and not at all deep down, the youngster, the booby, the little rascal, out of whom age has made this powerful monster.

PAUL VALÉRY

Children, Autistic

According to Dr. Bruno Bettelheim, who seems to have an unusual gift for handling autistic children, the cause of "autism" is that the child is convinced, rightly or wrongly, that its parents wish it did not exist. Consequently the world an autistic child creates is based upon total doubt. (*See* Belief.)

Many who have reflected on the autistic child's desire for sameness recognize that its purpose is to reduce anxiety. What is not stressed as much is that it stands for an ordering of things, an effort to establish laws by which things must happen.

With us, too, scientific law signifies that, given the same conditions, the same events will take place. If the search for natural laws has a purpose, it is to predict events and master nature so as to make our lives more secure. Social law, too, has no purpose except to safeguard our common existence. This—their intrinsic purpose—all our laws have in common with the laws the autistic child creates. He is firmly convinced that those he lives by are essential to his security. They must be observed or his life will fall apart, just as society would decay if no one accepted the law of the land. To prevent this, he must arrange his toys in the same way and with the same enunciation. What distinguishes his laws from ours is that his are non-adaptive and universal. One and the same law governs everything.

All autistic children demand that time must stop still. Time is the destroyer of sameness. If sameness is to be preserved, time must stop in its tracks. Therefore the autistic child's world consists only of space. Neither time nor causality exist there, because causality involves a sequence in time where events have to follow one another. In the autistic child's world the chain of events is not conditioned by the causality we know. But since one event does follow another, it must be because of some timeless cosmic law that ordains it. An eternal law. Things happen because they must, not because they are caused.

Time also implies hope. Without time there is no hope but also no disappointment nor the fear that things might get even worse. Hence infantile autism and the cosmic law. Once and for all, and absolutely, it ordains how things must be ordered. Sensible laws can be subjected to sensible revision and hence permit hope to arise. Thus it must be an insensible law that never changes. And the essential content of this law is "You must never hope that anything can change."

BRUNO BETTELHEIM

For anybody interested in language, the linguistic behavior of autistic children is of the greatest interest and significance.

Joey's language, step by step, became abstract, depersonalised, detached. He lost the ability to use personal pronouns correctly, later lost the use of them entirely.

While at first Joey named foods correctly, calling them, "butter", "sugar", "water", and so forth, he later gave this up. He then called sugar "sand", butter "grease", water "liquid" and so on. Thus he deprived food of taste and smell, and these qualities he replaced by the way they feel to the touch. Clearly he had the ability to engage in abstract thinking. It is also clear that in his transposing of names, as much as his giving up of pronouns, the autistic child creates a language to fit his emotional experience of the world. Far from not knowing how to use language correctly, there is a spontaneous decision to create a language which will match how he experiences things—and things only, not people.

(After a period of therapy Joey began to use personal pronouns again, but in reverse, as do most autistic children. He referred to himself as "you" and to the adult he was speaking to as "I".) Shortly after his treatment there was ended, he was able to use the "I" correctly and to name some of the children in addition to his therapist. But he never used names or personal pronouns in direct address, only in the indirect third person when referring to them. He never referred to anyone by name; other than simply "That person"; later, with some differentiation, "the small person" or "the big person".

By not permitting himself to be an "I", by not permitting himself to say "yes" to anything, the autistic child is complying with what he considers a parental wish that he should not exist. This is why the "you"—those others who are permitted to exist—and the "no" which is essentially a denial of existence, are so much more readily available to him.

BRUNO BETTELHEIM

Choirboys

As a boy, both before and after it broke, I had the luck to possess a voice which, though certainly not of solo quality, was good enough for a choir.

As a choirboy, I had to learn, not only to sight-read music, but also to enunciate words clearly—there is a famous tongue twister in the *Jubilate*—"For why, it is He that hath made us and not we ourselves"—and to notice the difference between their metrical values when spoken and when sung, so that, long before I took a conscious interest in poetry I had acquired a certain sensitivity to language which I could not have acquired in any other way.

The Choir Boy

And when he sang in choruses
   His voice o'ertopped the rest,
Which is very inartistic,
   But the public like that best.

ANON.

Like luxurious cygnets in their cloudy lawn, a score of young singing-boys were awaiting their cue: Low-masses, cheapness and economy, how they despised them, and how they would laugh at "Old Ends" who snuffed out the candles.

"Why should the Church charge higher for a short *Magnificat* than for a long *Miserere?*"

The question had just been put by the owner of a dawning moustache and a snub, though expressive, nose.

"Because happiness makes people generous, stupid, and often as not they'll squander, boom, but unhappiness makes them calculate. People grudge spending much on a snivel—even if it lasts an hour."

"It's the choir that suffers."

"This profiteering . . ." there was a confusion of voices.

"Order!" A slim lad, of an ambered paleness, raised a protesting hand. Indulged and made-much-of by the hierarchy, he was Felix Ganay, known as Chief-dancing-choir-boy to the cathedral of Clemenza.

"Aren't they awful?" he addressed a child with a very finished small head. Fingering a score of music he had been taking the lead in a mass of Palestrina; and had the vaguely distraught air of a kitten that had seen visions.

RONALD FIRBANK

Christmas

Love is plonte of pees, most precious of vertues,
For hevene holde hit ne mighte, so hevy hit semede,
Til hit hadde of erthe y-yoten hitselve.
Was nevere lef upon linde lighter therafter

As whanne hit hadde of the folde flesch and blode ytake.
Tho was hit portatif and persaunt as the pointe of a nelde:
May none armure hit lette, ne none hye walles.

WILLIAM LANGLAND

Of the Nativity of Christ

Rorate celi desuper!
Hevins, distill your balmy schouris,
For now is rissin the bricht day ster,
Fro the ros Mary, flour of flouris:
The cleir Sone, quhome no clud devouris,
Surminting Phebus in the est,
Is cumin of his hevinly touris:
Et nobis Puer natus est.

Archangellis, angellis, and dompnationis,
Tronis, potestatis, and marteiris seir,
And all ye hevinly operationis,
Ster, planeit, firmament, and speir,
Fyre, erd, air, and watter cleir,
To him gife loving, most and lest,
That come in to so meik maneir;
Et nobis Puer natus est.

Synnaris be glaid, and pennance do,
And thank your Makar hairtfully;
For he that ye mycht nocht cum to,
To yow is cummin full humly,
Your saulis with his blud to by,
And lous yow of the feind is arrest,
And only of his awin mercy;
Pro nobis Puer natus est.

All clergy do to him inclyne,
And bow unto that barne benyng,
And do your observance devyne

To him that is of kingis King;
Ensence his altar, reid and sing
In haly kirk, with mynd degest,
Him honouring attour all thing,
Qui nobis Puer natus est.

Celestiall fowlies in the are
Sing with your jottis upoun hicht;
In firthis and in forrestis fair
Be myrthful now, at all your mycht,
For passit is your dully nycht,
Aurora hes the cluddis perst,
The son is rissin with glaidsum lycht,
Et nobis Puer natus est.

Now spring up flouris fra the rute,
Revert yow upwart naturaly,
In honour of the blessit frute
That rais up fro the rose Mary;
Lay out your levis lustely,
Fro dei tak lyfe now at the lest
In weirschip of that Prince wirthy,
Qui nobis Puer natus est.

Syng hevin imperiall, most of hicht,
Regions of air mak harmony;
All fishe in flud and foull of licht
Be mirthful and mak melody:
All *Gloria in excelsis* cry,
Hevin, erd, se, man, bird, and best,
He that is crownit abone the sky
Pro nobis Puer natus est.

WILLIAM DUNBAR

The Nativity of Our Lord
and Saviour Jesus Christ

Where is this stupendous stranger,
　　Swains of Solyma, advise,
Lead me to my Master's manger,
　　Shew me where my Saviour lies? . . .

Nature's decorations glisten
　　Far above their usual trim;
Birds on box and laurel listen,
　　As so near the cherubs hymn.

Boreas now no longer winters
　　On the desolated coast;
Oaks no more are riv'n in splinters
　　By the whirlwind and his host.

Spinks and ouzels sing sublimely,
　　"We too have a Saviour born";
Whiter blossoms burst untimely
　　On the blest Mosaic thorn.

God all-bounteous, all-creative,
　　Whom no ills from good dissuade,
Is incarnate, and a native
　　Of the very world he made.

CHRISTOPHER SMART

Cities, Modern

◆§ミ◆

Some cities are really successful, and present the solid and definite achievement of the thing at which their builders aimed; and when they do this, they present, just as a fine statue presents, something

of the direct divinity of man, something immeasurably superior
to mere nature, to mere common mountains, to mere vulgar seas.
. . . The modern city is ugly, not because it is a city, but because
it is not enough of a city, because it is a jungle, because it is confused and anarchic, and surging with selfish and materialistic energies. In short, the modern town is offensive because it is a great
deal too like nature, a great deal too like the country.

G. K. CHESTERTON

Noise is manufactured in the city, just as goods are manufactured. The city is the place where noise is kept in stock, completely detached from the object from which it came.

MAX PICARD

The official acropolis outdoes the most colossal conceptions of
modern barbarity. It is impossible to describe the dull light produced by the unchanging grey sky, the imperial brightness of the
masonry, and the eternal snow on the ground. They have reproduced, in singularly outrageous taste, all the classical marvels of
architecture. I go to exhibitions of painting in places twenty
times vaster than Hampton Court. What painting! A Norwegian
Nebuchadnezzar designed the staircases of the ministries; the
minor officials I did see are prouder than Brahmins as it is, and
the looks of the guardians of colossi and of the building foremen
made me tremble. By their grouping of the buildings, in closed
squares, terraces, and courtyards, they have squeezed out the
bell-towers. The parks present primeval nature cultivated with
marvellous art. There are parts of the better district which are
inexplicable: an arm of the sea, without boats, rolls its sheet of
blue ground glass between quays covered with giant candelabra.
A short bridge leads to a postern immediately below the dome of
the Holy Chapel. This dome is an artistic framework of steel
about fifteen thousand feet in diameter.

From certain points on the copper foot-bridges, the platforms,
the stairways which wind round the covered markets and the pillars, I thought I could judge the depth of the city. This was the
marvel I was unable to verify: what are the levels of the other
districts above and below the acropolis? For the foreigner in our

times exploration is impossible. The commercial district is a circus all in the same style, with galleries of arcades. One can see no shops, but the snow on the roadway is trampled; a few nabobs, as rare as walkers on a Sunday morning in London, move towards a stage-coach made of diamonds. There are a few red velvet divans: polar drinks are served, whose prices range from eight hundred to eight thousand rupees. To my idea of looking for theatres in this circus, I reply that the shops must contain some pretty gloomy dramas. I think there is a police force; but the laws must be so strange that I give up trying to imagine what the adventurers of this place are like.

The outlying part, as elegant as a fine street in Paris, is favoured with the appearance of light; the democratic element numbers a few hundred souls. Here again, the houses are not in rows; the suburb loses itself oddly in the country, the 'County' which fills the endless west of forests and huge plantations where misanthropic gentlemen hunt for news by artificial light.

ARTHUR RIMBAUD
(trans. Oliver Bernard,
slightly modified by W.H.A.)

Here malice, rapine, accident conspire,
And now a rabble rages, now a fire;
Their ambush here relentless ruffians lay,
And here the fell attorney prowls for prey;
Here falling houses thunder on your head,
And here a female atheist talks you dead.

DR. JOHNSON

A Nocturnal Sketch

Even is come; and from the dark Park, hark,
The signal of the setting sun—one gun!
And six is sounding from the chime, prime time
To go and see the Drury-Lane Dane slain,—
Or hear Othello's jealous doubt spout out,—
Or Macbeth raving at that shade-made blade,
Denying to his frantic clutch much touch;—

Or else to see Ducrow with wide stride ride
Four horses as no other man can span;
Or in the small Olympic Pit, sit split
Laughing at Liston, while you quiz his phiz.

Anon Night comes, and with her wings brings things
Such as, with his poetic tongue, Young sung;
The gas up-blazes with its bright white light,
And paralytic watchmen prowl, howl, growl,
About the streets and take up Pall-Mall Sal,
Who, hasting to her nightly jobs, robs fobs.

Now thieves to enter for your cash, smash, crash,
Past drowsy Charley in a deep sleep, creep,
But frightened by Policeman B.3, flee,
And while they're going, whisper low, "No go!"

Now puss, while folks are in their beds, treads leads,
And sleepers waking, grumble—, "Drat that cat!"
Who in the gutter caterwauls, squalls, mauls
Some feline foe, and screams in shrill ill-will.

Now Bulls of Bashan, and of prize size, rise
In childish dreams, and a roar, gore, poor
Georgy, or Charley, or Billy, willy-nilly;—
But Nursemaid in a nightmare rest, chest-pressed,
Dreameth of one of her old flames, James Games,
And that she hears—what faith is man's—Ann's banns
And his, from Reverend Mr. Rice, twice, thrice:
White ribbons flourish, and a stout shout out
That upward goes, shows Rose knows those bows' woes.

THOMAS HOOD

Climber, An Amateur

❦§❧

Eskdale, Friday, Augt 6th (1802) at an Estate House called Toes.

There is one sort of Gambling, to which I am much addicted; and that not of the least criminal kind for a man who has children & a Concern.—It is this. When I find it convenient to descend from a mountain, I am too confident & too indolent to round about & wind about 'till I find a track or other symptom of safety; but I wander on, & where it is first possible to descend, there I go—relying upon fortune for how far down this possibility will continue. So it was yesterday afternoon. I passed down from Broadcrag, skirted the Precipices, and found myself cut off from a most sublime Crag-summit, that seemed to rival Sca'Fell Man in height, & to outdo it in fierceness. A Ridge of Hill lay low down, & divided this Crag (called Doe-crag) & Broad-crag—even as the Hyphen divides the words broad & crag. I determined to go thither; the first place I came to, that was not Direct Rock, I slipped down, & went on for a while with tolerable ease—but now I came (it was midway down) to a smooth perpendicular Rock about 7 feet high—this was nothing—I put my hands on the Ledge, & dropped down / in a few yards came just such another / I dropped that too / and yet another, seemed not higher —I would not stand for a trifle / so I dropped that too / but the stretching of the muscle(s) of my hand & arms, & the jolt of the Fall on my Feet, put my whole Limbs in a Tremble, and I paused, & looking down, saw that I had little else to encounter but a succession of these little Precipices—it was in truth a Path that in a very hard Rain is, no doubt, the channel of a most splendid Waterfall. / So I began to suspect that I ought not to go on / but then unfortunately tho' I could with ease drop down a smooth Rock 7 feet high, I could not climb it / so go on I must / and on I went / the next 3 drops were not half a Foot, at least not a foot more than my own height / but every Drop increased the Palsy of my Limbs—I shook all over, Heaven knows without the least influence of Fear / and now I had only two more to drop down / to return was impossible—but of these two the first was tremendous / it was twice my own height, & the Ledge at the bottome was (so) exceedingly narrow, that if I dropt down upon it I must of necessity have fallen backwards & of course killed myself. My Limbs were all in a tremble—I lay upon my Back to rest myself, & I was beginning according to my Custom to laugh at myself for a Madman, when the sight of the Crags above me on each side, & the impetuous Clouds just over them, posting so luridly & so rapidly northward, overawed me / I lay in a state of almost prophetic Trance & Delight—& blessed God aloud, for the powers of Reason & the Will, which remaining no Danger can overpower us! O God, I exclaimed aloud—how calm, how blessed am I now / I know not how to proceed, how to return / but I am calm & fearless & confident / if this reality were a Dream, if I were asleep, what agonies had I suffered! what screams!—When the Reason & the Will are away, what remains to us but Darkness & Dimness & a bewildering Shame, and Pain that is utterly Lord over us, or fantastic Pleasure, that draws the Soul along swimming through the air in man shapes, even as Flight of Starlings in a Wind. —I arose, and looking down saw at the bottom a heap of stones—which had fallen abroad—and rendered the narrow Ledge on which they had been piled, double dangerous / at the bottom of the third Rock that I dropt from, I met a dead Sheep quite rotten— This heap of Stones, I guessed, & have since found that I guessed aright, had been piled up by the Shepherd to enable him to climb & free the poor creature whom he had observed to be crag-fast—but seeing nothing but rock over rock, he had desisted & gone for help—& in the mean time the poor creature had fallen down & killed itself. —As I was looking at these I glanced my eye to my left & observed that the Rock was rent from top to bottom —I measured the breadth of the Rent, and found that there was no danger of my being wedged in / so I put my Knap-sack round to my side, & slipped down as between two walls, without any danger or difficulty—the next Drop brought me down on the Ridge called the How / I hunted out my Besom Stick, which I had flung before me when I first came to the Rocks—and wisely gave over all thoughts of ascending Doe-Crag—for the Clouds were again coming in most tumultuously—so I began to descend / when I felt an odd sensation across my whole Breast—not pain nor itching— & putting my hand on it I found it all bumpy—and on looking saw the whole of my Breast from my Neck (to my Navel)— & exactly all that my Kamell-hair Breast-shield covers, filled with great red heatbumps, so thick that no hair could lie between them. They still remain / but are evidently less— & I have no doubt will wholly disappear in a few Days. It was however a startling proof to me of the violent exertions which I had made. —I descended this low Hill which was all hollow beneath me—and was like the rough green Quilt of a Bed of waters—at length two streams burst out & took their way down, one on (one) side a high Ground upon this Ridge, the other on the other—I took that to my right (having on my left this high Ground, & the other Stream, & beyond that Doe-crag, on the other side of which is Esk Halse, where the head-spring of the Esk rises, & running down the Hill & in upon the Vale looks and actually deceived me, as a great Turnpike Road—in which, as in many other respects the Head of Eskdale much resembles Langdale & soon the channel sank all at once, at least 40 yards, & formed a magnificent Waterfall—and close under this a succession of Waterfalls 7 in number, the third of which is nearly as high as the first. When I had almost reached the bottom of the Hill, I stood so as to command the whole 8 Waterfalls, with the great triangle-Crag looking in above them, & on the one side of them the enormous more than perpendicular Precipices & Bull's-Brows, of Sc'Fell! And now the Thunder-storm was coming on, again & again! —Just at the bottom of the Hill I saw on before me in the Vale, lying just above the River on the side of a Hill, one, two, three, four Objects, I could not distinguish whether Peat-hovels, or hovel-shaped Stones—I thought in my mind, that 3 of them would turn out to be stones—but that the fourth was certainly a Hovel. I went on toward them, crossing & recrossing the Becks & the River & found that they were all huge Stones—the one nearest the Beck which I had determined to be really a Hovel, retained It's likeness when I was close beside / in size it is nearly equal to the famous Bowder stone, but in every other respect greatly superior to it—it has a complete Roof, & that perfectly thatched with wees, & Heath, & Mountain-Ash Bushes—I now was obliged to ascend again, as the River ran greatly to the Left, & the Vale was nothing more than the Channel of the River, all the rest of the interspace between the mountains was a tossing up and down of Hills of all sizes—and the place at which I am now writing is called—Te-as, & spelt, Toes—as the Toes of Sc'Fell—. It is not possible that any name can be more descriptive of the Head of Eskdale—I ascended close under Sca'Fell, & came to a little Village of Sheep-folds / there were 5 together / & the redding Stuff, & the Shears, & an old Pot, was in the Passage of the first of them. Here I found an imperfect Shelter from a Thunder-shower—accompanied with such Echoes! O God! what thoughts were mine! O how I wished for Health & Strength that I might wander about for a Month together in the stormiest month of the year, among these Places, so lonely & savage & full of sounds!

After the Thunder-storm I shouted out all your names in the Sheep-fold—when Echo came upon Echo / and then Hartley & Derwent & then I laughed and shouted Joanna / it leaves all the Echoes I ever heard far far behind, in number, distinctness & humanness of Voice— & then not to forget an old Friend I made them all say Dr. Dodd & c.—

S . T . C O L E R I D G E

Climber, A Professional

The Summit

There was no one to tell about it. There was, perhaps, nothing to tell. All the world we could see lay motionless in the muted splendor of the sunrise. Nothing stirred, only we lived; even the wind had forgotten us. Had we been able to hear a bird calling from some pine-tree, or sheep bleating in some valley, the summit stillness would have been familiar; now it was different, perfect. It was as if the world had held its breath for us. Yet we were so

tired . . . the summit meant first of all a place to rest. We sat
down just beneath the top, ate a little of our lunch, and had a
few sips of water. Ed had brought a couple of firecrackers all the
way up; now he wanted to set one off, but we were afraid it
would knock the cornices loose. There was so little to do, nothing we really had the energy for, no gesture appropriate to what
we felt we had accomplished: only a numb happiness, almost a
languor. We photographed each other and the views, trying even
as we took the pictures to impress the sight on our memories
more indelibly than the cameras could on the film. . . . I thought
then, much as I had when Matt and I sat on the glacier just after
flying in, that I wanted to know how the others felt and couldn't.
Trying to talk about it now would have seemed profane; if there
was anything we shared, it was the sudden sense of quiet and rest.
For each of us, the high place we had finally reached culminated ambitions and secret desires we could scarcely have articu-
lated had we wanted to. And the chances are our various dreams
were different. If we had been able to know each other's, perhaps
we could not have worked so well together. Perhaps we would
have recognised, even in our partnership, the vague threats of ambition, like boats through a fog: the unrealisable desires that
drove us beyond anything we could achieve, that drove us in the
face of danger; our unanswerable complaints against the universe
—that we die, that we have so little power, that we are locked
apart, that we do not know. So perhaps the best things that happened on the summit were what we could see happening, not anything beneath. Perhaps it was important for Don to watch me
walk across the top of the east ridge; for Matt to see Ed stand
with a cigarette in his mouth, staring at the sun; for me to notice
how Matt sat, eating only half of his candy bar; for Ed to hear
Don insist on changing to black-and-white film. No one else
could see these things; no one else could even ask whether or not
they were important. Perhaps they were all that happened.

DAVID ROBERTS

Commitment

&§§&

The "great" commitment is so much easier than the ordinary everyday one—and can all too easily shut our hearts to the latter. A willingness to make the ultimate sacrifice can be associated with, and even produce, a great hardness of heart.

DAG HAMMARSKJÖLD

Those who serve a cause are not those who love that cause. They are those who love the life which has to be led in order to serve it—except in the case of the very purest, and they are rare. For the idea of a cause doesn't supply the necessary energy for serving it.

SIMONE WEIL

The scrupulous and the just, the noble, humane and devoted natures, the unselfish and the intelligent, may begin a movement—but it passes away from them. They are not the leaders of a revolution. They are its victims.

JOSEPH CONRAD

The young man plays at busying himself with problems of the collective type, and at times with such passion and heroism that anyone ignorant of the secrets of human life would be led to believe that his preoccupation was genuine. But, in truth, all this is a pretext for concerning himself with himself, and so that he may be occupied with self.

During periods of crisis, positions which are false or feigned are very common. Entire generations falsify themselves to themselves; that is to say, they wrap themselves up in artistic styles, in doctrines, in political movements which are insincere and which fill the lack of genuine conviction. When they get to be about forty years old, those generations become null and void, because at that age one can no longer live on fictions.

ORTEGA Y GASSET

By all means let a poet, if he wants to, write *engagé* poems, protesting against this or that political evil or social injustice. But let him remember this. The only person who will benefit from them is himself; they will enhance his literary reputation among those who feel as he does. The evil or injustice, however, will remain exactly what it would have been if he had kept his mouth shut.

Conception, The Immaculate

Behind this ingenious doctrine lies, I cannot help suspecting, a not very savory wish to make the Mother of God an Honorary Gentile. As if we didn't all know perfectly well that the Holy Ghost and Our Lady both speak British English, He with an Oxford, She with a Yiddish, accent.

Conscience

Freud recognized that there was a profound difference between the Voice of Conscience, i.e., the Voice of the Holy Spirit, and the Voice of the Superego, but was too inclined, in my opinion, to identify the former with the Voice of Reason. The superego speaks loudly and either in imperatives or interjections—"DO THIS! DON'T DO THAT! BRAVO! YOU SON OF A BITCH!" Conscience speaks softly and in the interrogative—"Do you really think so? Is that really true?"

To say that their voices are different does not mean, of course, that they never coincide; indeed in a perfect society they always would coincide. The Pharisee with his strong surperego is a very lucky fellow; the Publican, whose superego is weak, a very unlucky one. The former, for example, cannot be said to be "tempted" to steal, for, should the idea of stealing occur to him, he will immediately dismiss it from his mind as something which is "not done"; every time the idea of stealing occurs to the Publican, it requires a moral effort to resist for which he may not have the strength. What is wrong with the Pharisee is his refusal to recognize his good fortune; he takes to himself the credit which is properly due to his parents and teachers.

The limitation of the superego as a guide to conduct is that, since it is a social creation, it is only effective so long as social conditions remain unchanged; if they change, it doesn't know what to say. At home the Spartans did not use money; consequently, when they traveled to countries that did they were helpless to resist the temptations of money, and it was said in the ancient world that a Spartan could always be bribed.

Cosmos, The Medieval

⟜❧⟝

. . . Go out on a starry night and walk about for half an hour trying to see the sky in terms of the old cosmology. Remember that now you have an absolute Up and Down. The Earth is really the centre, really the lowest place; movement to it from whatever direction is downward movement. As a modern you located the stars at a great distance. For distance you must now substitute that very special, and far less abstract, sort of distance which we call height; height which speaks immediately to our muscles and nerves. The Medieval Model is vertiginous. And the fact that the height of the stars in the medieval astronomy is very small compared with their distance in the modern, will turn out not to have the kind of importance you anticipated. For thought and imagination, ten million miles and a thousand million are much the same. Both can be conceived (that is, we can do sums with both) and neither can be imagined; and the more imagination we have the better we shall know this. The really important difference is that the medieval universe, while unimaginably large, was also unambiguously finite. And one unexpected result of this is to make the smallness of Earth more vividly felt. In our universe she is small, no doubt; but so are the galaxies, so is everything—and so what? But in theirs there was an absolute standard of comparison. The furthest sphere, Dante's *maggior corpo*, is, quite simply and finally, the largest object in existence. The word "small" as applied to Earth thus takes on a far more absolute significance. Again, because the medieval universe is finite, it has a shape, the perfect spherical shape, containing within itself an ordered variety. Hence to look out on the night sky with modern eyes is like looking out over a sea that fades away into mist, or looking about one in a trackless forest—trees forever and no horizon. To look up at the towering medieval universe is much more like looking at a great building. The "space" of modern astronomy may arouse terror, or bewilderment or vague reverie; the spheres of the old present us with an object in which the mind can rest, overwhelming in its greatness but satisfying in its harmony. That is the sense in which our universe is romantic, and theirs was classical.

C. S. LEWIS

Cuckoo, The

Before the cuckoo lays her egg she picks up an egg from the host's nest, holds it in her bill as she sits and flies off some distance to eat it. Country rhymes show that something of this was known long before British ornithologists studied the bird's behavior.

In Northamptonshire the cuckoo is called "Suck-egg". According to the Scots song,

> The cuckoo's a fine bird, he sings as he flies;
> He brings us good tidings, he tells us no lies.
> He sucks little birds' eggs to make his voice clear,
> And when he sings "cuckoo" the summer is near.

The Sussex version ends with,

> She picks up the dirt in the spring of the year,
> And eats little birds' eggs to make her voice clear.

In Devon it is said that the cuckoo "comes to eat up the dirt," and continental sayings of a similar nature show that the meaning is that the bird arrives when the land is drying up after the winter. Germans say that the cuckoo cannot call until he has eaten a bird's egg and a Spanish proverb declares, "I am like the cuckoo which cannot sing until I have my stomach full." Another continental tradition is that the cuckoo stammers late in the year because of an egg in its throat. . . .

All over the world the calling of various species of cuckoo is associated with rain and the birds are often called "rain-crow" or its equivalent—due, no doubt, to their loud, reiterative notes coinciding with the rainy season. . . .

From being associated with changes in the weather the cuckoo acquired a reputation as forecaster of the weather and other events. Hesiod advised the farmer to plough when the cuckoo called from the oaks, but more recent tradition attributes to it foresight concerning the whole season:

> When the cuckoo comes to the bare thorn,
> Sell your cow and buy your corn;
> But when she comes to the full bit,
> Sell your corn and buy your sheep.

There are Irish and Welsh rhymes to the same effect.

The next step in the chain of association was to assume that a bird so knowledgeable about future events was able to forecast tides in the affairs of men. . . . Practically throughout western Europe the bird is more or less playfully consulted concerning future events. Yorkshire and Guernsey children recite a rhyme asking the cuckoo to foretell by the number of its calls how long they have to live. This belief goes back at least to the 13th century, for it is mentioned in *Le Roman du Renart,* and is, or was, widespread in Europe. In England and on the continent, as, for example, in Portugal, it was believed that a girl could discover how long she would remain unmarried by counting the calls of the first cuckoo. No wonder the Danes say that the cuckoo does not build a nest because it is kept too busy answering the questions of young and old.

So percipient a bird may predict evil as well as blessedness; and in the magical world of portents your luck may turn on what might seem a trivial detail. In Scotland and Norway it is unlucky to hear the cuckoo before breakfast, but the Scots say that good fortune awaits you if you hear it while walking. . . . In the Hebrides it bodes ill to hear the cuckoo while hungry. Welshfolk used to say that a child born the first day the cuckoo calls would be lucky all his life, but in the Principality and also in Somerset, a cuckoo heard after midsummer may be a portent of death. To be gazing on the ground on hearing the first cuckoo was believed in Midlothian, Berwickshire and Cornwall to be a warning of an untimely fate. . . .

The point of the compass at which the cuckoo calls may be considered fraught with significance. In Cornwall a cuckoo heard on one's right was lucky, and in Ireland a cuckoo on one's left was unlucky. Irish folk thought that the direction in which you heard the first cuckoo indicated where you would live during the year. . . . According to a German tradition, if the first cuckoo were heard in the north, the year would be disastrous, if in the south, it would be a good butter year.

EDWARD A. ARMSTRONG

Cultures, The Two

Of course, there is only one. Of course, the natural sciences are just as "humane" as letters. There are, however, two languages, the spoken verbal language of literature, and the written sign language of mathematics, which is the language of science. This puts the scientist at a great advantage, for, since like all of us he has learned to read and write, he can understand a poem or a novel, whereas there are very few men of letters who can understand a scientific paper once they come to the mathematical parts.

When I was a boy, we were taught the literary languages, like Latin and Greek, extremely well, but mathematics atrociously badly. Beginning with the multiplication table, we learned a series of operations by rote which, if remembered correctly, gave the "right" answer, but about any basic principles, like the concept of number, we were told nothing. Typical of the teaching methods then in vogue is this mnemonic which I had to learn.

> Minus times Minus equals Plus:
> The reason for this we need not discuss.

Curtain Lines

The best actual curtain line I know of is the end of Cocteau's *Les Chevaliers de la Table Ronde*. Merlin, the villain, has been defeated, the Waste Land blooms again, and the birds once more start to sing. One of the Knights, Sagramour, used to understand the language of the birds. The others excitedly ask him to tell them what the birds are saying. After listening for a short while, he makes out their message: *"Paie, paie, paie. Il faut payer, payer, payer. Paie, paie, paie, paie."*

The best imaginary line, suggested to his brother by Max Beerbohm: "I'm leaving for the Thirty Years' War."

The most impossible line for an actor to say, the end of Drinkwater's *Abraham Lincoln:* "He's with the ages now." (Which word shall he accent?)

Probably apocryphal. Mrs. Fiske, who had the reputation for always demanding the last word, was to play Mrs. Alving in Ibsen's *Ghosts.* In rehearsals she was faithful to the text, but on opening night the finale went thus:

> OSWALD: Give me the sun, Mother.
> MRS. ALVING: NO!

Cygnet

ᗕᔿᔾᔿᗒ

A cygnet is born. He thinks himself a king, the restless lord of the sluggish marsh. He sits on his mother's back, comes and goes, an object of public solicitude.

He feeds on scraps and on boys' gifts thrown from the bridge. He wastes the time of the servants who hurry along the crowded road bringing articles for the kitchens;

For just born things please everyone; beauty reigns as a goddess on earth; what has the charm of being fresh and young captivates the eyes of the crowd.

Yet the parents of the young cygnet swim round their offspring in mistrust. They hiss, they scream, they stir the pool in threatening flight.

Let not our love be like that. The gods forbid the muses who
rule over men to know what the nymphs teach their voiceless
companions.

Poem in Latin by WILLIAM JOHNSON CORY
(trans. Frederick Brittain)

Dark Ages, Thank God for the

Theodosianism betrays a fatal confusion of ideas. For to envisage
the faith as a political principle was not so much to christianize
civilization as to "civilize" Christianity; it was not to consecrate
human institutions to the service of God but rather to identify
God with the maintenance of human institutions, i.e., with that of
the *pax terrena*. And, in this case, the *pax terrena* was represented
by the tawdry and meretricious empire, a system which, originat-
ing in the pursuit of human and terrestrial aims, had so far degen-
erated as to deny to men the very values which had given it birth;
and was now held together only by sheer and unmitigated force.
By so doing, it rendered the principle purely formal while, at the
same time, it suggested the application of conventional "political"
methods for its realization. While, therefore, under governmental
pressure, the empire rapidly shed the trappings of secularism to
assume those of Christianity, it remained at heart profoundly
pagan and was, to that extent, transformed merely into a whited
sepulchre.

C. N. COCHRANE

A. "*Dum has exitiorum communium clades suscitat turba
feralis, urbem aeternam Leontius regens, multa spectati judicis
documenta praebebat, in audiendo celer, in disceptando
justissimus, natura benevolus, licet autoritatis causa servandae
acer quibusdam videbatur, et inclinatior ad amandum.*"

(While that carrion crew was causing these catastrophes of
general destruction, Leontius, governor of the Eternal City,
gave many evidences of being an excellent judge—speedy in
hearings, most just in decisions, by nature benevolent, though
he seemed to some to be severe in the matter of maintaining
his authority and over-inclined toward sensual love.)

Ammianus

B. "Gravia tunc inter Toronicos bella civilia surrexerunt."
(Serious local fighting arose at that time between the inhabitants of the region of Tours.)   Gregory of Tours

A complete change has taken place since the days of Ammianus
and Augustine. Of course, as has often been observed, it is a de-
cadence, a decline in culture and verbal disposition; but it is not
only that. It is a reawakening of the directly sensible. Both style
and treatment of content had become rigid in late antiquity. An
excess of rhetorical devices, and the somber atmosphere which
enveloped the events of the time, gave the authors of late antiquity, from Tacitus and Seneca to Ammianus, a something that is
labored, artificial, overstrained. With Gregory the rigidity is dissolved. He has many horrible things to relate; treason, violence,
manslaughter are everyday occurrences; but the simple and
practical vivacity with which he reports them prevents the for-
mation of that oppressive atmosphere which we find in the late
Roman writers and which even the Christian writers can hardly
escape. When Gregory writes, the catastrophe has occurred, the
Empire has fallen, its organization has collapsed, the culture of
antiquity has been destroyed. But the tension is over. And it is
more freely and directly, no longer haunted by insoluble tasks,
no longer burdened by unrealizable pretensions, that Gregory's
soul faces living reality, ready to apprehend it as such and to
work in it practically. . . . [The sentence by Ammianus] surveys
and masters a many-faceted situation, as well as supplying in addition a clear connection between what came first and what followed. But how labored it is and how rigid! Is it not a relief to
turn from it to Gregory's . . . ? To be sure, his *tunc* is only a
loose and vague connective, and the language as a whole is unpol-
ished, for *bella civilia* is certainly not the proper term for the dis-

orderly brawls and thefts and killings which he has in mind. But things come to Gregory directly; he no longer needs to force them into the straitjacket of the elevated style; they grow or even run wild, no longer laced into the apparatus of the Diocletian-Constantinian reform, which brought only a new rule, being too late to bring a new life. Sensory reality, which, in Ammianus, where it was burdened by the fetters of tyrannical rules and the periodic style, could show itself only spectrally and metaphorically, can unfold freely in Gregory.

ERICH AUERBACH

Day, Times of

Daybreak

Dyonea, nycht hyrd, and wach of day,
The starnis chasit of the hevin away,
Dame Cynthea doun rolling in the see,
And Venus lost the bewte of hir E,
Fleand eschamyt within Cylenyus cave;
Mars onbydrew, for all his grundin glave,
Nor frawart Saturn, from his mortall speyr,
Durst langar in the firmament appeir,
Bot stall abak yond in his regioun far
Behynd the circulat warld of Jupiter;
Nycthemyne, affrayit of the lycht,
Went undir covert, for gone was the nycht;
As fresch Aurora, to mychty Tythone spous,
Ischit of hir safron bed and evir hous,
In crammysin cled and granit violat,
With sanguyne cape, the selvage purpurat,
Onschot the windois of hyr large hall,

Spred all wyth rosys, and full of balm ryall,
And eik the hevinly portis crystallyne
Upwarpis braid, the warld to illumyn.
The twinkling stremowris of the orient
Sched purpour sprangis with gold and asure ment,
Persand the sabill barmkyn nocturnall,
Bet doun the skyis clowdy mantill wall:
Eous the steid, with ruby hamis reid,
Abuf the seyis lyftis furth his heid,
Of cullour soyr, and sum deill broun as berry,
For to alichtyn and glaid our emyspery,
The flambe owtbrastyng at his neys thyrlys;
Sa fast Phaeton wyth the quhip him quhirlys,
To roll Apollo his faderis goldin chair,
That schrowdyth all the hevynnis and the ayr;
Quhill schortly, with the blesand torch of day,
Abilyeit in his lemand fresch array,
Furth of hys palyce ryall ischyt Phebus,
Wyth goldin croun and vissage gloryus,
Crysp haris, brycht as chrysolite or topace,
For quhais hew mycht nane behald his face,
The fyry sparkis brastyng fra his ene,
To purge the ayr, and gylt the tendyr grene,
Defundand from hys sege etheriall
Glaid influent aspectis celicall.
Before his regale hie magnificens
Mysty vapour upspringand, sweit as sens,
In smoky soppis of donk dewis wak,
Moich hailsum stovis ourheildand the slak;
The aureat fanys of hys trone soverane
With glytrand glans ourspred the occiane,
The large fludis lemand all of lycht
Bot with a blenk of his supernale sycht.
For to behald, it was a gloir to se
The stabillit wyndis and the cawmyt see,
The soft sessoun, the firmament serene,
The lowne illumynat air, and fyrth amene;
The sylver scalyt fyschis on the greit

Ourthwort cleir stremis sprynkland for the heyt,
Wyth fynnis schynand broun as synopar,
And chyssell talis, stowrand hery and thar;
The new cullour alychtyng all the landis,
Forgane thir stannyris schane the beryall strandis,
Quhill the reflex of the diurnal bemis
The bene bonkis kest ful of variant glemis,
And lusty Flora did hyr blomis spreid
Under the feit of Phebus sulyart steid;
The swardit soyll enbroud wyth selcouth hewis
Wod and forest obumbrat with thar bewis,
Quhois blissfull branchis, porturat on the grund,
With schaddois schene schew rochis rubycund:
Towris, turattis, kyrnellis, pynnaclis hie
Of kirkis, castellis, and ilke fair cite,
Stude payntit, every fyall, fane, and stage,
Apon the plane grund, by thar awin umbrage.

GAVIN DOUGLAS

Morning

'Tis the hour when white-horsed Day
    Chases Night her mares away,
When the Gates of Dawn (they say)
    Phoebus opes:
And I gather that the Queen
May be uniformly seen,
Should the weather be serene,
    On the slopes.

When the ploughman, as he goes
Leathern-gaitered o'er the snows,
From his hat and from his nose
    Knocks the ice;
And the panes are frosted o'er
And the lawn is crisp and hoar,
As has been observed before
    Once or twice.

When arrayed in breastplate red
Sings the robin, for his bread,
On the elmtree that hath shed
  Every leaf;
While, within, the frost benumbs
The still sleepy schoolboy's thumbs,
And in consequence his sums
  Come to grief.

But when breakfast-time hath come,
And he's crunching crust and crumb,
He'll no longer look a glum
  Little dunce;
But be as brisk as bees that settle
On a summer rose's petal:
Wherefore, Polly, put the kettle
  On at once.

C. S. CALVERLEY

Afternoon

When down from heaven more radiant gladness pours, a joy
approaches for human kind, so that they marvel at much that is
visible, higher, agreeable:

How beautifully with it does sacred song combine! How laugh-
ingly in hymns does the heart dwell upon the truth that in an
image is rejoicing—over the pathway sheep set out on

Their track, that takes them almost to glimmering woods. The
meadows, however, which are covered with flawless green, are
like that heath which habitually is to be found

Near the dark wood. There, on the meadows too these sheep
remain. The peaks that are round about, bare heights, are covered
with oaks and with rare pine-trees.

There, where the river's lively wavelets are, so that someone
passing there on his way looks at them happily, there the gentle
shape of the mountains and the vineyard rises high.

True, amidst the grape-vines the steps steeply ascend, where

the fruit-tree stands above it in blossom, and fragrance lingers
upon wild hedges, where the hidden violets burgeon;

But waters come trickling down, and a rustling is faintly audible
there all day long; the villages in that region, however, rest and
are silent throughout the afternoon.

HÖLDERLIN
(trans. Michael Hamburger)

Evening

The Day's grown old, the fainting Sun
Has but a little way to run,
And yet his Steeds, with all his skill,
Scarce lug the Chariot down the Hill.

With Labour spent, and Thirst opprest,
While they strain hard to gain the West,
From Fetlocks hot drops melted light,
Which turn the Meteors in the Night.

The Shadows now so long do grow,
That Brambles like tall Cedars show,
Mole-hills seem Mountains, and the Ant
Appears a monstrous Elephant.

A very little little Flock
Shades thrice the Ground that it would stock;
Whilst the small Stripling following them,
Appears a mighty *Polypheme*.

These being brought into the Fold,
And by the thrifty Master told,
He thinks his Wages are well paid,
Since none are either lost, or stray'd.

Now lowing Herds are each-where heard,
Chains rattle in the Villains Yard,
The Cart's on Tayl set down to rest,
Bearing on high the Cuckolds Crest.

The Hedge is stript, the Clothes brought in,
Nought's left without should be within,
The Bees are hiv'd, and hum their Charm,
Whilst every House does seem a Swarm.

The Cock now to the Roost is prest:
For he must call up all the rest;
The Sow's fast pegg'd within the Sty,
To still her squeaking Progeny.

Each one has had his Supping Mess,
The Cheese is put into the Press,
The Pans and Bowls clean scalded all,
Rear'd up against the Milk-house Wall.

And now on Benches all are sat
In the cool Air to sit and chat,
Till *Phœbus*, dipping in the West,
Shall lead the World the Way to Rest.

CHARLES COTTON

Night

Every star its diamond, every cloud its white plume,
    sadly the moon marches on.
Onward marches while it lights up fields, hills, meadows,
    rivers, where the day is failing.
Fails the day, the dark night falls, falls, little by little, over
    the green mountains.
Green and leafy, sprinkled with rivulets, beneath the shade
    of the branches.
Branches where sing the twittering birds that rise with the
    first light.
    Which all night sleep that the crickets may come out
    and trill among the shadows.

ROSALIA CASTRO
(trans. Gerald Brenan)

Death

Yonder he is through the stream, a man without a coat, a man without a belt, a man of hard slender legs, it is my woe that I cannot run.

Irish riddle

De Profundis

The metallic weight of iron;
The glaze of glass;
The inflammability of wood . . .

You will not be cold there;
You will not wish to see your face in a mirror;
There will be no heaviness,
Since you will not be able to lift a finger.

There will be company, but they will not heed you;
Yours will be a journey only of two paces
Into view of the stars again; but you will not make it.

There will be no recognition;
No one, who should see you, will say—
Throughout the uncountable hours—

'Why . . . the last time we met, I brought you some flowers!'

WALTER DE LA MARE

And smart as little Tommie be, one man kill the whole world—
Mr. Debt.

Jamaican riddle

Death, Dance of

∾

It is a commonplace of literary historians that, because of linguistic changes, the English poets between Chaucer and Wyatt were metrically all at sea. I can only say that if the rhythms of these stanzas are an accident it is a very lucky accident.

DEATH

O thou minstral, that cannest so note and pipe
Unto folkes for to do pleasaunce,
By the right honde anoone I shal thee gripe,
With these other to go upon my daunce.
Ther is no scape nouther avoidaunce,
On no side to contrarye my sentence,
For in music be crafte and accordaunce
Who maister is shall shew his science.

MINSTREL

This newe daunce is to me so straunge,
Wonder diverse and passingly contrarye;
The dredful foting dothe so ofte chaunge,
And the mesures so ofte sithes varye,
Whiche now to me is no thing necessarye
Yif hit were so that I might asterte:
But many a man, yif I shal not tarye,
Ofte daunceth, but no thinge of herte.

LYDGATE

Dejection

✦

March 22, 1782

I spent the time idly. *Mens turbata*. In the afternoon it snowed.

DR. JOHNSON

December 3, 1854

A very dark day. Mary Hales suffered torments from tooth-extraction, very unsuccessfully done, and was crying with pain at intervals throughout the day; my wife's voice had gone through a severe cold; my elder daughter was suffering from a boil, and I with rheumatism; the weather was dreadful, and it was becoming dark at three. All these things tried the tempers of the party so that I was not sorry to solace myself with the *Guardian* and a pipe after they had all gone to bed.

BENJAMIN JOHN ARMSTRONG

The deadliest of all things to me is my loss of faith in nature. No spring—no summer. Fog always, and the snow faded from the Alps.

RUSKIN

August 16, 1873

We hurried too fast and it knocked me up. We went to the College, the seminary being wanted for the secular priests' retreat: almost no gas, the retorts were being mended; therefore candles in bottles, things not ready, darkness and despair. In fact, being unwell, I was quite downcast: nature in all her parcels and faculties gaped and fell apart, *fatiscebat*, like a clod cleaving and holding only by strings of root.

GERARD MANLEY HOPKINS

The high hills have a bitterness
Now they are not known,
And memory is poor enough consolation
For the soul hopeless gone.
Up in the air there beech tangles wildly in the wind—
That I can imagine.
But the speed, the swiftness, walking into clarity,
Like last year's briony, are gone.

IVOR GURNEY

Wednesday, May 25, 1932

. . . since we came back, I'm screwed up into a ball; can't get into step; can't make things dance; feel awfully detached; see youth; feel old; no, that's not quite it: wonder how a year or so perhaps is to be endured. Think, yet people do live; can't imagine what goes on behind faces. All is surface hard; myself only an organ that takes blows, one after another; the horror of the hard raddled faces in the flower show yesterday: the inane pointlessness of all this existence: hatred of my own brainlessness and indecision; the old treadmill feeling, of going on and on and on, for no reason: Lytton's death; Carrington's; a longing to speak to him; all that cut away, gone: . . . women: my book on professions: shall I write another novel; contempt for my lack of intellectual power; reading Wells without understanding; . . . society; buying clothes; Rodmell spoilt; all England spoilt: terror at night of things generally wrong in the universe; buying clothes; how I hate Bond Street and spending money on clothes: worst of all is this dejected barrenness. And my eyes hurt: and my hand trembles.

VIRGINIA WOOLF

When the bells jussle in the tower,
  The hollow night amid,
Then on my tongue the taste is sour
  Of all I ever did.

A. E. HOUSMAN

Departure, Prose and Poetry of

❦

The world, we think; makes a great mistake on the subject of saying, or acting, farewell. The word or deed should partake of the suddenness of electricity; but we all drawl through it at a snail's pace. We are supposed to tear ourselves from our friends; but tearing is a process which should be done quickly. What is so wretched as lingering over a last kiss, giving the hand for the third time, saying over and over again, "Good-bye, John, God bless you; and mind you write!" Who has not seen his dearest friends standing round the window of a railway carriage, while the train would not start, and has not longed to say to them, "Stand not upon the order of your going, but go at once!" And of all such farewells, the ship's farewell is the longest and most dreary. One sits on a damp bench, snuffling up the odour of oil and ropes, cudgelling one's brains to think what further word of increased tenderness can be spoken. One returns again and again to the weather, to coats and cloaks, perhaps even to sandwiches and the sherry flask. All effect is thus destroyed, and a trespass is made even upon the domain of feeling.

I remember a line of poetry, learnt in my earliest youth, and which I believe to have emanated from a sentimental Frenchman, a man of genius, with whom my parents were acquainted. It was as follows:—

> *Are you go? Is you gone? And I left? Ver vell!*

Now the whole business of a farewell is contained in that line. When the moment comes, let that be said; let that be said and felt, and then let the dear ones depart.

A. TROLLOPE

Sufficiently seen. The vision has been encountered under all skies.

Sufficiently experienced. The sounds of cities, in the evening,
    and in the sunlight, and always.
Sufficiently known. The limits of life. O Sounds and Visions!
Departure into the new affection and the new noise.

ARTHUR RIMBAUD
(trans. Oliver Bernard,
modified by W.H.A.)

At that moment Elrond came out with Gandalf, and he called the
Company to him. "This is my last word," he said in a low voice.
"The Ring-Bearer is setting out on the Quest of Mount Doom.
On him alone is any charge laid: neither to cast away the Ring,
nor to deliver it to any servant of the Enemy nor indeed to let
any handle it, save members of the Company and the Council,
and only then in gravest need. The others go with him as free
companions, to help him on his way. You may tarry, or come
back, or turn aside into other paths, as chance allows. The further
you go, the less easy will it be to withdraw; yet no oath or bond
is laid on you to go further than you will. For you do not yet
know the strength of your hearts, and you cannot foresee what
each may meet upon the road."

"Faithless is he that says farewell when the road darkens," said
Gimli.

"Maybe," said Elrond, "but let him not vow to walk in the
dark, who has not seen the nightfall."

"Yet sworn word may strengthen the quaking heart," said
Gimli.

"Or break it," said Elrond. "Look not too far ahead! But go
now with good hearts! Farewell, and may the blessing of Elves
and Men and all Free Folk go with you. May the stars shine upon
your faces!"

J . R . R . TOLKIEN

Diaries, Fate of the Obscure in

The historical reputation of a public figure is based upon a large number of known data, some favorable, some unfavorable. Consequently, a single derogatory remark in a contemporary memoir affects his reputation, for better or worse, very little.

In the case of an obscure private individual, however, the single derogatory remark may damn him forever, because it is all we shall ever hear about him.

January 3, 1854

In the evening went to a party at Mr. Anfrere's. Very slow—small rooms, piano out of tune, bad wine, and stupid people.

BENJAMIN JOHN ARMSTRONG

Poor Mr. Anfrere! No doubt he had many virtues, but to posterity he is simply an incompetent host.

Dogs

Lupus and Aureus

The reticent exclusiveness and the mutual defence at any price are properties of the wolf which influence favorably the character of all strongly wolf-blooded dog breeds and distinguish them to their advantage from Aureus dogs, which are mostly "hail-fellow-well-met" with every man and will follow anyone who holds the other end of the lead in his hand. A Lupus dog, on the contrary, who has once sworn allegiance to a certain man is forever a one-man dog, and no stranger can win from him so much as a single wag of his bushy tail. Nobody who has once possessed the one-man love of a Lupus dog will ever be content with one of pure Aureus blood. Unfortunately, this fine characteristic of the Lupus dog has against it various disadvantages which are indeed the immediate results of the one-man loyalty. That a mature Lupus dog can never become *your* dog is a matter of course. But worse, if he is already yours and you are forced to leave him, the animal becomes literally mentally unbalanced, obeys neither your wife nor children, sinks morally, in his grief, to the level of an ownerless street cur, loses his restraint from killing and, committing misdeed upon misdeed, ravages the surrounding district.

Besides this, a predominantly Lupus-blooded dog is, in spite of his boundless loyalty and affection, never quite sufficiently submissive. He is ready to die for you, but not to obey you. . . . If you walk with a Lupus dog in the woods you can never make him stay near you. All he will do is to keep in very loose contact with you and honor you with his companionship only now and again.

Not so the Aureus dog; in him, as a result of his age-old domestication, that infantile affection has persisted which makes him a manageable and tractable companion. (Instead of the proud manly loyalty of the Lupus dog which is far removed from obedience, the Aureus dog will grant you that servitude which, day and night, by the hour and by the minute, awaits your command and even your slightest wish.) When you take him for a walk, an Aureus dog of a more highly domesticated breed will, without previous training, always run with you, keeping the same radius whether he runs before, behind or beside you, and adapting his speed to yours. He is naturally obedient—that is to say, he answers to his name not only when he wishes to and when you cajole him, but also because he knows he *must* come. The harder you shout, the more surely he will come, whereas a Lupus dog, in this case, comes not at all but seeks to appease you from a distance with a friendly gesture.

Opposed to these good and congenial properties of the Aureus dog are unfortunately some others which also arise from the permanent infantility of these animals and are less agreeable for an owner. . . . Like many spoilt human children who call every grown-up "uncle", they pester people and animals alike with overtures to play. . . . The worst part of it lies in the literally "dog-like" submission that these animals, who see in every man an "uncle", show towards anyone who treats them with the least sign of severity; the playful storm of affection is immediately transformed into a cringing state of humility. Everyone is acquainted with this kind of dog which knows no happy medium between perpetual exasperating "jumping up", and fawningly turning upon its back, its paws waving in supplication.

KONRAD LORENZ

Bibbles

. . . Oh Bibbles, oh Pips, oh Pipsey,
You little black love-bird!
Don't you love *everybody!*
Just everybody.
You love 'em all.
Believe in the One Identity, don't you,
You little Walt-Whitmanesque bitch?
First time I lost you in Taos plaza,
And found you after endless chasing,
Came upon you prancing round the corner in exuberant,
    bibbling affection
After the black-green skirts of a yellow-green old Mexican
    woman
Who hated you, and kept looking round at you and cursing
    you in a mutter,
While you pranced and bounced with love of her, you in-
    discriminating animal,
All your wrinkled *miserere* Chinese black little face beaming
And your black little body bouncing and wriggling
With indiscriminate love, Bibbles;
I had a moment's pure detestation of you. . . .

. . . . . .

Yet you're so nice,
So quick, like a little black dragon.

So fierce, when the coyotes howl, barking like a whole little
    lion, and rumbling,
And starting forward in the dusk, with your little black fur
    all bristling like plush
Against those coyotes, who would swallow you like an
    oyster.

And in the morning, when the bedroom door is opened,
Rushing in like a little black whirlwind, leaping straight as an
    arrow on the bed at the pillow
And turning the day suddenly into a black tornado of *joie de
    vivre*, Chinese dragon.

So funny
Lobbing wildly through deep snow like a rabbit,
Hurtling like a black ball through the snow,
Champing it, tossing a mouthful,
Little black spot in the landscape!

So absurd
Pelting behind on the dusty trail when the horse sets off
    home at a gallop:
Left in the dust behind like a dust-ball tearing along,
Coming up on fierce little legs, tearing fast to catch up, a
    real little dust-pig, ears almost blown away,
And black eyes bulging bright in a dust-mask
Chinese-dragon-wrinkled, with a pink mouth grinning, under
    jaw shoved out
And white teeth showing in your dragon-grin as you race,
    you split-face,
Like a trundling projectile swiftly whirling up.

         . . . . . .

Plenty of conceit in you.
Unblemished belief in your own perfection
And utter lovableness, you ugly-mug;
Chinese puzzle-face,

Wrinkled underhung physiog that looks as if it had done
with everything,
Through with everything.

Instead of which you sit there and roll your head like a
canary
And show a tiny bunch of white teeth in your underhung
blackness,
Self-conscious little bitch,
Aiming again at being loved. . . .

D. H. LAWRENCE

Tulip

She has two kinds of urination, Necessity and Social. Different
stances are usually, though not invariably, adopted for each. In
necessity she squats squarely and abruptly, right down on her
shins, her hind legs forming a kind of dam against the stream that
gushes out from behind; her tail curves up like a scimitar; her expression is complacent. For social urination, which is mostly preceded by the act of smelling, she seldom squats, but balances herself on one hind leg, the other being withdrawn or cocked up in
the air. The reason for this seems obvious; she is watering some
special thing and wishes to avoid touching it. It may also be that
in this attitude she can more accurately bestow her drops. Often
they are merely drops, a single token drop will do, for the social
flow is less copious. The expression on her face is business-like, as
though she were signing a cheque.

She attends socially to a wide range of objects. The commonest
group are the droppings, both liquid and solid, of other animals.
Fresh horse dung has a special attraction for her and is always
liberally sprayed. Then she sprinkles any food that has been
thrown about—buns, bones, fish, bread, vomit—unless it is food
she wishes to eat. Dead and decaying animals are carefully attended to. There are advanced stages of decay, when flesh turns
into a kind of tallow, which affect her so deeply that urination
appears to be an inadequate expression of her feelings. Try as she
may she cannot lift leg, and tottering round the object in a

swooning way would prostrate herself upon it if the meddling voice of authority did not intervene. . . .

She drips also upon drains, disinfectants and detergents (in a street of doorsteps it is generally the one most recently scoured which she selects), and pieces of newspaper. Once she spared a few drops for a heap of socks and shoes left on the foreshore of the river by some rowing men who had gone sculling. Following her antics with the utmost curiosity I used to wonder what on earth she was up to. I saw that, excepting perhaps for the newspapers, unless she was moved by printers' ink, all these objects had a quality in common, smell; even so, why did she pee on them? It could not be because other dogs had done so before her, for that only pushed the question further back: who began, and why? Nor did I think she was staking a kind of personal claim; nothing in her subsequent behaviour suggested appropriation. I came to the conclusion that she was simply expressing an appreciative interest; she was endorsing these delectable things with her signature, much as we underline a book we are reading. . . .

. . . Some people believe they [dogs] hate sex; others regard it as unnecessary, or odious, or positively dangerous. Some, hugging to themselves all the love, which dogs feel only for the human race, will not allow that there is a sexual instinct also. To this large category belong those nervous women who, far from being sympathetic to intimate canine relationships, prevent their creatures, male or female, even from speaking to their own kind. Never off the lead, they are twitched away from all communication with other dogs, in case of fights, contagion, or "nasty" behaviour, they are so greatly loved. Men, too, frequently exhibit the deepest aversion to such poor sexual satisfactions as are left to their beasts. I meet it constantly, the intolerant reaction to the natural conduct of a dog and a bitch. No sooner does some canine admirer begin to pay Tulip court than the master's stick will stir, the reproof will be uttered: "Come off it, Rex! Now stop it, I say! How often must I tell you?" Nor can "the feelings of others", though they may occasionally be the modest motive, always be advanced in excuse, for the same thing happens when there is no-one else about. "Do let them be!" I sometimes expostulate.

"They're doing no harm." But the stick stirs. One gentleman, fidgeting from foot to foot in the solitude of Putney Common, exclaimed: "I hate to see dogs do that!"

When Tulip is actually in the canine news—that is to say when she is on the verge of heat or just coming out of it—incidents are more frequent and more serious. The little dog approaches her and begins to flatter her. This she graciously permits. The master, who is stationary ten paces away watching the rowing crews on the river, notices and calls his dog. Both animals are safely on the pavement, they are clearly on the best of terms, the master is in no hurry. But the amount of totally unnecessary interference in canine lives, the exercise of authority for its own sake, has to be seen to be believed. The little creature cannot tear himself away. The master calls more harshly. The dog wags his tail but cannot go. Sensing trouble I summon Tulip and put her on the lead.

"It's not his fault," I say mildly. "I'm afraid my bitch is just coming into heat."

The master gives me a brief look but no reply. He calls a third time, and now that Tulip has been withdrawn, the little dog rejoins him, wagging his tail. . . .

"Come here!" says the master, upright in his aquascutum.

The little dog creeps forward to his very feet. The master lashes out. With a yelp the little dog shrinks away.

"Come here!" says the master.

Inch by inch, on his stomach, the little dog crawls once more up to his master's boots. The lash descends. Now the master is satisfied. A lesson has been taught. Two lessons, one lash for each: obedience, propriety. He squares his shoulders and their interrupted walk is resumed.

J. R. ACKERLEY

Sled Dogs

A dog has a wonderful mind of its kind but it lives on incident, and monotony is death to it. Yet monotony is an ever-present feature of the Barrier, where for 200 miles one is out of sight of land; where on a bright day there is nothing to see but the shadows of snow furrows or the painful glint of light reflected from ice crystals in the air or on the surface.

On a clouded day there is nothing but a blank whiteness from underfoot to overhead, not even a horizon to steady oneself. To a man this monotony is infinitely wearisome, to a dog it is almost insupportable, and he just longs for something, anything, however trivial, to claim his attention.

After a night sleeping on the snow still in his harness there is the men's tent to watch, their preparation for the start, the yelping of his companions, the general eagerness to be off, and there is the glorious gallop for the first half-mile when the sledge seems to weigh nothing and the driver has to mount it or be left behind. But after that first zest of movement things begin to pall. The place where the harness rubs begins to ache, the jerking of the sledge is annoying, the stumbles of his yoke-mate yank him viciously to the side, the caked snow on his belly-band feels rougher every minute. He could endure all these things if only there were something to see or to smell, but there is nothing in air or snow which can raise a single spark of interest for him.

When the going is really heavy the driver can walk ahead of the team and raise the dogs' spirits by giving them something to look at, but usually the only features in a day's march were the cairns every five miles raised by the pony-party ahead or the occasional pony droppings, black on the white snow, which, miraged up, would look like a penguin or a seal and cause ears to cock and footsteps to quicken. Captain Scott always said that the Barrier is no place for a Christian, and we may add that it is even worse for a dog.

FRANK DEBENHAM

Rover

The dog that lives with his master constantly, sleeping before his fire, instead of in the kennel, and hearing and seeing all that passes, learns if at all quick-witted to understand not only the meaning of what he sees going on, but also, frequently in the most wonderful manner, all that is talked of. I have a favourite retriever, a black water-spaniel, who for many years has lived in the house and been constantly with me; he understands and notices everything that is said, if it at all relates to himself or to the sporting plans for the day: if at breakfast time I say, without addressing the dog himself, "Rover must stop at home to-day, I cannot take him out," he never attempts to follow me; if, on the contrary, I say, however quietly, "I shall take Rover with me to-day," the moment that breakfast is over he is all on the *qui vive*, following me wherever I go, evidently aware that he is to be allowed to accompany me. When left at home, he sits on the step of the front door, looking out for my return, occasionally howling and barking in an ill-tempered kind of voice; his great delight is going with me when I hunt the woods for roe and deer. I had some covers about five miles from the house, where we were accustomed to look for roe: we frequently made our plans over night while the dog was in the room. One day, for some reason, I did not take him: in consequence of this, invariably when he heard us at night, forming our plan to beat the woods, Rover started alone very early in the morning, and met us up there. He always went to the cottage where we assembled, and sitting on a hillock in front of it, which commanded a view of the road by which we came, waited for us; when he saw us coming, he met us with a peculiar kind of grin on his face, expressing, as well as words could, his half doubt of being well received, in consequence of his having come without permission: the moment he saw that I was not angry with him, he threw off all his affectation of shyness, and barked and jumped upon me with the most grateful delight.

As he was very clever at finding deer, I often sent him with the beaters or hounds to assist, and he always plainly asked me on starting, whether he was to go with me to the pass, or to accompany the men. In the latter case, though a very exclusive dog in his company at other times, he would go with any one of the beaters, although a stranger to him, whom I told him to accompany, and he would look to that one man for orders as long as he was with him. I never lost a wounded roe when he was out, for once on the track he would stick to it, the whole day if necessary, not fatiguing himself uselessly, but quietly and deter-

minedly following it up. If the roe fell and he found it, he would
return to me, and then lead me up to the animal, whatever the
distance might be. With red-deer he was also most useful. The
first time that he saw me kill a deer he was very much surprised;
I was walking alone with him through some woods in Ross-shire,
looking for woodcocks; I had killed two or three, when I saw
such recent signs of deer, that I drew the shot from one barrel,
and replaced it with ball. Then I continued my walk. Before I
had gone far, a fine barren hind sprung out of a thicket, and as
she crossed a small hollow, going directly away from me, I fired
at her, breaking her backbone with the bullet; of course she
dropped immediately, and Rover, who was a short distance behind me, rushed forward in the direction of the shot, expecting
to have to pick up a woodcock; but on coming up to the hind,
who was struggling on the ground, he ran round her with a look
of astonishment, and then came back to me with an expression in
his face plainly saying, "What have you done now?—you have
shot a cow or something." But on my explaining to him that the
hind was fair game, he ran up to her and seized her by the throat
like a bulldog. Ever afterwards he was peculiarly fond of deer-
hunting, and became a great adept, and of great use. When I sent
him to assist two or three hounds to start a roe—as soon as the
hounds were on the scent, Rover always came back to me and
waited at the pass: I could enumerate endless anecdotes of his
clever feats in this way.

Though a most aristocratic dog in his usual habits, when staying with me in England once, he struck up an acquaintance with
a ratcatcher and his curs, and used to assist in their business when
he thought that nothing else was to be done, entering into their
way of going on, watching motionless at the rats' holes when the
ferrets were in, and as the ratcatcher told me, he was the best dog
of them all, and always to be depended on for showing if a rat
was in a hole, corn-stack, or elsewhere; never giving a false alarm,
or failing to give a true one. The moment, however, that he saw
me, he instantly cut his humble friends, and denied all acquaintance with them in the most comical manner.

C. G. W. ST. JOHN

Wanted: a dog that neither barks nor bites, eats broken glass and shits diamonds.

GOETHE

To be sure, the dog is loyal. But why, on that account, should we take him as an example? He is loyal to men, not to other dogs.

KARL KRAUS

Donkey, The

A horse translated into Dutch.

G. C. LICHTENBERG

Dons, Humor of

Dr. Spooner, who could still be seen in the streets of Oxford when I was an undergraduate, did not himself, it seems, make many spoonerisms (q.v.). His conversation, however, could be very odd. In his *Memories* Sir Maurice Bowra reports the following snatch of dialogue.

DR. SPOONER: I want you to come to tea next Thursday to meet Mr. Casson.
MR. CASSON: But I am Mr. Casson.
DR. SPOONER: Come all the same.

And here are three more anecdotes from the same source.

It was told that once, when he [Joseph Wells] heard a fearful row in the back quad, he walked up in the dark and said, "If you don't stop at once, I shall light a match." They stopped.

Symons never admitted that he was wrong. An undergraduate was found drunk, and Symons abused another, quite innocent man for it, who said that his name was not that by which Symons had called him, but Symons would not admit it. "You're drunk still. You don't even know your own name. Go to your room at once."

Brabant kept a car and drove it badly, even by academic standards, which, from myopia, or self-righteousness, or loquacity, or absorption in other matters, are notoriously low. Once when I was with him, he drove straight into a cow and knocked it down, fortunately without damage. When the man in charge of it said quite mildly, "Look out where you are going," Brabant said fiercely, "Mind your own business," and drove on.

MAURICE BOWRA

In Memoriam Examinatoris Cuisdam

Lo, where yon undistinguished grave
   Erects its grassy pile on
One who to all Experience gave
   An Alpha or Epsilon.

The world and eke the world's content,
   And all therein that passes,
With marks numerical (per cent)
   He did dispose in classes:

Not his to ape the critic crew
   Which vulgarly appraises
The Good, the Beautiful, the True
   In literary phrases:

He did his estimate express
   In terms precise and weighty,—
And Vice got 25 (or less),
   While Virtue rose to 80.

Now hath he closed his earthly lot
   All in his final haven,—
(And be the stone that marks the spot
   On one side only graven);

Bring papers on his grave to strew
   Amid the grass and clover,
And plant thereby that pencil blue
   Wherewith he looked them over!

There freed from every human ill
   And fleshly trammels gross, he
Lies in his resting place until
   The final Viva Voce:

So let him rest till crack of doom,
   Of mortal tasks aweary,—
And nothing write upon his tomb
   Save β–?

                A. D. GODLEY

An Election Address

(To Cambridge University, 1882)

I venture to suggest that I
   Am rather noticeably fit
To hold the seat illumined by
   The names of Palmerston and Pitt.

My principles are such as you
   Have often heard expressed before:
They are, without exception, true;
   And who can say, with candor, more?

My views concerning Church and State
   Are such as bishops have professed:

I need not recapitulate
  The arguments on which they rest.

Respecting Ireland, I opine
  That Ministers are in a mess,
That Landlords rule by Right Divine,
  That Firmness will relieve Distress.

I see with horror undisguised
  That freedom of debate is dead:
The Liberals are organised;
  The Caucus rears its hideous head.

Yet need'st thou, England, not despair
  At Chamberlain's or Gladstone's pride,
While Henry Cecil Raikes is there
  To organise the other side.

I never quit, as others do,
  Political intrigue to seek
The dingy literary crew,
  Or hear the voice of science speak.

But I have fostered, guided, planned
  Commercial enterprise: in me
Some ten or twelve directors and
  Six worthy chairmen you may see.

My academical career
  Was free from any sort of blot:
I challenge anybody here
  To demonstrate that it was not.

At classics, too, I worked amain,
  Whereby I did not only pass,
But even managed to obtain
  A very decent second class.

And since those early days, the same
   Success has crowned the self-same plan:
Profundity I cannot claim;
   Respectability I can.

J. K. STEPHEN

Double-Entendre, Unconscious

It is possible to make one through sheer inattention. While translating *Die Zauberflöte,* I wrote a stage direction which sent my collaborator, Mr. Chester Kallman, into fits of laughter. It ran: "Pamina's Chamber. Two Slaves are cleaning it." It must have been sheer inattention, too, that permitted Laurence Binyon to write: "Why hurt so hard by little pricks?"

Usually, however, the double-entendre is caused by an historical change in the meaning of a word. The most obvious example of this is the change, which has taken place during my lifetime, in the meaning of the word *fairy*. It is still possible to speak of fairy stories, but if one wishes to speak of fairies one must now refer to them as elves.

At a dinner party I once was seated next to Miss Rose Fyleman, author of "There Are Fairies at the Bottom of My Garden," and it was clear that nobody had told her what Beatrice Lillie had done with her song. Among her poems there are much more extraordinary examples.

There are no wolves in England any more;
The fairies have driven them all away.

and

My fairy muff is made of pussy-willow

and

The best thing the fairies do, the best thing of all
Is sliding down steeples—you know they're very tall.
Climb up the weather-cock and, when you hear it crow,
Fold your wings, and clutch your things, and then—Let go!

They've lots of other games: cloud-catching's one,
And mud-mixing after rain is lots and lots of fun.
But when you go to stay with them, then never mind the rest:
Take my advice—they're very nice—but steeple-sliding's
      best.

   The most (unconsciously) obscene poem in English that I
know of I ran across in Quiller-Couch's *Oxford Book of Victorian Verse*.

When love meets love, breast urged to breast,
God interposes
An unacknowledged guest,
And leaves a little child among our roses.

We love, God makes: in our sweet mirth
God spies occasion for a birth.
Then is it His, or ours?
I know not—He is fond of flowers.

T. E. BROWN

Dreams

There are four distinguishable stages of sleep, each with characteristic brainwave patterns. The first stage usually lasts a few minutes; the sleeper is easily awakened, the electric waves from the brain are low voltage and irregular. Stage II is characterised by "spindles"—sudden bursts of electrical activity—with a slow rolling of the eyes. Then Stage III gradually supervenes: large slow brainwaves emerge, about one per second, with five times the voltage of the waking rhythms. The heart rate slows, temperature and blood pressure drop, the muscles relax somewhat.

Finally, the sleeper enters Stage IV, the deepest sleep of all, when he is most impervious to noise and disturbance. A large portion of the first part of the night tends to be spent in this deep sleep. Curiously, it is also the phase in which sleepwalking starts.

The most dramatic events begin usually some 90 minutes after going to sleep. The sleeper begins to surface again, back through Stages III, II and I. But instead of entering into a light Stage I sleep, there appears what is virtually a new state of experience. It is signalled by rapid eye movements ("REMs"), quite distinct from the slow rolling of the eyes during deeper sleep. Perhaps the central discovery of sleep research was made in the early 1950's when Nathaniel Kleitman and Eugene Aserinsky, at the University of Chicago, discovered that people woken in this phase of sleep almost always reported a vivid dream.

The whole REM state has proved, on investigation, to be quite extraordinary. For instance, some muscles of the dreamer are, to begin with, completely flaccid. Yet a host of other physiological symptoms suggest that the REM state is one of intense emotional experience and inner concentration: hormones pour into the blood, the heartbeat becomes irregular, blood pressure varies considerably. Breathing may be shallow and rapid, oxygen consumption rises and so does the temperature deep within the brain (as it does on waking).

Luce and Segal call it an "internal storm", and there are usually four to five REM periods each night. They come at roughly 90-minute intervals, and last longer as the night proceeds. Most people thus spend about an hour and a half each night in this strange turmoil.

The peculiar muscular limpness which accompanies the REM state may account for a familiar type of nightmare in which the dreamer struggles to flee from some terror or to cry out, but finds himself paralysed.

But the most astonishing feature of these episodes began to emerge through a now-famous series of experiments by a former student of Kleitman, William Dement. He set out to discover what would happen if people were deprived of dreams by waking them as soon as the REM periods began. Some volunteers subjected to this treatment for a few nights became irritable and forgetful, began to concentrate poorly, reported obscure feelings of uneasiness. Tests with flickering lights produced grotesque hallucinations. Personality changes began to show. The striking thing, though, was that on falling asleep subjects made increasingly frequent "attempts" to dream: they would move almost instantly into the REM state.

On the first night of undisturbed sleep they were allowed, subjects spent an excessive amount of time in the REM state: they appeared to be catching up, not on sleep, but on dream. Control experiments with subjects awakened just as often, but from deep sleep rather than REM periods, showed far less ill effect: although here, too, there was a "rebound", and the subjects took more deep sleep than usual in the first undisturbed night.

Since then, a great deal of evidence has accumulated to show the functional but still obscure importance of the REM state. Even relatively primitive warm-blooded animals like the opossum show REM sleep and suffer if deprived of it. Young animals and human infants spend far more time in the REM state than adults (about half their sleep time in new-born babies). Premature infants take even more.

The day's events are often woven into REM dreams, although sometimes in disguised forms. As the night proceeds, the dreams seem to concern themselves with an increasingly distant past, as though the sleeper were moving back in time. Simultaneously, the dream content tends to become more vivid and laden with imagery.

Recently, workers at Mount Sinai Hospital in New York found that in men almost all REM periods are accompanied by an erection. The erections occur even when a dream appears to have no erotic content. . . . However, it has also been found that if the REM state is prevented, the erections will still occur at the time the REM periods are due, suggesting that some physiological clock is also involved. Indeed, there is the classical hen-and-egg problem here concerning the links between bodily and mental phenomena.

JOHN DAVY

Is sleep a mating with oneself?

NOVALIS

In dreams I do not recollect that state of feeling so common when awake, of thinking of one subject and looking at another.

S. T. COLERIDGE

I cannot say I was hostile to him, nor friendly either: I have never dreamed of him.

G. C. LICHTENBERG

If all the dreams which men had dreamed during a particular period were written down, they would give an accurate notion of the spirit which prevailed at that time.

G. W. F. HEGEL

"Dreaming permits each and every one of us to be quietly and safely insane every night of our lives." (Charles Fisher) Precisely. So far as my own experience goes, my dreams, however physiologically and psychologically necessary, seem to me, on waking, to be boring in exactly the same way that lunatics are, that is to say, repetitious, devoid of any sense of humor, and insanely egocentric. Only once in my life have I had a dream which, on conscious consideration, seemed interesting enough to write down.

A Nightmare—August 1936

I was in hospital for an appendectomy. There was somebody there with green eyes and a terrifying affection for me. He cut off the arm of an old lady who was going to do me an injury. I explained to the doctors about him, but they were inattentive, though, presently, I realized that they were very concerned about his bad influence over me. I decide to escape from the hospital, and do so, after looking in a cupboard for something, I don't know what. I get to a station, squeeze between the carriages of a train, down a corkscrew staircase and out under the legs of some boys and girls. Now my companion has turned up with his three brothers (there may have been only two). One, a smooth-faced, fine-fingernailed blond, is more reassuring. They tell me that they never leave anyone they like and that they often choose the timid. The name of the frightening one is Giga (in Icelandic *Gigur* is a crater), which I associate with the name Marigold and have a vision of pursuit like a book illustration and, I think, related to the long red-legged Scissor Man in *Schockheaded Peter*. The scene changes to a derelict factory by moonlight. The brothers are there, and my father. There is a great banging going on which, they tell me, is caused by the ghost of an old aunt who lives in a tin in the factory. Sure enough, the tin, which resembles my mess tin, comes bouncing along and stops at our feet, falling open. It is full of hard-boiled eggs. The brothers are very selfish and seize them, and only my father gives me half his.

I dreamed that I had landed from a fairly large boat on the shore of a fertile island with a luxuriant vegetation, where I had been told one could get the most beautiful pheasants. I immediately started bargaining for these birds with the natives, who killed them and brought them to me in great numbers. I knew they were pheasants, although, since dreams usually transform things, they had long tails covered with iridescent eyelike spots similar to those of peacocks or rare birds of paradise. The natives brought them on board and neatly arranged them so that their heads were inside the boat and the long gaily-colored feather tails hung outside. In the brilliant sunshine, they made the most splendid pile imaginable, and there were so many of them that there was hardly room for the steersman and the rowers. Then we glided over calm waters and I was already making a mental list of the names of friends with whom I meant to share these treasures. At last we reached a great port. I lost my way among huge masted ships, and climbed from one deck to another, looking for some place where I could safely moor my little boat.

GOETHE
(trans. W. H. A.
with Elizabeth Mayer)

I

Weary birds, large weary birds, perched upon a tremendous cliff that rises out of dark waters, await the fall of night. Weary birds turn their heads towards the blaze in the west. The glow turns to blood, the blood is mixed with soot. We look across the waters towards the west and upwards into the soaring arch of the sunset. Stillness—Our lives are one with that of this huge far-off world, as it makes its entry into the night.—Our few words, spoken or unspoken (My words? His words?), die away: now it is too dark for us to find the way back.

II

Night. The road stretches ahead. Behind me it winds up in curves towards the house, a gleam in the darkness under the dense trees of the park. I know that, shrouded in the dark out there, people are moving, that all around me, hidden by the night, life is a-quiver. I know that something is waiting for me in the house. Out of the darkness of the park comes the call of a solitary bird: and I go—up there.

III

Light without a visible source, the pale gold of a new day. Low bushes, their silk-grey leaves silvered with dew. All over the hills, the cool red of the cat's foot in flower. Emerging from the ravine where a brook runs under a canopy of leaves, I walk out onto a wide open slope. Drops, sprinkled by swaying branches, glitter on my hands, cool my forehead, and evaporate in the gentle morning breeze.

DAG HAMMARSKJÖLD
(trans. W. H. A.
with Leif Sjöberg)

She told me about a dream she had had a few nights before and as I listened I couldn't help feel that perhaps everything would work out alright.

"It was such a lovely warm dream," she said. "I dreamed that

Errol and I were married and that we had such a lovely home. Everything in the house was white. There was a white marble stairway and a completely white bedroom with white chiffon bedspreads. And I know this will please you, Mother. I also dreamed that I had a gold pipe organ to play, just like the one you always wanted me to have. But the best part of all was the baby I was going to have. Errol's baby. I wore this gorgeous black velvet top and gold trousers and gold shoes with the toes turned up. And I was so happy to have Errol's baby that I danced all through the halls of our lovely house."

FLORENCE AADLAND

Drinking Songs

Since the dawn of history alcoholic beverages have been among the greatest blessings of life, but there is not, to my knowledge, a single drinking song of first-rate poetic quality. About even the best of them there is an air of false *bonhomie,* characteristic of an all-male company, of "the boys" whooping it up. About the drinking song in *Antony and Cleopatra,* act II, scene vii, it is worth noting, firstly, that it is the worst lyric Shakespeare ever wrote, and, secondly, that in the context (Pompey's Galley) a good poem would have been dramatically wrong.

The only tolerable English example I can find seems to celebrate solitary drinking.

I have no pain, dear Mother, now,
But, Oh, I am so dry;
So connect me to a brewery,
And leave me there to die.

Oddly enough, there is a very good poem about drug taking.

Cocaine Lil and Morphine Sue

Did you ever hear tell about Cocaine Lil?
She lived in Cocaine town on Cocaine hill,
She had a cocaine dog and a cocaine cat,
They fought all night with a cocaine rat.

She had cocaine hair on her cocaine head.
She had a cocaine dress that was poppy red:
She wore a snowbird hat and sleigh-riding clothes,
On her coat she wore a crimson, cocaine rose.

Big gold chariots on the Milky Way,
Snakes and elephants silver and gray.
Oh the cocaine blues they make me sad,
Oh the cocaine blues make me feel bad.

Lil went to a snow party one cold night,
And the way she sniffed was sure a fright.
There was Hophead Mag with Dopey Slim,
Kankakee Liz and Yen Shee Jim.

There was Morphine Sue and the Poppy Face Kid,
Climbed up snow ladders and down they skid;
There was the Stepladder Kit, a good six feet,
And the Sleigh-riding Sister who were hard to beat.

Along in the morning about half past three
They were all lit up like a Christmas tree;
Lil got home and started for bed,
Took another sniff and it knocked her dead.

They laid her out in her cocaine clothes:
She wore a snowbird hat with a crimson rose;
On her headstone you'll find this refrain:
'She died as she lived, sniffing cocaine.'

Easter

৩§ৢ৯

Easter Day, April 17, 1870

The happiest, brightest, most beautiful Easter I have ever spent. As I had hoped, the day was cloudless, a glorious morning. My first thought was "Christ is Risen". It is not well to lie in bed on Easter morning, indeed it is thought very unlucky. I got up between five and six and was out soon after six. There had been a frost and the air was rimy with a heavy thick white dew on hedge, bank and turf, but the morning was not cold. Last night poor Mrs. Chalmers was in trouble because she had not been able to get any flowers to dress her husband's grave and Miss Chalmers was in deep distress about it. Some boys who had promised to bring them some primroses had disappointed them. So I thought I would go and gather some primroses this morning and flower the grave for them. I strolled down the lane till I came in sight of the full mill pond shining between the willow trunks like a lake of indefinite size. Here and there the banks and road sides were spangled with primroses and they shone like stars among the little brakes and bramble thickets overhanging the brook. A sheep and lamb having broken bonds were wandering about the lane by themselves and kept on fording and refording the brook where it crosses the road to get out of my way. The mill was silent except for the plash of the water from "the dark round of the dripping wheel". The mill pond was full, but I forgot to look at the sun to see if he was dancing as he is said to do on Easter morning. There was a heavy white dew with a touch of hoar frost on the meadows, and as I leaned over the wicket gate by the mill pond looking to see if there were any primroses in the banks but not liking to venture into the dripping grass suddenly I heard the cuckoo for the first time this year. He was near Peter's Pool and he called three times quickly one after another. It is very well to hear the cuckoo for the first time on Easter Sunday morning. I loitered up the lane again gathering primroses where I could from among the thorn and bramble thickets and along the brook banks, not without a good many scratches. Some few grew by the mill pond edge and there was one plant growing on the trunk of a willow some way from the ground. The children have almost swept the lane clear of primroses for the same purpose for which I wanted them. However I got a good handful with plenty of green leaves and brought them home.

The village lay quiet and peaceful in the morning sunshine, but by the time I came back from primrosing there was some little stir and people were beginning to open their doors and look out into the fresh fragrant splendid morning. Hannah Whitney's door was open. I tied my primroses up in five bunches, borrowed an old knife etc. and a can of water from Mary and went to Mrs. Powell's for the primroses Annie had tied for me last night, but no one in the house was up and the door was locked. Anthony and Richard Brooks were standing in the road by the churchyard wall and I asked them if they could show me Mr. Chalmers' grave. Richard Brooks came along with me and showed me where he believed it to be, and it proved to be the right grave. So I made a simple cross upon it with my five primrose bunches. There were a good many people about in the churchyard by this time finishing flowering the graves and looking at last night's work. John Davies and a girl seeing me at work came and dressed the rest of the four Chalmers graves. By this time Mrs. Powell was just opening her door so I went to the house with Charlie Powell and got the primroses which had been in water all night and were exquisitely fresh and fragrant. With these five bunches I made a primrose cross on the turf at the foot of the white marble cross which marks Mr. Henry Venables' grave. Then I went to the school.

It was now 8 o'clock and Mrs. Evans was down and just ready to set about finishing the moss crosses. She and Mary Jane went out to gather fresh primroses in the Castle Clump as last night's were rather withered. The moss had greatly improved and freshened into green during the night's soaking and when the crosses were pointed each with five small bunches of primroses they looked very nice and pretty because so simple. Directly they were finished I carried them to the churchyard and placed them standing, leaning against the stone tombs of the two Mr. Venables. People came up to look at the crosses and they were much admired. Then I ran home to dress and snatched a mouthful of breakfast.

There was a very large congregation at morning church, the largest I have seen for some time, attracted by Easter and the splendour of the day, for they have an immense reverence for Easter Sunday. The anthem went very well and Mr. Baskerville complimented Mr. Evans after church about it, saying that it was sung in good tune and time and had been a great treat. Mr. V read prayers and I preached from I. John III.2,3 about the Risen Body and Life. There were more communicants than usual: 29. This is the fifth time I have received the Sacrament within four days. After morning service I took Mr. V round the churchyard and showed him the crosses on his mother's, wife's, and brother's graves. He was quite taken by surprise and very much gratified. I am glad to see that our primrose crosses seem to be having some effect for I think I notice this Easter some attempt to copy them and an advance towards the form of the cross in some of the decorations of the graves. I wish we could get the people to adopt some little design in the disposition of the flowers upon the graves instead of sticking sprigs into the turf aimlessly anywhere, anyhow and with no meaning at all. But one does not like to interfere too much with their artless, natural way of showing their respect and love for the dead. I am thankful to find this beautiful custom on the increase, and observed more and more every year. Some years ago it was on the decline and nearly discontinued. On Easter Day all the young people come out in something new and bright like butterflies. It is almost part of their religion to wear something new on this day. It was an old saying that if you don't wear something new on Easter Day, the crows will spoil everything you have on. Mrs. Chalmers tells me that if it is fine on Easter Day it is counted in Yorkshire a sign of a good harvest. If it rains before morning church is over it is a sign of a bad harvest.

Between the services a great many people were in the churchyard looking at the graves. I went to Bettws Chapel in the afternoon. It was burning hot and as I climbed the hill the perspiration rolled off my forehead from under my hat and fell in drops on the dusty road. Lucretia Wall was in chapel looking pale and pretty after her illness. I went into the farmhouse after Chapel and when I came away Lucretia and Eliza both looking very pretty were leading little Eleanor about the farmyard between them, a charming home picture. Coming down the hill it was delightful, cool and pleasant. The sweet suspicion of spring strengthens, deepens, and grows more sweet every day. Mrs. Prig gave us lamb and asparagus at dinner.

FRANCIS KILVERT

Eating

The significance of the Mass. As biological organisms, we must all, irrespective of sex, age, intelligence, character, creed, assimilate other lives in order to live. As conscious beings, the same holds true on the intellectual level: all learning is assimilation. As children of God, made in His image, we are required in turn voluntarily to surrender ourselves to being assimilated by our neighbors according to their needs.

The slogan of Hell: Eat *or* be eaten.
The slogan of Heaven: Eat *and* be eaten.

Grub first: then ethics.

BERTHOLT BRECHT

Eating is touch carried to the bitter end.

SAMUEL BUTLER II

Soup and fish explain half the emotions of life.

SYDNEY SMITH

What is patriotism but the love of the good things we ate in our childhood?

LIN YUTANG

The discovery of a new dish does more for human happiness than the discovery of a new star.

BRILLAT-SAVARIN

There is more simplicity in the man who eats caviare on impulse than in the man who eats grapenuts on principle.

G. K. CHESTERTON

Dinnertime is the most wonderful period of the day and perhaps its goal—the blossoming of the day. Breakfast is the bud. The dinner itself, like life, is a curve: it starts off with the lightest courses, then rises to the heavier, and concludes with light courses again.

NOVALIS

. . . gastronomical perfection can be reached in these combinations: one person dining alone, usually upon a couch or a hillside; two people, of no matter what sex or age, dining in a good restaurant; six people, of no matter what sex or age, dining in a good home. . . .

The six should be capable of decent social behaviour: that is, no two of them should be so much in love as to bore the others, nor at the opposite extreme should they be carrying on any sexual or professional feud which could put poison on the plates all must eat from. A good combination would be one married couple, for warm composure; one less firmly established, to add a note of investigation to the talk; and two strangers of either sex, upon whom the better-acquainted could sharpen their questioning wits. . . .

Hunger and fair-to-good health are basic requirements, for no man stayed by a heavy midafternoon snack or gnawed by a gastric ulcer can add much to the general well-being.

M. F. K. FISHER

. . . A certain esteem for each other is clearly evident in all who eat together. This is already expressed by the fact of their *sharing*. The food in the common dish before them belongs to all of them together. Everyone takes some of it and sees that others take some too. Everyone tries to be fair and not to take advantage of anyone else. The bond between the eaters is strongest when it is *one* animal they partake of, one body which they knew as a living unit, or one loaf of bread. . . .

Modern man likes eating in restaurants, at separate tables, with his own little group, for which *he* pays. Since everyone else in the place is doing the same thing, he eats his meal under the pleasing illusion that everyone everywhere has enough to eat.

ELIAS CANETTI

When one despairs of the human race ever learning anything, it is some small comfort to recall that certain patriotic absurdities, common in the First World War, had disappeared in the Second. In the latter, for example, no restaurant proprietor on either side felt it necessary to Anglicize or Germanize the names of dishes. In the former, they did. Karl Kraus gives the following examples from Viennese menus:

Potage à la Colbert	*Suppe mit Wurzelwerk und verlorenem Ei*
Irish stew	*Hammelfleisch im Topf auf bürgerliche Art*
Ragout	*Mischgericht*
Vol-au-vent	*Blätterteighohlpastete*
Mired pickles	*Scharfes Allerlei*
Sauce mayonnaise	*Eieröltunke*
Pommes à la maître d'hôtel	*Erdapfel nach Haushofmeister-Art*
Rumpsteak	*Bereid-Doppelstück*
Macaroni	*Treubruchnudeln*
Romadour	*Hofratskäschen*

How much depends upon the way things are presented in this world can be seen from the very fact that coffee drunk out of wine-glasses is really miserable stuff, as is meat cut at the table

with a pair of scissors. Worst of all, as I once actually saw, is butter spread on a piece of bread with an old though very clean
razor.

G. C. LICHTENBERG

In 1855, George Musgrave, author of *A Ramble through Nor-
mandy,* watched a honeymoon couple on a river steamer at
Rouen consume the following meal:

Soup, fried mackerel, beefsteak, French beans and fried potatoes,
an omelette *fines herbes,* a fricandeau of veal with sorrel, a roast
chicken, garnished with mushrooms, a hock of pork served upon
spinach, an apricot tart, three custards, an endive salad, a small
roast leg of lamb, with chopped onion and nutmeg sprinkled
upon it, coffee, two glasses of absinthe, *eau dorée,* a Mignon
cheese, pears, plums, grapes and cakes. With the meal two bottles
of Burgundy and one of Chablis.

(Quoted by ELIZABETH DAVID
in *French Provincial Cooking*)

Once Archchancellor Cambacérès received two enormous stur-
geons, one weighing 324 pounds, the other 374, the same day.
There was to be a grand dinner that day, and the maître d'hôtel
closeted himself with His Highness to resolve the difficulty that
arose. If both were served at the same dinner, one would evidently belittle the other. On the other hand, it was unthinkable to
serve two fish of the same variety on succeeding days. He
emerged beaming from the conference. Here is how the problem
was solved.

The smaller sturgeon was bedded on flowers and foliage. A
concert of violins and flutes announced it. The flutist and the two
violinists, dressed like chefs, preceded the fish, which was flanked
by four footmen, bearing torches, and two kitchen assistants, bearing knives. The chef, halberd in hand, marched at the fish's head.

The procession paraded around the table, arousing such admiration that the guests, forgetting their respect for Monseigneur,
stood on their chairs to see the monster. But just as the tour was

completed, as the fish was about to be taken out for carving, one of the bearers made a false step, fell on one knee, and the fish slid to the floor.

A cry of despair rose from every heart, or rather from every stomach. There was a moment when everyone was talking, giving advice on how to save the situation. But the voice of Cambacérès dominated the tumult.

"Serve the other," he cried.

And the other, larger fish appeared, but with two flutists, four violinists, and four footmen. Applause succeeded cries of anguish as the first fish, weighing fifty pounds less, was taken away.

ALEXANDRE DUMAS
(trans. Louis Colman)

When a poor man eats a chicken, one of them is sick.

Yiddish proverb

Elizabeth found nothing to complain of in starvation corner as far as soup went: indeed Figgis's rationing had been so severe that she got a positive lake of it. She was pleased at having a man on each side of her, her host on her right, and Georgie on her left, whereas Lucia had quaint Irene on her right. Turbot came next; about that Figgis was not to blame, for people helped themselves, and they were all so inconsiderate that, when it came to Elizabeth's turn, there was little left but spine and a quantity of shining black mackintosh, and as for her first glass of champagne, it was merely foam. By this time, too, she was beginning to get uneasy about Benjy. He was talking in a fat contented voice, which she seldom heard at home, and neither by leaning back nor by leaning forward could she get any really informatory glimpse of him or his wine-glasses. She heard his gobbling laugh at the end of one of his own stories, and Susan said, "Oh fie, Major, I shall tell on you." This was not reassuring.

Elizabeth stifled her uneasiness and turned to her host.

"Delicious turbot, Mr. Wyse," she said. "So good. And did you see the *Hastings Chronicle* this morning about the great Roman discoveries of the *châtelaine* of Mallards. Made me feel quite a Dowager."

Mr. Wyse had clearly foreseen the deadly feelings that might be aroused by that article, and had made up his mind to be extremely polite to everybody, whatever they were to each other. He held up a deprecating hand.

"You will not be able to persuade your friends of that," he said. "I protest against your applying the word Dowager to yourself. It has the taint of age about it. The ladies of Tilling remain young for ever, as my sister Amelia so constantly writes to me."

Elizabeth tipped up her champagne-glass, so that he could scarcely help observing that there was nothing in it.

"Sweet of the dear Contessa," she said. "But in my humble little Grebe, I feel quite a country mouse, so far away from all that's going on. Hardly Tilling at all: my Benjy-boy tells me I must call the house 'Mouse-trap'."

Irene was still alert for attacks on Lucia.

"How about calling it Cat and Mouse trap, Mapp?" she enquired across the table.

"Why, dear?" said Elizabeth with terrifying suavity.

Lucia instantly engaged quaint Irene's attention, or something even more quaint might have followed, and Mr. Wyse made signals to Figgis and pointed towards Elizabeth's glass. Figgis thinking that he was only calling his notice to wine-glasses in general filled up Major Benjy's which happened to be empty, and began carving the chicken. The maid handed round the plates and Lucia got some nice slices off the breast. Elizabeth, receiving no answer from Irene, wheeled round to Georgie.

"What a day it will be when we are all allowed to see the great Roman remains," she said.

A dead silence fell on the table except for Benjy's jovial voice.

"A saucy little customer she was. They used to call her the Pride of Poona. I've still got her photograph somewhere, by Jove."

Rockets of conversation, a regular bouquet of them, shot up all round the table.

"And was Poona where you killed those lovely tigers, Major?" asked Susan. "What a pretty costume Elizabeth made of the best bits. So ingenious. Figgis, the champagne."

"Irene dear," said Lucia in her most earnest voice.

"I think you must manage your summer picture-exhibition this year. My hands are so full. Do persuade her to, Mr. Wyse."

"I see on all sides of me such brilliant artists and such competent managers—" he began.

"Oh, pray not me!" said Elizabeth. "I'm quite out of touch with modern art."

"Well, there's room for old masters and mistresses, Mapp," said Irene encouragingly. "Never say die."

Lucia had just finished her nice slice of breast when a well-developed drumstick, probably from the leg on which the chicken habitually roosted, was placed before Elizabeth. Black roots of plucked feathers were dotted about in the yellow skin.

"Oh, far too much for me," she said. "Just a teeny slice after my lovely turbot."

Her plate was brought back to her with a piece of the drumstick cut off. Chestnut ice with brandy followed, and the famous oyster savoury, and then dessert, with a compôte of figs and honey.

"A little Easter gift from my sister Amelia," explained Mr. Wyse to Elizabeth. "A domestic product of which the recipe is an heirloom of the Mistress of Castello Faraglione. I think Amelia had the privilege of sending you a spoonful or two of the Faraglione honey not so long ago."

The most malicious brain could not have devised two more appalling *gaffes* than this pretty speech contained. There was that unfortunate mention of the word "recipe" again, and everyone thought of lobster, and who could help recalling the reason why Countess Amelia had sent Elizabeth the jar of nutritious honey? The pause of stupefaction was succeeded by a fresh gabble of conversation, and a spurt of irresistible laughter from quaint Irene.

E. F. BENSON

I know a large, greedy, and basically unthinking man who spent all the middle years of his life working hard in a small town and eating in waffle shops and now and then gorging himself at friends' houses on Christmas Day. Quite late he married a large, greedy, and unthinking woman who introduced him to the dubious joys of whatever she heard about on the radio: Miracle Sponge Delight, Aunt Martha's Whipped Cheese Surprise, and all the homogenized, pasteurized, vitalized, dehydratized products intrinsic to the preparation of the Delights and the Surprises. My friend was happy.

He worked hard in the shop and his wife worked hard at the stove, her sink-side portable going full blast in order not to miss a single culinary hint. Each night they wedged themselves into their breakfast-bar-dinette and ate and ate and ate. They always meant to take up Canfield, but somehow they felt too sleepy. About a year ago he brought home a little set of dominoes, thinking it would be fun to shove the pieces around in a couple of games of Fives before she cleared the table. But she looked hard at him, gave a great belch, and died.

He was desperately lonely. We all thought he would go back to living in the rooming-house near the shop, or take up straight rye whisky, or at least start raising tropical fish.

Instead he stayed home more and more, sitting across from the inadequate little chromiumed chair his wife had died in, eating an almost ceaseless meal. He cooked it himself, very carefully. He listened without pause to her radio, which had literally not been turned off since her death. He wrote down every cooking tip he heard, and "enclosed twenty-five cents in stamps" for countless packages of Whipperoo, Jellerino, and Vita-glugg. He wore her tentlike aprons as he bent over the stove and sink and solitary table, and friends told me never, never, *never* to let him invite me to a meal.

But I liked him. And one day when I met him in the Pep Brothers' Shopping Basket—occasionally I fought back my claustrophobia-among-the-cans long enough to go there for the best frozen fruit in town—he asked me so nicely and straightforwardly to come to supper with him that I said I'd love to. He lumbered off, a look of happy purpose wiping the misery from his big face; it was like sunlight breaking through smog. I felt a shudder of self-protective worry, which shamed me.

The night came, and I did something I very seldom do when I am to be a guest: I drank a sturdy shot of dry vermouth and gin, which I figured from long experience would give me an appetite immune to almost any gastronomical shocks. I was agreeably mellow and uncaring by the time I sat down in the chair across from my great, wallowing, bewildered friend and heard him subside with a fat man's alarming *puff!* into his own seat.

I noticed that he was larger than ever. You like your own cooking, I-teased. He said gravely to me that gastronomy had saved his life and reason, and before I could recover from the shock of such fancy words on his strictly one-to-two syllable tongue, he had jumped up lightly, as only a fat man can, and started opening oven doors.

We had a tinned "fruit cup," predominantly gooseberries and obviously a sop to current health hints on station JWRB. Once having disposed of this bit of medical hugger-muggery, we surged on happily through one of the ghastliest meals I ever ate in my life. On second thought I can safely say, *the* ghastliest. There is no point in describing it, and to tell the truth a merciful mist has blurred its high points. There was too much spice where there should be none; there was sogginess where crispness was all-important; there was an artificially whipped and heavily sweetened canned-milk dessert where nothing at all was wanted.

And all through the dinner, in the small, hot, crowded room, we drank lukewarm Muscatel, a fortified dessert wine sold locally in gallon jugs, mixed in cheese-spread glasses with equal parts of a popular bottled lemon soda. It is incredible, but it happened.

I am glad it did. I know now what I may only have surmised theoretically before: there is indeed a gastronomic innocence, more admirable and more enviable than any cunning cognizance of menus and vintages and kitchen subtleties. My gross friend, untroubled by affectations of knowledge, served forth to me a meal that I was proud to partake of. If I felt myself at times a kind of sacrificial lamb, stretched on the altar of devotion, I was glad to be that lamb, for never was nectar poured for any goddess with more innocent and trusting enjoyment than was my hideous glass filled with a mixture of citric acid, carbon dioxide, and pure vinous hell for me. I looked into the little gray eyes of my friend and drank deep and felt the better for it.

M. F. K. FISHER

Echoes

❧

In a district as diversified as this, so full of hollow vales and hanging woods, it is no wonder that echoes should abound. Many we have discovered, that return the cry of a pack of dogs, the notes of a hunting horn, a tunable ring of bells, or the melody of birds very agreeably; but we were still at a loss for a polysyllabical articulate echo, till a young gentleman, who had parted from his company in a summer evening walk, and was calling after them, stumbled upon a very curious one in a spot where it might least be expected. At first he was very much surprised, and could not be persuaded but that he was mocked by some boys; but, repeating his trials in several languages, and finding his respondent to be a very adroit polyglot, he then discerned the deception.

This echo, in an evening before rural noises cease, would repeat ten syllables most articulately and distinctly, especially if quick dactyle were chosen. The last syllable of

Tityre, tu patulae recubans—

were as audibly and intelligibly returned as the first; and there is no doubt, could trial have been made, but that at midnight, when the air is very elastic, and a dead stillness prevails, one or two syllables more might have been obtained; but the distance rendered so late an experiment very inconvenient.

Quick dactyls, we observed, succeeded best; for when we came to try its powers in slow, heavy, embarrassed spondees of the same number of syllables

Monstrum horrendum, informe, ingens—

we could perceive a return of but four or five.

GILBERT WHITE

Eclipses

March 15, 1858

First-rate congregations yesterday. I question whether the solar
eclipse to-day had not something to do with it. The days have
gone when such a phenomenon would have brought a whole nation to its knees. But, notwithstanding the advancement of science, the generality know as little as ever.

BENJAMIN JOHN ARMSTRONG

June 30, 1927

We got out and found ourselves very high, on a moor, boggy,
heathery, with butts for grouse shooting. There were grass tracks
here and there and people had already taken up positions. So we
joined them, walking out to what seemed the highest point over-
looking Richmond. One light burned down there. Vales and
moors stretched, slope after slope, round us. It was like the Ha-
worth country. But over Richmond, where the sun was rising,
was a soft grey cloud. We could see by a gold spot where the
sun was. But it was early yet. We had to wait, stamping to keep
warm. Ray had wrapped herself in the blue striped blanket off a
double bed. She looked incredibly vast and bedroomish. Saxon
looked very old. Leonard kept looking at his watch. Four great
red setters came leaping over the moor. There were sheep feeding
behind us. Vita had tried to buy a guinea pig—Quentin advised a
savage—so she observed the animals from time to time. There
were thin places in the clouds and some complete holes. The
question was whether the sun would show through a cloud or
through one of these hollow places when the time came. We
began to get anxious. We saw rays coming through the bottom
of the clouds. Then, for a moment, we saw the sun, sweeping—it
seemed to be sailing at a great pace and clear in a gap; we had out
our smoked glasses; we saw it crescent, burning red; next moment
it had sailed fast into the cloud again; only the red streamers
came from it; then only a golden haze, such as one has often seen.

The moments were passing. We thought we were cheated; we looked at the sheep; they showed no fear; the setters were racing round; everyone was standing in long lines, rather dignified, looking out. I thought how we were like very old people, in the birth of the world—druids on Stonehenge; (this idea came more vividly in the first pale light though). At the back of us were great blue spaces in the cloud. These were still blue. But now the colour was going out. The clouds were turning pale; a reddish black colour. Down in the valley it was an extraordinary scrumble of red and black; there was the one light burning; all was cloud down there, and very beautiful, so delicately tinted. Nothing could be seen through the cloud. The 24 seconds were passing. Then one looked back again at the blue; and rapidly, very very quickly, all the colours faded; it became darker and darker as at the beginning of a violent storm; the light sank and sank; we kept saying this is the shadow; and we thought now it is over—this is the shadow; when suddenly the light went out. We had fallen. It was extinct. There was no colour. The earth was dead. That was the astonishing moment; and the next when as if a ball had rebounded the cloud took colour on itself again, only a sparky ethereal colour and so the light came back. I had very strongly the feeling as the light went out of some vast obeisance; something kneeling down and suddenly raised up when the colours came. They came back astonishingly lightly and quickly and beautifully in the valley and over the hills—at first with a miraculous glittering and ethereality, later normally almost, but with a great sense of relief. It was like recovery. We had been much worse than we had expected. We had seen the world dead. This was within the power of nature. Our greatness had been apparent too. Now we became Ray in a blanket, Saxon in a cap etc. We were bitterly cold. I should say that the cold had increased as the light went down. One felt very livid. Then—it was over till 1999. What remained was the sense of the comfort which we get used to, of plenty of light, and colour. This for some time seemed a definitely welcome thing. Yet when it became established all over the country, one rather missed the sense of its being a relief and a respite, which one had had when it came back after the darkness. How can I express the darkness? It was a sudden plunge, when

one did not expect it; being at the mercy of the sky; our own no-
bility; the druids; Stonehenge; and the racing red dogs; all that
was in one's mind.

VIRGINIA WOOLF

Education, Classical

The modern revolt against centering the school curriculum
around the study of Latin and Greek is understandable enough,
but deplorably mistaken.

In the Middle Ages Latin was the international language for
all topics, so that it was as obvious why a "clerk" must learn
it as it is obvious why a surgeon must learn anatomy. Then
came the sixteenth-century humanists, who turned Latin into a
dead, purely literary, language, incapable of dealing with any
matters which could not be expressed in the Ciceronian vocabulary. The study of Latin and, later, of Greek continued to have
a vocational value, but in a special, limited sense; a classical
education was thought of as providing a common cultural
background for a leisured ruling class.

Today, gentlemen are no longer in demand, but specialists
are, so that a classical education no longer appears to have an
obvious utility value. It has a great one, nevertheless. It is, no
doubt, a pleasure to be able to read the Greek and Latin poets,
philosophers, and historians in the original, but very few persons so educated in the past "kept up" their Greek and Latin
after leaving school. Its real value was something quite different. Anybody who has spent many hours of his youth translating into and out of two languages so syntactically and rhetoric-
ally different from his own, learns something about his mother
tongue which I do not think can be learned so well in any
other way. For instance, it inculcates the habit, whenever one
uses a word, of automatically asking, "What is its exact meaning?"

The people who have really suffered since a classical education became "undemocratic" are not the novelists and poets—their natural love of language sees them through—but all those, like politicians, journalists, lawyers, the man-in-the-street, etc., who use language for everyday and nonliterary purposes. Among such one observes an appalling deterioration in precision and conciseness.

Nobody, for example, who had had a classical education could have perpetrated this sentence by a film critic, quoted by Penelope Gilliatt in *The New Yorker*. "He [a film director] expresses the dichotomy between man and woman in the images of the bra and Dachau."

Elegies

◆§§◆

Poets seem to be more generally successful at writing elegies than at any other literary genre. Indeed, the only elegy I know of which seems to me a failure is "Adonais."

The Last Signal
(Oct. 11, 1886)
A Memory of William Barnes

Silently I footed by an uphill road
    That led from my abode to a spot yew-boughed;
Yellowly the sun sloped low down to westward,
        And dark was the east with cloud.

Then, amid the shadow of that livid sad east,
    Where the light was least, and a gate stood wide,
Something flashed the fire of the sun that was facing it,
        Like a brief blaze on that side.

Looking hard and harder I knew what it meant—
The sudden shine sent from the livid east scene;
It meant the west mirrored by the coffin of my friend there,
    Turning to the road from his green,

To take his last journey forth—he who in his prime
    Trudged so many a time from that gate athwart the land!
Thus a farewell to me he signalled on his grave-way,
    As with a wave of his hand.

THOMAS HARDY

I.M.
Walter Ramsden

ob. March 26th, 1947
Pembroke College, Oxford.

Dr. Ramsden cannot read *The Times* obituary to-day.
    He's dead.
Let monographs on silk worms by other people be
    Thrown away
    Unread
For he who best could understand and criticize them, he
    Lies clay
    In bed.

The body waits in Pembroke College where the ivy taps the
    panes
    All night;
That old head so full of knowledge, that good heart that kept
    the brains
    All right,
Those old cheeks that faintly flushed as the port suffused
    the veins,
    Drain'd white.

Crocus in the Fellows' Garden, winter jasmine up the wall
    Gleam gold.

Shadows of Victorian chimneys on the sunny grassplot fall
    Long, cold.
Master, Bursar, Senior Tutor, these, his three survivors, all
    Feel old.

They remember, as the coffin to its final obsequations
    Leaves the gates,
Buzz of bees in window boxes on their summer ministrations,
    Kitchen din,
    Cups and plates,
And the getting of bump suppers for the long-dead genera-
    tions
    Coming in,
    From Eights.

JOHN BETJEMAN

Enchantment

Where is your Self to be found? Always in the deepest enchantment that you have experienced.

HUGO VON HOFMANNSTHAL

The state of enchantment is one of certainty. When enchanted,
we neither believe nor doubt nor deny: we *know*, even if, as
in the case of a false enchantment, our knowledge is self-de-
ception.

All folk tales recognize that there are false enchantments as
well as true ones. When we are truly enchanted we desire
nothing for ourselves, only that the enchanting object or person
shall continue to exist. When we are falsely enchanted, we desire either to possess the enchanting being or be possessed by it.

We are not free to choose by what we shall be enchanted, truly or falsely. In the case of a false enchantment, all we can do is take immediate flight before the spell really takes hold.

Recognizing idols for what they are does not break their enchantment.

All true enchantments fade in time. Sooner or later we must walk alone in faith. When this happens, we are tempted, either to deny our vision, to say that it must have been an illusion and, in consequence, grow hardhearted and cynical, or to make futile attempts to recover our vision by force, i.e., by alcohol or drugs.

A false enchantment can all too easily last a lifetime.

Christ did not enchant men; He demanded that they believe in Him. Except on one occasion, the Transfiguration. For a brief while, Peter, James, and John were permitted to see Him in His glory. For that brief while they had no need of faith. The vision vanished, and the memory of it did not prevent them from all forsaking Him when He was arrested, or Peter from denying that he had ever known Him.

God loves all men but is enchanted by none.

My neighbor: someone who needs me but by whom I am not enchanted.

Enclosure

By far the most conspicuous element in the new landscape were the small hedged fields—small, that is, by comparison with the vast open fields that had preceded them, which usually ran to several hundred acres unbroken by a single hedge. As far as possible the enclosure commissioners formed square or squarish fields. Where we find long narrow fields they are nearly always adjacent to the village, lying behind or beside the "ancient homesteads," as they are called in the awards. These represent in most instances the crofts or separate paddocks of half an acre to an acre in size which have been hedged around since medieval times.

The new enclosures varied in size according to the size of the farms. On small farms of which there were great numbers in the Midlands and East Anglia—the holdings of the free peasantry—the new fields were usually five to ten acres in size. On large farms they ran up to fifty or sixty acres. But in grazing country these larger fields were soon reduced to a number of smaller fields of round about ten acres apiece. . . .

The conversion of the former arable fields to small enclosed fields of pasture had therefore two visible effects on the landscape. It tended to produce a monotonous field-pattern and it also produced "a continuous sheet of greensward," as William Marshall observed of Leicestershire in 1790, instead of the multi-coloured patchwork of the old arable strips. . . .

The new fields were hedged around with quickset, whitethorn, or hawthorn, to give its alternative names, with a shallow ditch on one side or both sides of the fence. In the upland stone country, dry-walling took the place of hedges. . . . Ash and elm were planted in the hedgerows, and the flashing grey-green willow along the banks of the streams.

The thousands of miles of new hedgerows in the Midland countryside, when they came to full growth after a generation, added enormously to the bird population, especially with the extermination of the larger hawks and kites, a process that is abundantly recorded in the churchwardens' accounts or the field-reeves' books of Midland villages. Millions of small birds now sing in the hedges and spinneys. But it was not all gain. The heathland birds have disappeared over large areas, and become rarer altogether. . . .

A great number of new by-roads came into existence as a result of the enclosure movement. They are immediately recognizable

on the one-inch map by the manner in which they run from village to village practically straight across the country, with perhaps an occasional sudden right-angled bend and then on again.
More significantly still, these straight roads sometimes do not run
to the nearest village but continue for some miles through open
country, reaching the villages by means of side-roads. There is
none of that apparently aimless wandering in short stretches,
punctuated by frequent bends, going halfway round the compass
to reach the next hamlet or village, which characterizes the by-
roads in country that has never been in open field or left it several centuries ago. . . .

There is, too, another feature of this piece of country which is
characteristic of all country enclosed from open fields or common of any kind. It is the complete absence of any *lanes*. . . .
Lanes—true lanes that is, deep and winding—are characteristic of
country fabricated piecemeal with small medieval implements. In
recently enclosed country we have instead an open regular mesh
of by-roads, and a few field-paths and bridle-roads to fill in the
larger spaces between the villages. In Leicestershire, the man who
wishes to forget income-tax, hydrogen bombs, and the relentless
onward march of science, walks the field-paths, to which special
maps and guides are provided; in Devon he takes to the deep
lanes between the farms. It is a fundamental difference in land-
scape-history.

W. G. HOSKINS

Eclogue: Two Farms in Woone

Robert

You'll lose your meäster soon, then, I do vind;
He's gwaï'n to leäve his farm, as I do larn,
At Miëlmas; an' I be sorry vor'n.
What, is he then a little bit behind?

Thomas

On no! at Miëlmas his time is up,
An' thik there sly wold fellow, Farmer Tup,

A-fearen that he'd get a bit o'bread,
'V a-been an' took his farm here over's head.

Robert

How come the Squire to treat your meäster zoo?

Thomas

Why, he an' meäster had a word or two.

Robert

Is Farmer Tup a-gwaï'n to leäve his farm?
He han't a-got noo young woones vor to zwarm.
Poor over-reachen man! why to be sure
He don't want all the farms in parish, do er?

Thomas

Why ees, all ever he can come across.
Last year, you know, he got away the eäcre
Or two o' ground a-rented by the beäker,
An' what the butcher had to keep his hoss;
An' vo'k do beä'nhan' now, that meäster's lot
Will be a-drow'd along wi' what he got.

Robert

That's it. In theäse here pleäce there used to be
Eight farms avore they were a-drow'd together,
An' eight farm-housen. Now how many be there?
Why after this, you know, there'll be but dree.

Thomas

An' now they din't imploy so many men
Upon the land as work'd upon it then,
Vor all they midden crop it worse, nor stock it.
The lan'lord, to be sure, is into pocket;
Vor half the housen be-en down, 'tis clear,
Don't cost so much to keep em up, a-near.
But then the jobs o' work in wood an' mortar
Do come I 'spose, you know, a little shorter;
An' many that were little farmers then,

Be now a-come all down to leäb'ren men;
An' many leäb'ren men, wi' empty hands,
Do live lik drones upon the workers' lands.

Robert

Aye, if a young chap, woonce, had any wit
To try an' screäpe together zome vew pound,
To buy some cows an' teäke a bit o' ground,
He mid become a farmer, bit by bit.
But, hang it! now the farms be all so big,
An' bits o' groun' so skeä'ce, woone got no scope;
If woone could seäve a poun', woone coudden hope
To keep noo live stock but a little pig.

Thomas

Why here wer vourteen men, zome years agoo,
A-kept a-drashen half the winter drough;
An' now, woone's drashels be'n't a bit o' good.
They got machines to drashy wi', plague teäke em!
An' he that vu'st vound out the way to meäke em,
I'd drash his busy zides vor'n if I could!
Avore they took away our work, they ought
To meäke us up the bread our leäbour bought.

Robert

They hadden need meäke poor men's leäbour less,
Vor work a'ready is uncommon skeä'ce.

Thomas

Ah! Robert! times be badish vor the poor;
Ah' worse will come, I be afeärd, if Moore
In theäse year's almanick do tell us right.

Robert

Why then we sartainly must starve. Good night!

WILLIAM BARNES

Enclosure

By Langley Bush I roam, but the bush hath left its hill,
On Cowper Green I stray, 'tis a desert strange and chill,
And the spreading Lea Close Oak, ere decay had penned its
    will,
To the axe of the spoiler and self-interest fell a prey,
And Crossberry Way and old Round Oak's narrow lane
With its hollow trees like pulpits I shall never see again,
Enclosure like a Buonaparte let not a thing remain,
It levelled every bush and tree and levelled every hill
And hung the moles for traitors—though the brook is run-
    ning still
It runs a naked stream, cold and chill.

JOHN CLARE

Eruptions

Eruption of the Öraefajökull

In the year 1727, on the 7th of August, which was the tenth Sunday after Trinity, after the commencement of divine service in
the church of Sandfell, as I stood before the altar, I was sensible
of a gentle concussion under my feet, which I did not mind at
first; but, during the delivery of the sermon, the rocking continued to increase, so as to alarm the whole congregation; yet they
remarked that the like had often happened before. One of them, a
very aged man, repaired to a spring, a little below the house,
where he prostrated himself on the ground, and was laughed at
by the rest for his pains; but, on his return, I asked him what it
was he wished to ascertain, to which he replied, "Be on your
guard, Sir; the earth is on fire!" Turning, at the same moment,
towards the church door, it appeared to me, and all who were

present, as if the house contracted and drew itself together. I now left the church, necessarily ruminating on what the old man had said; and as I came opposite to Mount Flega, and looked upwards, towards the summit, it appeared alternately to expand and be heaved up, and fall again to its former state. Nor was I mistaken in this, as the event shewed; for on the morning of the 8th, we not only felt frequent and violent earthquakes, but also heard dreadful reports, in no respect inferior to thunder. Everything that was standing in the houses was thrown down by these shocks; and there was reason to apprehend that mountains as well as houses would be overturned in the catastrophe. What most augmented the terror of the people was that nobody could divine in what place the disaster would originate, or where it would end.

After nine o'clock, three particularly loud reports were heard, which were almost instantaneously followed by several eruptions of water that gushed out, the last of which was the greatest, and completely carried away the horses and other animals that it overtook in its course. When these exudations were over, the ice mountain itself ran down into the plain, just like melted metal poured out of a crucible; and on settling, filled it to such a height, that I could not discover more of the well-known mountain Lounagrupr than about the size of a bird. The water now rushed down the east side without intermission, and totally destroyed what little of the pasture-grounds remained. It was a most pitiable sight to behold females crying, and my neighbours destitute both of counsel and courage: however, as I observed that the current directed itself towards my house, I removed my family up to the top of a high rock on the side of the mountain, called Dalskardstorfa, where I caused a tent to be pitched, and all the church utensils, together with our food, clothes and other things that were most necessary, to be conveyed thither; drawing the conclusion that, should the eruption break forth at some other place, this height would escape the longest, if it were the will of God, to whom we committed ourselves, and remained there.

Things now assumed quite a different appearance. The Jökull itself exploded, and precipitated masses of ice, many of which were hurled out to the sea; but the thickest remained on the plain at a short distance from the foot of the mountain. The noise and reports continuing, the atmosphere was so completely filled with fire and ashes, that day could scarcely be distinguished from night, by reason of the darkness that followed, and which was barely rendered visible by the light of the fire that had broken through five or six cracks in the mountain. In this manner the parish of Öraefa was tormented for three days together; yet it is not easy to describe the disaster as it was in reality; for the surface of the ground was entirely covered with pumice-sand, and it was impossible to go out in the open air with safety, on account of the red-hot stones that fell from the atmosphere. Any who did venture out, had to cover their heads with buckets, and such other wooden utensils as could afford them some protection.

On the 11th it cleared up a little in the neighbourhood; but the ice-mountain still continued to send forth smoke and flames. The same day I rode, in company with three others, to see how matters stood with the parsonage, as it was the most exposed, but we could only proceed with the utmost danger, as there was no other way except between the ice-mountain and the Jökull which had been precipitated into the plain, where the water was so hot that the horses almost got unmanageable: and, just as we entertained the hope of getting through by this passage, I happened to look behind me, when I descried a fresh deluge of hot water directly above me which, had it reached us, must inevitably have swept us before it. Contriving, of a sudden, to get on the ice, I called to my companions to make the utmost expedition in following me and, by this means, we reached Sandfell in safety.

The whole of the farm, together with the cottages of the tenants, had been destroyed; only the dwelling houses remained, and a few spots of the tuns. The people stood crying in the church. The cows which, contrary to all expectation, both here and elsewhere, had escaped the disaster, were lowing beside a few haystacks that had been damaged during the eruption. At the time the exudation of the Jökull broke forth, the half of the people belonging to the parsonage were in four nearly-constructed sheepcotes, where two women and a boy took refuge on the roof of the highest; but they had hardly reached it when, being unable to resist the force of the thick mud that was borne against it, it was carried away by the deluge of hot water and, as far as the eye could reach, the three unfortunate persons were seen clinging to the roof. One of the women was afterwards found among the substances that had proceeded from the Jökull, but burnt and, as it were, parboiled; her body was so soft that it could scarcely be touched. Everything was in the most deplorable condition. The sheep were lost; some of which were washed up dead from the sea in the third parish from Öraefa. The hay that was saved was found insufficient for the cows so that a fifth part of them had to be killed; and most of the horses which had not been swept into the ocean were afterwards found completely mangled. The eastern part of the parish of Sida was also destroyed by the pumice and sand; and the inhabitants were on that account obliged to kill many of their cattle.

The mountain continued to burn night and day from the 8th of August, as already mentioned, till the beginning of Summer in the month of April the following year, at which time the stones were still so hot that they could not be touched; and it did not cease to emit smoke till near the end of the Summer. Some of them had been completely calcined; some were black and full of holes; and others were so loose in their contexture that one could blow through them. On the first day of Summer 1728, I went in company with a person of quality to examine the cracks in the mountain, most of which were so large that we could creep into them. I found there a quantity of salpetre and could have collected it, but did not choose to stay long in the excessive heat. At one place a heavy calcined stone lay across a large aperture; and, as it rested on a small basis, we easily dislodged it into the chasm but could not observe the least sign of its having reached the bottom. These are the more remarkable particulars that have occurred to me with respect to this mountain; and thus God hath led me through fire and water, and brought me through much trouble and adversity to my eightieth year. To Him be the honour, the praise, and glory for ever.

JON THORLAKSSON
(Quoted by Sir George MacKenzie
in *Travels in Iceland*)

March 6, 1787

Reluctantly, but out of loyal comradeship, Tischbein accompanied me today on my ascent of Vesuvius. To a cultured artist like him, who occupies himself only with the most beautiful human and animal forms and even humanizes the formless—rocks and landscapes—with feeling and taste, such a formidable, shapeless heap as Vesuvius, which again and again destroys itself and declares war on any sense of beauty, must appear loathsome.

We took two cabriolets, since we didn't trust ourselves to find our own way through the turmoil of the city. The driver shouted incessantly, "Make way! Make way!" as a warning to donkeys, burdened with wood or refuse, carriages going in the opposite direction, people walking bent down under their loads or just strolling, children and aged persons, to move aside so that he could keep up a sharp trot.

The outer suburbs and gardens already gave sign that we had entered the realm of Pluto. Since it had not rained for a long time, the leaves of the evergreens were coated with a thick layer of ash-grey dust; roofs, fascias and every flat surface were equally grey; only the beautiful blue sky and the powerful sun overhead gave witness that we were still among the living.

At the foot of the steep slope we were met by two guides, one elderly, one youngish, but both competent men. The first took me in charge, the second Tischbein, and they hauled us up the mountain. I say "hauled," because each guide wears a stout leather thong around his waist; the traveller grabs on to this and is hauled up, at the same time guiding his own feet with the help of a stick.

In this manner we reached the flat base from which the cone rises. Facing us in the north was the debris of the Somma. One glance westward over the landscape was like a refreshing bath, and the physical pains and fatigue of our climb were forgotten. We then walked round the cone, which was still smoking and ejecting stones and ashes. So long as there was space enough to remain at a safe distance, it was a grand, uplifting spectacle. After a tremendous, thundering roar which came out of the depth of the cauldron, thousands of stones, large and small, and enveloped in clouds of dust, were hurled into the air. Most of them fell back into the abyss, but the others made an extraordinary noise as they hit the outer wall of the cone. First came the heavier ones, struck with a dull thud and hopped down the slope, then the lighter rattled down after them and, last, a rain of ash descended. This all took place at regular intervals, which we could calculate exactly by counting slowly.

However, the space between the cone and the Somma gradually narrowed till we were surrounded by fallen stones which made walking uncomfortable. Tischbein grew more depressed than ever when he saw that the monster, not content with being ugly, was now threatening to become dangerous as well.

But there is something about an imminent danger which challenges Man's spirit of contradiction to defy it, so I thought to myself that it might be possible to climb the cone, reach the mouth of the crater and return, all in the interval between two eruptions. While we rested safely under the shelter of a projecting rock and refreshed ourselves with the provisions we had brought with us, I consulted our guides. The younger one felt confident that we could risk it; we lined our hats with linen and silk handkerchiefs, I grabbed his belt, and, sticks in hand, we set off.

The smaller stones were still clattering, the ashes still falling about us as the vigorous youth hauled me up the glowing screes. There we stood on the lip of the enormous mouth; a light breeze blew the smoke away from us but also veiled the interior of the crater; steam rose all around us from thousands of fissures; now and then we could glimpse the cracked rock walls. The sight was neither instructive nor pleasing, but this was only because we could not see anything, so we delayed in the hope of seeing more. We had forgotten our slow count and were standing on a sharp edge of the monstrous abyss when, all of a sudden, thunder shook the mountain and a terrific charge flew past us. We ducked instinctively, as if that would save us when the shower of stones began. The smaller stones had already finished clattering down when, having forgotten that another interval had begun, and happy to have survived, we reached the foot of the cone under a rain of ashes which thickly coated our hats and shoulders. . . .

March 20

The news that another emission of lava had just occurred, invisible to Naples since it was flowing towards Ottaiano, tempted me to make a third visit to Vesuvius. On reaching the foot of the mountain, I had hardly jumped down from my two-wheeled, one-horse vehicle before the two guides who had accompanied us the last time appeared on the scene and I hired them both.

When we reached the cone, the elder stayed with our coats and provisions while the younger followed me. We bravely made our way towards the enormous cloud of steam, which was issuing from a point halfway below the mouth of the cone. Having reached it, we descended carefully along its edge. The sky was clear and at last, through the turbulent clouds of steam, we saw the lava stream.

It was only about ten feet wide, but the manner in which it flowed down the very gentle slope was most surprising. The lava on both sides of the stream cools as it moves, forming a channel. The lava on its bottom also cools, so that this channel is constantly being raised. The stream keeps steadily throwing off to right and left the scoria floating on its surface. Gradually, two levels of considerable height are formed, between which the fiery stream continues to flow quietly like a mill brook. We walked along the foot of this embankment while the scoria kept steadily rolling down its sides. Occasionally there were gaps through which we could see the glowing mass from below. Further down, we were also able to observe it from above.

Because of the bright sunshine, the glow of the lava was dulled. Only a little smoke rose into the pure air. I felt a great desire to get near the place where the lava was issuing from the mountain. My guide assured me that this was safe, because the moment it comes forth, a flow forms a vault of cooled lava over itself, which he had often stood on. To have this experience, we again climbed up the mountain in order to approach the spot from the rear. Luckily, a gust of wind had cleared the air, though not entirely, for all around us puffs of hot vapour were emerging from thousands of fissures. By now we were actually standing on the lava crust, which lay twisted in coils like a soft mush, but it projected so far out that we could not see the lava gushing forth.

We tried to go half a dozen steps further, but the ground under our feet became hotter and hotter and a whirl of dense fumes darkened the sun and almost suffocated us. The guide who was walking in front turned back, grabbed me, and we stole away from the hellish cauldron.

After refreshing our eyes with the view and our throats with wine, we wandered about observing other features of this peak of hell which towers up in the middle of paradise. I inspected some more volcanic flues and saw that they were lined up to the rim with pendent, tapering formations of some stalactitic matter. Thanks to the irregular shape of the flues, some of these deposits were in easy reach, and with the help of our sticks and some hooked appliances we managed to break off some pieces. At the lava dealer's, I had already seen similar ones, listed as true lavas, so I felt happy at having made a discovery. They were a volcanic soot, precipitated from the hot vapours; the condensed minerals they contained were clearly visible.

A magnificent sunset and evening lent their delight to the return journey. However, I could feel how confusing such a tremendous contrast must be. The Terrible beside the Beautiful, the Beautiful beside the Terrible, cancel one another out and produce a feeling of indifference. The Neapolitan would certainly be a different creature if he did not feel himself wedged between God and the Devil.

GOETHE
(trans. W. H. Auden
with Elizabeth Mayer)

Eskimos

❧❧❧

When a child is born it comes into the world with a soul of its own (*nappan*), but this soul is as inexperienced, foolish, and feeble as a child is and looks. It is evident, therefore, that the child needs a more experienced and wiser soul than its own to do the thinking for it and take care of it. Accordingly the mother, so soon as she can after the birth of the child, pronounces a magic formula to summon from the grave the waiting soul of the dead to become the guardian soul of the new-born child, or its *atka*, as they express it.

Let us suppose that the dead person was an old wise man by the name of *John*. The mother then pronounces the formula which may be roughly translated as follows: "Soul of John, come here, come here, be my child's guardian! Soul of John, come here, come here, be my child's guardian!" (Most magic formulae among the Eskimo must be repeated twice.)

When the soul of John, waiting at the grave, hears the summons of the mother, it comes and enters the child. . . . The spirit of John not only teaches the child to talk, but after the child learns to talk it is really the soul of John which talks to you and not the inborn soul of the child. The child, therefore, speaks with all the acquired wisdom which John accumulated in the long lifetime, plus the higher wisdom which only comes after death. Evidently, therefore, the child is the wisest person in the family or in the community, and its opinions should be listened to accordingly. What it says and does may seem foolish to you, but that is mere seeming and in reality the child is wise beyond your comprehension. . . . If it cries for a knife or a pair of scissors, it is not a foolish child that wants the knife, but the soul of the wise old man John that wants it, and it would be presumptuous of a young mother to suppose that she knows better than John what is good for the child, and so she gives it the knife. If she refused the knife (and this is the main point), she would not only be preferring her own foolishness to the wisdom of John, but also she would thereby give offense to the spirit of John, and in his anger John would abandon the child. Upon the withdrawal of his protection the child would become the prey to disease and would probably die, and if it did not die, it would become stupid or hump-backed or otherwise deformed or unfortunate. John must, therefore, be propitiated at every cost. . . .

As the child grows up, the soul with which he was born (the *nappan*) gradually develops in strength, experience, and wisdom, so that after the age of ten or twelve years it is fairly competent to look after the child and begins to do so; at that age it therefore becomes of less vital moment to please the guardian spirit (*atka*), and accordingly it is customary to begin forbidding children and punishing them when they come to the age of eleven or twelve years.

VILHJALMUR STEFANSSON

My husband and I were on a journey from Igdlulik to Ponds Inlet. On the way he had a dream, in which it seemed that a friend of his was being eaten by his own kin. Two days after, we came to a spot where strange sounds hovered in the air. At first we could not make out what it was, but coming nearer it was like the ghost of words; as if it were one trying to speak without a voice. And at last it said:

"I am one who can no longer live among human kind, for I have eaten my own kin."

We could hear now that it was a woman. Then searching round, we found a little shelter built of snow and a fragment of caribou skin. Close by was a thing standing up; we thought at first it was a human being, but saw it was only a rifle stuck in the snow. But all this time the voice was muttering. And going nearer again we found a human head, with the flesh gnawed away. And at last, entering into the shelter, we found the woman seated on the floor. Her face was turned towards us and we saw that blood was trickling from the corners of her eyes, so greatly had she wept.

"Kikaq," (a gnawed bone) she said, "I have eaten my husband and my children!"

She was but skin and bone herself, and seemed to have no life in her. And she was almost naked, having eaten most of her clothing. My husband bent down over her, and she said:

"I have eaten him who was your comrade when he lived."

And my husband answered: "You had the will to live, and you are still alive." Then we put up our tent close by, cutting off a piece of the fore-curtain to make a shelter for the woman; for she was unclean, and might not be in the tent with us. And we gave her frozen caribou meat to eat, but when she had eaten a mouthful or so, she fell to trembling all over, and could eat no more.

We ceased from our journey then and turned back to Igdlulik, taking her with us, for she had a brother there. She is still alive to this day and married to a great hunter, named Igtussarssua, and she is his favorite wife, though he had one before.

KNUD RASMUSSEN

Face, The Human

The countenances of children, like those of animals, are masks, not faces, for they have not yet developed a significant profile of their own.

Our notion of symmetry is derived from the human face. Hence, we demand symmetry horizontally and in breadth only, not vertically nor in depth.

B. PASCAL

Chins are exclusively a human feature, not to be found among the beasts. If they had chins, most animals would look like each other. Man was given a chin to prevent the personality of his mouth and eyes from overwhelming the rest of his face, to prevent each individual from becoming a species unto himself.

The ears are the last feature to age.

MALCOLM DE CHAZAL

Jack on one side, Tom on the other; and yet Jack cannot see Tom.

Bermudan riddle

Hair a-top, hair a-bottom; only a dance in the middle.

Jamaican riddle

If the eyes are often the organ through which the intelligence shines, the nose is generally the organ which most readily publishes stupidity.

M. PROUST

The noses of fat men do not follow suit with the rest of them as they age. The noses become, if anything, sharper, thinner.

MAX BEERBOHM

The glance embroiders in joy, knits in pain, and sews in boredom.

When indifferent, the eye takes stills, when interested, movies.

Laughter is regional: a smile extends over the whole face.

MALCOLM DE CHAZAL

The wink was not our best invention.

RALPH HODGSON

A man is always as good as the good which appears in his face, but he need not be as evil as the evil which appears in it, because evil does not always realize itself immediately; indeed, sometimes it never realizes itself at all.

MAX PICARD

Fatigue

I observed that, in proportion as our strength decayed, our minds exhibited symptoms of weakness, evinced by a kind of unreasonable pettishness with each other. Each of us thought the other weaker in intellect than himself, and more in need of advice and assistance. So trifling a circumstance as a change of place, recommended by one as being warmer and more comfortable, and refused by the other from a dread of motion, frequently called forth fretful expressions which were no sooner uttered than atoned for, to be repeated perhaps in the course of a few minutes. The same thing often occurred when we endeavoured to assist each other in carrying wood to the fire; none of us were willing to receive assistance, although the task was disproportionate to our strength.

JOHN FRANKLIN

Forgiveness

In contrast to revenge, which is the natural, automatic reaction to transgression and which, because of the irreversibility of the action process, can be expected and even calculated, the act of forgiving can never be predicted; it is the only reaction that acts in an unexpected way and thus retains, though being a reaction, something of the original character of action.

HANNAH ARENDT

Many promising reconciliations have broken down because, while both parties came prepared to forgive, neither party came prepared to be forgiven.

CHARLES WILLIAMS

No one ever forgets where he buried the hatchet.

KIN HUBBARD

PRIEST: "Do you forgive your enemies?"
A DYING SPANIARD: "I have no enemies. I have shot them all."

Tout comprendre, c'est tout pardonner. No commonplace is more untrue. Behavior, whether conditioned by an individual neurosis or by society, can be understood; that is to say, one knows exactly why such and such an individual behaves as he does. But a personal action or deed is always mysterious. When we really act, precisely because it is a matter of free choice, we can never say exactly why we do this rather than that. But it is only deeds that we are required to forgive. If someone does me an injury, the question of forgiveness only arises if I am convinced (a) that the injury he did me was a free act on his part and therefore no less mysterious to him than to me, and (b) that it was me personally whom he meant to injure. Christ does not forgive the soldiers who are nailing him to the Cross; he asks the Father to forgive them. He knows as well as they do *why* they are doing this—they are a squad, detailed to execute a criminal. They do not know *what* they are doing, because it is not their business, as executioners, to know *whom* they are crucifying.

If the person who does me an injury does not know *what* he is doing, then it is as ridiculous for me to talk about forgiving him as it would be for me to "forgive" a tile which falls on my head in a gale.

Friday, Good

Our crucifixes exhibit the pain, but they veil, perhaps necessarily, the obscenity: but the death of the God-Man was both.

CHARLES WILLIAMS

Christmas and Easter can be subjects for poetry, but Good Friday, like Auschwitz, cannot. The reality is so horrible, it is not surprising that people should have found it a stumbling block to faith. The Manicheans of the third century argued: "Jesus was the Christ, the Son of God. Therefore, he cannot have been really crucified. The body on the cross was either a phantom body or Judas Iscariot." The liberal humanists of the eighteenth century argued: "Jesus was crucified. Therefore, he cannot have been the Son of God."

Poems about Good Friday have, of course, been written, but none of them will do. "The Dream of the Rood" turns Christ into an epic hero, but no epic hero would say "I thirst" or "My God, my God, why hast Thou forsaken me?" The *"Stabat Mater,"* which sentimentalizes the event, is the first poem in medieval literature which can be called vulgar and "camp" in a pejorative sense.

Just as we were all, potentially, in Adam when he fell, so we were all, potentially, in Jerusalem on that first Good Friday before there was an Easter, a Pentecost, a Christian, or a Church. It seems to me worth while asking ourselves who we should have been and what we should have been doing. None of us, I'm certain, will imagine himself as one of the Disciples, cowering in agony of spiritual despair and physical terror. Very few of us are big wheels enough to see ourselves as Pilate, or good churchmen enough to see ourselves as a member of the Sanhedrin. In my most optimistic mood I see myself as a Hellenized Jew from Alexandria visiting an intellectual friend. We are walking along, engaged in philosophical argument. Our path takes us past the base of Golgotha. Looking up, we see an all too familiar sight—three crosses surrounded by a jeering crowd. Frowning with prim distaste, I say, "It's disgusting the way the mob enjoy such things. Why can't the authorities execute criminals humanely and in private by giving them hemlock to drink, as they did with Socrates?" Then, averting my eyes from the disagreeable spectacle, I resume our fascinating discussion about the nature of the True, the Good, and the Beautiful.

Friendship

❖❖❖

What friends really mean to each other can be demonstrated better by the exchange of a magic ring or a horn than by psychology.

HUGO VON HOFMANNSTHAL

In friendship, nobody has a double.

F. SCHILLER

Our friends show us what we can do; our enemies teach us what we must do.

GOETHE

Glossolalia

❖❖❖

It is extraordinary that sects of religious enthusiasts, from the Montanists down to the Catholic Apostolics, should have imagined that to make verbal noises which nobody else could understand was evidence of Divine Inspiration, a repetition of the miracle of Pentecost. What happened at Pentecost was exactly the opposite, the miracle of instantaneous translation—everybody could understand what everybody else was saying.

In his great book *Enthusiasm,* Father Ronald Knox gives us two examples of "speaking with tongues": *"Hippo gerosto niparos boorasti farini O fastor sungor boorinos epoongos menati,"* and *"Hey amei hassan alla do hoc alors lovre has heo massan amor ho ti prov hir aso me."* Of these, he says, "The philology of another world does not abide our question, but if we are to judge these results by merely human standards, we must admit that a child prattles no less convincingly."

Goat, Nanny

❧❀❧

There she is, perched on her manger, looking over the boards into the day
Like a belle at her window.
And immediately she sees me she blinks, stares, doesn't know me, turns her head and ignores me vulgarly with a wooden blank on her face.

What do I care for her, the ugly female, standing up there with her long-tangled sides like an old rug thrown over a fence?
But she puts her nose down shrewdly enough when the knot is untied,
And jumps staccato to earth, a sharp, dry jump, still ignoring me,
Pretending to look round the stall.

Come on, you, crapa! I'm not your servant!

She turns her head away with an obtuse, female sort of deafness, bête.
And then invariably she crouches her rear and makes water.
That being her way of answer, if I speak to her. —Self-conscious!
Le bestie non parlano, poverine! . . .

D. H. LAWRENCE

God

⟨⟩

Speculations over God and the World are almost always idle, the thoughts of idlers, spectators of the theatre of life. "Is there a God?" "Has Man a soul?" "Why must we die?" "How many hairs has the Devil's Grandmother?" "When is the Day of Judgment?"—all these are idle questions, and one fool can ask more of them than a hundred wise men can answer. Nevertheless, teachers, parents, bishops, must give answers to such questions because, otherwise, the idlers will spread their corruption. Every idle question can ensnare at least one innocent heart. The Church Councils found themselves in the position of parents whose daughters are on the point of being seduced by young louts. The dogmas of the Church have to deal with blasphemous scoundrels, and therefore they have to speak their language, the language of shamelessness.

EUGEN ROSENSTOCK-HUESSY

Nicea then was a double climax. The spectacle of magnificence was accompanied by an intellectual ostentation of dogma. "The great and sacred Synod" exhibited itself in the two worlds. Christ was throned in heaven and in Constantinople. Yet at times, as the jewels seem only jewels, so the words seem only words. "Father," "Son," "Holy Spirit," "person," "essence and nature," "like and unlike"—what has such a pattern of definition to do with a Being that must exist always in its incomprehensibility? It is not surprising that the human mind should revolt against the jewels and words. It is, of course, a revolt of immature sensibility, an ignorant, a young-romantic revolt, but it is natural. "The great and sacred Synod" looms sublimely anti-pathetic. From such revolts there have sprung the equally immature and romantic devotions to the simple Jesus, the spiritual genius, the broad-minded international Jewish working-man, the falling-sparrow and grass-of-the-field Jesus. They will not serve. The Christian idea from the beginning had believed that his Nature reconciled earth and

heaven, and all things met in him, God and Man. A Confucian
Wordsworth does not help there. Jewels and words are but images, but then so are grass and sparrows. And jewels and words
are no less and no more necessary than cotton and silence.

CHARLES WILLIAMS

Theologians are in the difficult position of having to use language, which by its nature is anthropomorphic, to deny anthropomorphic conceptions of God. Dogmatic theological statements are neither logical propositions nor poetic utterances.
They are "shaggy dog" stories; they have a point, but he who
tries too hard to get it will miss it.

From a Christian point of view the whole of learned theology is
really a corollary; and is declined like *mensa*.

SØREN KIERKEGAARD

Among medieval and modern philosophers anxious to establish the
religious significance of God, an unfortunate habit has prevailed
of paying him metaphysical compliments.

A. N. WHITEHEAD

It is generally agreed among theologians that in giving men
freedom of will, freedom to reject His love and defy His commandments, God has, in a sense, chosen to limit His omnipotence. But unless, at the same time, He has chosen to limit His
omniscience, the Calvinist doctrine of predestination is an inevitable conclusion. May it not be that, just as we have to have
faith in Him, God has to have faith in us and, considering the
history of the human race so far, may it not be that "faith" is
even more difficult for Him than it is for us?

To talk *about* God, except in the context of prayer, is to take His
name in vain.

One may, indeed, talk to a child about God, but this is on a par
with telling him that he was brought to his mother by a stork.

FERDINAND EBNER

It is as difficult to be quite orthodox as it is to be quite healthy. Yet the need for orthodoxy, like the need for health, is imperative.

There is a great deal of scepticism in believers, and a good deal of belief in non-believers; the only question is where we decide to give our better energy. "Lord, I believe; help thou mine unbelief" may, and should, be prayed both ways.

CHARLES WILLIAMS

An atheist may be simply one whose faith and love are concentrated on the impersonal aspects of God.

SIMONE WEIL

God does not die on the day when we cease to believe in a personal deity, but we die on the day when our lives cease to be illuminated by the steady radiance, renewed daily, of a wonder, the source of which is beyond all reason.

DAG HAMMARSKJÖLD

You can change your faith without changing gods, and vice versa.

STANISLAUS LEC

It always strikes me, and it is very peculiar, that, whenever we see the image of indescribable and unutterable desolation—of loneliness, poverty, and misery, the end and extreme of things— the thought of God comes into one's mind.

VAN GOGH

We have to believe in a God who is like the true God in everything except that he does not exist, since we have not reached the point where God exists.

SIMONE WEIL

"God is Love," we are taught as children to believe. But when we first begin to get some inkling of how He loves us, we are repelled; it seems so cold, indeed, not love at all as we understand the word.

All the passions produce prodigies. A gambler is capable of watching and fasting almost like a saint; he has premonitions, etc. There is a great danger of loving God as the gambler loves his game.

SIMONE WEIL

Every time a priest adds his *personal fervor* to the "canons" something terrible results (a hypocrite, a Torquemada); only when the priest is "slack" is it right. Why is this so? Why so *here?*

V. ROZANOV

There is always a danger of intense love destroying what I might call the "polyphony" of life. What I mean is that we should love God eternally with our whole hearts, but not so as to compromise or diminish our earthly affections, but as a kind of *cantus firmus* to which the other melodies of life provide the counterpoint. Earthly affection is one of these contrapuntal themes, a theme which enjoys an autonomy of its own.

DIETRICH VON BONHOEFFER

The word of him who wishes to speak with men without speaking to God is not fulfilled; but the word of him who wishes to speak with God without speaking with men goes astray.

MARTIN BUBER

In this world, so long as we are vigorous enough to be capable of action, God, surely, does not intend us to sit around thinking of and loving Him like anything. Aside from rites of public worship in which we bring our bodies to God, we should direct our mental attention towards Him only for so long as it takes us to learn what He wills us to do here and now. This may take only a moment if the task he sets us is easy; if hard, a little longer. But once we know what it is, we should forget all about Him and concentrate our mental and physical energies upon our task.

The "dead" God: a god Who never existed but in Whom, undoubtedly, many people who thought of themselves as Christians believed—a Zeus without Zeus's vices. Science has certainly killed Him.

The Christian God is not *both* transcendent and immanent. He is a reality other than being Who is present to being, by which presence He makes being to be.

LESLIE DEWART

In German the word *sein* signifies both things: to be and to belong to Him.

KAFKA

Hands

⋙❀⋘

The fingers must be educated; the thumb is born knowing.

The thumb takes the responsibility, the index finger the initiative.

The little finger looks through a magnifying glass, the index finger through a lorgnette.

The gestures of an adult are those of a carpenter, the gestures of an infant those of a mason.

MALCOLM DE CHAZAL

Hangman, The

⋙❀⋘

The story of Edward Dennis (in *Barnaby Rudge*) is not an invention. There was such a man, and he did take part in the Gordon riots. He said himself that his profession was known to the other rioters; and when he was arrested, the Brideswell in Tothill Fields would not take him in because (said the keeper, who recognized him) the other prisoners would cut him up as soon as he got inside. Dennis was tried and sentenced to death, but naturally he was pardoned, and went back to work hanging the rioters.

Nor is Dennis alone at the dark intersection of crime and punishment. At least three other hangmen in England in the eighteenth century were found guilty of hanging crimes, and one of them was actually hanged. To bring the bizarre register up to date, let me match these with contemporary cases. In 1948 the busy public executioner in East Berlin was found to have organized gangs of young delinquents who stole, robbed, and (at a pinch) murdered. Shortly after this, a prisoner in gaol in Brunswick with time on his hands applied for the job of executioner there, and under the heading of "Previous Experience" claimed that he had murdered thirty-three people. He had overstated his qualifications, as applicants will: it turned out that he had really murdered only twelve.

More characteristically, perhaps, and more modestly (he was after all an Englishman), the assistant hangman in Nottingham in 1954 was sentenced for running a sideline in sadistic books and obscene photographs.

J. BRONOWSKI

Hare, Hunting a

Hunting a hare. Our dogs are raising a racket;
Racing, barking, eager to kill, they go,
And each of us in a yellow jacket
Like oranges against the snow.

One for the road. Then, off to hound a hare,
My cab-driver friend who hates a cop, I,
Buggins' brother and his boy, away we tear.
Our jalopy,

That technological marvel goes bounding,
Scuttling along on its snow-chains. Tallyho!
After a hare we go.
Or is it ourselves we're hounding?

I'm all dressed up for the chase
In boots and jacket: the snow is ablaze.
But why, Yuri, why
Do my gun-sights dance? Something is wrong, I know,
When a glassful of living blood has to fly
In terror across the snow.

The urge to kill, like the urge to beget,
Is blind and sinister. Its craving is set
Today on the flesh of a hare: tomorrow it can
Howl the same way for the flesh of a man.

Out in the open the hare
Lay quivering there
Like the gray heart of an immense
Forest or the heart of silence:

Lay there, still breathing,
Its blue flanks heaving,
Its tormented eye a woe,
Blinking there on the cheek of the snow.

Then, suddenly, it got up,
Stood upright: suddenly,
Over the forest, over the dark river,
The air was shivered
By a human cry.

Pure, ultrasonic, wild,
Like the cry of a child.
I knew that hares moan, but not like this:
This was the note of life, the wail
Of a woman in travail,

The cry of leafless copses
And bushes hitherto dumb,
The unearthly cry of a life
Which death was about to succumb.

Nature is all wonder, all silence:
Forest and lake and field and hill
Are permitted to listen and feel,
But denied utterance.

Alpha and Omega, the first and last
Word of Life as it ebbs away fast,
As, escaping the snare, it flies
Up to the skies.

For a second only, but while
It lasted we were turned to stone
Like actors in a movie-still.

The boot of the running cab-driver hung in mid-air,
And four black pellets halted, it seemed,
Just short of their target:
Above the horizontal muscles, the blood-clotted fur of the
    neck,
A face flashed out.

With slanting eyes, set wide apart, a face
As in frescoes of Dionysus,
Staring at us in astonishment and anger,
It hovered there, made one with its cry,
Suspended in space,

The contorted transfigured face
Of an angel or a singer.

Like a long-legged archangel a golden mist
Swam through the forest.
"Shit!" spat the cab-driver. "The little faking freak!"
A tear rolled down the boy's cheek.

Late at night we returned,
The wind scouring our faces: they burned
Like the traffic lights as, without remark,
We hurtled through the dark.

ANDREI VOZNESENSKY
(trans. W.H.A.)

Hell

᠊ᕒᣍᕕ᠊

Ethics does not treat of the world. Ethics must be a condition of
the world, like logic.

LUDWIG WITTGENSTEIN

Men are not punished for their sins, but by them.

E. HUBBARD

All theological language is necessarily analogical, but it was
singularly unfortunate that the Church, in speaking of sin and
punishment for sin, should have chosen the analogy of criminal
law, for the analogy is incompatible with the Christian belief
in God as the creator of Man.

Criminal laws are *laws-for,* imposed on men, who are already
in existence, with or without their consent, and, with the possible exception of capital punishment for murder, there is no
logical relation between the nature of a crime and the penalty
inflicted for committing it.

If God created man, then the laws of man's spiritual nature must, like the laws of his physical nature, be *laws-of,* laws, that is to say, which he is free to *defy* but no more free to *break* than he can break the law of gravity by jumping out of the window, or the laws of biochemistry by getting drunk, and the consequences for defying them must be as inevitable and as intrinsically related to their nature as a broken leg or a hangover.

To state spiritual laws in the imperative—Thou *shalt* love God with all thy being, Thou *shalt* love thy neighbor as thyself—is simply a pedagogical technique, as when a mother says to her small son, "Stay away from the window!" because the child does not yet know what will happen if he falls out of it.

In the case of physical laws, we learn very soon the painful consequences of defying them, though even this certain knowledge does not prevent some of us from destroying ourselves with alcohol or drugs. But in the case of spiritual laws, where the consequences of defiance are not perceptible to the senses and take effect only gradually, we are all too inclined to behave, either like madmen who imagine they are magicians who can fly, or like suicides who smash themselves up out of despair or, more often, out of spite.

All sin tends to be addictive, and the terminal point of addiction is what is called damnation.

Since God has given us the freedom either to accept His love and obey the laws of our created nature or to reject it and defy them, He cannot prevent us from going to Hell and staying there if that is what we insist upon.

Origen, sensing the horror of the idea of Hell as a criminal prison and torture chamber, but failing to realize that the analogy was false, tried to mitigate the horror by saying that Hell would not be eternal, that in the end God's love would prove too strong and the devils and the damned would repent and be saved. If, however, it were ever possible for God's love to be compulsive, then He would be a monster for ever letting things get so far; He should never have allowed Eve to taste of the Tree in the first place.

History, Political

❧

To read History is to run the risk of asking, "Which is more honorable? To rule over people, or to be hanged?"

J. G. SEUME

Politics is what a man does in order to conceal what he is and what he himself does not know.

KARL KRAUS

> Political history is far too criminal and pathological to be a fit subject of study for the young. All teachers know this. In consequence, they bowdlerize, but to bowdlerize political history is not to simplify but to falsify it. Children should acquire their heroes and villains from fiction. I have read somewhere that Hitler's boyhood hero was Sulla.

Hitler

❧

I have the gift of reducing all problems to their simplest foundations.

Why babble about brutality and be indignant about tortures? The masses want that. They need something that will give them a thrill of horror.

The day of individual happiness has passed.

Don't waste your time over "intellectual" meetings and groups drawn together by mutual interests. Anything you may achieve with such folk to-day by means of reasonable explanation may be erased tomorrow by an opposite explanation. But what you tell the people in the mass, in a receptive state of fanatic devotion, will remain words received under an hypnotic influence, ineradicable, and impervious to every reasonable explanation.

A new age of magic interpretation of the world is coming, of interpretation in terms of the will and not of the intelligence. There is no such thing as truth, either in the moral or in the scientific sense.

I am restoring to force its original dignity, that of the source of all greatness and the creatrix of order.

Quoted by H. RAUSCHNING

August 31, 1944

I think it's pretty obvious that this war is no pleasure for me. For five years I have been separated from the rest of the world. I haven't been to the theatre, I haven't heard a concert, and I haven't seen a movie.

Quoted by FELIX GILBER

We have forged with fire a sword of steel out of ice.

(From a speech)

When I come to power, I promise you, every German girl shall get a German husband.

(From a speech)

Holmes, Sherlock

"He appears to have a passion for definite and exact knowledge."

"Very right too."

"Yes, but it may be pushed to excess. When it comes to beating the subjects in the dissecting-rooms with a stick, it is certainly taking rather a bizarre shape."

"Beating the subjects!"

"Yes, to verify how far bruises may be produced after death. I saw him at it with my own eyes."

"And yet you say he is not a medical student?"

Among these unfinished tales is that of Mr. James Phillimore, who, stepping back into his own house to get his umbrella, was never more seen in this world. No less remarkable is that of the cutter *Alicia*, which sailed one spring morning into a small patch of mist from where she never again emerged, nor was anything further ever heard of herself and her crew. A third case worthy of note is that of Isadore Persana, the well-known journalist and duellist, who was found stark staring mad with a match box in front of him which contained a remarkable worm said to be unknown to science.

I deprecate, however, in the strongest way the attempts which have been made lately to get at and destroy these papers. The source of these outrages is known, and if they are repeated I have Mr. Holmes's authority for saying that the whole story concerning the politician, the lighthouse, and the trained cormorant will be given to the public. There is at least one reader who will understand.

ARTHUR CONAN DOYLE

Home

Home is the only place where you can go out and in. There are places you can go into, and places you can go out of, but the one place, if you do but find it, where you may go out and in both, is home.

GEORGE MACDONALD

. . . "How quick," to someone's lip
The words came, "will the beaten horse run home!"

The word "home" raised a smile in us all three,
And one repeated it, smiling just so
That all knew what he meant and none would say.
Between three counties far apart that lay
We were divided and looked strangely each
At the other, and we knew we were not friends
But fellows in a union that ends
With the necessity for it, as it ought.

Never a word was spoken, not a thought
Was thought, of what the look meant with the word
"Home" as we walked and watched the sunset blurred.
And then to me the word, only the word,
"Homesick," as it were playfully occurred:
No more.

   If I should ever more admit
Than the mere word I could not endure it
For a day longer: this captivity
Must somehow come to an end, else I should be
Another man, as often now I seem,
Or this life be only an evil dream.

EDWARD THOMAS

Homer and the Definite Article

❧§❧

In Greece, the verbal—and that is to say: the intellectual—seeds of scientific language are of a very ancient date. To take one example: we could scarcely imagine the existence of Greek science or Greek philosophy if there had been no definite article. For how could scientific thought get along without such phrases as *to hydro* (water), *to psychron* (the cold), *to noein* (thought)? If the definite article had not permitted the forming of these 'abstractions' as we call them, it would have been impossible to develop an abstract concept from an adjective or a verb, or to formulate the universal as a particular. As far as the use of the definite article is concerned, Homer's speech is already more advanced than the classical Latin of Cicero. Cicero finds it very difficult to reproduce the simplest philosophical concepts, for no other reason than the lack of an article. To express ideas which to a Greek come easily and naturally, he has to fall back upon circumlocutions: his translation of *to agathon* (the good) is: *id quod (re vera) bonum est.*

Its [the definite article's] evolution from the demonstrative pronoun, via the specific article, into the generic article was slow and halting. *The* horse, in Homer, is never the concept of a horse, but always a particular horse. This demonstrative use of the article enables Homer to promote an adjective to the status of a noun, as in the case of the superlative: *ton ariston Achaion*, 'the best of the Achaeans'. In the same way Homer is free to say: *ta t' eonta ta t' essomena pro t' eonta*, 'the present, the future, the past'. The plural number shows that Homer does not yet 'abstract' permanent being, but merely draws together the sum total of all that is now, and distinguishes it from all that will be.

BRUNO SNELL

Homer and Seeing

 ঙ৪৯

. . . Homer uses a great variety of verbs to denote the operation of sight. . . . Of these several have gone out of use in later Greek, at any rate in prose literature and living speech: *derkesthai, leussein, ossesthai, paptainein*. Only two words make their appearance after the times of Homer: *blepein* and *theorin*. The

words which were discarded tell us that the older language recognized certain needs which were no longer felt by its successor.
Derkesthai means: to have a particular look in one's eye. *Drakon*,
the snake, whose name is derived from *derkesthai*, owes this des-
ignation to the uncanny glint in his eye. He is called 'the seeing
one', not because he can see particularly well, but because his
stare commands attention. By the same token Homer's *derkesthai*
refers not so much to the function of the eye as to its gleam noticed by someone else. The verb is used of the Gorgon whose
glance incites terror, and of the raging boar whose eyes radiate
fire. . . . Many a passage in Homer reveals its proper beauty only
if this meaning is taken into consideration [e.g., Odysseus]: [*pon-
ton ep' atrugeton derkesketo dakrua leibon. Derkesthai* means: 'to
look with a specific expression,' and the context suggests that the
word here refers to the nostalgic glance which Odysseus, an exile
from his homeland, sends across the seas. . . . Of the eagle it may
be said that *ozutaton derketai*, he looks very sharply; but whereas
in English the adjective would characterize the function and ca-
pacity of the visual organ, Homer has in mind the beams of the
eagle's eye, beams which are as penetrating as the rays of the sun
which are also called 'sharp' by Homer; like a pointed weapon
they cut through everything in their path. *Derkesthai* is also used
with an external object; in such a case the present would mean:
'his glance rests upon something,' and the aorist: 'his glance falls
upon an object,' 'it turns toward something,' 'he casts his glance
on someone.' . . .

The same is true of another of the verbs which we have mentioned as having disappeared in later speech. *Paptainein* is also a
mode of looking, namely a 'looking about' inquisitively, carefully,
or with fear. Like *derkesthai*, therefore, it denotes a visual attitude, and does not hinge upon the function of sight as such.
Characteristically enough neither word is found in the first person. . . . A man would notice such attitudes in others rather than
ascribing them to himself. *Leusso* behaves quite differently. Ety-
mologically it is connected with *leukos*, 'gleaming,' 'white'; three
of the four cases in the *Iliad* where the verb is followed by an ac-
cusative object pertain to fire and shining weapons. The meaning
clearly is: to see something bright. It also means: to let one's eyes

travel. . . . Pride, joy, and a feeling of freedom are expressed in it. Frequently *leusso* appears in the first person, which distinguishes it from *derkesthai* and *paptainein*, those visual attitudes which are mostly noticed in others. . . . It is never used in situations of sorrow or anxiety.

It goes without saying that even in Homer men used their eyes 'to see,' i.e., to receive optical impressions. But apparently they took no decisive interest in what we justly regard as the basic function, the objective essence, of sight. . . .

BRUNO SNELL

Honor, Sense of

᭞

Christos Milionis

Three little birds are perched on the ridge by the klepht's
  stronghold,
One looks on Armyro, the other on to Valto;
The third, the fairest, sings a dirge and says:
'Lord, what has become of Christos Milionis?
At Valto he is not seen, nor in Kryavrisi.
They told us he had gone away and entered into Arta,
And taken captive the kadi, and two agas as well.'
The Musselim heard of it, and sorely was he troubled;
He called Mavromati and Mukhtar Klisura:
'If you wish for bread, and if you would have captaincies,
First do you kill Christos, kill Captain Milionis:
So does our Sultan order it, and he has sent me a firman.'
Friday dawned,—would it had dawned never!—
And Suleiman was sent to go to find him.
At Armyro he overtook him and as friends they greeted each
  other;
And all night they drank, until dawn.

And as the dawn began to shine, they went up to the *limeria*,
And Suleiman shouted to Captain Milionis:
'Christos, the Sultan wants you, the Agas too want you.'
'While life is in Christos, to Turks he does not do homage.'
With gun in hand they ran to meet, as one would eat the
    other;
Fire answered fire and they fell dead on the spot.

Note: Mukhtar had entrusted the task of killing Christos
    Milionis to the Albanian Suleiman, a former brother in
    arms of Milionis.

The Klephtic Ballads
(trans. John Baggally)

Horse, Evolution of the

The evolution of the horse must have involved organic changes
of many kinds, but naturally we can know only those that show
themselves in the fossilized skeleton, and of these, four are outstanding. They are: an increase in size, a reduction of toes or digits on all four feet, an elongation of the facial region, and finally a
marked change in the teeth. The earliest horse, *Eohippus*, was
about the size of a fox-terrier, had four digits on each foot, and
low-crowned teeth adapted to browsing off comparatively succu-
lent vegetation. Subsequent development, culminating in the
horse we know and protracted over some fifty million years, was
towards a progressively larger animal with a more highly developed brain. Accompanying these changes there arose a tendency
towards supporting the weight more and more on the tips of the
toes, in such a way as to make the lateral digits less and less necessary. This gave the creature enhanced speed, and it ended with
the single-toed horse of to-day with vestigial splint-bones, invisible externally, as the sole remnants of the lateral digits. As for the
teeth, they underwent a change from the low-crowned sort with

a simple surface-pattern, to a new type longer in proportion to their width and with an intricate surface-pattern suitable for the mastication of harder and drier grasses. All these changes were adaptive, for the later horses were grazing as opposed to browsing creatures, and their development can be correlated with a changing habitat during the Miocene Period when forests were tending to disappear and drier, open, grassy plains, admirable for galloping over, were taking their place. Life on these plains set a premium on speed and on the ability to chew tough-stemmed grasses. But it must not be supposed that there was this one line of development only. On the contrary there were many lines, but none persisted for as long as that which gave rise to the large, one-toed, grazing horses. One line continued from the original forest-living browsers, which remained as such. They too developed, but differently and less rapidly, reaching a sort of culmination, with three toes instead of four, at about the time when the future grazers were beginning to take to the plains. Finally they became extinct.

Where then does pre-adaptation figure in this story? Very notably. One example of it has already been referred to, namely that the forest-dwelling browsers, while they could still so be described, had undergone a reduction in the number of digits from four to three. But that is by no means all, for the interesting and highly significant conclusion emerging from study of the skeletons of the many kinds of horse destined in time to develop into the animal that we know to-day, is that their evolution was materially assisted by organic changes that had already begun to manifest themselves while they yet lived in forests and browsed off leaves. In other words those structural changes fitting them so admirably for life on the plains—increase in size and reduction of digits; the transition from low- to high-crowned, grinding teeth; elongation of the facial region, giving space for more teeth—began to develop before the conditions responsible for their final perfection had begun to appear.

LESLIE REID

Hospital Talk

"My name's Butler, Captain Ernest Butler. Been in here six weeks —you going to be long? Now take my case," and before I had time to accept or reject 'his case,' Captain Butler was in full swing again; "now take my case, four years ago they said it was hopeless, absolutely hopeless, not a chance in a thousand. Not a chance in a thousand. Then I was sent to see Mr. Carver, really through my uncle's wife's daughter, she was a nurse . . . well, it was her who first mentioned Mr. Carver; and Mr. Carver says, 'Captain Butler, I'm interested in your case, very interested. I should like to do an . . .'"; at this point Captain Butler flashed a medical word of some six syllables, two of which rang with accentuated diphthongs, "I'd like to do it on Monday, that was four weeks ago yesterday, I beg your pardon, tomorrow; you get so confused with days in hospital after all this time." This last remark faded into the ward, attempting self-pity, but in fact swollen with pride for his four weeks' seniority and suffering. "So there I was for the 'chopper,' not a bit nervous, but first of all, two days before the op, they did a lot of X-rays." At this moment his face lit up with an enthusiasm rarely expressed by X-ray plates. "They've got a smashing set-up there; they first of all pump in a lot of blue stuff, well, you might say it was purple, I've always been a little colour blind, they first of all pump in a lot of this blue stuff into your arteries—only the ones they're going to X-ray of course—then they blow them up." At this last remark he seemed to grow larger and more important. "They did fourteen, that was in the afternoon, and six more next morning, which doesn't include the ones they'd done the first day I arrived."

At this point Captain Butler paused to allow his point, and the blue-cum-purple injections, to be fully injected. "You could tell they knew their job," again Captain Butler managed to effect the feeling that they had learnt this special knowledge for his benefit alone, "Oh they knew their job all right. It's a smashing set-up over there; of course it's a long journey but they take you by ambulance." Captain Butler was filled with delighted remembrance of that ambulance ride when he had been helped down the three steps by a fair, pretty nurse on arrival. "Now my boy's good at photography and all that sort of thing; you may think I'm boasting if I tell you he won the Tech. College prize for his colour photos—his Spanish holiday and all that—but it's a fact. Well, when I told him about the set-up over there, in the X-ray department, you should have seen his face . . ."

Captain Butler's eyes misted over and he was back in that world of egocentrical, X-ray seclusion, where his whole history of suffering was exposed, and permanently fixed by chemicals, on twenty semi-matt dark sheets of negative, and which, now that his Captain's rank was one of name and not authority, was his sole link with the world of importance; for a short time everything had revolved round him in a way that it had only done during the war. Consequently he treasured his disease most preciously and nursed it indulgently. His eyes unmisted a little and he continued, "Mind you, they can't do this op on everyone, it just doesn't work." The last four words were uttered as if he had watched all the cases on which it had not worked. I saw body after body expiring, with blue-cum-purple-blood spurting, which no doctor could stem.

"But I was lucky; it was a risk, mind you, but I took it," he added hastily, "now look at my legs; of course they'll never be the same . . . still . . ." and his voice faded.

ANTHONY ROSSITER

Hosts

₰

The men and women who make the best boon companions seem to have given up hope of doing something else. They have, perhaps, tried to be poets or painters; they have tried to be actors, scientists, and musicians. But some defect of talent or opportunity has cut them off from their pet ambition and has thus left them with leisure to take an interest in the lives of others. Your ambitious man is selfish. No matter how secret his ambition may be, it makes him keep his thoughts at home. But the heartbroken people—if I may use the word in a mild benevolent sense—the people whose wills are subdued to fate, give us consideration, recognition and welcome.

JOHN JAY CHAPMAN

Humanists

. . . It is largely to the humanists that we owe the curious conception of the 'classical' period in a language, the correct or normative period before which all was immature or archaic and after which all was decadent. Thus Scalinger tells us that Latin was 'rude' in Plautus, 'ripe' from Terence to Virgil, decadent in Martial and Juvenal, senile in Ausonius. . . . When once this superstition was established it led naturally to the belief that good writing in the fifteenth or sixteenth century meant writing which aped as closely as possible that of the chosen period in the past. All real development of Latin to meet the changing needs of new talent and new subject-matter was thus precluded; with one blow of 'his Mace petrific' the classical spirit ended the history of the Latin tongue. This was not what the humanists intended. They had hoped to retain Latin as the living esperanto of Europe while putting back the great clock of linguistic change to the age of Cicero. From that point of view, humanism is a great archaizing movement parallel to that which Latin had already undergone at the hands of authors like Apuleius and Fronto. But this time it was too thorough. They succeeded in killing the medieval Latin: but not in keeping alive the schoolroom severities of their restored Augustanism. Before they had ceased talking of a rebirth it became evident that they had really built a tomb. . . . A negative

194 {Bloom} A CERTAIN WORLD

conception of excellence arose: it was better to omit a beauty than to leave in anything that might have the shadow of an offence. . . . Men vied with one another in smelling out and condemning 'unclassical' words, so that the permitted language grew steadily poorer. . . .

Gravity, prudence, the well ordered *civitas;* on the other hand boorishness and rusticity—these are the clues. Whatever else humanism is, it is emphatically not a movement towards freedom and expansion. It is the impulse of men who feel themselves simple, rustic, and immature, towards sophistication, urbanity, and ripeness. In a word, it is the most complete opposite we can find to the Romantic desire for the primitive and the spontaneous. . . .

The humanists' revolt against medieval philosophy was not a philosophical revolt. What it really was can best be gauged by the language it used. Your philosophers, says Vives . . . are straw-splitters, makers of unnecessary difficulties, and if you call their jargon Latin, why then we must find some other name for the speech of Cicero. 'The more filthie barbarisme they haue in their style . . . the greater theologians they doe account themselues,' says Erasmus. . . . 'Calle ye Thomas Aquinas a doctor?' said Johan Wessel. 'He knew no tongue but the Latin and barely that!'. . . . These are not the terms in which a new philosophy attacks an old one: they are, unmistakably, the terms in which at all times the merely literary man, the bellettrist, attacks philosophy itself. No humanist is now remembered as a philosopher. They jeer and do not refute. The schoolman advanced, and supported, propositions about things: the humanist replied that his words were inelegant. Of the scholastic terminology as an instrument of thought—that instrument which, according to Condorcet, has created *une précision d'idées inconnue aux anciens*—no reasoned criticism was usually vouchsafed. Words like *realitas* and *identificatio* were condemned not because they had no use but because Cicero had not used them.

. . . The medieval philosophy is still read as philosophy, the history as history, the songs as songs: the hymns are still in use. The 'barbarous' books have survived in the only sense that really matters: they are used as their authors meant them to be used. It would be hard to think of one single text in humanists' Latin, except the *Utopia*, of which we can say the same. Petrarch's Latin poetry, Politian, Buchanan, even sweet Sannazarus, even Erasmus himself, are hardly ever opened except for an historical purpose. We read the humanists, in fact, only to learn about humanism; we read the 'barbarous' authors in order to be instructed or delighted about any theme they choose to handle.

C. S. LEWIS

The men of the Renaissance discovered suddenly that the world for ten centuries had been living in an ungrammatical manner, and they made it forthwith the end of human existence to be grammatical. And it mattered thenceforth nothing what was said, or what was done, so only that it was said with scholarship, and done with system. Falsehood in a Ciceronian dialect had no opposers; truth in patois no listeners. A Roman phrase was thought worth any number of Gothic facts.

RUSKIN

Humility

A brother asked the abbot Alonius, "What is contempt?" And the old man said, "To be below the creatures that have no reason, and to know that they are not condemned."

The Desert Fathers
(trans. Helen Waddell)

We do not have to acquire humility. There is humility in us—only we humiliate ourselves before false gods.

SIMONE WEIL

Humor, Scatological

❧

Most of it is only for children, but this verse, which so delighted myself and my brothers when we were little, still seems to me funny.

While shepherds watched their flocks by night,
    All shitting on the ground,
An angel of the Lord came down
    And handed paper round.

And this anonymous Neapolitan lyric is, surely, beautiful.

Strunz' . . .
Nel sole fumante
Come un incenso
A Dio . . .
Una mosca
Ti canta
Una ninna-nanna . . .
Zzz . . . Zzz . . .
Ma . . . tu non ascolti . . .
Strunz' . . . .

(Turd, smoking in the sun to God like a thurifer . . . A fly sings you a hush-a-bye . . . Zzz . . . Zzzz . . . but . . . you don't listen . . . Turd! . . . .)

Hurdy-Gurdy

❧

When I was a child the streets of any city were full of street vendors and street entertainers of every kind, and of the latter the Italian organ-grinder with his monkey was one of the most endearing. Today, officialdom seems to have banished them all, and the only persons who still earn their living on the streets are prostitutes and dope peddlers.

Over there, beyond the village, a hurdy-gurdy man stands,
Grinding away with numbed fingers as best he can.
He staggers barefoot on the ice
And his little plate remains ever empty.
No one wants to hear him, no one looks at him,
And the dogs snarl about the old man.
But he lets the world go by,
He turns the handle, and his hurdy-gurdy is never still.
Strange old man—shall I go with you?
Will you grind your music to my songs?

WILHELM MÜLLER
(trans. S. S. Prawer)

Hygiene, Personal

Errol was exceptionally tidy in his personal habits. Sometimes he shaved twice a day and he took constant showers. But one day Beverly said to me: "Mama, isn't it strange? He doesn't use anything under his arms. You'd think a man who's been around would know about a little thing like that, wouldn't you?"

I certainly agreed. He wasn't offensive—far from it. But it proved to me once again that those women he'd run around with for years—all those top sex charmers—were a bunch of dummies in some departments. You'd think one of them might have gotten around to giving Errol the message. But not one of them knew how to tell him.

With Beverly herself it was simply no problem. She was such a sweet person she didn't need an under-arm deodorant, but she used one just to be safe.

One night when she and Errol were preparing to go somewhere in New York, she suddenly brought up the subject. It was always her way to be quite frank with him.

"Errol," she said, "why don't you use Mennen's under the arms, or something like that?"

He took it as quite an insult. He had been shaving and he turned away from the washbowl and gave her a hurt look.

"Well," he said sarcastically, "I've always considered myself a fairly clean man."

"But why not use one," said Beverly.

Her persistence made him a little angry.

"Damn it," he said. "Who uses that stuff anyway? Besides, how come you know so much about what men are supposed to put on?" He looked at her half-suspiciously, half-jokingly. "I thought you were supposed to be a virgin before you met me. So how come you know all about this? Who told you?"

"My *father!*" snapped Beverly. "That's who! He's the cleanest man that ever was. He always asks me to give him Mennen toilet water for Christmas!"

FLORENCE AADLAND

Icebergs

The Berg

A Dream

I saw a ship of martial build
(Her standards set, her brave apparel on)
Directed as by madness mere
Against a stolid iceberg steer,
Nor budge it, though the infatuate ship went down.
The impact made huge ice-cubes fall
Sullen, in tons that crashed the deck;

But that one avalanche was all—
No other movement save the foundering wreck.

Along the spurs of ridges pale,
Not any slenderest shaft and frail,
A prism over glass-green gorges lone,
Toppled; nor lace of traceries fine,
Nor pendant drops in grot or mine
Were jarred, when the stunned ship went down.
Nor sole the gulls in cloud that wheeled
Circling one snow-flanked peak afar,
But nearer fowl the floes that skimmed
And crystal beaches, felt no jar.
No thrill transmitted stirred the lock
Of jack-straw needle-ice at base;
Towers undermined by waves—the block
Atilt impending—kept their place.
Seals, dozing sleek on sliddery ledges
Slipt never, when by loftier edges
Through very inertia overthrown,
The impetuous ship in bafflement went down.

Hard Berg (methought), so cold, so vast,
With mortal damps self-overcast;
Exhaling still thy dankish breath—
Adrift dissolving, bound for death;
Though lumpish thou, a lumbering one—
A lumbering lubbard, loitering slow,
Impingers rue thee and go down,
Sounding thy precipice below,
Nor stir the slimy slug that sprawls
Along thy dead indifference of walls.

HERMAN MELVILLE

Imagination

I will not refrain from setting among these precepts a new device for consideration which, although it may appear trivial and almost ludicrous, is nevertheless of great utility in arousing the mind to various inventions.

And this is that if you look at any walls spotted with various stains or with a mixture of different kinds of stones, if you are about to invent some scene you will be able to see in it a resemblance to various different landscapes adorned with mountains, rivers, rocks, trees, plains, with valleys and various groups of hills. You will also be able to see divers combats and figures in quick movement, and strange expressions of faces, and outlandish costumes and an infinite number of things which you can then reduce into separate and well-conceived forms. With such walls and blends of different stones, it comes about as it does with the sound of bells in whose clanging you may discover every name and word you can imagine.

LEONARDO DA VINCI

He hath consumed a whole night in lying looking at his great toe, about which he hath seen Tartars and Turks, Romans and Carthaginians, fight in his imagination.

BEN JONSON

A nurse was having difficulty in measuring two quantities against each other on a scales. The left dish insisted upon outweighing the other, and I saw it as the bully in life, the one with "the whip hand"; the right dish, uncomfortably aloft, seemed to stand small chance, as does the "little man" in life, of exerting its influence. Then, quite suddenly, a small miracle occurred. The nurse equated the scales more nearly to a perfect balance, there was a tremor of delight as the two opposing dishes made a final frictional effort to disagree, and then there was perfection as the dual forces married in harmony. Even in my drowsy state, my heart stirred with joy at this revelation and perfection.

ANTHONY ROSSITER

Think of a white cloud as being holy, you cannot love it; but think of a holy man within the cloud, love springs up in your thoughts, for to think of holiness distinct from man is impossible to the affections. Thought alone can make monsters, but the affections cannot.

WILLIAM BLAKE

While we were enjoying the unlimited vistas, we noticed a commotion on the water at some distance to our left and, somewhat nearer on our right, a rock rising out of the sea; one was Charybdis, the other Scylla. Because of the considerable distance in nature between these two objects which the poet has placed so close together, people have accused poets of fibbing. What they fail to take into account is that the human imagination always pictures the objects it considers significant as taller and narrower than they really are, for this gives them more character, importance and dignity. A thousand times I have heard people complain that some object they had known only from a description was disappointing when seen in reality, and the reason was always the same. Imagination is to reality what poetry is to prose: the former will always think of objects as massive and vertical, the latter will always try to extend them horizontally.

GOETHE

It is better to say, "I'm suffering," than to say, "This landscape is ugly."

Imaginary evil is romantic and varied; real evil is gloomy, monotonous, barren, boring. Imaginary good is boring, real good is always new, marvellous, intoxicating. "Imaginative literature," therefore, is either boring or immoral or a mixture of both.

SIMONE WEIL

Good can imagine Evil, but Evil cannot imagine Good.

Inverted Commas, Transformation by

❦

As the editors of the anthology *The Stuffed Owl* were the first to realize, there is a certain kind of bad poetry which, had it been written with the conscious satiric intention of being bad, instead of in all earnestness, would be very good.

When I was twenty, I wrote a line which, had I intended it to be a caption for a Thurber cartoon, I should today be very proud of; alas, I did not, so that I now blush when I recall it: "And Isobel who with her leaping breasts pursued me through a summer."

Again, anyone wishing to write a satire on the "socially conscious" poetry of the thirties, could hardly do better than the final line of Miss Genevieve Taggard's poem "On Planting a Tree in Vermont": *"Bloom for the People. Don't be a family shrub."*

With inverted commas round his verses, William McGonagall (1830–?) becomes one of the greatest comic poets in English. For example:

Then as for Leith Fort, it was erected in 1779, which was
    really grand,
And which is now the artillery headquarters in Bonnie Scot-
    land;
And as for the Docks, they are magnificent to see,
They comprise five docks, two piers, 1,141 yards long re-
    spectively . . .

Besides, there are sugar refineries and distilleries,
Also engineer works, saw-mills, rope-works, and breweries,
Where many of the inhabitants are daily employed,
And the wages they receive make their hearts feel overjoyed.

    or

Friends of humanity, of high and low degree,
I pray ye all come listen to me;

And truly I will relate to ye
The tragic fate of the Rev. Alexander Heriot Mackonochie.

Who was on a visit to the Bishop of Argyle
For the good of his health, for a short while;
Because for the last three years his memory had been affected,
Which prevented him from getting his thoughts collected.

Inscape

⤠⤠⤠

Rings

A veärry ring so round's the zun
   In summer leäze did show his rim,
An' near, at hand, the weäves did run
   Athirt the pond wi' rounded brim:
An' there by round built ricks ov haÿ,
   By het a-burn'd, by zuns a-brown'd,
We all in merry ring did plaÿ,
   A-springen on, a-wheelen round.

As there a stwone that we did fling
   Did zweep, in flight, a lofty bow,
An' vell in water, ring by ring
   O' weäves bespread the pool below,
Bezide the bridge's arch, that sprung
   Between the banks, within the brims,
Where swung the lowly benden swing,
   On elem boughs, on mossy limbs.

WILLIAM BARNES

Jackdaws

Once the social order of rank amongst the members of a colony has been established, it is most conscientiously observed by jackdaws, much more so than by hens, dogs or monkeys. A spontaneous reshuffling, without outside influence, and due only to the discontent of one of the lower orders, has never come to my notice. Only once, in my colony, did I witness the dethroning of the hitherto ruling tyrant, Goldgreen. It was a returned wanderer, who, having lost in his long absence his former deeply imbued respect for his ruler, succeeded in defeating him in their first encounter. In the autumn of 1931 the conqueror "Double Aluminum"—he derived this strange name from the rings on his feet—came back, after having been away the whole summer. He returned home strong in heart and stimulated by his travels, and at once subdued the former autocrat. . . .

The way in which my attention was drawn to this revolution was quite unusual. Suddenly, at the feeding-tray, I saw, to my astonishment, how a little, very fragile, and, in order of rank, low-standing lady sidled ever closer to the quietly feeding Goldgreen, and finally, as though inspired by some unseen power, assumed an attitude of self-display, whereupon the large male quietly and without opposition vacated his place. Then I noticed the newly returned hero, Double-Aluminum,—and saw that he had usurped the position of Goldgreen, and I thought at first that the deposed despot, under the influence of his recent defeat, was so subdued that he had allowed himself to be intimidated by the other members of the colony, including the aforesaid young female. But the assumption was false: Goldgreen had been conquered by Double-Aluminum only, and remained forever second in command. But Double-Aluminum, on his return, had fallen in love with the young female and within the course of two days was publicly engaged to her. Since the partners in a jackdaw marriage support each other loyally and bravely in every conflict, and as no pecking order exists between them, they automatically rank as of equal status in their disputes with all other members of the colony; a wife is therefore, of necessity, raised to her husband's position. But the contrary does not hold good—an inviolable law dictates that no male may marry a female that ranks above him. The extraordinary part of the business is not the promotion as such, but the amazing speed with which the news spreads that such a little jackdaw lady, who hitherto had been maltreated by eighty per cent of the colony, is, from to-day, the "wife of the president" and may no longer receive so much as a black look from any other jackdaw. But, more curious still—the promoted bird knows of its promotion . . . that little jackdaw knew within forty-eight hours exactly what she could allow herself, and I'm sorry to say that she made the fullest use of it. She lacked entirely that noble or even blasé tolerance which jackdaws of high rank should exhibit towards their inferiors. She used every opportunity to snub former superiors, and she did not stop at gestures of self-importance, as high-rankers of long standing nearly always do. No—she always had an active and malicious plan of attack ready at hand. In short, she conducted herself with the utmost vulgarity.

KONRAD LORENZ

Journalism

❦

THWAITES: Then, before leaving you—since you are so reluctant to leave me—let me make a very necessary apology. (*The reporters get their notebooks and pencils ready.*) I thought, while you were questioning me, how much better the world would be if you and your employers were utterly abolished. But I am sorry to have thought that. Without you, we should have no way of knowing what we are like—no mirror in which to study the diseases of our skins. You are our spite, our greed, our pleasure in the pains of others, our love of lies, our perfect emptiness.

3RD REPORTER: Sir Augustus! Statements of that sort are of no interest to our readers.

THWAITES: In you, our fear of taking any decisive steps finds its perfect illustration. We know that you are too disgusting to live, but we are so afraid that your suppression might lead to something just a shade *more* disgusting that we have not the courage to do away with you. Thus, the liberty which you enjoy is the reflection of our own cowardice, and until we are brave enough to trample you down, you will always be present to reflect the yellowness of our hearts, the corruption of our manliness, and the collapse of our powers of decision.

3RD R (*good-humouredly*): We are grateful for all that information, Sir Augustus. But we have heard it many times before.

LADY R: Very many times before. (*She takes her mirror from her handbag, studies her face, then applies lipstick.*)

THWAITES: It is not dramatic? It is not interesting? It is not personal?

3RD R (*still good-humouredly*): I'm afraid not.

THWAITES: Then may I draw your attention to something that is?

3RD R: I'm sure we'd all be much obliged.

THWAITES (*moving to the 3rd R and pointing*): There is something the matter with your left arm. Has it been withered from birth?

(*There is an astonished gasp from the others.*)

3RD R (*after a pause*): Yes.

THWAITES: But how dramatic! How interesting! How personal! I wish *my* readers could hear about it. They love stories about cripples. May I photograph it? And perhaps you will tell me the influence it has had on your life? A story of shame, suffering and courage—always such a pleasure to others. (*The 3rd R turns sharply and goes out.*) Oh! He is gone! (*He turns to the Lady R.*) Madam. Did you see the pain in his face? Where was your camera? He is degraded! He is humiliated! He feels the whole world knows. How will he recover, now? (*He crosses to the Lady R.*) Answer me that, madam—you with your poor,

tired, stretched face. Ah, Madam, yours was an unhappy marriage, was it not? And the child? Never born? Ah, so sad—but to
read about at breakfast time—*your* kidneys on *my* toast.

LADY R (*clenching her fists, furiously*): It's not true!

THWAITES (*shrugging*): Pooh, pooh, pooh! Who cares what's
true?

NIGEL DENNIS

Journalists write because they have nothing to say, and they have
something to say because they write.

A journalist is stimulated by a dead-line: he writes worse when
he has time.

The public doesn't understand German; and in Journalese I can't
tell them so.

KARL KRAUS

With all that can be said, justly, against journalists, there is
one kind of journalist to whom civilization owes a very great
debt, namely, the brave and honest reporter who unearths and
makes public unpleasant facts, cases of injustice, cruelty, corruption, which the authorities would like to keep hidden, and
which even the average reader would prefer not to be compelled to think about.

Justice and Injustice

Whoever suffers from the malady of being unable to endure any
injustice, must never look out of the window, but stay in his
room with the door shut. He would also do well, perhaps, to
throw away his mirror.

J. G. SEUME

Justice: to be ever ready to admit that another person is something quite different from what we read when he is there, or when we think about him. Or rather, to read in him that he is certainly something different, perhaps something completely different, from what we read in him.

Justice consists in seeing that no harm is done to men. Whenever a man cries inwardly, "Why am I being hurt?", harm is being done to him. He is often mistaken when he tries to define the harm, and why and by whom it is being inflicted upon him. But the cry itself is infallible.

SIMONE WEIL

To commit violent and unjust acts, it is not enough for a government to have the will or even the power; the habits, ideas, and passions of the time must lend themselves to their committal.

ALEXIS DE TOCQUEVILLE

Injustice cannot reign if the community does not furnish a due supply of unjust agents.

HERBERT SPENCER

The dispensing of injustice is always in the right hands.

STANISLAUS LEC

A Review only continues to have life in it so long as each issue annoys at least one fifth of its subscribers. Justice lies in seeing that this fifth is not always the same one.

CHARLES PÉGUY

Kilns

Severn has kilns set all along her banks
Where the thin reeds grow and rushes in ranks;

And the carts tip rubbish there from the town;
It thunders and raises white smoke and goes down.
I think some of those kilns are very old,
An age is on those small meres, and could unfold
Tales of the many tenders of kilns, and tales
Of the diggers and earth-delvers of those square weals
Or oblong of Severn bank. And all the flowers
June ever imagined stand and fulfil June's hours.
I think of the countless slabs gone out from all of them;
Farm house, cottage, loved of generations of men,
Fronting day as equal, or in dusk shining dim;
Of the Dane-folk curious of the sticky worthy stuff;
Kneading, and crumbling till the whim wearied enough.
Of the queer bricks unlearned hands must have made;
Spoiling clay, wasting wood, working out the war's trade;
With one hand the clear eyes fending, keeping in shade
Fierce Fire that grazes and melts with its regardings rough.
Or the plays children had of Dane-Saxon breed,
Chasing round the square kilns with devil-may-care
Headlong roughness of heedless body-reckless speed;
Grazing knees and knuckles to disaster there,
Of the creeping close to parents when November azure
Melancholy made company, and stillness, a new pleasure,
And the wonder of fire kept the small boys to stay sure.

And the helping of fathers build well of the new brick,
The delight in handling over thin and thick—the youthful
   critic.

Of the Normans, how they liked kilns, that thrust to endure
Endless abbeys and strong chapels up in the air,
And Domesday questioners who worried the too evasive
Owner as to tales and day's work to a story unplausive,
As to the fuels used, and the men there and the hours, the
   wage hours.

IVOR GURNEY

Landscape: Basalt

Far and wide through the moors of the northern counties run the dykes and sills of hard black basaltic rock called whinstone. Nature has forced it between softer layers of rock much as cement is driven between the crumbling stones of a cathedral wall. But this volcanic grouting is so much harder than sedimentary rock, and the operation was carried out so many hundreds of thousands of years ago, that the basaltic bonds have outlasted the layers which they compact, and now project beyond them. Dykes are vertical layers of whinstone, which out-top the moor's surface by 20 or 40 feet, like a wall. Sills show where the molten greenstone was forced between horizontal beds; where it emerges, the sill's edge so stubbornly resists erosion that it forms a hard black cliff-face. Sometimes the whinstone is roughly columnar, and suggests the more perfect basaltic architecture of the Giant's Causeway. Often the sill forms only part of the cliff, but has protected by its durability the softer limestone beneath it, and to a less extent above. Sometimes the heat of the rock has turned the limestone next it, not merely into marble—for marble is baked limestone—but into a crumbling layer like white sugar. Where moorland streams meet these cliffs or sills, they form waterfalls. In a few miles of Upper Teesdale, the Tees plunging over two whinstone cliffs forms the two grandest waterfalls in England—Caldron Snout and High Force. Beside these two falls, voluminous and naked, Lodore, or Scale Force, in the Lake Country is but an exquisite wild toy.

It gives a fresh attraction to rambles through all that wide, wild country from Eden Valley, near Applesby, over the Pennine backbone, and away to the coast of Northumberland, to pencil down from a geological map the course of the great outcrops of whinstone. When we meet them again it is pleasant to feel that

they are old friends, and impressive, in the light of day, to think
of that vast sheet of hard volcanic rock which probably underlies
hundreds of square miles of the moorlands between the unknown
point at which the earth's fiery stomach disgorged it, and the
outcrops by which we stand. The Tees at High Force pours over
a line of crag which runs far eastward through County Durham.
Northumberland has the Acklington Dyke, about thirty-five
miles long, from the Cheviot to the coast near the mining village
of Acklington. But the most famous of all these basaltic bands is
the Great Whin Sill. Its outcrop begins in the moors between
Middleton-in-Teesdale and Appleby, and is leaped by the Tees at
Caldron Snout. Soon a descending beck carves the narrow gap of
High Cup Nick, which gives access across the moors from High
Force to Appleby, and forms the finest of the longer approaches
to the Lake Mountains. Turning east, the Sill runs for nearly fifty
miles through Northumberland, carrying the Roman Wall on its
crest. It rears up on the brink of salt water into the splendid and
storied rock of Bamburgh, and sinks at last beneath the North
Sea, after throwing up the Castle Rock on Holy Island, like a
Bamburgh in miniature, and the seafowl-haunted pinnacles of the
Farnes.

ANTHONY COLLETT

Landscape, Cultivated

✑§§✑

From Swindon we came up into the *down-country;* and these
downs rise *higher* even than the Cotswold. . . . My companion,
though he had been to London, and even to France, had never
seen *downs* before; and it was amusing to me to witness his surprise at seeing the immense flocks of sheep, which were now (ten
o'clock) just going out from their several folds to the downs for
the day, each having its shepherd, and shepherd his dog. We
passed the homestead of a farmer WOODMAN, with *sixteen* banging

wheat-ricks in the rick-yard, two of which were old ones; and rick-yard, farm-yard, waste-yard, horse-paddock, and all round about, seemed to be swarming with fowls, ducks and turkeys, and on the whole of them, *not one feather but was white!* Turning our eyes from the sight, we saw, just going out from the folds of this farm, three separate and numerous flocks of sheep, one which (the *lamb*-flock) we passed close by the side of. The shepherd told us, that his flock consisted of *thirteen score and five;* but, apparently, he could not, if it had been to save his soul, tell us how many *hundreds* he had: and, if you reflect a little, you will find that his way of counting is much the easiest and best. This was a most beautiful flock of lambs; short-legged, and, in every respect, what they ought to be. George, though born and bred among sheep-farms, had never before seen sheep with dark-colored faces and legs; but his surprise, at this sight, was not nearly so great as the surprise of both of us, at seeing numerous and very large pieces (sometimes 50 acres together) of very good early turnips, *Swedish* as well as *White!* All the three counties of Worcester, Hereford and Gloucester (except on the Cotswold) do not, I am convinced, contain as great a weight of turnip bulbs, as we here saw in one single *piece;* for here there are, for miles and miles, no hedges, and no fences of any sort.

Doubtless they must have had *rain* here in the months of June and July; but, as I once before observed, (though I forget when), a *chalk bottom* does not suffer the surface to *burn,* however shallow the top soil may be. It seems to me to absorb and to *retain* the water, and to keep it ready to be drawn up by the heat of the sun. At any rate, the fact is, that the surface above it *does not burn;* for, there never yet was a summer, not even this last, when the downs did not *retain their greenness to a certain degree,* while the rich pastures, and even the meadows (except actually watered) were burnt so as to be *as brown as the bare earth.*

This is a most pleasing circumstance attending the *down-countries;* and there are no *downs* without a chalk bottom.

Along here, the country is rather *too bare;* here, until you come to AUBURN or ALDBOURNE, there are *no meadows* in the valleys, and *no trees,* even round the homesteads. This, therefore, is too naked to please me; but I love the *downs* so much, that, if I had *to choose*, I would live even here, and especially I would *farm* here, rather than on the banks of the WYE in Herefordshire, in the vale of Gloucester, or Worcester, or of Evesham, or, even in what the Kentish men call their "*garden of Eden.*" I have now seen (for I have, years back, seen the vales of Taunton, Glastonbury, Honiton, Dorchester and Sherborne) what are deemed the richest and most beautiful parts of England; and, if called upon to name the spot, which I deem the brightest and most beautiful and, of its extent, *best* of all, I should say, the villages of *North Bovant and Bishops-strow*, between Heytesbury and Warminster in Wiltshire; for there is, as appertaining to rural objects, *every thing* that I delight in. Smooth and verdant down in hills and valleys of endless variety as to proportion, and these watered at pleasure; and, lastly, the homesteads and villages, sheltered in winter and shaded in summer by lofty and beautiful trees; to which may be added, roads never dirty and a stream never dry.

WILLIAM COBBETT

Caltanissetta, April 28, 1787

At last we can say we have seen with our own eyes the reason why Sicily earned the title of "The Granary of Italy." Soon after Girgenti, the fertility began. There are no great level areas, but the gently rolling uplands were completely covered with wheat and barley in one great unbroken mass. Wherever the soil is suitable to their growth, it is so well tended and exploited that not a tree is to be seen. Even the small hamlets and other dwellings are confined to the ridges, where the limestone rocks make the ground untillable. The women live in these hamlets all the year round, spinning and weaving, but during the season of field labour, the men spend only Saturdays and Sundays with them; the rest of the week they spend in the valleys and sleep at night in reed huts. . . .

A few more geological observations. As one descends from Girgenti, the soil turns whitish; the older type of limestone appears to be followed immediately by gypsum. Then comes a new type of limestone, more friable, slightly decomposed and, as one can see from the tilled fields, varying in colour from a light yellow to a darker, almost violet tint. Halfway between Girgenti

and Caltanissetta, gypsum reappears. This favours the growth of a
beautiful purple, almost rose-red sedum, while the limestone har-
bours a bright yellow moss. . . .

The valleys are beautiful in shape. Even though their bottoms
are not completely level, there is no sign of heavy rain, for it immediately runs off into the sea; only a few little brooks, which
one hardly notices, trickle along.

The dwarf-palms and all the flowers and shrubs of the south-
western zone had disappeared and I did not see much red clover.
Thistles are allowed to take possession only of the roads, but all
the rest is Ceres' domain. . . . They plough with oxen and it is
forbidden to slaughter cows or calves. We have met many goats,
donkeys and mules on our trip, but few horses. Most of these
were dapple greys with black feet and black manes. They have
magnificent stables with built-in stone mangers.

Manure is only used in growing beans and lentils; the other
crops are grown after they have been harvested. Red clover and
sheaves of barley, in the ear but still green, are offered for sale to
passing riders.

GOETHE

Landscape: Fens

❦

A certain sadness is pardonable to one who watches the destruction of a grand natural phenomenon, even though its destruction
brings blessings to the human race. Reason and conscience tell us
that it is right and good that the Great Fen should have become,
instead of a waste and howling wilderness, a garden of the Lord,
where

> All the land in flowery squares,
> Beneath a broad and equal-blowing wind,
> Smells of the coming summer.

And yet the fancy may linger, without blame, over the shining meres, the golden reed-beds, the countless waterfowl, the strange and gaudy insects, the wild nature, the mystery, the majesty—for mystery and majesty there were—which haunted the deep fens for many a hundred years. Little thinks the Scotsman, whirled down by the Great Northern Railway from Peterborough to Huntingdon, what a grand place, even twenty years ago, was that Holme and Whittlesea, which is now but a black, unsightly, steaming flat, from which the meres and reed-beds of the old world are gone, while the corn and roots of the new world have not as yet taken their place.

But grand enough it was, that black ugly place, when backed by Caistor Hanglands and Holme Wood, and the patches of the primaeval forest; while dark-green alders, and pale-green reeds, stretched for miles round the broad lagoon, where the coot clanked, and the bittern boomed, and the sedge-bird, not content with its own sweet song, mocked the notes of all the birds around; while high overhead hung, motionless, hawk beyond hawk, buzzard beyond buzzard, kite beyond kite, as far as eye could see. Far off, upon the silver mere, would rise a puff of smoke from a punt, invisible from its flatness and its white paint. Then down the wind came the boom of the great stanchion-gun; and after that sound another sound, louder as it neared; a cry as of all the bells of Cambridge, and all the hounds of Cottesmore; and overhead rushed and whirled the skein of terrified wild-fowl, screaming, piping, clacking, croaking, filling the air with the hoarse rattle of their wings, while clear above all sounded the wild whistle of the curlew, and the trumpet note of the great wild swan.

They are all gone now. No longer do the ruffs trample the sedge into a hard floor in their fighting-rings, while the sober reeves stand round, admiring the tournament of their lovers, gay with ears and tippets, no two of them alike. Gone are ruffs and reeves, spoonbills, bitterns, avosets; the very snipe, one hears, disdains to breed. Gone too, not only from Whittlesea but from the whole world is that most exquisite of English butterflies, Lycaena dispar—the great copper; and many a curious insect more. Ah, well, at least we shall have wheat and mutton instead, and no more typhus and ague; and, it is to be hoped, no more brandy-drinking and opium-eating; and children will live and not die. For it was a hard place to live in, the old Fen; a place wherein one heard of "unexampled instances of longevity," for the same reason that one hears of them in savage tribes—that few lived to old age at all, save those iron constitutions which nothing could break down.

CHARLES KINGSLEY

Landscape: Limestone

. . . Mountain limestone has almost as much scenery within it as without. There is stranger and more fantastic climbing within the portals of Gaping Gill in the West Riding than anywhere on the sunny side of the caverns' dome. Exploration of limestone caverns is often interrupted by the stream which has formed them, plunging suddenly through a widened joint in the rock to new halls at unknown depths. When every peak on earth has been mapped, and climbed, there are still likely to be strands that no foot has trodden in caves beneath the peaceful surface of a Mendip or Craven sheepwalk.

The fuller the channels beneath the limestone surface, the drier they run above, and the chief limestone districts are full of streams that dive into swillets or swallow-holes, to emerge again, in putative identity, miles away and many fathoms lower. Buttertubs Pass, between Wensleydale and Swaledale, gains its racy name from swallow-holes of this kind. In wet weather one of these leaky stream-beds may make a fair show of holding water; the natural sinks cannot take all that comes, and it is not until the stranger returns to slake his thirst on a hot day that he discovers it has vanished. Elsewhere streams make their dive where the trap in the rock is concealed by a substantial layer of surface soil, and forms a conspicuous funnel. Elms and ashes spring luxuriant on the sides of the pit, with ivied trunks that mark by a muddy stain the highest recent freshet. Months may pass without the surface-water seeking this singular exit; then bursts the autumn rain, and the brown flood eddying round the trunks forms a restless whirl-pool. Great limestone gorges, like that at Cheddar, may be the channels of ancient subterranean rivers, of which the roofs have fallen in. Through all the mountain limestone country the interest of its surface moulding and the attraction of its plant and insect life is heightened by the sense of the unknown sculpture in the roots of the rocks—the unpolluted rivers running, through caverns measureless, to sunless seas.

Thin though moist is the turf of the grey limestone hills, and it is characteristic of their scenery for the live rock to break out freely at the surface. Sometimes its slabs and bands assume a dreary largeness, and, reducing the turf and herbage to narrow terraced strips, look like misshapen masonry. The long white tilted layers of the limestone hills near Carnforth have a touch of that power first to repel and at last to fascinate which is possessed by all barren and thirsty places. Elsewhere the rock juts through its cloak of turf in warm lichened bosses. Beside them the sheep couch, for dryness, and upon them the tawny wall butterflies, which delight in a limestone country, fan and shift in the rays of the sun. Limestone and chalk are close enough akin to have nurtured the same delicate flora, though some of the rarest that love lime are confined to the sunnier slopes of the southern chalk. Both on limestone hills and chalk downs the thyme fills the turf with its delicate summer scent that floats even in January among the withered tufts when the sun shines warm on the hillside. Many orchids love both soils—the bee, the butterfly, the pyrami-dal and the fragrant, among the commoner kinds. The limestones of the west and north were the last haunts of the almost extinct lady's slipper, and the chalk still guards the lizard and the military orchids, now almost equally rare. Equally common on both these warm and porous rocks, and of a finer growth than when we find it straggling among coarser gravels, the delicate golden cistus, or rock-rose, shakes out, morning by morning, its crumpled petals to the midsummer sunshine. When limestone rises among red rocks, or chalk from blue clay, the change of soil is instantly signalled by these yellow blossoms. On one side of a brook the turf may be sprinkled by the almost universal flowers—buttercups, milfoil, knapweed, clover—undistinguished either in number or kind; but immediately beyond the thread of mint-tinged water the grey rock shows its side, and the hill turf is variegated with rock-roses, and scented with the wandering prostrate thyme-threads.

ANTHONY COLLETT

Landscape, West of England

Larches

Larches are most fitting to small red hills
That rise like swollen ant-heaps likeably
And modest before big things like near Malvern
Or Cotswold's farther early Italian
Blue arrangement, unassuming as the
Cowslip, celandines, buglewort and daisies
That trinket out the green swerves like a child's game.
O, never so careless or lavish as here . . .

IVOR GURNEY

Landscape, Wild

The Precipice

Such precipices are among the most impressive as well as the most dangerous of mountain ranges; in many spots inaccessible with safety either from below or from above; dark in colour, robed with everlasting mourning, for ever tottering like a great fortress shaken by war, fearful as much in their weakness as in their strength, and yet gathered after every fall into darker frowns and unhumiliated threatening; for ever incapable of comfort or healing from herb or flower, nourishing no root in their crevices, touched by no hue of life on buttress or ledge, but, to the utmost, desolate; knowing no shaking of leaves in the wind, nor of grass beside the stream,—no motion but their own mortal shivering, the dreadful crumbling of atom from atom in their corrupting stones; knowing no sound living voice or living tread, cheered neither by the kid's bleat nor the marmot's cry; haunted only by uninterrupted echoes from far off, wandering hither and thither, among their walls, unable to escape, and by the hiss of angry torrents, and sometimes the shriek of a bird that flits near the face of them, and sweeps frightened back from under their shadow into the gulph of air; and, sometimes, when the echo has fainted, and the wind has carried the sound of the torrent away, and the bird has vanished, and the mouldering stones are still for a little time,—a brown moth, opening and shutting its wings upon a grain of dust, may be the only thing that moves, or feels, in all that waste of weary precipice, darkening five thousand feet of the blue depth of heaven.

RUSKIN

Lead Mine, Visit to a

⋅⋅§⋅⋅

Parties of ladies and gentlemen desirous of visiting the mines, can have suitable dresses provided by the landlord of the inn. A coat, pair of trowsers, and hat suffice for a gentleman, while the softer sex are often indebted to the landlady's wardrobe. Old shawls, hats, aprons, and even bedgowns, are taken to the mining shop, and the fair form of beauty and fashion is there disguised in such heterogeneous garments as to create no small share of amusement. The grotesque and novel appearance, both of ladies and gentlemen, frequently contributes not a little to the mirth of the company, and also tends to dissipate any timorous feeling. As mines, like states and empires, "have their periods of declension, and feel in their turn what distress and poverty are," it is thought better not to limit this sketch of a subterranean visit to any particular mine, but rather to describe such features as are generally presented in the Alston Mines. Permission to view the mines is in the most instances readily obtained.

The author ventures from his own observation to premise, that visitors will generally be gratified with the rustic but kind civility and attention of the miners, and in some instances also with their intelligence, due allowance being made for local dialect and limited education. Their readiness to afford information and to render assistance greatly contributes to the interest and comfort of the excursion, by imparting knowledge to the inquirer, and confidence to the timorous.

Arrived at the mine, the visitor has a full view of the various apparatus used in washing the ore. A lofty heap of stones, clay, and other earthy substances, called *the dead heap*, forms a prominent feature at the entrance of all extensively wrought mines. A railway carried on a frame-work gallery over several deposits of *bouse*, or mixed stone and ore, forms the *bouse teams*, and the work of the separate partnerships of miners is divided by partitions. From these *bouse teams* the contents are carried away to undergo the various and, it may be said, amusing processes of washing; for strangers who have leisure to examine them are usually much entertained with the ingenious and cunning devices to obtain every particle of ore. In stone recesses called *bing steads*, sundry heaps of shining ore are laid, some in broken lumps, and others in fine powder. These are ready to be conveyed to the smelt-mills, there to be converted into lead and silver, provided the latter exists in sufficient proportion to repay the expense of refining.

The party being suitably arrayed, have sometimes to wait a little until the waggons come out, and in the mean time are each furnished with a candle, round which a piece of clay is fixed to hold it by. At length the rumbling noise of the approaching waggons rapidly increases, and their contents having been deposited, they are prepared for the visitors, the inside being cleaned, and a board placed at each end for a seat. The entrance to the mine, or *the level mouth*, resembles an open arched door-way, into which the waggons are driven at a moderate pace, and the visitors experience the novel sensations which so unusual a conveyance is apt to create. The jolting, tottering motion of the waggon, the splashing of the water, and the dark and narrow passage, all concur to produce a strange effect, which, however, soon wears off, and the subterranean traveller finds leisure to observe the rugged roof and walls of the level, or to listen to the guide urging forward his horse, in tones which the echoes of the mine often render musical. Even the fragment of a song from the driver sometimes enlivens the journey, but, on no account, is whistling allowed to be heard in a mine. The same prejudice exists among seamen, but whence its origin is probably unknown.

After advancing some distance into the interior, the visitor passes the rise foots, in some of which a store of *bouse* is laid ready to be taken away, and at length the waggons stop, and the company get out at one of these openings. A powerful vociferation of "*put nought down*," is sent forth as a warning to those above to throw no work down, and a further summons brings a few miners to render their assistance. When a signal is to be made to some distance, it is done by beating on the rails or posts, five beats, the first two slow, and other three quick, and this is repeated several times. The same signal is used in the Newcastle coal-mines, where it is denominated "jowling."

The ascent of a rise is frequently attended with some difficulty, especially to ladies; but the gallantry of the gentlemen and the effective civility of the miners soon overcome the apparent dangers, and, one by one, they are raised into the workings of the vein. Hence the party are conducted along the mine drift of the vein, and this part of the expedition must of course greatly vary in different mines; in all, however, the stranger is apt to be impressed with feelings of awe at the idea of being so far underground. The contemplative mind cannot but find many interesting subjects of reflection on the distribution of so much wealth in a country otherwise so barren—the various uncertainties which are the means of so extensive employment—the fluctuations of

fortune so often resulting from mining adventures, and the ingenuity displayed in prosecuting them, are all circumstances which
may engage the attention of a reflecting mind. To the mineralo-
gist, the interior of a mine, especially if it contain any spar-en-
crusted caverns, is a sort of "home, sweet home," where the lovers of that science and of geology may derive copious stores of
intellectual enjoyment.

Blende and calamine, the ores of zinc, are sometimes found
spreading their glossy sparkling blackness in the veins; and fluor
spar and quartz are the principal, almost the only, sparry ornaments that abound. The traveller at Alston is not gratified by
the sight of such beautiful caverns as are found in the Coalcleugh
and Allendale mines. The latter, however, being private property,
and worked by the proprietor, cannot be considered as generally
accessible to public curiosity, though intelligent strangers of scientific pursuits will doubtless receive every attention from the
hospitality and liberal-minded feeling of the resident agents.

The progress along vein workings is often "with cautious steps
and slow," especially among the intricacies of flat workings. The
friendly caution of "take care ye dinna *fall* down the *rise*," sometimes calling the visitor's attention (absorbed perhaps in other
thoughts) to a yawning gulf not to be passed over without some
caution. Sometimes an almost perfect stillness is suddenly broken
by a noise like distant thunder, the report of a blast, which, rolling through the workings of the mine, at length, after many re-
verberations, dies away. The noise of work "*falling down a rise*,"
and the rumblings of waggons occasionally salute the ear; the
sound of the latter, gradually increasing and lessening, resembles
the solemn effect of distant thunder.

The process of blasting has been already described. The miners
usually describe this and other modes of entertainment of the visitor; but, when near at hand, the effect is by no means so striking
as when distance softens the noise and adds repeated echoes to it.
At length arrived at the far end or *forehead* of the vein, the party
usually rest, and a pleasant company is occasionally formed by
the accession of two or three partnerships. Spirits or other re-
freshments are sometimes taken by the visitors; and those who
choose to spend half an hour in the company of miners may fre-

quently derive both information and amusement. Most of the miners are well acquainted with practical mining, and with this is necessarily blended a knowledge of many facts in geology and mineralogy. But many of them are also tolerably well informed on other subjects, and a friend of the author's was much surprised in one of these forehead meetings, to hear Blackstone's Commentaries quoted by a miner both with accuracy and direct reference to the subject of discussion.

The miners work by what is often in other trades called piece-work, so that the time spent with strangers is taken from their own labour, and the prodigal expenditure of light is also at their own cost. By the latter is meant the custom of miners of not putting out their candles, however numerous the company may be, and a forehead assemblage presents a brilliant illumination, twenty or thirty candles being sometimes placed against the wall. If any partners of the mine are present, many are the speculations on the goodness and improving of the *grove*. The *bonny donk* and *excellent rider*, as well as the ore, come in for a share of gratulation, and are often considered harbingers of the vein being still more productive. Many a lively song and joke are often added to the entertainment of such an assemblage as we are now describing. One example, spoken by a miner, may suffice as a specimen of dialect and humor. "An folk wad nobbit let folk like folk as weel as folk wad like to like folk, folk wad like folk as weel as folk ever liked folk sin folk was folk!" It may here be remarked, that the conversation of miners sometimes has a curious effect from their assuming, as it were, a sort of volition in the mineral world. Thus they speak of a vein being *frightened* to climb the hill, and that she therefore *swings away* to the sun side, (a feminine appellation being generally used). The throw of the strata is attributed, as it were, to an *act* of the vein,—"*she throws* the north cheek up." These are homely but they are also expressive modes of describing what they have frequent occasion to speak of, and they save a world of words.

Ladies seldom pursue a subterranean excursion further than the main workings, or such others as are easily accessible, while their more adventurous companions frequently accompany the guides into other parts of the mine. In so doing, obstacles present themselves more difficult of accomplishment than those already described. Lofty rises with rude and slippery *stemples* are sometimes found extremely awkward to climb, and still more so to descend. It sometimes happens that the *stemples* are covered over with boards to prevent their being injured by falling ore, etc. thrown from the workings above, and the only footholds then to be had are the spaces between these boards. The attention of the miners, however, who climb and descend with perfect confidence, prevents any real danger, though to a stranger the idea of climbing fifty or a hundred feet on so perilous a footing is seldom unattended with some sense of fearful apprehension.

Journeying through the drifts of a narrow vein is a less dangerous but often equally fatiguing task, especially if, by reason of accumulated work, the hands and knees are to be put in requisition for several fathoms over sharp angular blocks of rock, which all but fill the narrow passage. At the end or forehead of such drifts, buried as it were in a deep and lonely cavern, a single miner is often found pursuing his solitary labours at a string or thin vein of ore, which, like a bright silvery stream, is seen traversing the rock. It is considered that in general a solid rib of ore two or three inches wide, will pay for working, and as a much greater space is required for *vein room*, the procuring of this slender thread of ore is attended with a great proportion of unprofitable labour, hence the inconvenient but economical narrowness of the drift. The persevering visitor, who would explore every part of a mine, after *descending the rise* to the level, is probably next taken to a sump head, where he is required to trust his person to a substantial rope hung on the axle of a hand whimsey, often of seemingly frail construction, and is thus lowered down into the deeper workings of the mine, the aspect of which is similar to those above.

The subterranean researches of our visitors being at length completed, the waggons are again entered, and the eye accustomed to such scenery surveys with greater clearness the strata of the roof and sides,—pendent drops are seen hanging from above, and the wooden posts, which in some places support the level roof, are covered with woolly snow-like fungi. The timorous sensations felt on entering are now dissipated, and the party can fearlessly look at these and other swiftly passing objects, on which at length a faint white gleam of light is seen to blend with the yellower rays of the candles. The rocky prominences become more and more illuminated, and the solar light, together with the sparkling drops of water impart so bright and silvery an aspect as to excite the greatest admiration. This rapidly increases until, amid the splashing of water and the noisy rattling of their rugged cars, the party emerge from the dark chambers of the earth to the magnificent and almost overpowering brightness of "THE DAY."

T. SOPWITH

Liturgy, Reform of

✑§§✑

I don't know if it is any better with the Anglican Church in England, but the Episcopalian Church in America seems to have gone stark raving mad. Here are some features of a proposed reformed Holy Communion service.

(I) The Prayer of Humble Access and the General Confession have been cut. Roman Catholics have to go to auricular confession before taking communion. We do not. Surely, some verbal act of contrition is required.

(II) The Prayer for the Church Militant has become an interminable and boring attempt to pray for all sorts and conditions of men, a futile attempt, since if we were really to pray for them *all*, we should never get away. Thus, we pray for farmers, but not for barbers.

(III) Presumably out of ecumenical good will, the *Filioque* clause is omitted from the Creed. How often does a member of the Greek Orthodox Church turn up in a parish church?

(IV) Worst of all, the Epistle and Gospel are read in some appalling "modern" translation. In one such, the Greek word which St. Paul uses in Romans VIII and which the Authorized Version translates as *flesh* turns into *our lower nature,* a concept which is not Christian, but Manichean.

And why? The poor Roman Catholics have had to start from scratch, and, as any of them with a feeling for language will admit, they have made a cacophonous horror of the Mass. We had the extraordinary good fortune in that our Book of Common Prayer was composed at exactly the right historical moment. The English language had already become more or less what it is today, so that the Prayer Book is no more difficult to follow than Shakespeare, but the ecclesiastics of the sixteenth century still possessed a feeling for the ritual and ceremonious which today we have almost entirely lost. Why should we spit on our luck?

Logic

⋖ᢒᢒᢒᢖ

If language had been the creation, not of poetry, but of logic, we should only have one.

HEBBEL

Grammar and logic free language from being at the mercy of the tone of voice. Grammar protects us against misunderstanding the sound of an uttered name; logic protects us against what we say having a double meaning.

EUGEN ROSENSTOCK-HUESSY

In logic (mathematics) process and result are equivalent. Hence no surprises.

LUDWIG WITTGENSTEIN

It is always easy to be on the negative side. If a man were not to deny that there is salt on the table, you could not reduce him to an absurdity.

DR. JOHNSON

Logic is the art of going wrong with confidence.

Anon.

A proof tells us where to concentrate our doubts.

Anon.

Sufficient unto the day is the rigor thereof.

E. H. MOORE

Logic is like the sword—those who appeal to it shall perish by it. Faith is appealing to the living God, and one may perish by that too, but somehow one would rather perish that way than the other, and one has got to perish sooner or later.

SAMUEL BUTLER II

Four Logical Exercises

1) Everything, not absolutely ugly, may be kept in a drawing-room;
2) Nothing, that is encrusted with salt, is ever quite dry;
3) Nothing should be kept in a drawing-room, unless it is free from damp;
4) Bathing machines are always kept near the sea;
5) Nothing that is made of mother-of-pearl can be absolutely ugly;
6) Whatever is kept near the sea gets encrusted with salt.

1) I call no day "unlucky" when Robinson is civil to me;
2) Wednesdays are always cloudy;
3) When people take umbrellas, the day never turns out fine;
4) The only days when Robinson is uncivil to me are Wednesdays;

5) Everybody takes his umbrella with him when it is raining;
6) My lucky days always turn out fine.

1) No shark ever doubts that it is well fitted out;
2) No fish, that cannot dance a minuet, is contemptible;
3) No fish is quite certain it is well fitted out, unless it has three rows of teeth;
4) All fishes, except sharks, are kind to children;
5) No heavy fish can dance a minuet;
6) A fish with three rows of teeth is not to be despised.

1) All the human race, except my footmen, have a certain amount of common-sense;
2) No one, who lives on barley-sugar, can be anything but a mere baby;
3) None but a hop-scotch player knows what real happiness is;
4) No mere baby has a grain of common-sense;
5) No engine-driver ever plays hop-scotch;
6) No footman of mine is ignorant of what true happiness is.

LEWIS CARROLL

Love, Romantic

No notion of our Western culture has been responsible for more human misery and more bad poetry than the supposition, initiated by the Provençal poets, though not fully vulgarized by them, that a certain mystical experience called falling or being "in love" is one which every normal man and woman can expect to have. As a result, thousands and thousands of unfortunate young persons have persuaded themselves they were "in love" when their real feelings could be more accurately described in much cruder terms, while others, more honest, knowing that they have never been "in love," have tormented themselves with the thought that there must be something wrong with them.

The experience certainly does occur, but only, I should guess, to those with a livelier imagination than the average. In the case of a man, its proper effect should be to stimulate all his powers, physical and intellectual. The warrior who is "in love" should, like Troilus, become a better warrior, the scientist a better scientist. Under its influence, the poet, too, should write better poetry—about something else. Alas, he all too often tries to write about the experience itself, and the results are seldom satisfactory, even if he is a great poet. I must confess that I find the personal love poems of Dante, Shakespeare, Donne, for all their verbal felicities, embarrassing. I find the romantic vocabulary only tolerable in allegorical poems where the "Lady" is not a real human being. For instance:

She commaunded her minstrelles right anone to play
Mamours, the swete and the gentill daunce;
With La Bell Pucell that was faire and gaye
She me recommaunded with all pleasaunce
To daunce true mesures without variaunce.
O Lorde God, how glad than was I,
So for to daunce with my swete lady.

By her propre hande soft as ony silke
With due obeisaunce I dide her than take.
Her skinne was white as whalles bone or milke;
My thought was ravisshed; I might not aslake
My brenninge hert: she the fire dide make.
These daunces truely Musicke hath me tought:
To lute or daunce but it availed nought.

For the fire kindled and waxed more and more;
The dauncinge blewe it with her beaute clere;
My hert sekened and began waxe sore:
A minute six houres, and six houres a yere,
I thought it was, so hevy was my chere;

But yet for to cover my great love aright,
The outwarde countenance I made gladde and light.

STEPHEN HAWES

Simple, or elaborate, praise of physical beauty is always charming, but when it comes to writing about the emotional relation between the sexes, whether in verse or prose, I prefer the comic or the coarse note to the hot-and-bothered or the whining-pathetic.

Wulf and Edwacer

The men of my tribe would treat him as game:
if he comes to the camp: they will kill him outright.
    Our fate is forked.

Wulf is on one island, I on another.
Mine is a fastness: the fens girdle it
and it is defended by the fiercest men.
If he comes to the camp they will kill him for sure.
    Our fate is forked.

It was rainy weather, and I wept by the hearth,
thinking of my Wulf's far wanderings;
one of the captains caught me in his arms.
It gladdened me then; but it grieved me too.

Wulf, my Wulf, it was wanting you
that made me sick, your seldom coming,
the hollowness at heart; not the hunger I spoke of.

Do you hear, Edwacer? Our whelp
    Wulf shall take to the wood.
What was never bound is broken easily,
    our song together.

Anon. Anglo-Saxon
(trans. Michael Alexander)

In Secreit Place This Hyndir Nycht

In secreit place this hyndir nycht,
I hard ane beyrne say till ane bricht,
'My huny, my hart, my hoipmny heill,
I have bene lang your luifar leill,
And can of yow get confort nane;
How lang will ye with danger deill?
Ye brek my hart, my bony ane!'

His bony beird was kemmit and croppit
Bot all wit cale it was bedroppit,
And he wes townysche, peirt, and gukit;
He clappit fast, he kist, and chukkit,
As with the glaikis he wer ouirgane;
Yit be his feirris he wald have fukkit;
'Ye brek my hart, my bony ane!'

Quod he, 'My hairt, sweit as the hunye,
Sen that I borne wes of my mynnye,
I nevir wowit weycht bot yow;
My wambe is of your lufe sa fow,
That as ane gaist I glour and grane,
I trymble sa, ye will not trow;
Ye brek my hart, my bony ane!'

'Tehe!' quod scho, and gaif ane gawfe,
'Be still my tuchan and my calfe,
My new spanit howffing fra the sowk,
And all the blythnes of my bowk;
My sweit swanking, saif yow allane
Na leyd I luiffit all this owk;
Fow leis me that graceless gane.'

Quod he, 'My claver, and my curldodie,
My huny soppis, my sweit possodie,
Be not oure bosteous to your billie,
Ne warme hairtit and not ewill willie;

Your heylis, quhyt as quhalis bane,
Garris ryis on loft my quhillelillie;
Ye brek my hart, my bony ane!'

Quod scho, 'My clype, my unspaynit gyane,
With moderis mylk yit in your mychane,
My belly huddrun, my swete hurle bawsy,
My huny gukkis, my slawsy gawsy,
Your musing waild perse and harte of stane,
Tak gud confort, my grit heidit slawsy,
Fow leis me that graceless gane.'

Quod he, 'My kid, my capirculyoun,
My bony baib with the ruch brylyoun,
My tendir gurle, my wallie gowdye,
My tirlie myrlie, my crowdie mowdie;
Quhone that oure mouthis dois meit at ane,
My stang dois storkyn with your towdie;
Ye brek my hairt, my bony ane!'

Quo scho, 'Now tak me be the hand,
Welcum! my golk of Marie land,
My chirrie and my maikles munyoun,
My sowklar sweit as ony unyoun,
My strumill stirk, yit new to spane,
I am applyit to your opunyoun;
I luif rycht weill your graceless gane.'

He gaiff to hir ane apill rubye;
Quod scho, 'Gramercye! my sweit cowhubye.'
And thai twa to ane play began,
Quhilk men dois call the dery dan;
Quhill that thair myrthis met baythe in ane.
"Wo is me!" quod scho, 'quhair will ye, man?
Bot now I luif that graceless gane.'

WILLIAM DUNBAR

La Bella Bona Roba

I cannot tell who loves the Skeleton
Of a poor Marmoset, nought but boan, boan.
Give me a nakedness with her cloath's on.

Such whose white-sattin upper coat of skin,
Cuts upon Velvet rich Incarnadin,
Ha's yet a Body (and of Flesh) within.

Sure it is meant good Husbandry in men,
Who do incorporate with Aëry leane,
T' repair their sides, and get their Ribb agen.

Hard hap unto that Huntsman that Decrees
Fat joys for all his swet, when as he sees,
After his Say, nought but his Keepers Fees.

Then Love I beg, when next thou tak'st thy Bow,
Thy angry shafts, and dost Heart-chasing go,
Passe *Rascall Deare*, strike me the largest Doe.

RICHARD LOVELACE

Language has not the power to speak what love indites:
The soul lies buried in the ink that writes.

JOHN CLARE

As I walked out one night, it being dark all over,
The moon did show no light I could discover,
Down by a river-side where ships were sailing,
A lonely maid I spied, weeping and bewailing.

I boldly stept up to her, and asked what grieved her,
She made this reply, None could relieve her,
'For my love is pressed,' she cried, 'to cross the ocean,
My mind is like the Sea, always in motion.'

He said, 'My pretty fair maid, mark well my story,
For your true love and I fought for England's glory,
By one unlucky shot we both got parted,
And by the wounds he got, I'm broken hearted.

'He told me before he died, his heart was broken,
He gave me this gold ring, take it for a token,—
"Take this unto my dear, there is no one fairer,
Tell her to be kind and love the bearer."

Soon as these words he spoke she ran distracted,
Not knowing what she did, nor how she acted,
She run ashore, her hair showing her anger,
'Young man, you've come too late, for I'll wed no stranger.'

Soon as these words she spoke, his love grew stronger,
He flew into her arms, he could wait no longer,
They both sat down and sung, but she sung clearest,
Like a nightingale in spring, 'Welcome home, my dearest.'

He sang, 'God bless the wind that blew him over.'
She sang, 'God bless the ship that brought him over.'
They both sat down and sung but she sung clearest,
Like a nightingale in spring, 'Welcome home, my dearest.'

Anon.

Take Him

LINDA

Take him, you don't have to pay for him,
Take him, he's free.
Take him, I won't make a play for him,
He's not for me.
True that his head is like lumber,
True that his heart is like ice:
You'll find this little number
Cheap at half the price.

Take him, and just for the lure of it
Marry him too.
Keep him for you can be sure of it,
He can't keep you.
So take my old jalopy,
Keep him from falling apart.
Take him, but don't ever take him to heart.

VERA

Thanks, little Mousie,
For the present and all that,
But in this housie
I would rather keep a rat.
Only a wizard
Could reform that class of male:
They say a lizard
Cannot change his scale.

LINDA

Take him, I won't put a price on him,
Take him, he's yours.
Take him, pyjamas look nice on him,
But how he snores.
Though he is well-adjusted,
Certain things make him a wreck:
Last year his arm was busted,
Reaching from a check.

His thoughts are seldom consecutive,
He just can't write.
I know a movie executive
Who's twice as bright.
Lots of good luck, you'll need it,
And you'll need aspirin too.
Take him, but don't ever let him take you.

DUET

I hope that things will go well with him,
I bear no hate.

All I can say is:—"To hell with him,
He gets the gate."
So take my benediction,
Take my old Benedict too.
Take him away, he's too good to be true.

LORENZ HART

. . . "Give me my diamond anemones," the Queen commanded, and motioning to her Maid: "Pray conclude, mademoiselle, those lofty lines."

With a slight sigh, the lectress took up the posture of a Dying Intellectual.

"*Live with an aim, and let that aim be high!*" she reiterated in tones tinged perceptibly with emotion.

"But not *too* high, remember, Mademoiselle de Nazianzi . . ."

There was a short pause. And then—

"Ah, Madam. What a dearest he is!"

"I think you forget yourself," the Queen murmured with a quelling glance. "You had better withdraw."

"He has such strength! One could niche an idol in his dear, dinted chin."

"Enough!"

And a moment later the enflamed girl left the room warbling softly: *Depuis le Jour.*

A Fragment of Sappho

"I'm not going to inflict upon you a speech," the professor said, breaking in like a piccolo to Miss Compostella's harp.

"Hear, hear!" Mr. Sophax approved.

"You have heard, of course, how, while surveying the ruins of Crocodileopolis Arsinoe, my donkey, having—"

And then, after what may have been an anguishing obbligato, the Professor declaimed impressively the imperishable lines.

"Oh, delicious!" Lady Listless exclaimed, looking quite perplexed. "Very charming indeed!"

"Will anyone tell me what it means," Mrs. Thumbler queried, "in plain English? Unfortunately, my Greek—"

"In plain English," the Professor said, with some reluctance, "it means: 'Could not' (he wagged a finger) 'Could not, for the fury of her feet!' "

"Do you mean she ran away?"

"Apparently!"

"O-h!" Mrs. Thumbler seemed inclined to faint.

RONALD FIRBANK

The maxim for any love affair is: "Play and pray; but on the whole do not pray when you are playing and do not play when you are praying." We cannot yet manage such simultaneities.

CHARLES WILLIAMS

Machines

⚬§₿⚬

Machines are beneficial to the degree that they eliminate the need for labor, harmful to the degree that they eliminate the need for skill.

I cannot imagine a housewife not being glad to come by a dish-washing machine. But for some couples the electric dish-washer eliminated the one thing they did together every day; one of them washed while the other dried. As one woman put it, she now enjoys not only less fatigue but a pure gift of time. Yet she added wistfully, "But it *was* cozy, just the two of us together for that little while every night after we got the kids to bed. . . ." The comfortable intimacy that went with the chore was hardly noticed until it vanished. But just as obviously, the arrival of the machine in the home meant the couple would have to find some other occasion for spending their brief while together. Only then would the machine truly add, and not detract from their lives with each other. This, as I say, is obvious. But in how many families does this "obvious" become an actuality?

Just as modern machines can no longer be recognized as obvious extensions of our bodily organs, or as performing bodily functions more efficiently—though that may have been their origin—so in modern delusions we find more and more non-human projections. For example, a characteristic feature of modern insanity is the "influencing machine", a device that supposedly puts thoughts into a person's head as if they were his own, or forces him to act against his conscious will. . . .

It can be shown that the influencing machine, too, began as a projection of the human body, but the essential point is that it does not retain this image; it becomes ever more complex and the psychotic person ends up feeling controlled by mechanical devices that no longer resemble anything human or even animal-like. Thus modern man, when he is haunted, whether sane or profoundly disturbed, is no longer haunted by other men or by grandiose projections of man, but by machines.

BRUNO BETTELHEIM

Machines are better than people. People go further than they should.

An autistic child

Madness

The last thing that can be said of a lunatic is that his actions are causeless. If any human acts may loosely be called causeless, they are the minor acts of a healthy man; whistling as he walks; slashing the grass with a stick; kicking his heels or rubbing his hands. It is the happy man who does the useless things; the sick man is not strong enough to be idle. It is exactly such careless and causeless actions that the madman could never understand; for the madman (like the determinist) generally sees too much cause in everything. The madman would read a conspiratorial significance into these empty activities. He would think that the lopping of the grass was an attack on private property. He would think that the kicking of the heels was a signal to an accomplice. If the madman could for an instant become careless, he would become sane. Every one, who has had the misfortune to talk with people in the heart or on the edge of mental disorder, knows that their most sinister quality is a horrible clarity of detail; a connecting of one thing with another in a map more elaborate than a maze. If you argue with a madman, it is extremely probable that you will get the worst of it; for in many ways his mind moves all the quicker for not being delayed by the things that go with good judgment. He is not hampered by a sense of humor or by charity, or by the dumb certainties of experience. He is more logical for losing certain sane affections. Indeed, the common phrase for insanity is in this respect a misleading one. The madman is not the man who has lost his reason. The madman is the man who has lost everything except his reason.

The madman's explanation of a thing is always complete, and often in a purely rational sense satisfactory. Or, to speak more strictly, the insane explanation, if not conclusive, is at least unanswerable; this may be observed specially in the two or three commonest kinds of madness. If a man says (for instance) that men have a conspiracy against him, you cannot dispute it except by saying that all the men deny that they are conspirators; which is exactly what conspirators would do. His explanation covers the facts as much as yours. Or if a man says that he is the rightful King of England, it is no complete answer to say that the existing authorities call him mad; for if he were King of England, that might be the wisest thing for the existing authorities to do. Or if a man says that he is Jesus Christ, it is no answer to tell him that the world denies his divinity; for the world denied Christ's.

G. K. CHESTERTON

It was utterly wonderful to me to find that I could go so heartily and headily mad; for you know I had been priding myself on my peculiar sanity! And it was more wonderful yet to find the madness made up into things so dreadful out of things so trivial. One of the most provoking and disagreeable of the spectres was developed out of the fire-light on my mahogany bed-post; and my fate, for all futurity, seemed continually to turn on the humour of dark personages who were materially nothing but the stains of damp on the ceiling. But the sorrowfullest part of the matter was, and is, that while my illness at Matlock encouraged me by all its dreams in after work, this one has done nothing but humiliate and terrify me; and leaves me nearly unable to speak any more except of the natures of stones and flowers.

RUSKIN
(*Letter to Carlyle, June 23, 1878*)

I seemed to read messages in chairs, stoves, tables, pots, pans, flowers, in anything. It is the way in which you act upon this revelation which determines your sanity. If you see these messages as contacts with deeper realities, you are using them correctly, as symbols expressing something greater than themselves. If you kneel down in front of a dressing-gown crucifixion, you are very near insanity.

ANTHONY ROSSITER

Sanity is perhaps the ability to punctuate.

PARRY IDRIS

Asylum Dialogue

JONES (*Laughs loudly, then pauses*): I'm McDougal myself.

SMITH: What do you do for a living, little fellow? Work on a ranch or something?

J: No, I'm a civilian seaman. Supposed to be high muckamuck society.

S: A singing recording machine, huh? I guess a recording machine sings sometimes. If they're adjusted right. Mm-hm. I thought that was it. My towel, mm-hm. We'll be going back to sea in about—eight or nine months though. Soon as we get our— destroyed parts repaired. (*Pause*)

J: I've got lovesickness, secret love.

S: Secret love, huh? (*Laughs*)

J: Yeah.

S: I ain't got any secret love.

J: I fell in love, but I don't feed any woo—that sits over—looks something like me—walking around over there.

S: My, oh, my only one, my only one is the shark. Keep out of the way of him.

J: Don't they know I have a life to live. (*Long pause*)

S: Do you work at the air base? Hm?

J: You know what I think of work. I'm thirty-three in June, do you mind?

S: June?

J: Thirty-three years old in June. This stuff goes out of the window after I live this, uh—leave the hospital. So I lay off cigarettes. I'm a spatial condition, from outer space, myself, no shit.

S (*Laughs*): I'm a real space ship from across.

J: A lot of people talk, uh—that way like crazy, but Believe It or Not by Ripley, take it or leave it—alone it's in the *Examiner*, it's in the comic section, Believe It or Not by Ripley, Robert E. Ripley, Believe It or Not, but we don't have to believe anything unless I feel like it. (*Pause*) Every little rosette—too much alone. (*Pause*)

S: Could be possible. (*Phrase inaudible because of aeroplane noise*)

J: I'm a civilian seaman.

S: Could be possible. (*Sighs*) I take my bath in the ocean.

J: Bathing stinks. You know why? Cause you can't quit when you feel like it. You're in the service.

S: I can quit whenever I feel like quitting. I can get out when I feel like getting out.

J (*Talking at the same time*): Take me, I'm a civilian. I can quit.

S: Civilian?

J: Go my—my way.

S: I guess we have, in port, civilian. (*Long pause*)

J: What do they want with us?

S: Hm?

J: What do they want with you and me?

S: What do they want with you and me? How do I know what they want with you? I know what they want with me. I broke the law, so I have to pay for it. (*Silence*)

Quoted by J. HALEY

'Tis very difficult to write like a madman, but 'tis a very easy matter to write like a fool.

NATHANIEL LEE

> I have observed that poets on the verge of madness are often easier to translate into another tongue than sane ones, since, even in their own language, much of their poetic effect comes from their odd associations of ideas and images, which are equally odd in any language. The following poem by Hölderlin, for example, even in a prose translation, "comes across" in a way that Goethe very rarely does.

Heavenly Love, you the tender! If I should forget you, if ever I should, O you fateful ones, you fiery ones that are full of ashes and even before were deserted and lonely,

Beloved islands, eyes of the world of marvels! For you have become my one and only concern, your shores where the idolatrous, where Love does penance, but to the Heavenly alone.

For, all too thankful, there the holy ones served in the days of beauty, and the wrathful heroes; and many trees, and the cities, stood in that place,

Visible, like a pondering man; now the heroes are dead, the islands of Love are almost disfigured, Thus everywhere must Love be tricked and exploited, silly. . . .

HÖLDERLIN
(trans. Michael Hamburger)

Man

✺

One log has nine holes.

Turkish riddle

Man was created in order that a beginning might be made.

ST. AUGUSTINE

Man is an exception, whatever he is. If it is not true that a divine being fell, then we can only say that one of the animals went entirely off its head.

Men are men, but Man is a woman.

G. K. CHESTERTON

To breed an animal with the right to make promises—is not this the paradoxical problem nature has set herself with regard to man?

NIETZSCHE

Man only plays when, in the full meaning of the word, he is a man, and he is only completely a man when he plays.

F. SCHILLER

Man is the only animal that laughs and weeps; for he is the only animal that is struck by the difference between what things are and what they might have been.

WILLIAM HAZLITT

Man is only man at the surface. Remove his skin, dissect, and immediately you come to machinery.

PAUL VALÉRY

. . . Bedizened or stark

naked, man, the self, the being we call human, writing-
master to this world, griffons a dark
"Like does not like like that is obnoxious"; and writes error
with four
r's. Among animals, *one* has a sense of humor.
Humor saves a few steps, it saves years. Unignorant,
modest and unemotional, and all emotion,
he has everlasting vigor,
power to grow,
though there are few creatures who can make one
breathe faster and make one erecter.

Not afraid of anything is he,
and then goes cowering forth, tread paced to meet
an obstacle
at every step. Consistent with the
formula—warm blood, no gills, two pairs of hands
and a few hairs—that
is a mammal; there he sits in his own habitat,
serge-clad, strong-shod. The prey of fear, he, always
curtailed, extinguished, thwarted by the dusk, work
partly done,
says to the alternating blaze,
"Again the sun!
anew each day; and new and new and new,
that comes into and steadies my soul."

MARIANNE MOORE

In the Beginning

When is Tellus
to give her dear fosterling
her adaptable, rational, elect
and plucked-out otherling
a reasonable chance?
Not yet—but soon, very soon
as lithic phases go.

So before then?
　　　　　Did the fathers of those
who forefathered them
　　　　　　　　(if by genital or ideate begetting)
set apart, make other, oblate?

By what rote, if at all
　　　　had they the suffrage:
　　　　Ascribe to, ratify, approve
in the humid paradises
　　　　of the Third Age?
But who or what, before these?
　　　　Had they so far to reach the ground?
and what of the pelvic inclination of their co-laterals, whose
far cognates went—on how many feet?—in the old time
before *them?*
For all WHOSE WORKS FOLLOW THEM
　　　　　among any of these or them
dona eis requiem.

　　　　　(He would lose, not any one
　　　　　　　　　　　from among them.
Of all those given him
　　　　he would lose none.)

　　　　　By the uteral marks
that make the covering stone an artefact.
　　　　　By the penile ivory
and by the viatic meats.
　　　　　Dona ei requiem.
Who was he? Who?
Himself at the cave-mouth
　　　　　　　　the last of the father-figures
to take the diriment stroke
　　　　　　　　of the last gigantic leader of
thick-felled cave-fauna?
Whoever he was
　　　　　Dona ei requiem
sempiternam.

(He would not lose him

           . . . non perdidi

ex eis quemquam.)

           Before the melt-waters
had drumlin-dammed a high hill-water for the water-maid
to lave her maiden hair.

Before they morained Tal-y-llyn, cirqued a high hollow for
Idwal, brimmed a deep-dark basin for Peris the Hinge and for
old Paternus.

Long ages since they'd troughed, in solid Ordovician
his Bala bed for Tacitus.
Long, long ago they'd turned the flow about.
But had they as yet morained
           where holy Deva's entry is?
Or pebbled his mere, where
           still the Parthenos
she makes her devious exit?

Before the Irish sea-borne sheet lay tattered on the gestatorial
couch of Camber the eponym
           lifted to every extremity of the sky
by pre-Cambrian oreos-heavers
           for him to dream
the Combroges' epode.
In his high *sêt* there.
           Higher than any of 'em
south of the Antonine limits.
Above the sealed hypogéum
           where the contest was
over the great *mundus* of sepulture (there the *ver-tigérnus*
                         was)

here lie dragons and old Pendragons
           very bleached.
His unconforming bed, as yet
           is by the muses kept.

And shall be, so these Welshmen say, till the thick rotundities
give, and the bent flanks of space itself give way
      and the whitest of the Wanderers
falters in her transit
      at the Sibyl's *in favilla*–day.

Before the drift
      was over the lime-face.
Sometime between the final and the penultimate débâcle.
      (Already Arcturus deploys his reconnoitering
chills in greater strength: soon his last *Putsh* on any scale.)
Before this all but proto-historic transmogrification of the
land-face.
Just before they rigged the half-lit stage for dim-eyed Clio
to step with some small confidence the measures of her
brief and lachrymal pavan.

DAVID JONES

The life of mankind could very well be conceived as a speech in
which different men represented the various parts of speech (that
might also be applied to the nations in the relations to one another). How many people are merely adjectives, interjections,
conjunctions, adverbs; and how few are substantives, verbs, etc.;
how many are copula?

In relation to each other men are like irregular verbs in different languages; nearly all verbs are slightly irregular.

There are people whose position in life is like that of the in-
terjection, without influence on the sentence— They are the hermits of life, and at the very most take a case, eg, *O me miserum*.

Our politicians are like Greek reciprocals (alleeloin) which are
wanting in the nominative singular and all subjective cases. They
can only be thought of in the plural and possessive cases.

The sad thing about me is that my life (the condition of my
soul) changes according to declensions where not only the endings change but the whole word is altered.

SØREN KIERKEGAARD
(trans. A. Dru)

Marriage

✎🎋✎

Like everything which is not the involuntary result of fleeting emotion but the creation of time and will, any marriage, happy or unhappy, is infinitely more interesting and significant than any romance, however passionate.

Love is an ideal thing, marriage a real thing; a confusion of the real with the ideal never goes unpunished.

It is a mistake for a taciturn, serious-minded woman to marry a jovial man, but not for a serious-minded man to marry a light-hearted woman.

GOETHE

If you are afraid of loneliness, don't marry.

A. CHEKHOV

No trap so mischievous to the field preacher as wedlock, and it is laid for him at every hedge corner. Matrimony has quite maimed poor Charles [Wesley], and might have spoiled John [Wesley] and George [Whitefield], if a wise Maker had not graciously sent them a pair of ferrets. Dear George has now got his liberty again, and he will 'scape well if he is not caught by another tenter-hook. Eight or nine years ago, having been grievously tormented with housekeepers, I truly had thought about looking out for a Jezebel myself. But it seemed highly needful to ask advice of the Lord. So falling down on my knees beside a table, with a Bible between my hands, I besought the Lord to give me direction . . . This method of procuring divine intelligence is much flouted by flimsy professors who walk at large, and desire not that sweet and secret access to the mercy-seat which babes of the Kingdom do find.

BERRIDGE OF EVERTON

What did I get married for?
    That's what I want to know:
I was led to the altar
    Like a lamb to the slaughter.
We met on a Friday;
    My luck was out, I'm sure:
I took her for better or worse, but she
    Was worse than I took her for.

                                        Anon.

Wenn der Rabbi trennt,
Schocklen sich die Wend,
Und alle Hassidim
Kleppen mit die Hend.

(When the Rabbi has marital intercourse, the walls shake, and all
the Hassidim clap their hands.)

                                        Anon.

In England a few years ago, during a suit for damages involv-
ing the proprietor of a circus and a midget, whose midget wife
had been injured by an elephant, a witness said it was a well-
known fact among circus people that midget married couples
are so devoted that if one of them is sick, the other cannot be
expected to work.

When asked about "the quiet affection" which is supposed to
replace passion in marriage, Charles Williams said, "Well, it
certainly isn't quiet, and it isn't exactly affection, but the phrase
will have to do."

When I hear that "Possession is the grave of love," I remember
that a religion may begin with the resurrection.

                                        F. H. BRADLEY

When the husband drinks to the wife, all would be well; when
the wife drinks to the husband, all is.

                                        English proverb

The wife carries the husband on her face; the husband carries the wife on his linen.

Bulgarian proverb

With all her experience, every woman expects to do better when she marries a second time, and some do.

WILLIAM FEATHER

Remarried widowers, it has been observed, tend to confound the persons of their wives. The reason, I suppose, is that they identify the substance.

F. H. BRADLEY

Arnold Bennett says that the horror of marriage lies in its "dailiness." All acuteness of relationship is rubbed away by this. The truth is more like this: life—say 4 days out of 7—becomes automatic; but on the 5th day a bead of sensation (between husband and wife) forms which is all the fuller and more sensitive because of the automatic customary unconscious days on either side. That is to say the year is marked by moments of great intensity. Hardy's "moments of vision." How can a relationship endure for any length of time except under these conditions?

VIRGINIA WOOLF

Charlotte played the piano extremely well. Eduard performed not quite so well on the flute; for, although he practiced diligently from time to time, he was by nature not patient or persevering enough to train such a talent successfully. Therefore he played his part unevenly—some passages well but perhaps too quickly; in others he had to slow down because he was not familiar enough with the music; and it would have been difficult for any one but Charlotte to go through an entire duet with him. But Charlotte knew how to cope with it; she slowed down, and then allowed him to run away with her, fulfilling in this way the double duty of a good conductor and an intelligent house-wife, both of whom always know how to preserve a general moderate measure, even if single passages may not always be in the right tempo.

GOETHE
(trans. Elizabeth Mayer and Louise Bogan)

She Revisits Alone the Church of Her Marriage

I have come to the church and chancel,
      Where all's the same!
—Brighter and larger in my dreams
Truly it shaped than now, meseems,
      Is its substantial frame.
But, anyhow, I made my vow,
      Whether for praise or blame,
Here in this church and chancel
      Where all's the same.

Where touched the check-floored chancel
      My knees and his?
The step looks shyly at the sun,
And says, " 'Twas here the thing was done,
      For bale or else for bliss!"
Of all those there I least was ware
      Would it be that or this
When touched the check-floored chancel
      My knees and his!

Here in this fateful chancel
      Where all's the same,
I thought the culminant crest of life
Was reached when I went forth the wife
      I was not when I came.
Each commonplace one of my race,
      Some say, has such an aim—
To go from a fateful chancel
      As not the same.

Here, through this hoary chancel
        Where all's the same,
A thrill, a gaiety even, ranged
That morning when it seemed I changed
        My nature with my name.
Though now not fair, though gray my hair,
        He loved me, past proclaim,
Here in this hoary chancel,
        Where all's the same.

THOMAS HARDY

Tokens

Green mwold on zummer bars do show
    That they've a-dripp'd in winter wet;
The hoof-worn ring o' groun' below
    The tree, do tell o' storms or het;
The trees in rank along a ledge
Do show where woonce did bloom a hedge;
An' where the vurrow-marks do stripe
The down, the wheat woonce rustled ripe.
Each mark ov things a-gone vrom view—
To eyezight's woone, to soulzight two.

The grass ageän the mwoldren door
    'S a token sad o' vo'k a-gone,
An' where the house, bwoth wall an' vloor.
    'S a-lost, the well mid linger on.
What tokens, then, could Meäry gi'e
That she'd a-liv'd an' liv'd for me,
But things a-done vor thought an' view?
Good things that nwone ageän can do,
An' every work her love ha' wrought
To eyezight's woone, but two to thought.

WILLIAM BARNES

Asphodel, That Greeny Flower

             . . . All women are not Helen,
                       I know that,
but have Helen in their hearts.
             My sweet,
                       you have it also, therefore
I love you
             and could not love you otherwise.
                       Imagine you saw
a field made up of women
             all silver-white.
                       What should you do
but love them?
             The storm bursts
                       or fades! it is not
the end of the world.
             Love is something else,
                       or so I thought it,
a garden which expands,
             though I knew you as a woman
                       and never thought otherwise,
until the whole sea
             has been taken up
                       and all its gardens.
It was the love of love,
             the love that swallows up all else,
                       a grateful love,
a love of nature, of people,
             animals,
                       a love engendering
gentleness and goodness
             that moved me
                       and *that* I saw in you.
I should have known,
             though I did not,
                       that the lily-of-the-valley

is a flower that makes many ill
        who whiff it.
                We had our children,
rivals in the general onslaught.
        I put them aside
                though I cared for them
as well as any man
        could care for his children
                according to my lights.
You understand
        I had to meet you
                after the event
and have still to meet you.
        Love
                to which you too shall bow
along with me—
        a flower
                a weakest flower
shall be our trust
        and not because
                we are too feeble
to do otherwise
        but because
                at the height of my power
I risked what I had to do,
        therefore to prove
                that we love each other
while my very bones sweated
        that I could not cry to you
                in the act.
Of asphodel, that greeny flower,
        I come, my sweet
                to sing to you!
My heart rouses
        thinking to bring you news
                of something
that concerns you
        and concerns many men. Look at

                    what passes for the new.
You will not find it there but in
           despised poems.
                    It is difficult
to get the news from poems
                    yet men die miserably every day
                             for lack
of what is found there.
                    Hear me out
                             for I too am concerned
and every man
           who wants to die at peace in his bed
                    besides.

W I L L I A M   C A R L O S   W I L L I A M S

My dear Heart,—My sad parting was so far from making me
forget you, that I scarce thought upon myself since, but wholly
upon you. Those dear embraces which I yet feel, and shall never
lose, being the faithful testimonies of an indulgent husband, have
charmed my soul to such a reverence of your remembrance, that
were it possible, I would, with my own blood, cement your dead
limbs to live again, and (with reverence) think it no sin to rob
Heaven a little longer of a martyr. Oh! my dear, you must now
pardon my passion, this being my last (oh fatal word!) that ever
you will receive from me; and know, that until the last minute
that I can imagine you shall live, I shall sacrifice the prayers of a
Christian, and the groans of an afflicted wife. And when you are
not (which sure by sympathy I shall know), I shall wish my own
dissolution with you, so that we may go hand in hand to Heaven.
'Tis too late to tell you what I have, or rather have not done for
you; how being turned out of doors because I came to beg for
mercy; the Lord lay not your blood to their charge.

I would fain discourse longer with you, but dare not; passion
begins to drown my reason, and will rob me of my devoirs,
which is all I have left to serve you. Adieu, therefore, ten thousand times, my dearest dear; and since I must never see you more,
take this prayer—May your faith be so strengthened that your
constancy may continue; and then I know Heaven will receive

you; whither grief and love will in a short time (I hope) translate,

My dear,

   Your sad, but constant wife, even to love your ashes when
dead,

ARUNDEL PENRUDDOCK

May the 3rd, 1655, eleven o'clock at night. Your children beg
your blessing and present their duties to you.

> [Her husband, John Penruddock, a Royalist who joined the
> insurrection of 1655, was taken at South Molton, and beheaded
> at Exeter.]

Medicine

ᣰᣆᣓ

I can remember my father, who was a physician, quoting to me
when I was a young boy an aphorism by Sir William Osler:
"Care more for the individual patient than for the special features of his disease." In other words, a doctor, like anyone else
who has to deal with human beings, each of them unique,
cannot be a scientist; he is either, like the surgeon, a craftsman,
or, like the physician and the psychologist, an artist. As Novalis wrote, "Every sickness is a musical problem; every cure
a musical solution. . . ." This means that in order to be a good
doctor a man must also have a good character, that is to say,
whatever weaknesses and foibles he may have, he must love
his fellow human beings in the concrete and desire their good
before his own. A doctor, like a politician, who loves other
men only in the abstract or regards them simply as a source
of income can, however clever, do nothing but harm.

   It is precisely those members of the medical profession who
make the bogus claim that they are "scientific" who are most
likely to refuse to consider new evidence. To its shame, the

profession has always had its unacknowledged "Holy Office," which has dealt with the heterodox, like Kaspar Wolff and Semmelweis, every bit as unscrupulously and ruthlessly as the Inquisition ever dealt with heretics.

PRIEST: "*Croyez-vous?*"

A DYING 18TH-CENTURY PHYSICIAN: "*Je crois à tout, sauf le médecin.*"

Memory

❧❦❧

When Hoare was a young man of about five-and-twenty, he one day tore the quick of his finger-nail—I mean, he separated the fleshly part of the finger from the nail—and this reminded him that many years previously while quite a child he had done the same thing. Thereon he fell to thinking of that time, which was impressed upon his memory partly because there was a great disturbance in the house about a missing five-pound note, and partly because it was while he had the scarlet fever.

Having nothing to do he followed the train of thought aroused by his torn finger, and asked himself how he tore it. After a while it came back to him that he had been lying ill in bed as a child of about seven years old at the house of an aunt who lived in Hertfordshire. His arms often hung out of the bed and as his hands wandered over the wooden frame of the bed he felt there was a place where a nut had come off so that he could stuff his fingers in; one day, in trying to stuff a piece of paper into this hole, he stuffed it so far and so tightly that he tore the quick of his nail. The whole thing came back so vividly, though he had not thought of it for twenty years, that he could see the room in his aunt's house, and remembered how his aunt used to sit by his bedside writing at a little table from which he had got the piece of paper which he had stuffed into the hole.

So far so good; but then there flashed upon him an idea that was not so pleasant. I mean it came upon him with irresistible force that the piece of paper he had stuffed into the hole in the bedstead was the missing five-pound note about which there had been so much disturbance. At that time he was so young that a five-pound note was to him only a piece of paper; when he heard that five pounds were missing he had thought it was five sovereigns; or perhaps he was too ill to know anything, or to be questioned. I forget what I was told about this—at any rate he had no idea of the value of the piece of paper he was stuffing into the hole but now that the matter had recurred to him at all he felt so sure it was the note that he immediately went down to Hertfordshire where his aunt was living, and asked to the surprise of everyone to be allowed to wash his hands in the room he had occupied as a child. He was told there were friends staying with them who had the room at present, but, on his saying he had a reason, and particularly begging to be allowed to remain alone a little while in this room, he was taken upstairs and left there.

He immediately went to the bed, lifted up the chintz which then covered the frame, and found his old friend the hole.

A nut had been supplied and he could no longer get his fingers into it.

He rang the bell and, when the servant came, asked for a bed-key. All this time he was rapidly acquiring the reputation of being a lunatic throughout the whole house, but the key was brought, and by the help of it Hoare got the nut off. When he had done so, there sure enough, by dint of picking with his pocket-knife, he found the missing five-pound note.

SAMUEL BUTLER II

Middle-Class, English

❧§❧

In spite of Belloc's description of Lord Heygate as "The sort of peer who well might pass/For someone of the Middle-Class," the label does not, thank God, carry with it the pejorative associations of the label *bourgeois*. Both in France and England, until very recently, nearly all the writers, painters, composers, scientists, and philosophers came from this class, but we do not, like our unfortunate French colleagues, have to apologize for the fact.

One may sneer as one will at its narrow-mindedness, its repressions, its dullness, but let it be remembered that it was the middle-class who first practiced, if it did not invent, the virtue of financial honesty, the first class to be scrupulous about paying bills and taxes. The aristocracy paid its gambling debts but not its tailors' bills; the poor stole.

We even have our martyr, Sir Walter Scott, who, when made bankrupt through no fault of his own, worked himself to death to pay off his creditors. In our modern economy it seems unlikely that the middle-class morality about money will be able to survive. I, for example, was brought up never to buy anything until I had the cash to pay for it. If everyone did the same, i.e., bought nothing on credit, our economy would go smash.

Mind, The Human

> Over the water,
> Under the water,
> Round the world it ranges,
> Never been seen by the eye of man,
> But oftentimes it changes.
>
> Nova Scotian riddle

Mind is rather a little bourgeois, yet you can't dispense with the *tiers état*.

V. ROZANOV

A man is infinitely more complicated than his thoughts.

Consciousness reigns but doesn't govern.

Cogito, ergo sum. This is not a piece of reasoning. It's a fist coming down on the table, to corroborate the words in the mind.

A *thinker* is a *talker* before the fact.

PAUL VALÉRY

Speech is the Mother, not the handmaid, of Thought.

KARL KRAUS

When we think a thing, the thing we think is not the thing we think we think, but only the thing we think we think we think.

Anon.

The highest and deepest thoughts do not "voluntarily move harmonious numbers," but run rather to grotesque epigram and doggerel.

COVENTRY PATMORE

The proper, unique, and perpetual object of thought: that which does not exist, that which is not before me, that which was, that which will be, that which is possible, that which is impossible.

PAUL VALÉRY

In the study of ideas, it is necessary to remember that insistence on hard-headed clarity issues from sentimental feeling, as it were a mist, cloaking the perplexities of fact. Insistence on clarity at all costs is based on sheer superstition as to the mode in which human intelligence functions.

It is a profoundly erroneous truism, repeated by all copy-books and by eminent people when they are making speeches, that we should cultivate the habit of thinking what we are doing. The precise opposite is the case. Civilization advances by extending the number of important operations which we can perform without thinking about them.

A. N. WHITEHEAD

Thinking is more interesting than knowing, but less interesting than looking.

GOETHE

The Climate of Thought

The climate of thought has seldom been described.
It is no terror of Caucasian frost,
Nor yet that brooding Hindu heat
For which a loin-rag and a dish of rice
Suffice until the pestilent monsoon.
But, without winter, blood would run too thin;
Or, without summer, fires would burn too long.
In thought the seasons run concurrently.

Thought has a sea to gaze, not voyage on;
And hills, to rough the edge of the bland sky,
Not to be climbed in search of blander prospect;
Few birds, sufficient for such caterpillars
As are not fated to turn butterflies;
Few butterflies, sufficient for such flowers
As are the luxury of a full orchard;
Wind, sometimes, in the evening chimneys, rain
On the early morning roof, on sleepy sight;
Snow streaked upon the hilltop, feeding
The fond brook at the valley-head
That greens the valley and that parts the lips;
The sun, simple, like a country neighbour;
The moon, grand, not fanciful with clouds.

ROBERT GRAVES

It seems to me that the soul, when alone with itself and speaking to itself, uses only a small number of words, none of them extraordinary. This is how one recognizes that there *is* a soul at that moment, if at the same time one experiences the sensation that everything else—everything that would require a larger vocabulary —is mere possibility.

PAUL VALÉRY

Whenever I hear people talking about "liberal" ideas, I am always astounded that men should so love to fool themselves with empty sounds. An idea should never be liberal: it must be vigorous, positive, and without loose ends so that it may fulfill its divine mission and be productive. The proper place for liberality is in the realm of emotions.

GOETHE

The Jansenists put a rigor into the *heart* that belongs to the mind.

PAUL VALÉRY

Every abstract thinker tears love and time asunder.

The primary questions for an adult are not *why* or *how*, but *when* and *where*.

EUGEN ROSENSTOCK-HUESSY

I have drawn from the well of language many a thought which I do not have and which I could not put into words.

In mathematical analysis we call x the undetermined part of line a; the rest we don't call y, as we do in common life, but $a-x$. Hence mathematical language has great advantages over the common language.

G. C. LICHTENBERG

We are all capable of evil thoughts, but only very rarely of evil deeds: we can all do good deeds, but very few of us can think good thoughts.

CESARE PAVESE

Thou hast commanded that an ill-regulated mind should be its own punishment.

ST. AUGUSTINE

Mnemonics

✺

Mnemonics, or aids to memory, should be quoted from memory, which means that I cannot vouch for the accuracy of any of my examples.

Some of the earliest poetry I can remember are the mnemonic rhymes in Kennedy's *Shorter Latin Primer*. For example, the list of prepositions taking the ablative:

A,ab,absque,coram,de,
Palam,clam,cum,ex, and e.
Sine,tenus,pro and prae,
Add super,subter,sub and in
When State not Motion 'tis they mean.

or

Nouns denoting males in *a*
Are by meaning Mascula,
And masculine is found to be
Hadria, the Adriatic Sea.

I can also recall a prose, somewhat surrealistic, mnemonic I made up myself when studying chemistry in order to remember the metals in group II.

Are (arsenic) any (antimony) taxis (tin) made (manganese) like (lead) corpulent (copper) business (bismuth) charlatans (cadmium)?

The oddest mnemonics I have come across are in Sigmund Spaeth's *Great Symphonies and How to Recognize Them,* intended, apparently, to help schoolchildren taking classes in musical appreciation.

Beethoven still is great
In the symphony he numbers Eight.

This music is real, and not just a dream:
'Tis Schubert, not Mozart, who composed this theme.

This music has a less pathetic strain,
It sounds more sane and not so full of pain,
Sorrow is ended, grief may be mended,
It seems Tchaikovsky will be calm again.

I am a little puzzled by his words for Tchaikovsky's Fifth
Symphony. Admirable as the sentiments may be, I cannot see
how they can help a student to remember either the name of
the composer or the number of the Symphony.

Tell every nation, all of creation,
That it is time we should end all warfare:
Utter it loudly, utter it proudly,
Ye who are wise, may ye bring your powers to bear,
No more inciting madmen to fighting . . .

Mole, The

⋇⧜⋇

A Dead Mole

Strong-shouldered mole,
That so much lived below the ground,
Dug, fought and loved, hunted and fed,
For you to raise a mound
Was as for us to make a hole;
What wonder now that being dead
Your body lies here stout and square
Buried within the blue vault of the air?

ANDREW YOUNG

Money

The King's Coins

They laid the coins before the council.
Kay, the king's steward, wise in economics, said:
"Good; these cover the years and the miles
and talk one style's dialects to London and Omsk.
Traffic can hold now and treasure be held,
streams are bridged and mountains of ridged space
tunnelled; gold dances deftly over frontiers.
The poor have choice of purchase, the rich of rents,
and events move now in a smoother control
than the swords of lords or the orisons of nuns.
Money is the medium of exchange."

Taliessin's look darkened; his hand shook
while he touched the dragons; he said, "We had a good
          thought.
Sir, if you made verse, you would doubt symbols.
I am afraid of the little loosed dragons.
When the means are autonomous, they are deadly; when
          words
escape from verse they hurry to rape souls;
when sensation slips from intellect, except the tyrant;
the brood of carriers levels the good they carry.
We have taught our images to be free; are ye glad?
are we glad to have brought convenient heresy to Logres?"

The Archbishop answered the lords;
his words went up through a slope of calm air:
"Might may take symbols and folly make treasure,
and greed bid God, who hides himself for man's pleasure
by occasion, hide himself essentially: this abides—
that the everlasting house the soul discovers
is always another's; we must lose our own ends;

we must always live in the habitation of our lovers,
my friend's shelter for me, mine for him.
This is the way of this world in the day of that other's;
make yourselves friends by means of the riches of iniquity,
for the wealth of the self is the health of the self exchanged.
What saith Heraclitus?—and what is the City's breath?—
dying each other's life, living each other's death.
Money is a medium of exchange."

CHARLES WILLIAMS

Money is human happiness in the abstract: he, then, who is no longer capable of enjoying human happiness in the concrete devotes himself utterly to money.

SCHOPENHAUER

Everyone, even the richest and most munificent of men, pays much by cheque more lightheartedly than he pays little in specie.

MAX BEERBOHM

Nothing knits man to man like the frequent passage from hand to hand of cash.

W. SICKERT

I am not sure just what the unpardonable sin is, but I believe it is a disposition to evade the payment of small bills.

E. HUBBARD

Many priceless things can be bought.

MARIA VON EBNER-ESCHENBACH

You will never find people laboring to convince you that you may live very happily upon a plentiful fortune.

DR. JOHNSON

Two evenings spent at *La Scala*, Milan, one of them standing up, the other sitting down. On the first evening, I was continuously conscious of the existence of the spectators who were seated. On the second evening, I was completely unconscious of the existence of the spectators who were standing up (and of those who were seated also).

SIMONE WEIL

If the rich could hire other people to die for them, the poor could make a wonderful living.

Yiddish proverb

Names, Proper

⋅ᵉᵍᵉ⋅

Proper names are poetry in the raw. Like all poetry they are untranslatable. Someone who is translating into English a German novel, the hero of which is named *Heinrich,* will leave the name as it is; he will not Anglicize it into *Henry.*

The early epic poets, composing for an audience with the same mythology, heroic legends, topography as themselves, had half their poetic work done for them. Later, when the poet's audience became a cultured elite, their cultural background was still the same as his own: Milton, for example, could assume that any name taken from Greek and Roman mythology or from the Bible would be familiar to his readers. A modern poet, on the other hand, can hardly use a single proper name without wondering whether he ought not to footnote it. In 1933 I wrote a poem in which the name *Garbo* appeared, assuming, I think rightly, that at that time her name was a household word. When, after the War, Mr. Richard Hoggart included the poem in a selection he had made from my work, he felt it necessary to gloss the name.

With knowledge of the name comes a distincter recognition and knowledge of the thing.

H. D. THOREAU

Words do not change their meaning so drastically in the course of centuries as, in our minds, names do in the course of a year or two.

M. PROUST

The first book of Moses cites as one of the distinctive marks of man: to give animals names. Now it is characteristic of the ordinary man, the man of the people, to have that gift. If the ordinary man sees a bird for some years, which is not normally seen, he immediately gives it a name, and a characteristic name. But take ten learned men and how incapable they are of finding a name. What a satire on them when one reads scientific works and sees the names which come from the people, and then the silly miserable names when once in a while a learned man has to think of a name. Usually they can think of nothing better than calling the animal or the plant after their own names.

SØREN KIERKEGAARD
(trans. A. Dru)

NAMES FOR THE GREEN WOODPECKER

Sprite
Hickway
Woodspite
Popinjay
Yaffle
Highoe
Rindtabberer
Yaffingale
Green Peck
Yuckel
Cutbill
Rain Pie
Nickerpecker
Woodweele

NAMES FOR THE CUCKOO-PINT

Aaron
Adam-and-Eve
Adders Meat
Bloody-Man's-Finger
Bobbin-Joan
Bulls-and-Cows
Calf's-Foot
Friar's-Cowl
Lamb-in-a-Pulpit
Lily Grass
Nightingales
Wake-Robin

NAMES OF VEINS IN THE LEAD-MINING DISTRICT OF TIDESWELL, DERBYSHIRE

Dirtland Rake
Bacchus Pipe
Kettle-End Vein
Moss Rake

Dinah's Rake
Hunt's Coldberry
Barbara Load
Friarfold Hush

Chapmaiden Rake	Reformer's
Tideslaw	Legrim's Palfrey
Pearson's Venture	Horse-buttock
Hubnub	Blobber
Pyenest	Flappy
Old Nestor's Pipe	Modesty Flat

NAMES FOR THE GENITALS

Male	*Female*
Bald-headed Hermit	Ace of Spades
Dr. Johnson	Almanack
Fiddle-bow	Cabbage
Silent (one-eyed) Flute	Fart-Daniel
Goose's Neck	Fig
Hampton Wick	Front-Attic (Garden)
Jack-in-the-Cellar	Fumbler's Hall
Ladyweave	Garden Gate
Nimrod	Goldfinch's Nest
Stargazer	Grotto
Tackle	Gyvel
Titmouse	Jacob's Ladder
Donkey	Leather Lane
Giggle-Stick	Lobster Pot
Impudence	Mother of St. Patrick
Power	Milliner's Shop
Rector	Jack Nasty-Face
	Oyster
	Penwiper
	Purse
	Receipt of Custom
	Regulator
	Hans Carvel's Ring
	Saddle
	Sportsman's Gap
	Sugar Basin
	Teazle
	Growler

Trench Nomenclature

Genius named them, as I live! What but genius could compress
In a title what man's humour said to man's supreme distress?
Jacob's Ladder ran reversed, from earth to a fiery pit extending,
With not angels but poor Angles, those for the most part descending.
Thence *Brocks Benefit* commanded endless fireworks by two nations,
Yet some voices there were raised against the rival coruscations.
Picturedome peeped out upon a dream, not Turner could surpass,
And presently the picture moved, and greyed with corpses and morass.
So down south; and if remembrance travel north, she marvels yet
At the sharp Shakespearean names, and with sad mirth her eyes are wet.
The Great Wall of China rose, a four-foot breastwork, fronting guns
That, when the word dropped, beat at once its silly ounces with brute tons;
Odd *Krab Krawl* on paper looks, and odd the foul-breathed alley twisted,
As one feared to twist there too, if *Minnie*, forward quean, insisted.
Where the Yser at *Dead End* floated on its bloody waters
Dead and rotten monstrous fish, note (east) *The Pike and Eel* headquarters.
Ah, such names and apparitions! name on name! what's in a name?
From the fable's vase the genie in his shattering horror came.

EDMUND BLUNDEN

Naming Animals

Birds are given human christian names in accordance with the species to which they belong more easily than are other zoological classes, because they can be permitted to resemble men for the very reason that they are so different. They are feathered, winged, oviparous, and they are also physically separated from human society by the element in which it is their privilege to move. As a result of this fact, they form a community which is independent of our own but, precisely because of this independence, appears to us like another society, homologous to that in which we live: birds love freedom; they build themselves homes in which they live a family life and nurture their young; they often engage in social relations with other members of their species; and they communicate with them by acoustic means recalling articulate language.

Consequently everything objective conspires to make us think of the bird world as a metaphorical human society. . . . Now, this metaphorical relation which is imagined between the society of birds and the society of men, is accompanied by a procedure of naming, itself of a metonymical order . . . when species of birds are christened "Pierrot," "Margot," or "Jacquot," these names are drawn from a portion which is the preserve of human beings and the relation of bird names to human names is thus that of part to whole.

The position is exactly the reverse in the case of dogs. Not only do they not form an independent society; as "domestic" animals they are part of human society, although with so low a place in it that we should not dream of following the example of some Australians and Amerindians in designating them in the same way as human beings—whether what is in question are proper names or kinship terms. On the contrary, we allot them a special series: "Azor," "Medor," "Sultan," "Fido," "Diane" (the last of these is of course a human christian name but in the first instance conceived as mythological). Nearly all these are like stage names, forming a series parallel to the names people bear in ordinary life or, in other words, metaphorical names. Consequently, when the relation between (human and animal) species is socially conceived as metaphorical, the relation between the respective systems of naming takes on a metonymical character; and when the relation between species is conceived as metonymical, the system of naming assumes a metaphorical character.

Let us now consider another case, that of cattle, the social position of which is metonymical (they form part of our technical and economic system) but different from that of dogs in that cattle are more overtly treated as "objects" and dogs as "subjects". . . . Now, the names given to cattle . . . are generally descriptive terms, referring to the colour of their coats, their bearing or temperament: "Rustaud," "Rousset," "Blanchette," "Douce," etc. These names often have a metaphorical character but they differ from the names given to dogs in that they are epithets coming from the syntagmatic chain, while the latter come from a paradigmatic series; the former thus tend to derive from speech, the latter from language.

Finally, let us consider the names given to horses—not ordinary horses whose place approximates more or less closely to that of cattle or that of dogs according to the class and occupation of their owner, and is made even more uncertain by the rapid technological changes of recent times, but racehorses, whose sociological position is clearly distinguishable from the cases already examined. The first question is how to define their position. They cannot be said to constitute an independent society after the manner of birds, for they are products of human industry and they are born and live as isolated individuals juxtaposed in stud farms devised for their sake. On the other hand, they do not form part of human society either as subjects or as objects. Rather, they constitute the desocialized condition of a private society: that which lives off race-courses or frequents them. Another difference, in the system of naming, corresponds to these, although two reservations must be made in drawing this comparison: the names given to racehorses are chosen in accordance with particular rules which differ for thoroughbreds and half-breds and they display an eclecticism which draws on learned literature rather than oral tradition. This said, there is no doubt that there is a significant contrast between the names of racehorses and those of birds, dogs or cattle. They are rigorously individualized since . . .

two individuals cannot have the same name; and, although they share with the names given to cattle the feature of being formed by drawing upon the syntagmatic chain: "Ocean," "Azimuth," "Opera," "Belle-de-Nuit," "Telegraphe," "Luciole," "Orvietan," "Weekend," "Lapis-Lazuli," etc., they are distinguished from them by the absence of descriptive connotation.

Their creation is entirely unrestricted so long as they satisfy the requirement of unambiguous individuation and adhere to the particular rules referred to above. Thus, while cattle are given descriptive names formed out of words of discourse, the names assigned to racehorses are words from discourse which rarely, if ever, describe them. The former type of name perhaps resembles a nickname [*surnom*] and these latter perhaps merit the title of sub-names [*sous-nom*] as it is in this second domain that the most extreme arbitrariness reigns.

To sum up: birds and dogs are relevant in connection with human society either because they suggest it by their own social life (which men look on as an imitation of theirs), or alternatively because, having no social life of their own, they form part of ours.

Cattle, like dogs, form part of human society, but as it were, asocially, since they verge on objects. Finally racehorses, like birds, form a series disjoined from human society, but like cattle, lacking in intrinsic sociability. If, therefore, birds are *metaphorical human beings* and dogs, *metonymical human beings*, cattle may be thought of as *metonymical inhuman beings* and racehorses as *metaphorical inhuman beings*. . . .

LÉVI-STRAUSS

Star Names

For the names of the group of the Hyades the following explanations have been offered.

(1) The Hyades are so called because they were the sisters of Hyas, whose untimely end—of which there is more than one account—they are ever lamenting; whence their association with a season of moisture. This is a possible explanation of the name Hyades, but does not help us to find one for the name Hyas.

(2) The shape of the Hyades reminds us of a capital V, and must have reminded the ancient Greek of their letter Upsilon. The name of Hyades, therefore, must originally mean simply the "the V stars".

This explanation has found a modern supporter in the great scholar Buttmann, whose argument, however, seems to lead decidedly rather towards its rejection than its acceptance.

He points out that the bright stars of Cassiopeia, if viewed the right way up, form a conspicuous capital W. Is it not certain, he asks, that if we had now for the first time to name the constellations, unbiassed, as we are now, by the tales of our grandfathers, we should call this bright and unmistakeable group, "the W"?

Perhaps we might, but as a matter of fact we do not. And that our ancestors under similar conditions would have done so seems much less probable. For on the one hand, whereas nowadays we can all read—even alas! in these days base advertisements scrawled upon the sky itself—it is exceedingly doubtful whether in pre-Homeric times, from which the name of the Hyades certainly descends, the vast majority of the people who used the name had any familiarity at all with written characters. And on the other hand, it is a pure assumption that the first people to notice that the Hyades were like a V were not already provided with a name for the group.

(3) The word Hyades ('Υάδες) is connected with ὕειν, "to rain". It means therefore "the rainy stars", just as the Pleiades, connected with πλεῖν, "to sail", means "the stars of the sailing season". It may seem strange that two groups, so near each other in the sky, should have such different meteorological characters, but whereas it is the morning rising of the Pleiades that may have inaugurated the sailing season, it is the morning setting of the Hyades which may have been taken to announce, or even to cause, the rains. This took place in November.

There can, I think, be no doubt that such meteorological explanation is far more satisfactory as applied to the Hyades than it is in the case of the Pleiades. For one thing, there is evidence that the Hyades were actually regarded by plain men as bringers of rain: in the *Ion* of Euripides we find them described as the surest of all such signs possessed by the seaman. And for another, the reasons for this surety are apparent: the opening of a rainy season is a much more definite and observable thing than that of good boating weather, and moreover the Hyades are not, like the Pleiades, a close swarm of faint stars, but contain one conspicuous member, the bright star now known as Aldebaran, remarkable to the ancients, as to us, not only for its magnitude but for its color. The date on which such a star could for the last time be seen to go down, before the light of dawn made it invisible, could be fixed with comparative precision.

But for all that, I cannot believe that the rainy Hyades had no name before they were found to be rainy, and greatly prefer the next explanation, namely:

(4) The word Ὑάδες is connected, not with ὕειν, "to rain", but with ὗς, "a swine". The Hyades were originally seen as a litter of pigs, or perhaps rather as a "sounder" of wild swine.

Perhaps the reluctance of critics, ancient and modern, to accept this explanation may have been partly caused by a feeling that there is nothing at all celestial about the pig as he is usually regarded by civilised man. This feeling must certainly go back as far as the time of Circe. But the domestic pig is degenerate. No one who has seen the wild boar in freedom has ever thought of him as an ignoble animal, and no one has expressed admiration of him more warmly than it is expressed in Homer. Why is it more unlikely that the Greeks should have seen Aldebaran and his companions as swine than that the Arabs, according to Al Sufi, should have seen them as camels? And that they did so is strongly suggested by the curious fact that the old Roman name for the group seems to have been *suculae*, "little pigs". It is true that Cicero disdains this piece of evidence, apparently considering that *suculae* is merely a mistranslation of the Greek ὑάδες. But this seems very improbable. The natural meaning of Cicero's words and those of Pliny after him is that *nostri*, the Romans of their day, did really call the Hyades *suculae*, and that *suculae* did really mean "little pigs".

The object of this chapter has been to show, not merely that it is untrue to say, with the old scholiast, that most star-names have been given for purposes of instruction, but that it is actually the reverse of the truth. Even if we rank among instructors such rude folk as Kepler's sailors and husbandmen, we shall find that the names they used have for the most part no connection with the functions which the stars bearing these names have been found to discharge. The vast majority of star-names, it is here contended, are of popular origin and have usually a descriptive meaning.

C . C . J . WEBB

Napoleon

Now that all the facts about Napoleon's life, including his table conversation, have been unearthed and published, it seems a thousand pities that, when he surrendered to them, the British did not immediately hang him from the yardarm and sink his body in the sea, as an enemy of civilization.

Just how appalling political and social conditions in England at the time must have been is indicated by the fact that many liberal-minded young Englishmen could think of him as a liberator. How would one feel if, in the following poem, the refrain ran, *Since Hitler killed himself in Berlin?*

Song

When working blackguards come to blows,
And give or take a bloody nose,
Shall injuries try such gods as those,
    Now Nap lies at Saint Helena?

No, let the Great Unpaid decide,
Without appeal, on tame bull's hide,
Ash-planted well, or fistified,
    Now Nap died at Saint Helena.

When Sabbath stills the dizzy mill,
Shall Cutler Tom, or Grinder Bill,

On footpaths wander where they will,
    Now Nap lies at Saint Helena?

No, let them curse, but *feel* our power;
Dogs! let them spend their idle hour
Where burns the highways' dusty shower;
    For Nap died at Saint Helena.

Huzza! the rascal Whiglings work
For better man than Hare and Burke,
And envy Algerine and Turk,
    Since Nap died at Saint Helena.

Then close each path that sweetly climbs
Suburban hills, where village chimes
Remind the rogues of other times,
    Ere Nap died at Saint Helena.

We tax their bread, restrict their trade;
To toil for us, their hands are made;
Their doom is sealed, their prayer is prayed;
    Nap perished at Saint Helena.

Dogs! would they toil and fatten too?
They grumble still, as dogs will do:
We conquered *them* at Waterloo;
    And Nap lies at Saint Helena.

But shall the villains meet and prate
In crowds about affairs of state?
Ride, yeomen, ride! Act, magistrate!
    Nap perished at Saint Helena.

EBENEZER ELLIOTT

Narcissus

A mirror has no heart but plenty of ideas.

MALCOLM DE CHAZAL

Narcissus leant over the spring, enthralled by the only man in whose eyes he had ever dared—or been given the chance—to forget himself.

Narcissus leant over the spring, enchanted by his own ugliness which he prided himself upon having the courage to admit.

DAG HAMMARSKJÖLD

Egoism puts the feelings in Indian file.

MALCOLM DE CHAZAL

Every man likes the smell of his own farts.

Icelandic proverb

Every stink that fights the ventilator thinks it is Don Quixote.

STANISLAUS LEC

Nature

Many years ago, as now, my mind strove with eager delight to study and discover the creative life of Nature. It is eternal unity in manifold manifestation; the great is little, the little is great, and everything after its kind; ever changing and yet preserving itself, near and far, and far and near, and so shaping and re-shaping itself—to marvel at it is what I am here for.

The reason why I prefer the society of nature to any other is that nature is always right and the error, if any, can only be on my side. But if I hold converse with men, they will err, then I will, and so on forever, and we never get to see matters clearly.

Everything factual is, in a sense, theory. The blue of the sky exhibits the basic laws of chromatics. There is no sense in looking for something behind phenomena: they *are* theory.

GOETHE

There is no nature at an instant.

A. N. WHITEHEAD

Repetition is the only form of permanence that nature can achieve.

G. SANTAYANA

In the physical world, one cannot increase the size or quantity of anything without changing its quality. Similar figures exist only in pure geometry.

PAUL VALÉRY

Nature has wit, humor, fantasy, etc. Among animals and plants one finds natural caricatures. Nature is at her wittiest in the animal kingdom; there she is humorous throughout. The mineral and vegetable kingdoms bear more the stamp of fantasy; in the world of man, rational nature is bejeweled with fantasy and wit.

Are not plants, perhaps, the product of a feminine nature and a masculine spirit, animals the product of a masculine nature and a feminine spirit? Are not plants, as it were, the girls, animals the boys, of nature?

NOVALIS

How do we distinguish the oak from the beech, the horse from the ox, but by the bounding outline? How do we distinguish one face or countenance from another, but by the bounding line and its infinite inflections and movements. Leave out the line, and you leave out life itself; all is chaos again, and the line of the Almighty must be drawn out upon it before man or beast can exist.

WILLIAM BLAKE

The one who loves and understands a thing best will incline to use the personal pronouns in speaking of it. To him there is no neuter gender.

H. D. THOREAU

All colors are the friends of their neighbors and the lovers of their opposites.

No scent is a virgin.

MALCOLM DE CHAZAL

The extrahuman in the experience of the greatness of Nature. This does not allow itself to be reduced to an expression of our human reactions, nor can we share in it by expressing them. Unless we each find a way to chime in as one note in the organic whole, we shall only observe ourselves observing the interplay of its thousand components in a harmony outside our experience of it as harmony.

DAG HAMMARSKJÖLD

> And ich bowede my body · by-holdynge al a-boute,
> And seih the sonne and the see · and the sand after,
> Wher that briddes and bestes · by here makes yeden,
> Wilde wormes in wodes · and wonderful foules
> With fleckede fetheres · and of fele colours; . . .
> Briddes ich by-helde · in bosshes maden nestes,
> Hadde neuere weye wit · to worche the leste.
> Ich hadde wonder at wham · and wher that the pye
> Lernede legge styckes · that leyen in here neste;
> Ther is no wryght, as ich wene · sholde worche here nest
>   to paye.
> Yf eny mason therto · makede a molde
> With all here wyse castes · wonder me thynketh!
>   And yut ich meruaillede more · menye of tho bryddes

Hudden and heleden · durneliche here egges,
For no foul sholde hem funde · bote hus fere and hym-self.
And some treden, ich tok kepe · and on trees bredden,
And brouhten forth here bryddes · al aboue the grounde.
In maries and in mores · in myres and in wateres
Dompynges dyueden · 'deere god,' ich sayde,
'Where hadden these wilde suche witt · and at what scole?'
And when the pocok caukede · ther-of ich took kepe,
How vn-corteisliche the cok · hus kynde forth strenede,
And ferliche hadde of hus fairnesse · and of hus foule ledene.
    And siththe ich loked on the see · and so forth on the
        sterres,
Meny selcouth ich seih · aren nouht to seggen nouthe;
Ne what on floures in feldes · and of hure faire coloures,
How out of greot and of gras · grewe so meny huwes,
Somme soure and somme swete · selcouth me thouhte;
Of here kynde and of here colours · to carpen hit were to
    longe.

WILLIAM LANGLAND

If nature be regarded as the teacher and we poor human beings as her pupils, the human race presents a very curious picture. We all sit together at a lecture and possess the necessary principles for understanding it, yet we always pay more attention to the chatter of our fellow students than to the lecturer's discourse. Or, if our neighbor copies something down, we sneak it from him, stealing what he himself may have heard imperfectly, and add to it our own errors of spelling and opinion.

G. C. LICHTENBERG

In relation to nature, early man was so weak and nature so strong as to make man almost her slave. It was natural, therefore, that he should have dreamed of a future in which their relative positions would be reversed, a time when he would be the master and nature the slave.

We have already reached the point where there is almost nothing we cannot compel nature to do, but we are finding to our cost that nature cannot be enslaved without enslaving ourselves. If nobody or nothing in the universe is responsible for man, then we must conclude that man is responsible, to God, for the universe, just as Adam was made responsible for the Garden of Eden. This means that it is our task to discover what everything in the universe, from electrons upwards, could, to its betterment, become, but cannot become without our help. This means reintroducing into science the notion of teleology, long a dirty word. For our proper relation to nonliving things, the right analogy might be that of the sculptor. Every sculptor thinks of himself, not as someone who forcibly imposes a form on stone, but as someone who reveals a form already latent in it. For our relation to living creatures, the analogy might be that of the good trainer of animals. A well-trained, well-treated sheep dog is more of a dog than a wild one, just as a stray, terrified by ill-usage, or a spoilt lap dog has had its "dogginess" debased. We have to realize that every time we make an ugly lampstand, we are torturing helpless metal, every time we make a nuclear bomb we are corrupting the morals of a host of innocent neutrons below the age of consent.

Rhea

On her shut lids the lightning flickers,
Thunder explodes above her bed,
An inch from her lax arm the rain hisses;
Discrete she lies,

Not dead but entranced, dreamlessly
With slow breathing, her lips curved
In a half-smile archaic, her breast bare,
Hair astream.

The house rocks, a flood suddenly rising
Bears away bridges: oak and ash
Are shivered to the roots—royal green timber.
She nothing cares.

(Divine Augustus, trembling at the storm,
Wrapped sealskin on his thumb; divine Gaius
Made haste to hide himself in a deep cellar,
Distraught by fear.)

Rain, thunder, lightning: pretty children.
'Let them play,' her mother-mind repeats;
'They do no harm, unless from high spirits
Or by mishap.'

ROBERT GRAVES

Neighbor, Love of One's

Belief in the existence of other human beings as such is love.

To love our neighbor as ourselves does not mean that we should love all people equally, for I do not have an equal love for all the modes of existence of myself. Nor does it mean that we should never make them suffer, for I do not refuse to make myself suffer. But we should have with each person the relationship of one conception of the universe to another conception of the universe, and not to a part of it.

Standing in front of a human being, whoever it may be—not to wish him either immortal or dead.

SIMONE WEIL

We are not commanded (or forbidden) to love our mates, our children, our friends, our country because such affections come naturally to us and are good in themselves, although we may corrupt them. We are commanded to love our neighbor because our "natural" attitude toward the "other" is one of either indifference or hostility.

Most people really believe that the Christian commandments (e.g., to love one's neighbor as oneself) are intentionally a little too severe—like putting the clock ahead half an hour to make sure of not being late in the morning.

SØREN KIERKEGAARD

Two brethren made their way to the city to sell their handi-work: and when, in the city, they went different ways, divided one from the other, one of them fell into fornication. After a while came his brother, saying, "Brother, let us go back to our cell." But he made answer, "I am not coming." And the other questioned him, saying, "Wherefore, brother?" And he answered, "Because when thou dids't go from me, I ran into temptation, and I sinned in the flesh." But the other, anxious to help him, began to tell him, saying, "But so it happened with me: when I was sepa-rated from thee, I too ran into fornication. But let us go, and do penance together with all our might: and God will forgive us that are sinful men." And they came back to the monastery and told the old men what had befallen them, and they enjoined on them the penance they must do. But the one began his penance, not for himself but for his brother, as if he himself had sinned. And God, seeing his love and labor, after a few days revealed to one of the old men that for the great love of this brother who had not sinned He had forgiven the brother who had.

The Desert Fathers
(trans. Helen Waddell)

We found ourselves on the track with several car-loads of Japa-nese wounded. These unfortunates were on their own and with-out medical care.

No longer fit for action in Burma, they had been packed into railway cars which were being returned to Bangkok. They had been packed up and dropped off according to the make-up of the trains. Whenever one of them died en route he was thrown off into the jungle. The ones who survived to reach Bangkok pre-sumably would receive some kind of medical treatment. But they were given none on the way.

They were in a shocking state. I have never seen men filthier. Uniforms were encrusted with mud, blood and excrement. Their wounds, sorely inflamed and full of pus, crawled with maggots. The maggots, however, in eating the putrefying flesh, probably prevented gangrene.

It was apparent why the Japanese were so cruel to their prisoners. If they didn't care a tinker's damn for their own, why should they care for us?

The wounded men looked at us forlornly as they sat with their heads against the carriages, waiting for death. They had been discarded as expendable, the refuse of war. These were the enemy. They were more cowed and defeated than we had ever been.

Without a word most of the officers in my section unbuckled their packs, took out part of their ration and a rag or two, and, with water canteens in their hands, went over to the Japanese train.

Our guards tried to prevent us, bawling, "No goodka! No goodka!" But we ignored them and knelt down by the enemy to give water and food, to clean and bind up their wounds. Grateful cries of "Aragotto!" ("Thank you!") followed us when we left.

An allied officer from another section of the train had been taking it all in.

"What bloody fools you are!" he said to me.

"Have you never heard the story of the man who was going from Jerusalem to Jericho?" I asked him. . . .

"But that's different," the officer protested angrily. "That's in the Bible. These are the swine who have starved us and beaten us. These are our enemies." . . . He gave me a scornful glance and, turning his back, left me. . . .

I regarded my comrades with wonder. Eighteen months ago they would have joined readily in the destruction of our captors had they fallen into their hands. Now these same officers were dressing the enemy's wounds.

ERNEST GORDON

Numbers

❧⊱🙞❧

Numbers, Friendly and Perfect

Pythagoras, when asked what a friend was, replied: "One who is the other I, such are 220 and 284." Expressed in modern terminology this meant: the divisors of 284 are 1, 2, 4, 71, and 142, and these add up to 220; while the divisors of 220 are 1, 2, 4, 5, 10, 11, 20, 22, 44, 55, and 110, and these in turn add up to 284. Such numbers the Pythagoreans called *amicable* numbers.

. . . The general question whether there exists an infinity of such couples has not been settled to this day, although almost a hundred are known. . . .

Then there were the *perfect* numbers. Consider first a number such as 14; add up its divisors which are 1, 2, and 7; we get 10. The number 14 therefore is greater than the sum of its divisors, and is for this reason called *excessive*. On the other hand the sum of the divisors of 12 is 16—greater than 12, and for this reason 12 is said to be *defective*. But in a *perfect* number there is neither excess nor deficiency; the number equals the sum of its own divisors.

The smallest perfect numbers are 6 and 28, and were known to the Hindus as well as to the Hebrews. Some commentators of the Bible regard 6 and 28 as the basic numbers of the Supreme Architect. They point to the 6 days of creation and the 28 days of the lunar cycle. Others go so far as to explain the imperfection of the second creation by the fact that eight souls, not six, were rescued in Noah's ark.

Said St. Augustine:

> Six is a number perfect in itself, and not because God created all things in six days; rather the converse is true; God created all things in six days because this number is perfect, and it would have been perfect even if the work of the six days did not exist.

The next two perfect numbers seem to have been the discovery of Nicomachus. We quote from his *Arithmetica*.

> . . . the perfect are both easily counted and drawn up in a fitting order: for only one is found in the units, 6; and only one in the tens, 28; and a third in the depth of the hundreds, 496; as a fourth the one, on the border of the thousands, that is short of the ten thousand, 8128. It is their uniform attribute to end in 6 or 8, and they are invariably even.

If Nocomachus meant to imply that there was a perfect number in every decimal class, he was wrong, for the fifth perfect number is 33, 550, 336. But his guess was excellent in every other respect. While the impossibility of an odd perfect number was never proved, no example of such a number is known. Furthermore it is true that an even perfect number must end in either 6 or 8. . . .

Numbers, Irrational

. . . From Egypt the Pythagoreans imported the "golden" triangle, the sides of which were in the ratio 3:4:5. Soon other "Pythagorean" triangles, such as 5:12:13 and 8:15:17, were discovered. The conviction that all triangles were *rational* had evidence to feed on. . . .

The contemplation of such triangles led to a capital discovery, which to this day bears the name of Pythagoras and which is one of the basic theorems of classical geometry. It reads: *In any right triangle the sum of the squares built on the legs is equal to the square built on the hypothenuse.* . . .

[Pythagoras] and his disciples attached the greatest importance to it; for *therein they saw the inherent union between geometry and arithmetic*, a new confirmation of their dictum: "Number rules the universe."

But the triumph was short-lived. Indeed, one of the immediate consequences of the theorem was another discovery: *the diagonal of the square is incommensurable with its side.* Who it was that first established this, and how it was done, will probably remain a mystery forever. . . . But . . . there is little doubt that it caused great consternation in the ranks of the Pythagoreans. . . . *Alogon*, the *unutterable*, these incommensurables were called, and the members of the order were sworn not to divulge their existence to outsiders. . . .

Says Proclus:

> It is told that those who first brought out the irrationals from concealment into the open perished in shipwreck, to a man. For the unutterable and the formless must needs be concealed. . . .

Zero

. . . Any attempt to make a permanent record of a counting-board operation would meet the obstacle that such an entry as ≡ = may represent any one of several numbers: 32, 302, 320, 3002, and 3020 among others. In order to avoid this ambiguity it is essential to have some method of representing the gaps, i.e., what is needed is a *symbol for an empty column*.

We see therefore that no progress was possible until a symbol was invented for an *empty* class, a symbol for *nothing*, our modern *zero*. The concrete mind of the ancient Greeks could not conceive the void as a number, let alone endow the void with a symbol.

And neither did the unknown Hindu see in zero the symbol of nothing. The Indian term for zero was *sunya*, which meant *empty* or *blank*, but had no connotation of "void" or "nothing." And so, from all appearances, the discovery of zero was an accident brought about by an attempt to make an unambiguous permanent record of a counting-board operation. . . .

. . . When the Arabs of the tenth century adopted the Indian numeration, they translated the Indian *sunya* by their own *sifr*, which meant empty in Arabic. When the Indo-Arabic numeration was first introduced into Italy, *sifr* was latinized into *zephirum*. This happened at the beginning of the thirteenth century, and in the course of the next hundred years the word underwent a series of changes which culminated in the Italian *zero*.

About the same time Jordanus Nemerarius was introducing the

Arabic system into Germany. He kept the Arabic word, changing it slightly to *cifra*. That for some time in the learned circles of Europe the word *cifra* and its derivatives denoted zero is shown by the fact that the great Gauss, the last of the mathematicians of the nineteenth century who wrote in Latin, still used *cifra* in this sense. In the English language the word *cifra* has become *cipher* and has retained its original meaning of zero.

The attitude of the common people toward this new numeration is reflected by the fact that soon after its introduction into Europe, the word *cifra* was used as a secret sign. . . . The verb *decipher* remains as a momument of these early days.

. . . the essential part played by zero in this new system [of reckoning] did not escape the notice of the masses. Indeed, they identified the whole system with its most striking feature, the *cifra*, and this explains how this word in its different forms, *ziffer*, *chiffre*, etc., came to receive the meaning of numeral, which it has in Europe today.

This double meaning, the popular *cifra* standing for numeral and the *cifra* of the learned signifying zero, caused considerable confusion . . . the matter was eventually settled by adopting the Italian zero in the sense in which it is used today.

The same interest attaches to the word *algorithm*. As the term is used today, it applies to any mathematical procedure consisting of an indefinite number of steps, each step applying to the result of the one preceding it. But between the tenth and fifteenth centuries *algorithm* was synonymous with positional numeration. We now know that the word is merely a corruption of Al Kworesmi, the name of the Arabian mathematician of the ninth century whose book (in Latin translation) was the first work on this subject to reach Western Europe.

Today, when positional numeration has become a part of our daily life, it seems that the superiority of this method, the compactness of its notation, the ease and elegance it introduced into calculations, should have assured the rapid and sweeping acceptance of it. In reality, the transition, far from being immediate, extended over long centuries. The struggle between the *Abacists*, who defended the old traditions, and the *Algorists*, who advocated the reform, lasted from the eleventh to the fifteenth century. . . . In some places Arabic numerals were banned from official documents; in others, the art was prohibited altogether. And, as usual, *prohibition* did not succeed in abolishing, but merely served to spread *bootlegging,* ample evidence of which is found in the thirteenth century archives of Italy, where, it appears, merchants were using the Arabic numerals as a sort of secret code.

Binary System (Torres Straits)

1 urapun
2 okosa
3 okosa-urapun
4 okosa-okosa
5 okosa-okosa-urapun
6 okosa-okosa-okosa

Quinary System
(Api Language of the New Hebrides)

tâi
lua
tolu
vari
luna (hand)
otai (other hand)
olua
otolu
oviar
lua luna (hands)

Vigesimal System (Maya Language)

1	hun
20	kal
400	bak
8000	pic
160,000	calab

| 3,200,000 | kinchel |
| 64,000,000 | alce |

TOBIAS DANTZIG

Counting Rhymes

Eena, deena, deina, duss,
Catala, weena, weina, wuss,
Spit, spot, must be done,
Twiddlum, twaddlum, twenty-one.

Un, deux, trois, j'irai dans le bois,
Quatre, cinq, six, chercher des cerises,
Sept, huit, neuf, dans mon panier neuf;
Dix, onze, douze, elles seront toutes rouges;
Treize, quatorze, quinze, pour mon petit Prince;
Seize, dix-sept, dix-huit, je les apporterai tout de suite.
Dix-neuf, vingt, pour qu'elles prennent leurs bains.

Eine kleine weisse Bohne wollte gern nach Engelland,
Engelland war zugeschlossen, und der Schlüssel war zer-
       brochen.
Bauer bind den Pudel an,
Dass er mich nicht beissen kann.
Beisst er mich, so kost es dich
Tausend Thaler sicherlich.

Nursery Library, My

As readers, we remain in the nursery stage so long as we cannot distinguish between taste and judgment, so long, that is,
as the only possible verdicts we can pass on a book are two:
this I like; this I don't like.

For an adult reader, the possible verdicts are five: I can see this is good and I like it; I can see this is good but I don't like it; I can see this is good and, though at present I don't like it, I believe that with perseverance I shall come to like it; I can see that this is trash but I like it; I can see that this is trash and I don't like it.

NONFICTIONAL PROSE

T. Sopwith	*A Visit to Alston Moor*
?	*Underground Life*
?	*Machinery for Metalliferous Mines*
His Majesty's Stationary Office	*Lead and Zinc Ores of Northumberland and Alston Moor*
?	*The Edinburgh School of Surgery*
?	*Dangers to Health* (a Victorian treatise, illustrated, on plumbing, good and bad)

FICTION

Beatrix Potter	All her books
Hans Andersen	*The Snow Queen*
Morris and Magnusson	*Icelandic Stories*
Lewis Carroll	The two *Alice* books
George Macdonald	*The Princess and the Goblin*
Jules Verne	*The Child of the Cavern, Journey to the Centre of the Earth*
Rider Haggard	*King Solomon's Mines, She*
Dean Farrar	*Eric, or Little by Little*
Ballantyne	*The Cruise of the Cachelot*
Conan Doyle	The *Sherlock Holmes* stories

POETRY

Hoffmann	*Struwel Peter*
Hilaire Belloc	*Cautionary Tales*
Harry Graham	*Ruthless Rhymes for Heartless Homes*

O*pera, Soap*

❧❧❧

While it flourished, it seemed awful, but now that television
has killed it, one remembers it with a nostalgic regret.

DISEASES OF

The people of Soapland are subject to a set of special ills. Temporary blindness, preceded by dizzy spells and headaches, is a
common affliction of Soapland people. The condition usually
clears up in six or eight weeks, but once in a while it develops
into brain tumor and the patient dies. One script writer, apparently forgetting that General Mills was the sponsor of his serial,
had one of his women characters go temporarily blind because of
an allergy to chocolate cake. There was hell to pay, and the
writer had to make the doctor in charge of the patient hastily
change his diagnosis. Amnesia strikes almost as often in Soapland
as the common cold in our world. There have been as many as
eight or nine amnesia cases on the air at one time. The hero of
Rosemary stumbled around in a daze for months last year. When
he regained his memory, he found that in his wanderings he had
been lucky enough to marry a true-blue sweetie. The third major
disease is paralysis of the legs. This scourge usually attacks the
good males. Like mysterious blindness, loss of the use of the legs
may be either temporary or permanent. The hero of *Life Can Be
Beautiful* was confined to a wheel chair until his death last
March, but young Dr. Malone, who was stricken with paralysis a
year ago, is up and around again. I came upon only one crippled
villain in 1947: Spencer Hart rolled through a three-month sequence of *Just Plain Bill* in a wheel chair. When their men are
stricken, the good women become nobler than ever. A disabled
hero is likely to lament his fate and indulge in self-pity now and
then, but his wife or sweetheart never complains. She is capable

of twice as much work, sacrifice, fortitude, endurance, ingenuity, and love as before. Joyce Jordan, M. D., had no interest in a certain male until he lost the use of both legs and took to a wheel chair. Then love began to bloom in her heart. . . .

The children of the soap towns are subject to pneumonia and strange fevers, during which their temperatures run to 105 or 106. Several youngsters are killed every year in automobile accidents or die of mysterious illnesses. Infantile paralysis and cancer are never mentioned in serials, but Starr, the fretful and errant wife in *Ma Perkins*, died of tuberculosis in March as punishment for her sins. There are a number of Soapland ailments that are never named or are vaguely identified by the doctors as "island fever" or "mountain rash." A variety of special maladies affect the glands in curious ways. At least three Ivorytown and Rinsoville doctors are baffled for several months every year by strange seizures and unique symptoms.

Next to physical ills, the commonest misfortune in the world of soap is false accusation of murder. . . .

TIME IN

Compared to the swift flow of time in the real world, it is a glacier movement. It took one male character in a soap opera three days to get an answer to the simple question, "Where have you been?" If, in *When a Girl Marries*, you missed an automobile accident that occurred on a Monday broadcast, you could pick it up the following Thursday and find the leading woman character still unconscious and her husband still moaning over her beside the wrecked car. In one sequence of *Just Plain Bill*, the barber of Hartville said, "It doesn't seem possible to me that Ralph Wilde arrived here only yesterday." It didn't seem possible to me, either, since Ralph Wilde had arrived, as mortal time goes, thirteen days before. Bill recently required four days to shave a man in the living room of the man's house. A basin of hot water Bill had placed on a table Monday (our time) was still hot on Thursday, when his customer stopped talking and the barber went to work.

JAMES THURBER

Owls, Barn

Up to the year 1813, the barn owl had a sad time of it at Walton Hall. Its supposed mournful notes alarmed the aged housekeeper. She knew full well what sorrow it had brought into other houses when she was a young woman; and there was enough of mischief in the midnight wintry blast, without having it increased by the dismal screams of something which people knew very little about, and which everybody said was far too busy in the churchyard at night-time. Nay, it was a well-known fact, that if any person were sick in the neighbourhood, it would be for ever looking in at the window, and holding a conversation outside with some-body, they did not know whom. The gamekeeper agreed with her in everything she said on this important subject; and he al-ways stood better in her books, when he had managed to shoot a bird of this bad and mischievous family. However, in 1813, on my return from the wilds of Guiana, having suffered myself and learned mercy, I broke in pieces the code of penal laws which the knavery of the gamekeeper and the lamentable ignorance of the other servants had hitherto put in force, far too successfully, to thin the numbers of this poor, harmless, unsuspecting tribe. On the ruin of the old gateway, against which, tradition says, the waves of the lake have dashed for the better part of a thousand years, I made a place with stone and mortar about four feet square, and affixed a thick oaken stick firmly into it. Huge masses of ivy now quite cover it. In about a month or so after it was fin-ished, a pair of barn owls came and took up their abode in it. I threatened to strangle the keeper if ever, after this, he molested either the old birds or their young ones; and I assured the house-keeper that I would take upon myself the whole responsibility of all the sickness, woe, and sorrow that the new tenants might bring into the Hall. She made a low curtsy, as much as to say, "Sir, I fall into your will and pleasure." But I saw in her eye, that she had made up her mind to have to do with things of fearful and portentous shape, and to hear many a midnight wailing in the surrounding woods. I do not think that, up to the day of this old lady's death, which took place in her eighty-fourth year, she ever looked with pleasure or contentment on the barn owl, as it flew round the large sycamore trees which grew near the old ruined gateway.

CHARLES WATERTON

Paradise, The Earthly

There is an island far away, around which the sea-horses glisten, flowing on their white course against its shining shore; four pillars support it.

It is a delight to the eye, the plain which the hosts frequent in triumphant ranks; coracle races against chariot in the plain south of Findargad.

Pillars of white bronze are under it, shining through aeons of beauty, a lovely land through the ages of the world, on which many flowers rain down.

There is a huge tree there with blossom, on which the birds call at all hours; it is their custom that they all call together in concert every hour.

Colours of every hue gleam throughout the soft familiar fields; ranged round the music, they are ever joyful in the plain south of Argadnél.

Weeping and treachery are unknown in the pleasant familiar land; there is no fierce harsh sound there, but sweet music striking the ear.

Without sorrow, without grief, without death, without any sickness, without weakness, that is the character of Emhaim; such a marvel is rare.

Loveliness of a wondrous land, whose aspects are beautiful, whose view is fair, excellent; incomparable is its haze.

Then if one sees Airgthech, on which dragon-stones and crystals rain down, the sea makes the wave foam against the land, with crystal tresses from its mane.

Riches, treasures of every colour are in Cíuin, have they not been found? Listening to sweet music, drinking choice wine.

Golden chariots race across the plain of the sea rising with the tide to the sun; chariots of silver in Magh Mon, and of bronze without blemish.

Horses of golden yellow there on the meadow, other horses of purple colour; other noble horses beyond them, of the colour of the all-blue sky.

There comes at sunrise a fair man who lights up the level lands, he strides over the bright plain which the sea washes so that it becomes blood.

There comes a host across the clear sea, to the land they display their rowing; then they row to the bright stone from which a hundred songs arise.

Through the long ages it sings a melody which is not sad; the music swells up in choruses of hundreds, they do not expect decay nor death.

Emhnae of many shapes, beside the sea, whether it is near or whether it is far, where there are many thousands of motley-dressed women; the pure sea surrounds it.

If one has heard the sound of the music, the song of little birds from Imchíuin, a troop of women comes from the hill to the playing-field where it is.

Holiday-making and health come to the land around which laughter echoes; in Imchíuin with its purity come immortality and joy.

Through the perpetual good weather silver rains on the lands; a very white cliff under the glare of the sea, over which its heat spreads from the sun.

The host rides across Magh Mon, a lovely sport which is not weakly; in the many-coloured land with great splendour they do not expect decay nor death.

Listening to music in the night, and going to Ildathach the many-coloured land, a brilliance with clear splendour from which the white cloud glistens.

ANON.
Seventh–eighth-century Irish
(trans. K. H. Jackson)

Ambition not in thee
Do we expect to find,
Hydroptic of the wind;
Nor Envy with her food,
The Egyptian serpent brood;
Nor her, who though a human face surmounts,
Is a wild beast below,
A Sphinx persuasive, who
Makes the Narcissus new
Solicit echoes and disdain the founts;
Nor her who wastes, impertinent, in show
All the essential powder of her age.
O foolish Courtesy!
At whom the villagers sincere may laugh
Over their crooked staff.
O well found hermitage,
Whatever hour it be.

GÓNGORA
(trans. E. M. Wilson)

Penis Rivalry

Whether, as some psychologists believe, some women suffer from penis envy, I am not sure. I am quite certain, however, that all males without exception, whatever their age, suffer from penis rivalry, and that this trait has now become a threat to the future existence of the human race.

Behind every quarrel between men, whether individually or collectively, one can hear the taunt of a little urchin: "My prick (or my father's) is bigger than yours (or your father's), and can pee further."

Nearly all weapons, from the early spear and sword down to the modern revolver and rocket, are phallic symbols. Men, to be sure, also fashion traps, most forms of which are vaginal symbols, but they never take a pride in them as they do in their weapons. The epic poets frequently give a loving and detailed description of some weapon, and, when heroes exchange gifts in earnest of friendship, weapons figure predominantly. But where in literature can one find a loving description of a trap, or hear of one as a precious gift?

Today our phallic toys have become too dangerous to be tolerated. I see little hope for a peaceful world until men are excluded from the realm of foreign policy altogether and all decisions concerning international relations are reserved for women, preferably married ones.

I would go further and say that, while men should still as in the past be permitted to construct machines, it should be for women to decide what kinds of machines shall be constructed.

Phrase Books, Foreign

Compared with the compilers of phrase books for tourists traveling abroad, the so-called surrealist poets are amateurs. For example:

At the Doctor's

Is your digestion all right?
The medicine was no good.
Shake the bottle.
For external use only.
You have broken your arm.
He has fractured his skull.
I have had a bad concussion.
I am injured.
Have you sprained your ankle?
I must bandage your foot.
You are badly bruised.
He has an internal ulcer.
The illness gets better (worse).
Are you feeling better?
The cut is healed but you can see the scar.
I must bandage your wounds.
I can't hear.
I am deaf.
She is deaf and dumb.
You must go to an ear specialist.
Your middle-ear is inflamed.
Where does the oculist live?
I am shortsighted.
He is longsighted.
She is blind.
I need spectacles.
He squints a little.

VIOLA ELLIS
Serbo-Croatian Phrase Book

In 1945 an Italian-English phrase book was hastily compiled in Florence to promote a better understanding between the Florentines and British and American troops. It contained the following entry:

ITALIAN   ENGLISH
Posso presentare il conte.   Meet the cunt.

Plants

◄§§►

Most poems about plants are even more indifferent to their natural properties than poems about animals. (In both cases D. H. Lawrence is a happy exception.)

The Fear of Flowers

The nodding oxeye bends before the wind,
The woodbine quakes lest boys their flowers should find,
And prickly dog-rose, spite of its array,
Can't dare the blossom-seeking hand away,
While thistles wear their heavy knobs of bloom
Proud as a war-horse wears its haughty plume,
And by the roadside danger's self defy;
On commons where pined sheep and oxen lie,
In ruddy pomp and ever thronging mood
It stands and spreads like danger in a wood,
And in the village street, where meanest weeds
Can't stand untouched to fill their husks with seeds,
The haughty thistle o'er all danger towers,
In every place the very wasp of flowers.

JOHN CLARE

The Lettuce

People have included this among your praises—that once upon a time you are said to have cured Augustus when he was ill. I certainly would not have wished you to heal that man, infamous from having banished Ovid and slain Cicero. But I imagine that you knew neither of them, and I do not wonder that you were willing to confer a favour on the tyrant of the world. You are indeed a useful medicine to all tyrants, and madness flees when touched with your divine coolness. Gird, I pray you, their heads with a better crown; and, if you can, bring succour through them to this world. At your command, love, the greatest of tyrants, sometimes abandons inflamed hearts. It is a false love, for you do not attempt to expel true love, which has the title of a just king and deserves to be loved. That dog-star lust which slays green things with its fire and gives birth to monsters is rightly hated by you.

ABRAHAM COWLEY
(trans. from Latin by Frederick Brittain)

The ageing of a plant is quite different from that of an animal. In an animal the processes of growth occur all over the body until maturity, and the animal may then continue to live a long time even though growth has stopped. In a plant the processes of growth are localised at the growing tips of the stems. In a corn plant, for example, cells at the tip are continually dividing to form new leaves. Above the youngest leaves there always remains a zone of newly formed cells, called the meristem, from which subsequent growth will come. The manner of growth of a corn plant from its tip is, to use a far-fetched analogy, rather like the growth of a knitted woolen sock from the needles at one end. It follows, therefore, that a plant is not the same age all over; its lower leaves may be three or four months old while the uppermost leaf is only a few hours old. So long as the plant is growing, new meristem cells are being formed at the tip of the stem.

Thus in time-age the tip is perpetually young. But it is certainly not perpetually young in physiological age. In a young plant the meristem cells give rise to juvenile leaves; in an older plant they give rise to adult leaves and eventually to flowers. And it appears that this inexorable process of ageing goes on even when the plant has a constant supply of nutrients and constant conditions of light.

. . . Recently at the University of Manchester we have begun to study the ageing of a plant under constant environmental conditions. The plant we use is the common floating duckweed, which can be found in almost any stagnant pond. Each leaflike frond produces a "daughter" frond from a pocket to its side; when this "daughter" is fully grown, a second daughter is produced from a similar pocket on the other side of the parent. By the time the second daughter is grown the first daughter frond has broken away and become a separate plant, and out of the empty pocket a third daughter appears. This is followed by a fourth daughter in the pocket formerly occupied by the second daughter. In this way a mother frond may bring forth up to five daughter fronds, after which the mother frond dies. The life expectation of a mother frond is about 45 days. The five daughter fronds produced in this time are similar to five leaves on a normal plant.

The remarkable fact is that even in the most carefully controlled artificial environment each of the daughter fronds is smaller than the one before, so that the fourth and fifth daughters are less than half the size of the first daughter. To put it another way, the meristem cells of the mother frond are, as it were, "running down".

. . . But that is not the entire story. If it were, then successive generations in a colony of duckweed plants would become smaller and smaller and ultimately disappear. This does not happen; indeed the average size of fronds in a colony remains about the same. The reason is that the impoverished fourth or fifth daughter fronds reverse the trend and produce "grandaughter" fronds that are larger than themselves. The process of ageing during the life of a frond is followed by a process of rejuvenation. Each new frond in a duckweed colony is in fact part of a cycle of ageing and rejuvenation. Physiological age, unlike time-age, can be put in reverse.

ERIC ASHBY

Pleasure

It is nonsense to speak of "higher" and "lower" pleasures. To a hungry man it is, rightly, more important that he eat than that he philosophize. All pleasures are equally good, but there is no pleasure which the Evil One cannot, according to our natures, use to tempt us into evil. If we yield, no matter what the particular pleasure be, the same thing always happens: what at first was a pleasurable activity becomes an addiction which gives us no pleasure but from which we cannot break loose. Compulsive eaters, drinkers, and smokers no longer enjoy food, alcohol, tobacco; compulsive seducers, like Don Giovanni, no longer enjoy sexual pleasure. But it is usually by the bait of pleasure that the Evil One first leads us astray. There is a certain kind of Catholic novelist who would rewrite the fall of Eve like this:

> And when the woman saw that the tree was poisonous and that it was hideous to look at, she took of the fruit thereof and did eat.

We are not born quite so corrupt as that.

All pleasures are good; but there is an antithesis between "holy" and "unholy" joy.

Praise, Epithets of

&§&

All peoples in the cultural phase which one might call "epic" give praise-epithets to any being they regard as numinous. In Greek and Norse epic poetry, praise-epithets are reserved for gods and heroic warriors. But to the cattle-raising tribe of the Bahima in Uganda, cattle are just as numinous as heroes, and therefore accorded praise-epithets.

Abatangaaza

(by Kagarame, son of Buzoora, chief herdsman of the Omugabe Kahaya. c. 1918)

1 At Katunguru near Rurangizi, She Who Teases lay back on her horns and so did She Who Approaches The Fighters;

2 At Kahama near Kambarango, we deceived The One Who Drives Back The Others with the calf of The One Whose Horns Are Well Spread pretending it was hers.

3 At Rwenfukuzi near Ndeego, the lazy ones of Migina marvelled at the white patch on the daughter of The One With The Blaze On Her Forehead as she gambolled;

4 At Kabura and Nyansheko, they marvelled at the horns of the strawberry beast of Rwaktungu, She Whose Horns Are Not Stunted,

5 At Kiyegayega near Migina, the varied herd made a noise as they went to Rusheesha;

6 At Rwekubo near Kinanga, the herd walked proudly having killed a loaned beast,

7 She Whose Horns Stand Out Above The Herd gave birth and so did She Who Has Straightened Our Her Horns.

8 She Who Prevents Others' Approaching became friendly with The One Whose Horns Are As Straight As Planks.

9 At Akkabare at Nyamukondo's, they prepared their camps;

10 At Igwanjura and Wabinyonyi, they had slim bodies.

11 At Byembogo, they played with the antelopes;

12 At Ntarama, they borrowed the dress of the sorcerers,

13 At Kakona near Rubaya, we gave them another bell when they refused to increase.

14 At Shagama and Rwabigyemana, they displayed the tips of their horns;

15 At Bunonko in Rwanda, they danced about and played in the light rain;

16 At Nsikizi in Rwanda, they prevented the bell of The Leader from ringing.

17 At Burunga at the home of The One Who Is Not Dissuaded From Fighting *,

18 At Rwoma and Ihondaniro, they returned facing Kaaro;

19 At Nyumba and Rwemiganda, they were patient in death;

20 At Obukomago and Nyambindo, they died as the princes died in Buganda;

* The name of a person, not a cow.

21 Alas! I am heartbroken by the groaning of The One Who
Returns Home with Pride. . . .

The Heroic Recitations of the Bahima of Ankole (Uganda)

H. F. MORRIS

Prayer, Nature of

To pray is to pay attention to something or someone other than
oneself. Whenever a man so concentrates his attention—on a
landscape, a poem, a geometrical problem, an idol, or the True
God—that he completely forgets his own ego and desires, he is
praying. Choice of attention—to pay attention to *this* and
ignore *that*—is to the inner life what choice of action is to the
outer. In both cases, a man is responsible for his choice and
must accept the consequences, whatever they may be. The
primary task of the schoolteacher is to teach children, in a
secular context, the technique of prayer.

Intellectual adherence is never owed to anything whatsoever, for
it is never in any degree a voluntary thing. Attention alone is voluntary. It alone forms the subject of an obligation.

SIMONE WEIL

Tell me to what you pay attention and I will tell you who you
are.

ORTEGA Y GASSET

To pray is to think about the meaning of life.

LUDWIG WITTGENSTEIN

Prayers, Petitionary

Our wishes and desires—to pass an exam, to marry the person we love, to sell our house at a good price—are involuntary and, therefore, not in themselves prayers. They only become prayers when addressed to a God whom we believe to know better than ourselves whether we should be granted or denied what we ask. A petition does not become a prayer unless it ends with the words, spoken or unspoken, "nevertheless not as I will but as Thou wilt."

Your cravings as a human animal do not become a prayer just because it is God whom you ask to attend to them.

DAG HAMMARSKJÖLD

The Father will never give the child a stone that asks for bread; but I am not sure that He will never give a child a stone who asks for a stone. If the Father say, "My child, that is a stone; it is no bread," and the child answer, "I am sure it is bread; I want it," may it not be well that he should try his "bread"?

GEORGE MACDONALD

He took his hands from his head, and clasping them together, said a little prayer. It may be doubted whether he quite knew for what he was praying. The idea of praying for her soul, now that she was dead, would have scandalised him. He certainly was not praying for his own soul. I think he was praying that God might save him from being glad that his wife was dead.

A. TROLLOPE

Make me chaste and continent, but not just yet.

ST. AUGUSTINE

"Heaven help me," she prayed, "to be decorative and to do right."

RONALD FIRBANK

The Lord's Prayer

Doctor Thornton's Tory Translation, Translated out of its disguise in the Classical & Scotch languages into the vulgar English.

Our Father Augustus Caesar, who art in these thy Substantial Astronomical Telescopic Heavens, Holiness to Thy Name or Title, & reverence to thy Shadow. Thy Kingship come upon Earth first & then in Heaven. Give us day by day our Real Taxed Substantial Money bought Bread; deliver from the Holy Ghost whatever cannot be Taxed; for all is debts & Taxes between Caesar & us & one another; lead us not to read the Bible, but let our Bible be Virgil & Shakespeare; & deliver us from Poverty in Jesus, that Evil One. For thine is the Kingship or Allegoric Godship, & the Power, or War, & the Glory, or Law, Ages after Ages in thy descendants; for God is only an Allegory of Kings & nothing Else. Amen.

WILLIAM BLAKE

Almighty God, Father of all mercies, we pray Thee to be gracious with those who fly this night. Guard and protect those of us who venture out into the darkness of Thy heaven. Uphold them on Thy wings. Keep them safe both in body and soul and bring them back to us. Give to us all the courage and strength for the hours that are ahead; give to them rewards according to their efforts. Above all else, our Father, bring peace to Thy world. May we go forward trusting in Thee and knowing we are in Thy presence now and forever. Amen.

Prayer by CHAPLAIN DOWNEY, *ending the briefing session preliminary to the bombing of Nagasaki*

Prose, Annihilating

✦❦✦

To be real, it must be written in response to some specific event or person that has aroused the author's anger and scorn. This,

I think, disqualifies Housman's savage remarks, funny though they are, because it seems that he wrote them *in vacuo* before he had found the victim to whom they would apply.

Mr. James Macpherson,—I received your foolish and impudent letter. Any violence offered me I shall do my best to repel; and what I cannot do for myself, the law shall do for me. I hope I shall never be deterred from detecting what I think a cheat, by the menaces of a ruffian.

What would you have me retract? I thought your book an imposture; I think it an imposture still. For this opinion I have given my reasons to the public, which I here dare you to refute. Your rage I defy. Your abilities, since your Homer, have not been so formidable; and what I hear of your morals, inclines me to pay regard not to what you shall say, but to what you shall prove. You may print this if you will.

DR. JOHNSON

We do not suppose all preservers of game to be so bloodily inclined that they would prefer the death of a poacher to his staying away. Their object is to preserve game; they have no objection to preserving the lives of their fellow-creatures also, if both can exist at the same time; if not, the least worthy of God's creatures must fall—the rustic without a soul—not the Christian partridge—not the immortal pheasant—not the rational woodcock, or the accountable hare.

SYDNEY SMITH

The freedoms of the young three—who were, by-the-way, not in their earliest bloom either—were thus bandied about in the void of the gorgeous valley without even a consciousness of its shrill, its recording echoes. . . . The immodesty was too colossal to be anything but inane. And they were alive, the slightly stale three: they talked, they laughed, they sang, they shrieked, they romped, they scaled the pinnacle of publicity and perched on it, flapping their wings, whereby they were shown in possession of many of the movements of life.

HENRY JAMES

Prose, Impressionistic

Dined *versus* six o' the clock. Forgot that there was a plum-pudding (I have added, lately, *eating* to my "family of vices") and had dined before I knew it. Drank half of a bottle of some sort of spirits—probably spirits of wine; for what they call brandy, rum, etc., etc., here is nothing but spirits of wine, colored accordingly. Did *not* eat two apples, which were placed by way of dessert. Fed the two cats, the hawk, and the tame (but not tamed) crow. Read Mitford's *History of Greece*—Xenophon's *Retreat of the Ten Thousand*. Up to this present moment writing, 6 minutes before 8 o' the clock—French hours, not Italian.

Hear the carriage—order pistols and great coat—necessary articles. Weather cold—carriage open, and inhabitants rather savage—rather treacherous and highly inflamed by politics. Fine fellows though—good materials for a nation. Out of chaos God made a world, and out of high passions come a people.

Clock strikes—going out to make love. Somewhat perilous but not disagreeable. Memorandum—a new screen put up today. It is rather antique but will do with a little repair.

LORD BYRON

Prose, Judges'

Mr. Gluckstein can take an action at law if he likes. If he hesitates to take that course, or takes it and fails, then his only recourse lies in an appeal to that sense of honour which is popularly supposed to reside among robbers of a humbler type.

MR. JUSTICE MACNAUGHTEN

If the defendant is to be believed, he combined the forbearance of a Christian Martyr with the dignity of a Grandee of Spain. The defendant, it will be remembered, is a company promoter.

Another judge

Prose, Purple

⋅⋦⋧⋗

Oh, young boys, if your eyes ever read these pages, pause and beware. The knowledge of evil is ruin, and the continuance in it hell. That little matter—that beginning of evil—it will be like the snow-flake detached by the breath of air from the mountain-top, which, as it rushes down, gains size and strength and impetus, till it has swollen to the mighty and irresistible avalanche that overwhelms garden and field and village in a chaos of undistinguishable death.

Kibbroth-Hattavah! Many and many a young Englishman has perished there. Many and many a happy English boy, the jewel of his mother's heart—brave, and beautiful, and strong—lies buried there. Very pale their shadows rise before us—the shadows of our young brothers who have sinned and suffered. From the sea and the sod, from foreign graves and English churchyards, they start up and throng around us in the paleness of their fall. May every schoolboy who reads this page be warned by the waving of their wasted hands, from that burning marl of passion where they found nothing but shame and ruin, polluted affections, and an early grave.

F . W . F A R R A R

Prose, Woozy

—§§—

No St George any more to be heard of; no more dragon-slaying possible: this child *, born on St George's Day, can only make manifest the dragon, not slay him, sea-serpent as he is; whom the English Andromeda, not fearing, takes for her lord. The fairy English Queen once thought to command the waves, but it is the sea-dragon now who commands her valleys; of old the Angel of the Sea ministered to them, but now the Serpent of the Sea; where once flowed clear springs now spreads the black Cocytus pool; and the fair blooming of the Hesperid meadows fades into ashes beneath the Nereid's Guard.

Yes, Albert of Nuremberg; the time has at last come. Another nation has arisen in the strength of its Black anger; another hand has portrayed the spirit of its toil. Crowned with fire, and with the wings of the bat.

RUSKIN

Puns

—§§—

M. Denis de Rougemont told me of this dedication by a French authoress to her publisher. I have, unfortunately, forgotten her name.

> *Je méditerai,*
> *Tu m'éditeras.*

I would have said that a pathetic pun was impossible, until I came across this verse by Praed:

---

* This child: Turner

Tom Mill was used to blacken eyes
   Without the fear of sessions;
Charles Medlar loathed false quantities
   As much as false professions;
Now Mill keeps order in the land,
   A magistrate pedantic;
And Medlar's feet repose unscanned
   Beneath the wide Atlantic.

Puritanism

⋖§§⋗

. . . Theologically, Protestantism was either a recovery, or a development, or an exaggeration (it is not for the literary historian to say which) of Pauline theology. . . . In the mind of a Tyndale or Luther, as in the mind of St. Paul himself, this theology was by no means an intellectual construction made in the interests of speculative thought. It springs directly out of a highly specialized religious experience; and all its affirmations, when separated from that context, become meaningless or else mean the opposite of what was intended. . . . The experience is that of catastrophic conversion. The man who has passed through it feels like one who has waked from nightmare into ecstasy. Like an accepted lover, he feels that he has done nothing, and never could have done anything, to deserve such astonishing happiness. Never again can he 'crow from the dunghill of desert'. All the initiative has been on God's side; all has been free, unbounded grace. . . . His own puny and ridiculous efforts would be as helpless to retain the joy as they would have been to achieve it in the first place. Fortunately they need not. Bliss is not for sale, cannot be earned. 'Works' have no 'merit', though, of course faith, inevitably, even unconsciously, flows out into works of love at once. He is not saved because he does works of love: he does works of love because he is saved. It is faith alone that has saved him: faith bestowed by sheer gift. From this buoyant humility, this fare-well to the self with all its good resolutions, anxiety, scruples, and motive-scratchings, all the Protestant doctrines originally sprang. . . .

It follows that nearly every association which now clings to the word *puritan* has to be eliminated when we are thinking of the early Protestants. Whatever they were, they were not sour, gloomy, or severe; nor did their enemies bring any such charge against them. On the contrary, Harpsfield (in his *Life of More*) describes their doctrines as 'easie, short, pleasant lessons' which lulled their unwary victim in 'so sweete a sleepe as he was euer after loth to wake from it'. For More, a Protestant was one 'dronke of the new must of lewd lightnes of minde and vayne gladnesse of harte'. . . . Luther, he said, had made converts pre-cisely because 'he spiced al the poison' with 'libertee'. . . . Protes-tantism was not too grim, but too glad, to be true; 'I could for my part be verie wel content that sin and pain all were as short-lye gone as Tyndale telleth us.'

C. S. LEWIS

Reformation, Vocabulary of the

❧

The Reformation seems, with its insistence on the *inwardness* of all true grace, to have been but another manifestation of that steady shifting inwards of the centre of gravity of human con-sciousness which we have already observed in the scientific out-look. That shift is, in a larger sense, the story told by the whole history of the Aryan languages. Thus *religion* itself, which had formerly been used only of external observances or of monastic orders, took on at about this time its modern, subjective meaning. Now it was that *piety*, differentiating itself from *pity*, began to acquire its present sense. *Godly*, *godlinesss*, and *godless* are first found in Tyndale's writings, and *evangelical* and *sincere* are words which have been noted by a modern writer as being new at this time and very popular among the Protestants. The great word *Protestant* itself was applied formerly to the German Princes who had dissented from the decision of the Diet of Spires in 1529, and together with *Reformation* it now acquired its new and special meaning, while the old words, *dissent* and *disagree*, were transferred at about the same time from material objects to matters of opinion. . . .

Very soon after the Reformation we find alongside the syllables of tenderness and devotion a very pretty little vocabulary of abuse. *Bigoted, faction, factious, malignant, monkish, papistical, pernicious, popery* are among the products of the struggle between Catholic and Protestant; and the terms *Roman, Romanist,* and *Romish* soon acquired such a vituperative sense that it became necessary to evolve *Roman Catholic* in order to describe the adherents of that faith without giving offence to them. The later internecine struggles among the Protestants themselves gave us *Puritan, precise, libertine*—reminiscent of a time when "liberty" of thought was assumed as a matter of course to include licence of behaviour—*credulous, superstitious, selfish, selfishness* and the awful Calvinistic word *reprobate*. It was towards the end of the Puritan ascendancy that *atone* and *atonement* (at-onement) acquired their present strong suggestion of legal expiation, and it may not be without significance that the odious epithet *vindictive* was then for the first time applied approvingly to the activities of the Almighty Himself.

OWEN BARFIELD

Renaissance, The

&§&

The Middle Ages paid their normal attention to the ordinary affairs of men, as all normal attention must be paid, *semper, ubique, ab omnibus*. When, however, they thought about those affairs, they imagined them in terms of God and grace. And eventually their energy could not live up to the dazzling circle of dogma within which it operated. God was everywhere the circumstance of all lives. Men had been over-nourished on such metaphysics, and the Renascence abandoned the idea of that universal Circumstance to attend to lesser circumstances. Change, sin, and intelligent delight in the creation had been at work, and now they did not so much break bounds as withdraw from the bounds. The thought of the Middle Ages was not limited, but perhaps its philosophical vocabulary was. Persistently and universally the stress changed. The Lord Alexander VI was not worse than some of the medieval Popes but he was—ever so little—different. He and Julius II and Leo X all accepted the Mass. But it is difficult to think of any of them as being primarily and profoundly concerned with the Mass. They were probably—even Julius—more humane than Urban VI but they were also more human. . . . Erasmus was as Christian as—and much less anti-Papal (so to call it) than—Dante. But the monks, the heavy and certainly stupid monks, who denounced Erasmus were, in a sense, right. There was a good deal to be said from their point of view, though (as so often happens) they themselves were precisely the wrong people to say it. Erasmus can be studied and admired as a devout scholar. He can hardly be ranked as a scholarly devotee. Leonardo was probably a pious, if sceptical, scientist. But he could hardly be said, except in a highly mathematical manner, to exalt piety by science. The opponents of either were no more pious or devout than scholarly or scientific. The habitual and rather worn religious intelligence of the time was not so high that it could afford to abuse Leonardo or Erasmus, as those periods might have done, with a better chance, to which grace was still a dreadful reality. . . . The Middle Ages had desired greatness and glory and gold as much as their children; virtue after them was not so very much impaired. But the metaphysical vision which had illuminated those otherwise base things was passing; they were no longer mythological beyond themselves. Man was left to take glory in, and to glorify, himself and his works. Had chances been different, there might have been a revival of the old wisdom of

Christ as *anthropos;* the secrets of Christendom might have enriched with new significance the material world. It was not to be; the *anthropos* had been forgotten for the *theos,* and now the other *anthropos,* the Adam of Augustine, the *homo sapiens* of science, preoccupied European attention.

CHARLES WILLIAMS

The Renaissance was, as much as anything, a revolt from the logic of the Middle Ages. We speak of the Renaissance as the birth of rationalism; it was in many ways the birth of irrationalism. It is true that the medieval Schoolmen, who had produced the finest logic that the world has ever seen, had in later years produced more logic than the world can ever be expected to stand. They had loaded and lumbered up the world with libraries of mere logic; and some effort was bound to be made to free it from such endless chains of deduction. Therefore, there was in the Renaissance a wild touch of revolt, not against religion but against reason. . . . When all is said, there is something a little sinister in the number of mad people there are in Shakespeare. We say that he uses his fools to brighten the dark background of tragedy; I think he sometimes uses them to darken it. . . . What is felt faintly even in Shakespeare is felt far more intensely in the other Elizabethan and Jacobean dramatists; they seem to go in for dancing ballets of lunatics and choruses of idiots, until sanity is the exception rather than the rule. . . .

The Elizabethan epoch was of intense interest, of intensive intelligence; of piercing sharpness and delicacy in certain forms of diplomacy and domestic policy, and the arts of the ambassador and the courtier; and especially in one or two great men, of vivid and concentrated genius in the study of certain particular problems of character. But it was not spacious. . . . Its special and specialist studies involved men in almost everything except fresh air. In literature it was the age of conceits. In politics it was the age of conspiracies. . . . It is almost in a double sense that we talk of Shakespeare's plots. In almost every case, it is a plot about a plot.

G. K. CHESTERTON

Revbnge

Revenge

✥

. . . The lord of Chateau-roux in France maintained in the castle a man whose eyes he had formerly put out, but who, by long habit, recollected the ways of the castle, and the steps leading to the towers. Seizing an opportunity of revenge, and meditating the destruction of the youth, he fastened the inward doors of the castle, and took the only son and heir of the governor of the castle to the summit of a high tower, from whence he was seen with the utmost concern by the people beneath. The father of the boy hastened thither, and, struck with terror, attempted by every possible means to procure the ransom of his son, but received for answer, that this could not be effected, but by the same mutilation of those lower parts, which he had likewise inflicted on him. The father, having in vain entreated mercy, at length assented, and caused a violent blow to be struck on his body; and the people around him cried out lamentably, as if he had suffered mutilation. The blind man asked him where he felt the greatest pain? When he replied in his reins, he declared it was false and prepared to precipitate the boy. A second blow was given, and the lord of the castle asserting that the greatest pain was at his heart, the blind man expressing his disbelief, again carried the boy to the summit of the tower. The third time, however, the father, to save his son, really mutilated himself; and when he exclaimed that the greatest pain was in his teeth; "It is true," said he, "as a man who has had experience should be believed, and thou hast in part revenged my injuries. I shall meet death with more satisfaction, and thou shalt neither beget any other son, nor receive comfort from this." Then, precipitating himself and the boy from the summit of the tower, their limbs were broken, and both instantly expired. The knight ordered a monastery built on the spot for the soul of the boy, which is still extant, and called De Doloribus. . . .

GIRALDUS CAMBRENSIS

Roads

⚬❦⚬

Up hill, down hill,
Stands still, but goes to mill every day.

Ozarks riddle

Tracing the Remains of the Roman Roads

Evidence of the alignment is of course the fundamental characteristic, and it is the rigidly straight length of modern road ending suddenly for no apparent reason and continuing only as a winding road that directs attention upon the map to many a Roman line. A word of caution is necessary, however, for straight lengths of roads across commons, or the enclosed land of former commons, often show very similar features, the straight length terminating at the end of the area with which the enclosure surveyors were dealing, but a little experience will soon enable such roads to be easily recognised.

Where substantial remains of the *agger* still exist, even if derelict, overgrown or under plough, the road can generally be recognised fairly easily, but in many cases the typical indications are very inconspicuous, although really very definite, and call for some observational experience in recognising them. Most often the *agger* will then appear as a very slight broad ridge, hardly more than a gentle swelling in the ground; there may be indications of metalling if ploughing has scattered it, and the hard surface may be felt on probing just below the tilth. Or the road may have been removed, either for the sake of the stone which could be usefully employed elsewhere, or to clear the land for better cultivation; in these cases a wide shallow hollow may mark its course, especially on a hill where water action would tend to deepen the original slight excavation. If the road is running along a hillside a slight terracing may remain even if it is crossing a field long under plough, but the break in the slope may be so slight that it will perhaps only be apparent when viewed in certain lights and from a favourable angle. The ditches of the road frequently disappear by silting, and the resultant increase in the top-soil depth may result in excessive growth of the crop at that point, with consequent "lodging" in wet weather. These are the kinds of signs which necessarily show most clearly from the air and so can best be studied on air photographs when these are available. It must be emphasized, however, that many such signs are seasonal in character, owing to the growth of the crops, whilst the time of day may also be important in its effect upon the lighting of the picture: thus it does not follow that such photographs, taken at any time not suitably chosen, will show the details required.

The road when derelict is nearly always covered with soil, owing to the accumulation of fallen leaves and weed growth, and when it is under grass this may become parched in dry weather, owing to the stony layer beneath, and appear as a brown or light-coloured strip, recognizable as one walks over it and showing very plainly indeed from the air.

Hedgerow lines, sometimes of considerable length, and lanes or minor roads, with footpaths and tracks, often mark parts of the course and are very significant if a long line of them can be traced across country, even when in discontinuous lengths upon the same alignment. Parish boundaries, often of very early Saxon origin, follow Roman roads very frequently and are sometimes a useful indication that the line is really old.

In some places however, especially in forest areas upon soft soil, the road will be entirely invisible, not even a hedgerow marking its course, but it does not follow that the road is not there. Experience has shown that it may have survived with its metalled surface quite intact but entirely buried below the level of cultivation. Such roads are necessarily hard to trace, and indeed this can only be done when some other parts of the route are more normally visible so that the alignment can be established. Probing along the line may then enable the invisible portions to be recovered. In some areas it seems probable that routes at present incompletely known will eventually be proved in this way.

When the roads have remained in use there is usually much less of interest to be found. The alignment will be clearly shown by the course of the road, and probably the most distinctive sign of its Roman origin will be the abrupt changes of direction, always taking place at a high point from which the sighting could be done. Often the road can be seen to be well raised, especially if it is a minor road which has not suffered greatly from wear, but if the soil is soft, and especially in hilly regions, the road may have greatly worn down during the centuries of neglect and far from being raised, will now be found in a deep hollow. Sometimes the hollow has become too waterlogged for use and a new road has taken its place alongside, in which case the hollow will be so over-grown that its existence may hardly be suspected as one passes it. Another indication of Roman origin in a road still in use is its behaviour when an obstacle is encountered; the road will negoti-ate this by short straight lengths, resuming the original line upon the far side, and if a steep hill has to be climbed the road may do so in a distinct zig-zag course which will very likely have been modified in later times to ease the gradient and hairpin bends, but it may still be traceable in its original form, now partly aban-doned, as terraces upon the hillside. Narrow enclosed plots along the side of a road are nearly always evidence that the road is old, and they may mask its original straightness considerably.

Place names are, of course, very useful evidence for the exis-tence of a Roman road. To the Saxon a "street" was a road with a paved or metalled surface, and since the only examples of these he could meet were Roman it follows that his Streathams, Strat-fords, Strattons, Strettons, Old Streets, and so on, indicate Roman roads with much certainty. Similar names derived from "Stone" or "Stane" such as Stanford, Stanstead, Stone Street, Stane Street, are also significant. The name High Street where it occurs in open country and does not mean the village street is another, re-ferring probably to the raised roadway, as do also such names as Ridgeway, The Ridge, Causeway, Long Causeway, Devil's Causeway, etc., while a derelict length of road may bear the name Green Street. Names such as Street Farm and Street Field in country areas are very significant, as the name almost certainly refers to such a road, and in the case of a field may establish its like position very closely.

IVAN D. MARGARY

Roads

I love roads:
The goddesses that dwell
Far along invisible
Are my favourite gods.

Roads go on
While we forget, and are
Forgotten like a star
That shoots and is gone.

On this earth 'tis sure
We men have not made
Anything that doth fade
So soon, so long endure.

The hill road wet with rain
In the sun would not gleam
Like a winding stream
If we trod it not again.

They are lonely
While we sleep, lonelier
For lack of the traveller
Who is now a dream only.

From dawn's twilight
And all the clouds like sheep
On the mountains of sleep
They wind into the night.

The next turn may reveal
Heaven: upon the crest

The close pine clump, at rest
And black, may Hell conceal.

Often footsore, never
Yet of the road I weary,
Though long and steep and dreary,
As it winds on for ever.

Helen of the roads,
The mountain ways of Wales
And the Mabinogian tales,
Is one of the true gods,

Abiding in the trees,
The threes and fours so wise,
The larger companies,
That by the roadside be,

And beneath the rafter
Else uninhabited
Excepting by the dead;
And it is her laughter

At morn and night I hear,
When the thrush cock sings
Bright irrelevant things,
And then the chanticleer

Calls back to their own night
Troops that make loneliness
With their light footsteps' press,
As Helen's own are light.

Now all roads lead to France *
And heavy is the tread
Of the living; but the dead
Returning lightly dance:

* The poem was written during World War I.

Whatever the road bring
To me or take from me,
They keep me company
With their pattering,

Crowding the solitude
Of the loops over the downs,
Hushing the roar of towns
And their brief multitude.

EDWARD THOMAS

The Middleness of the Road

The road at the top of the rise
Seems to come to an end
And take off into the skies.
So at the distant bend

It seems to go into a wood,
The place of standing still
As long the trees have stood.
But say what Fancy will,

The mineral drops that explode
To drive my ton of car
Are limited to the road.
They deal with near and far,

But have almost nothing to do
With the absolute flight and rest
The universal blue
And local green suggest.

ROBERT FROST

Sometimes a new road will follow an old one for miles together,
ignoring the crossing tracks, and sometimes, turning suddenly
where four roads meet, it leaves its own prolongation to the
traffic of rare farm carts and lurching gipsy vans. If we follow

the obsolete routes at such a crossing, between their high banks full of flowers and birds' nests, we often see how they lead to some feature of vanished importance—some dry common where we still trace the pit-dwellings, some deep and easily accessible spring, or some sly passage between the hills which a new road strides over. The old tracks have almost died out of use with the gradual shifting of the population. But it is by following their covert windings, and not by rushing along new coach-roads, or still newer motor-roads, that we often discover the finest speci-mens of old local architecture, and the seats of legend. This is true of the by-lanes in most English counties, but doubly true in Wales. Of old dwellings, indeed, we shall not here find many, ex-cept of the humblest kind. In Wales, the houses of ancient kings and chiefs, or of the later squires who inherited their lands and their leadership, are often shrunken and insignificant. But if we care for the ancient traditions, this farmhouse was the summer palace of an extinguished dynasty, that cottage with white walls beneath the sycamores, was the birthplace of a famous bard; and we can still see the stream of rustic life flowing persistently through the old hollow lanes. Here the fine new road that runs down the middle of the valley only dates from the coaching days, though English traffic began to be wrested into new and directer channels by the Romans some sixteen hundred years earlier.

Let us fly westward on the wings of the imagination into the heart of the Mid-Welsh kingdom of Powys, or else take train or car to Welshpool and on to Llanfair Caereinion, and push thence from railhead towards the sea. Boldly above the Banwy river looms the great hill called Moel Bentych, with its legend of a dull-witted dragon or "gwyber" (i.e., wyvern), which was be-fooled and slain by a cunning blacksmith with a spiky tar-baby. Our road cuts over a low pass behind it to a substantial stone bridge at Llanerfyl, and another at Garthbeibio, three miles be-yond. But do not think that it was by this fine high road, or by any road on the site of it, that in the days when the kings of Powys held the fat lands of Shropshire they came riding in the spring weather from Pengwern, which we call Shrewsbury, to their "hafod" of Llyssun, half-way down that sunny bank sprin-kled with red Hereford oxen. If they had occasion to call at

Llanfair, they did not cross the shining Banwy by Neuadd Bridge, as we do today, because there was no bridge then, but joined the track from Meifod, and then followed the steep and delightful lane which winds at the dry feet of the hills round all the crooks and crannies of the rocky river until it reaches Llyssun. Thenceforward the old road and the new coincide as far as the hamlet called the Foel, that is, the bare hill-top; for beyond Llangadfan the river runs through marshy meadows, and the new road no more tries to cut straight across them than the old did. Between the Foel and Garthbeibio church, high on the hillside, the peat-stained Twrch (not the same Twrch which we met at Llanuwchllyn) comes marching like a highlander into the vale. But before we reach Foel Bridge the old road has left us; it creeps to the right, up the Twrch stream, and crosses it where its bounding rocks meet closest, by a pack-bridge of a single span. Then we know why Garthbeibio church is perched so high on the hill. Though inconveniently placed for most of its modern congregation, it stands on the direct route from the old bridge, up the opposite side of the valley, over the moors that lead to the Dovey and the Dee. And the strange thing is that though the new road has invited them for more than a hundred years, the tramps and vagrants who form more of a separate caste in Wales than in England have never learnt to use it. On the high road, you would almost think that vagrancy had ceased. Follow the hill-trails between the little ancient bridges, high over the curlew-haunted moors among the roots of the mountains, and there, twice or thrice in a week, you will meet that shuffling, half-savage figure, red-haired and sullen of visage, following the trails that his fathers followed before the Romans came, and scowling still at the stranger.

To-day all hollow lanes form rivulets after rain, but it is clear from the lie of the land that some were traced by human feet before the water followed. They prick down the crests of narrow bridges, with a view over the valleys on each side. These were tracks before they were streams; but it is also likely that other watery lanes in the hill-countries were streams before they were tracks. There are advantages in the continuity and the hard bottom of a rivulet descending from the moor to the valley which more than compensate for a little additional water. Follow the bank above the wet lane, in the fields or on the moor above it, and see how much more tiresome is the going. The soil turns to mud after every storm of rain, and there are bogs on the moor in which we stumble from rush-clump to rush-clump. We return gladly to the rocky floor of the track, where the water has cut through the soft earth down to firm rock and gravel. In the shelter of the hollow lane there is comfort against keen north wind and driving rain-storms; and the wild life of the valleys and dingles spreads up the lanes to the very shoulder of the moor. Sheltered banks and running water make many of these lanes a wild garden, and they are sought out by the beasts and the birds. Here on spring mornings we meet the hare and the hedgehog—the hare daintily tripping to us among the wet pebbles with that strange incapacity of her sidelong vision to see danger in front, and the hedgehog just emerged from its leafy winter lair, and too eager to search the turf for beetles, or for brother hedgehogs, to wait for night. Weasels wind along the banks on their blood-quests; and from behind the curtains of dry bracken we hear the needle-sharp ejaculations of the shrew.

ANTHONY COLLETT

Royalty

◆§ఠ◆

The Queen had a passion for motoring. She would motor for hours and hours with her crown on; it was quite impossible to mistake her. . . .

"Just hark to the crowds!" the Prince evasively said. And never too weary to receive an ovation, he skipped across the room towards the nearest window, where he began blowing kisses to the throng.

"Give them the Smile Extending, darling," his mother beseeched.

"Won't you rise and place your arm about him, Madam?" the Countess suggested.

"I'm not feeling at all up to the mark," her Dreaminess demurred, passing her fingers over her hair.

"There is sunshine, ma'am . . . and you have your *anemones* on . . ." the Countess cajoled, "and to please the people, you ought indeed to squeeze him." And she was begging and persuading the Queen to rise as the King entered the room preceded by a shapely page (of sixteen) with cheeks fresher than milk.

"Go to the window, Willie," the Queen exhorted her Consort, fixing an eye on the last trouser button that adorned his long, straggling legs. The King, who had the air of a tired pastry-cook, sat down.

"We feel," he said, "to-day, we've had our fill of stares!"

"One little bow, Willie," the Queen entreated, "that wouldn't kill you."

"We'd give perfect worlds," the King went on, "to go, by Ourselves, to bed."

". . . and now, let me hear your lessons: I should like," Mrs. Montgomery murmured, her eyes set in detachment upon the floor, "the present-indicative tense of the Verb *To be!* Adding the words, Political H-Hostess;—more for the sake of the pronunciation than for anything else."

And after considerable persuasion, prompting, and "bribing" with various sorts of sweets:

> "I am a Political Hostess,
> Thou art a Political Hostess,
> He is a Political Hostess,
> We are Political Hostesses,
> Ye are Political Hostesses,
> They are Political Hostesses."

"Very good, dear, and only one mistake. *He* is a Political H-Hostess: can you correct yourself? the error is so slight. . . ."

But alas the Prince was in no mood for study; and Mrs. Montgomery very soon afterwards was obliged to let him go.

RONALD FIRBANK

For some reason he [Edward VII] spoke English with a heavy German accent, very guttural. . . . When he was still Prince of Wales and living at Marlborough House, Sir Sidney Lee, the Shakespearean scholar, came to the Prince with a proposal. It was on the eve of the publication of the *Dictionary of National Biography*. It was Sir Sidney's idea that the Prince ought to give a dinner to those responsible for the completion of this monumental work. The monumental work had escaped the Prince's attention, don't you know, and Sir Sidney had painfully to explain to him what it was. The Prince, you know, was not an omnivorous reader. Sir Sidney managed to obtain his grudging consent. "How many?" asked the Prince. "Forty," said Sir Sidney. The Prince was appalled. "For-r-ty!" he gasped. "For-r-ty wr-ri-ter-rs! I can't have for-r-ty wr-ri-ter-rs in Marlborough House! Giff me the list!" Sir Sidney gave it him, and the Prince, with a heavy black pencil, started slashing off names. Sir Sidney's heart sank when he saw that the first name the Prince had slashed was that of Sir Leslie Stephen. He conveyed, as tactfully as he could, that this was a bad cut, since Stephen was the animating genius of the whole enterprise. Reluctantly, the Prince allowed Sir Leslie to come. Eventually, Sir Sidney put over his entire list. The dinner took place. Among the contributors present was Canon Ainger, a distinguished cleric whose passion was Charles Lamb, on whom he was considered a very great authority indeed. He had written the articles on Charles and Mary Lamb for the *Dictionary*. Sir Sidney sat at the Prince's right and found it heavy weather, don't you know. The Prince must have found it heavy going also; to be having dinner with forty writers was not his idea of a cultivated way to spend an evening. His eye roamed the table morosely, in self-objurgation for having let himself in for a thing like this. Finally, his eye settled on Canon Ainger. "Who's the little parson?" he asked Lee. "Vy is *he* here? He's not a wr-ri-ter!" "He is a very great authority", said Lee, apologetically, "on Lamb." This was too much for the Prince. He put down his knife and fork in stupefaction; a pained outcry of protest heaved from him: "on *lamb!*"

MAX BEERBOHM
(as reported by S. N. Behrman)

Here is an incident which may make some of you smile. It happened shortly after the death of Prince Henry of Battenberg, the husband of Queen Victoria's daughter, Princess Beatrice. His death had greatly upset the Queen, for she had grown very fond of her son-in-law. He had brought a great deal of interest and life into the rather mournful atmosphere which still prevailed at Court.

On this particular afternoon to which I refer—a dark, dank afternoon in February—the Queen was at Osborne, and she went for her customary drive with Lady Errol, who was then in waiting. These dear, elderly ladies, swathed in crêpe, drove in an open carriage, called a sociable. The Queen was very silent, and Leila (Lady Errol) thought it time to make a little conversation. So she said, "Oh, Your Majesty, think of when we shall see our dear ones again in Heaven!"

"Yes," said the Queen.

"We will all meet in Abraham's bosom," said Leila.

"I will *not* meet Abraham," said the Queen.

An entry in Queen Victoria's diary for this day runs: "Dear Leila, not at all consolatory in moments of trouble!"

PRINCESS MARIE LOUISE

We were unaware, Sir, that the corridors of our palace were damp.

(Attributed to GEORGE V,
on contemplating a visitor at a time
when turned-up trousers had just become fashionable)

Abroad is bloody.

(Attributed to GEORGE VI)

Saints

Health is the state about which medicine has nothing to say; sanctity is the state about which theology has nothing to say.

I have met in my life two persons, one a man, the other a woman, who convinced me that they were persons of sanctity. Utterly different in character, upbringing and interests as they were, their effect on me was the same. In their presence I felt myself to be ten times as nice, ten times as intelligent, ten times as good-looking as I really am.

Reading *The Penguin Book of Saints,* I am sorry to learn that St. Catherine of the Catherine wheel never existed. Another nonexistent saint is St. Uncumber, who, according to legend, miraculously grew a beard in order to avoid marriage. Whom now are wives to invoke when their husbands are too sexually importunate?

Of my own saint, St. Wystan, all that appears to be known is that he objected to the uncanonical marriage of his widowed mother to his godfather, whereupon they bumped him off. A rather Hamlet-like story.

Catholicism baptized polytheism by substituting for the old pagan cults the cults of local and patron saints. Such cults can and have led to abuses, but they are infinitely more healthy than the cult of the fashionable film star or pop singer, which is all that Protestantism has to offer in their stead.

In our era, the road to holiness necessarily passes through the world of action.

DAG HAMMARSKJÖLD

Science

Art is I; Science is We.

CLAUDE BERNARD

Science is spectrum analysis: Art is photosynthesis.

KARL KRAUS

Someone remarked to me once: "Physicians shouldn't say, I have cured this man, but, this man didn't die under my care." In physics too, instead of saying, I have explained such and such a phenomenon, one might say, I have determined causes for it the absurdity of which cannot be conclusively proved.

G. C. LICHTENBERG

Many scientific theories have, for very long periods of time, stood the test of experience until they had to be discarded owing to man's decision, not merely to make other experiments, but to have different experiences.

ERIC HELLER

The hunger of the Eighteenth Century to believe in the power of reason, to wish to throw off authority, to wish to secularise, to take an optimistic view of man's condition, seized on Newton and his discoveries as an illustration of something which was already deeply believed in quite apart from the law of gravity and the laws of motion. The hunger with which the Nineteenth Century seized on Darwin had very much to do with the increasing awareness of history and change, with the great desire to naturalise man, to put him into the world of nature, which pre-existed long before Darwin and which made him welcome. I have seen an example in this century where the great Danish physicist Niels Bohr found in the quantum theory when it was developed thirty years ago this remarkable trait: it is consistent with describing an atomic system, only much less completely than we can describe large-scale objects. We have a certain choice as to which traits of the atomic system we wish to study and measure and which to let go; but we have not the option of doing them all. This situation, which we all recognise, sustained in Bohr his long-held view of the human condition: that there are mutually exclusive ways of using our words, our minds, our souls, any one of which is open to us, but which cannot be combined: ways as different, for example, as preparing to act and entering into an introspective search for the reasons for action. This discovery has not, I think, penetrated into general cultural life. I wish it had; it is a good example of something that would be relevant, if only it could be understood.

J. ROBERT OPPENHEIMER

Although this may seem a paradox, all exact science is dominated by the idea of approximation.

BERTRAND RUSSELL

Scientific reasoning is completely dominated by the pre-supposition that mental functionings are not properly part of nature.

A. N. WHITEHEAD

When we speak of the picture of nature in the exact science of our age, we do not mean a picture of nature so much as a picture of our relationship with nature. Science no longer confronts nature as an objective observer, but sees himself as an actor in this interplay between man and nature. The scientific method of analysing, explaining and classifying has become conscious of its human limitations, which arise out of the fact that by its intervention science alters and refashions the object of its investigation. In other words, method and object can no longer be separated. *The scientific world view has ceased to be a scientific view in the true sense of the word.*

WERNER HEISENBERG

Without my work in natural science I should never have known human beings as they really are. In no other activity can one come so close to direct perception and clear thought, or realize so fully the errors of the senses, the mistakes of the intellect, the weaknesses and greatnesses of human character.

GOETHE

It just so happens that during the 1950's, the first great age of molecular biology, the English Schools of Oxford and particularly of Cambridge produced more than a score of graduates of quite outstanding ability—much more brilliant, inventive, articulate, and dialectically skillful than most young scientists; right up in the [James D.] Watson class. But Watson had one towering advantage over all of them: in addition to being extremely clever he had something important to be clever *about*. This is an advantage which scientists enjoy over most people engaged in intellectual pursuits.

P. B. MEDAWAR

Freeman Dyson, in an article, *Innovation in Physics*, recalled that in 1958 the German physicist Werner Heisenberg and Pauli, put forward an unorthodox theory of particles which would explain the violations of parity in weak interactions. Pauli was lecturing in New York on these new ideas to a group of scientists that included Niels Bohr. In the discussion that followed the talk, younger scientists were sharply critical of Pauli.

Bohr rose to speak. "We are all agreed," he said to Pauli, "that your theory is crazy. The question which divides us is whether it is crazy enough to have a chance of being correct. My own feeling is that it is not crazy enough."

Dyson commented in his article:

"The objection that they are not crazy enough applies to all the attempts which have so far been launched at a radically new theory of elementary particles. It applies especially to the crackpots. Most of the papers which are submitted to *The Physical Review* are rejected, not because it is impossible to understand them, but because it is possible. Those which are impossible to understand are usually published."

MARTIN GARDNER

Generally speaking and to a varying extent, scientists follow their temperaments in their choice of problems.

CHARLES HERMITE

Experimental typhus of the guinea-pig is a very minimal disease. It is reduced to small changes in the temperature curve, and could not be diagnosed without a thermometer, since the animal does not seem to suffer or have any other symptoms.

Now it happened occasionally that we discovered amongst our guinea-pigs, inoculated with the same virus, some who had no fever at all. The first time we discovered this, we thought it was due to an accident in the inoculation or to the particular resistance of the inoculated animal. These were the two hypotheses by which all bacteriologists of that era would have explained this phenomenon.

When the phenomenon kept recurring, we felt that our explanations had been too superficial, and that it must be due to another specific reason. We kept in mind the table of sensitivity to typhus of various races and species that we had observed or infected. At the top of the scale was the European adult who had immigrated to regions where typhus is endemic, and in whom the disease is most severe and often fatal. Below him appeared the aboriginal adult who is seriously infected but who, when there are no complications, generally escapes death. Then there comes the indigenous child for whom typhus, with few exceptions, is only a mild disease. Below our species there figures the chimpanzee, less sensitive still than the child, followed by even less sensitive small monkeys, and finally the guinea-pig whose infection is reduced to a thermometer curve. Could there not be below this hardly recognizable disease an even smaller degree of sensitivity, where, in the absence of fever, the only means of diagnosing typhus would be the positive results of an inoculation of blood into an animal of definite sensitivity? That this was the case was soon proved by experiment. Other experiments very soon proved to us that latent typhus, exceptional as it was in the case of guinea-pigs, was the only form of typhus in some other species.

This latent typhus which we were the first to discover is a typhus of first infection. We were able to demonstrate the existence of the same sub-clinical type in other guinea-pigs, that had had primary typhus and were then reinoculated. The natural recurrence in man can also be of the sub-clinical type.

Subsequently we, and others after us, extended the notion of latent infection to a number of bacterial infections. The list increases daily.

Thus there exists a whole pathology that cannot be reached by clinical methods. If we add that it is in these unrecognizable forms that contagious and epidemic diseases are preserved, the practical importance of this new information is obvious. Now the starting-point of our discovery had been the simple absence of a temperature rise in some examples of a species which commonly becomes feverish after being inoculated with a virus.

CHARLES NICOLLE

The scientific method cannot lead mankind because it is based upon experiment, and every experiment postpones the present moment until one knows the result. We always come to each other and even to ourselves too late so soon as we wish to know in advance what to do.

EUGEN ROSENSTOCK-HUESSY

That's an old besetting sin; they think calculating is inventing. And that because they have been right so often, their wrongheadedness is right-minded. And that because their science is exact, none of them can be crazy.

We need a categorical imperative in the natural sciences just as much as we need one in ethics.

GOETHE

Science alone, and only in its purest rigor, can give a precise content to the notion of providence, and in the domain of knowledge, it can do nothing else.

SIMONE WEIL

Seasons, The Four

❧

Explore deep mountain chasms, soar high in the air in the wake of clouds; to brook and valley the Muse calls—a thousand and a thousand times.

When a fresh calyx newly blooms, it calls for new songs; and though streaming time flees from us, the seasons come again.

GOETHE
(trans. David Luke)

Winter to Spring: the west wind melts the frozen rancour,
    The windlass drags to sea the thirsty hull;
Byre is no longer welcome to beast or fire to ploughman,
    The field removes the frost-cap from his skull.

Venus of Cythera leads the dances under the hanging
    Moon and the linked line of Nymphs and Graces
Beat the ground with measured feet while the busy Fire-God
    Stokes his red-hot mills in volcanic places.

Now is the time to twine the spruce and shining head with
    myrtle,
    Now with flowers escaped the earthly fetter,
And sacrifice to the woodland god in shady copses
    A lamb or a kid, whichever he likes better.

Equally heavy is the heel of white-faced Death on the
    pauper's
    Shack and the towers of kings, and O my dear,
The little sum of life forbids the ravelling of lengthy
    Hopes. Night and the fabled dead are near

And the narrow house of nothing, past whose lintel
    You will meet no wine like this, no boy to admire

Like Lycidas, who today makes all young men a furnace
   And whom tomorrow girls will find a fire.

HORACE
(trans. Louis MacNeice)

The Objects of the Summer Scene

The objects of the summer scene entone
   Or image present peace or dear regrets;
Something that life to be content must own,
   Smiles near, though restless grief remotely frets;
Green sycamores brooding in the quiet sun;
   And on gray hills beyond the golden sheaves,
Lone poplars, sisters of fallen Phaeton,
   Quivering innumerate inconsolable leaves.

In wintry evening walks I turn where rest
   Within one tomb affection's first, and last;
As in a wind, of some dead wind in quest,
   I homeward pace companioned by the past.
For earth's great grave far ocean seems to moan;
   And the sad mind but marks anear, afar,
The tinkle of the dead leaf by the lone
   Sea road, the sad look of the setting star.

W. C. IRWIN

Summer

   Winter is cold-hearted,
   Spring is yea and nay,
Autumn is a weathercock
   Blown every way.
   Summer days for me
When every leaf is on its tree;

   When Robin's not a beggar,
   And Jenny Wren's a bride,

And larks hang singing, singing, singing
    Over the wheat-fields wide,
    And anchored lilies ride,
    And the pendulum spider
    Swings from side to side.

And blue-black beetles transact business,
    And gnats fly in a host,
And furry caterpillars hasten
    That no time be lost,
    And moths grow fat and thrive,
    And ladybirds arrive.

Before green apples blush,
Before green nuts embrown,
Why, one day in the country
Is worth one month in town;
Is worth a day and a year
Of the dusty, musty, lag-last fashion
    That days drone elsewhere.

CHRISTINA ROSSETTI

The Fall

The length o' days ageän do shrink
    An' flowers be thin in meäd, among
    The eegrass, a-sheenèn bright, along
Brook upon brook, an' brink by brink.

Noo starlens do rise in vlock on wing—
    Noo goocoo in nest-green leaves do sound—
    Noo swallows be now a-wheelèn round—
Dip after dip, an' swing by swing.

The wheat that did leätely rustle thick
    Is now up in mows that still be new,
    An' yollow bevore the sky o' blue—
Tip after tip, an' rick by rick.

While shooters do rove bezide the knoll
    Where leaves be a-rolled on quivren grass;
    Or down where the sky-blue stream do pass,
Vall after vall, an' shoal by shoal;

Their brown-dappled dogs do briskly trot
    By russet-brown boughs, while gun smoke grey
    Do melt in the aïr o' sunny day,
Reef after reef, an' shot by shot.

While now I can walk a dusty mile
    I'll teäke me a day, while days be clear,
    To vind a vew friends that still be dear,
Feäce after feäce, an' smile by smile.

                 WILLIAM BARNES

Look how the snow lies deeply on glittering
Soracte. White woods groan and protestingly
    Let fall their branch-loads. Bitter frost has
      Paralysed rivers: the ice is solid.

Unfreeze the cold! Pile plenty of logs in the
Fireplace! And you, dear friend Thaliarchus, come
    Bring out the Sabine wine-jar four years
      Old and be generous. Let the good gods

Take care of all else. Later, as soon as they've
Calmed down this contestation of winds upon
    Churned seas, the old ash-trees can rest in
      Peace and the cypresses stand unshaken.

Try not to guess what lies in the future, but
As Fortune deals days enter them into your
    Life's book as windfalls, credit items,
      Gratefully. Now that you are young, and peevish

Grey hairs are still far distant, attend to the
Dance-floor, the heart's sweet business; for now is the

Right time for midnight assignations,
    Whispers and murmurs in Rome's piazzas

And fields, and soft, low laughter that gives away
The girl who plays love's games in a hiding-place—
    Off comes a ring coaxed down an arm or
        Pulled from a faintly resisting finger.

HORACE
(trans. James Michie)

Winter Cold

Cold, cold, chill to-night is wide Moylurg; the snow is higher than a mountain, the deer cannot get at its food.

Eternal cold! The storm has spread on every side; each sloping furrow is a river and every ford is a full mere.

Each full lake is a great sea and each mere is a full lake; horses cannot get across the ford of Ross, no more can two feet get there.

The fishes of Ireland are roving, there is not a strand where the wave does not dash, there is not a town left in the land, not a bell is heard, no crane calls.

The wolves of Cuan Wood do not get repose or sleep in the lair of wolves; the little wren does not find shelter for her nest on the slope of Lon.

The keen wind and the cold ice have burst out upon the company of little birds; the blackbird does not find a bank it would like, shelter for its side in the Woods of Cuan.

Snug is our cauldron on its hook, ramshackle the hut on the slope of Lon: snow has crushed the wood here, it is difficult to climb up Benn Bó.

The eagle of brown Glen Rye gets affliction from the bitter wind; great is its misery and its suffering, the ice will get in its beak.

It is foolish for you—take heed of it—to rise from quilt and feather-bed; there is much ice on every ford; that is why I say "Cold!"

ANON. tenth century
(trans. K. H. Jackson)

Serpent, The

◄◄§ê►

There are myriads lower than this, and more loathsome, in the scale of being; the links between dead matter and animation drift everywhere unseen. But it is the strength of the base element that is so dreadful in the serpent; it is the very omnipotence of the earth. That rivulet of smooth silver—how does it flow, think you? It literally rows the earth, with every scale for an oar; it bites the dust with the ridges of its body. Watch it, when it moves slowly: —A wave, but without wind! a current, but with no fall! all the body moving at the same instant, yet some of it to one side, some to another, or some forward, and the rest of the coil backwards; but all with the same calm will and equal way—no contraction, no extension; one soundless, causeless march of sequent rings, and spectral procession of spotted dust, with dissolution in its fangs, dislocation in its coils. Startle it;—the winding stream will become a twisted arrow;—the wave of poisoned life will lash through the grass like a cast lance. It scarcely breathes with its one lung (the other shrivelled and abortive); it is passive to the sun and shade, and is cold or hot like a stone; yet, "it can outclimb the monkey, outswim the fish, outleap the jerboa, outwrestle the athlete, and crush the tiger." It is a divine hieroglyph of the demoniac power of the earth,—of the entire earthly nature. As the bird is the clothed power of the air, so this is the clothed power of the dust; as the bird is the symbol of the spirit of life, so this of the grasp and sting of death.

RUSKIN

Shakespeare and the Computers

I read in a newspaper that a certain Mrs. Winifred Venton, with the help of the Enfield College of Technology computer, has at last cracked the cipher of the *Sonnets*.

The Message: Shakespeare was really King Edward VI, who did not die, as the history books say, when he was sixteen, but at the age of 125. In addition to writing "Shakespeare," he wrote not only all of Ben Jonson and Bacon, but *Don Quixote* as well.

Sin

We can reach the point where it becomes possible for us to recognise and understand Original Sin, that dark counter-centre of evil in our nature—that is to say, though it *is* not our nature, it is *of* it—that something within us which rejoices when disaster befalls the very cause we are trying to serve, or misfortune overtakes even those we love.

Life in God is not an escape from this, but a way to gain full insight concerning it. It is not our depravity which forces a fictitious religious explanation upon us, but the experience of religious reality which forces the "Night Side" out into the light.

It is when we stand in the righteous all-seeing light of love that we can dare to look at, admit, and *consciously* suffer under this something in us which wills disaster, misfortune, defeat to everything outside the sphere of our narrowest self-interest.

DAG HAMMARSKJÖLD

You talk of Gayety and Innocence!
The moment when the fatal fruit was eaten,
They parted ne'er to meet again; and Malice
Has ever since been playmate to light Gayety,
From the first moment when the smiling infant
Destroys the flower or butterfly he toys with,
To the last chuckle of the dying miser,
Who on his deathbed laughs his last to hear
His wealthy neighbor has become a bankrupt.

WALTER SCOTT

Sin is nothing else but the refusal to recognise human misery: It is unconscious misery, and for that very reason guilty misery.

All sins are attempts to fill voids.

Evil is to love what mystery is to intelligence.

SIMONE WEIL

Certain sins can manifest themselves as their mirror opposites which the sinner is able to persuade himself are virtues. Thus Gluttony can manifest itself as Daintiness, Lust as Prudery, Sloth as Senseless Industry, Envy as Hero Worship.

My senses tell me that the world is inhabited by a number of human individuals whom I can count and compare with each other, and I do not doubt the evidence of my senses. It requires, however, an act of faith on my part to believe that they enjoy a unique personal existence as I do, that when they say "I" they mean what I mean when I say it, for this my senses cannot tell me. Vice versa, my own personal existence is to me self-evident; what, where I am concerned, calls for an act of faith, is to believe that I, too, am a human individual like the others, brought into the world by an act of sexual intercourse and exhibiting socially conditioned behavior. The refusal to make this double act of faith constitutes the Primal Sin, the Sin of Pride.

Society, High

The Challenge

A COURT BALLAD
TO THE TUNE OF "TO ALL YOU LADIES NOW AT LAND"

To *one* fair Lady out of Court,
   And *two* fair Ladies in,
We think the *Turk* and *Pope* a Sport,
   And Wit and Love no Sin;
Come, these soft Lines, with nothing stiff in,
To *Bellenden, Lepell,* and *Griffin.*
     With a fa, la, la.

What passes in the dark third Row,
   And what behind the Scene,
Couches and crippled Chairs I know,
   And Garrets hung with Green;
I know the Swing of sinful Hack,
Where many Damsels cry Alack.
     With a fa, la, la.

Then why to Court should I repair,
   Where's such ado with *Townshend,*
To hear each Mortal stamp and swear,
   And every speech with *Zowns* end;
To hear 'em rail at honest *Sunderland,*

And rashly blame the Realm of *Blunderland.*
  With a fa, la, la.

Alas! like *Schutz,* I cannot pun,
 Like *Grafton* court the *Germans;*
Tell *Pickenbourg* how Slim she's grown,
 Like *Meadowes* run to Sermons;
To Court ambitious Men may roam,
But I and *Marlbro'* stay at Home.
  With a fa, la, la.

In Truth, by what I can discern,
 Of Courtiers 'twixt you *Three,*
Some Wit you have, and more to learn
 From Court, than *Gay* or *Me:*
Perhaps, in Time, you'll leave high Diet,
To sup with us on Milk and Quiet.
  With a fa, la, la.

At *Leicester-Fields,* a House full high,
 With door all painted green,
Where Ribbons wave upon the Tye,
 (A *Milliner* I mean);
There may you meet us *Three* to *Three,*
For *Gay* can well make *Two* of Me.
  With a fa, la, la.

But shou'd you catch the Prudish Itch,
 And each become a Coward,
Bring sometimes with you Lady *Rich,*
 And sometimes Mistress *Howard;*
For Virgins to keep Chaste, must go
Abroad with such as are not so.
  With a fa, la, la.

And thus, fair Maids, my Ballad ends;
 God send the King safe Landing;
And make all honest Ladies friends
 To Armies that are Standing;

Preserve the Limits of these Nations,
And take off Ladies Limitations.
   With a fa, la, la.

      ALEXANDER POPE

Solitude and Loneliness

He who does not enjoy solitude will not love freedom.

      SCHOPENHAUER

Man is a gregarious animal, and much more so in his mind than in his body. He may like to go alone for a walk, but he hates to stand alone in his opinions.

      G. SANTAYANA

Solitude. In what does its value actually consist? For we are in the presence of ordinary matter (even the sky, the stars, the moon, trees in flower), things of lesser value perhaps than a human spirit. Its value consists in the superior possibility of attention. If one could be attentive to the same degree in the presence of a human being . . . (?)

      SIMONE WEIL

In natural objects we feel ourselves, or think of ourselves, only by *likenesses*—among men too often by *differences*. Hence the soothing love-kindling effect of rural nature and the bad passions of human societies.

      S. T. COLERIDGE

Letting rip a fart—
It doesn't make you laugh
When you live alone.

    Anon. Japanese
(trans. Geoffrey Bownas)

Where I could think of no thoroughfare,
Away on the mountain up far too high,
A blinding headlight shifted glare
And began to bounce down a granite stair
Like a star fresh fallen out of the sky.
And I away in my opposite wood
Am touched by that unintimate light
And made feel less alone than I rightly should,
For traveler there could do me no good
Were I in trouble with night tonight.

ROBERT FROST

A lonely man always deduces one thing from the other and thinks everything to the worst.

MARTIN LUTHER

Loneliness is not the sickness-unto-death. No, but can it be cured except by death? And does it not become the harder to bear the closer one comes to death?

DAG HAMMARSKJÖLD

Songs

The French *Symbolistes* asserted that poetry should be as like music as possible. Some of them, however, made the mistake of writing about music itself, thereby showing that they had no understanding whatever of that art. To them, music was not an organized structure of sound, but a stimulus to vague erotic reverie. By *la poésie pure,* I take it that they meant the kind of poetry we enjoy, not because of anything it tells us about the world we live in, but as a purely verbal experience, a paradise of language. The best examples, in English poetry at least, are songs, poems written with the intention that they be set to

music, either by the poet himself, if, like Campion, he be also
a composer, or by another musician. The song writer has to be
much more conscious of the metrical values of words and the
sounds of syllables than the writer of a lyric which is intended
to be spoken or read.

A New Year Carol

Here we bring new water
　from the well so clear,
For to worship God with,
　this happy New Year,
Sing levy dew, sing levy dew,
　the water and the wine;
The seven bright gold wires
　and the bugles that do shine.

Sing reign of Fair Maid,
　with gold upon her toe,—
Open you the West Door,
　and turn the Old Year go.

Sing reign of Fair Maid
　with gold upon her chin,—
Open you the East Door,
　and let the New Year in.
Sing levy dew, sing levy dew,
　the water and the wine;
The seven bright gold wires
　and the bugles they do shine.

Anon.

Bethsabe's Song

Hot sun, cool fire, tempered with sweet air,
Black shade, fair nurse, shadow my white hair:
Shine, sun; burn, fire; breathe, air, and ease me;
Black shade, fair nurse, shroud me, and please me:

Shadow, my sweet nurse, keep me from burning,
Make not my glad cause cause of my mourning.
    Let not my beauty's fire
    Inflame unstaid desire,
    Nor pierce any bright eye
    That wandereth lightly.

GEORGE PEELE

Weep, O mine eyes, and cease not,
These your spring tides, alas, methinks increase not:
O when, O when begin you
To swell so high that I may drown me in you.

Anon.
(set by John Bennet)

About the maypole new, with glee and merriment,
    While as the bagpipe tooted it,
Thyrsis and Cloris fine together footed it.
    And to the wanton instrument
Still they went to and fro and finely flaunted it,
And then both met again, and thus they chaunted it:
    Fa la la!

The shepherds and the nymphs them round enclosed had,
    Wondring with what facility
About they turned them in such strange agility.
    And still, when they unloosed had,
With words full of delight they gently kissed them,
And thus sweetly to sing they never missed them:
    Fa la la!

Anon.
(set by Thomas Morley)

Dance, dance, and visit the shadows of our joy,
All in height, and pleasing state, your changed forms employ.
And as the bird of Jove salutes, with lofty wings, the morn,
So mount, so fly, these trophies to adorn.
Grace them with all the sounds and motions of delight,

Since all the earth cannot express a lovelier sight.
View them with triumph, and in shades the truth adore:
No pomp or sacrifice can please Jove's greatness more.
Turn, turn, and honor now the life these figures bear:
Lo, how heavenly natures far above all art appear:
Let their aspects revive in you the fire that shined so late,
Still mount and still retain your heavenly state.
Gods were with dance and with music served of old,
Those happy days derived their glorious style from gold:
This pair, by Hymen joined, grace you with measures then,
Since they are both divine and you are more than men.

T. CAMPION

To Musick, to becalme a sweet-sick-youth

Charms, that call down the moon from out her sphere,
On this sick youth work your enchantment here:
Bind up his senses with your numbers, so,
As to entrance his paine, or cure his woe.
Fall gently, gently, and a while him keep
Lost in the civill Wildernesse of sleep:
That done, then let him, dispossest of paine,
Like to a slumbring Bride, awake againe.

ROBERT HERRICK

Hunter's Song

The toils are pitched, and the stakes are set,
    Ever sing merrily, merrily;
The bows they bend, and the knives they whet,
    Hunters live so cheerily.

It was a stag, a stag of ten,
    Bearing its branches sturdily;
He came stately down the glen,
    Ever sing hardily, hardily.

It was there he met with a wounded doe,
    She was bleeding dreadfully;
She warned him of the toils below,
    O so faithfully, faithfully!

He had an eye, and he could heed,
    Ever sing warily, warily;
He had a foot, and he could speed—
    Hunters watch so narrowly.

WALTER SCOTT

Time's Song

O'er the level plains, where mountains greet me as I go,
O'er the desert waste, where fountains at my bidding flow,
On the boundless beam by day, on the cloud by night,
I am riding hence away! Who will chain my flight?

War his weary watch was keeping;—I have crushed his spear:
Grief within her bower was weeping;—I have dried her tear:
Pleasure caught a minute's hold;—then I hurried by,
Leaving all her banquet cold, and her goblet dry.

Power had won a throne of glory;—where is now his fame?
Genius said,—"I live in story";—who hath heard his name?
Love, beneath a myrtle bough, whispered,—"Why so fast?"
And the roses on his brow withered as I past.

I have heard the heifer lowing o'er the wild wave's bed;
I have seen the billow flowing where the cattle fed;
Where began my wanderings?—Memory will not say!
Where will rest my weary wings?—Science turns away!

W. M. PRAED

Mandrake's Song

Folly hath now turned out of door
Mankind and Fate, who were before

Jove's Harlequin and clown;
The World's no stage, no tavern more—
Its sign the Fool ta'en down.

With poppy rain and cypress dew
Weep all, for all, who laughed for you,
For goose-grass is no medicine more,
But the owl's brown eye's the sky's new blue.
Heigho! Foolscap!

T. L. BEDDOES

During Wind and Rain

They sing their dearest songs—
He, she, all of them—yea,
Treble and tenor and bass,
And one to play;
With the candles mooning each face. . . .
Ah, no; the years O!
How the sick leaves reel down in throngs!

They clear the creeping moss—
Elders and juniors—aye,
Making the pathways neat
And the garden gay;
And they build a shady seat. . . .
Ah, no; the years, the years;
See the white storm-birds wing across!

They are blithely breakfasting all—
Men and maidens—yea,
Under the summer tree,
With a glimpse of the bay,
While pet fowl come to the knee. . . .
Ah, no; the years O!
And the rotten rose is ript from the wall.

They change to a high new house,
He, she, all of them—aye,

Clocks and carpets and chairs
   On the lawn all day,
And brightest things that are theirs. . . .
   Ah, no; the years, the years;
Down their carved names the rain-drop ploughs.

THOMAS HARDY

Spa

The Warwickshire Avon falls into the Severn here, and on the
sides of both, for many miles back, there are the finest meadows
that ever were seen. In looking over them, one wonders *what can
become of all the meat?* By riding on about eight or nine miles
further, however, this wonder is a little diminished; for here we
come to one of the devouring WENS; namely CHELTENHAM,
which is what they call a "watering place"; that is to say, a place
to which East India plunderers, West India floggers, English tax-
gorgers, together with gluttons, drunkards, and debauchees of all
descriptions, *female* as well as male, resort, at the suggestion of
silently laughing quacks, in the hope of getting rid of the bodily
consequences of their manifold sins and iniquities. When I enter a
place like this, I always feel disposed to squeeze up my nose with
my fingers. It is nonsense, to be sure; but I conceit that every
two-legged creature, that I see coming near me, is about to cover
me with the poisonous proceeds of its impurities. To places like
these come all that is knavish and all that is foolish and all that is
base; gamesters, pick-pockets, and harlots; young wife-hunters in
search of rich and ugly and old women, and young husband-
hunters in search of rich and wrinkled or half-rotten men, the
former resolutely bent, be the means what they may, to give
the latter heirs to their lands and tenements. These things are no-
torious; and, SIR WILLIAM SCOTT, in his speech of 1802, *in favour
of the non-residence of the Clergy*, expressly said, that they and

their families ought to appear at *watering places*, and that this was amongst the means of *making them respected by their flocks!* Memorandum: he was a member for Oxford when he said this!

WILLIAM COBBETT

Sparrows

━━━━━

❧⚶☙

3 sorts The common house Sparrow The Hedge Sparrow & Reed Sparrow often calld the fen sparrow The common sparrow is well known but not so much in a domesticated state as few people think it worth while bringing up a sparrow When I was a boy I kept a tamed cock sparrow 3 years it was so tame that it would come when calld & flew where it pleasd when I first had the sparrow I was fearful of the cat killing it so I usd to hold the bird in my hand toward her & when she attempted to smell of it I beat her she at last woud take no notice of it & I ventured to let it loose in the house they were both very shy at each other at first & when the sparrow venturd to chirp the cat woud brighten up as if she intended to seize it but she went no further than a look or smell at length she had kittens & when they were taken away she grew so fond of the sparrow as to attempt to caress it the sparrow was startld at first but came to by degrees & ventured so far at last as to perch upon her back puss would call for it when out of sight like a kitten & woud lay mice before it the same as she woud for her own young & they always livd in harmony so much the sparrow woud often take away bits of bread from under the cat's nose & even put itself in a posture of resistence when offended as if it reckoned her no more than one of its kind. In winter when we coud not bear the door open to let the sparrow come out & in I was alowd to take a pane out of the window but in the spring of the third year my poor tom Sparrow for that was the name he was calld by went out & never returnd I went day after day calling out for tom & eagerly eying

every sparrow on the house but none answerd the name for he
woud come down in a moment to the call & perch upon my hand
to be fed I gave it out that some cat which it mistook for its old
favourite betrayed its confidence & destroyed it

JOHN CLARE

Spider, The

Little City

Spider, from his flaming sleep,
staggers out into the window frame;
swings out from the red den where he slept
to nest in the gnarled glass.
Fat hero, burnished cannibal
lets down a frail ladder and ties a knot,
sways down to a landing with furry grace.

By noon this corner is a bullet-colored city
and the exhausted architect
sleeps in his pale wheel,
waits without pity for a gold visitor
or coppery captive, his aerial enemies
spinning headlong down the window to the trap.

The street of string shakes now and announces
a surprised angel in the tunnel of thread,
Spider dances down his wiry heaven to taste the moth.
A little battle begins and the prison trembles.
The round spider hunches like a judge.
The wheel glistens.
But this transparent town that caves in at a breath
is paved with perfect steel.

The victim hangs by his feet, and the spider
circles invisible avenues, weaving a grave.

By evening the web is heavy with monsters,
bright constellations of wasps and bees,
breathless, surrendered.
Bronze skeletons dangle on the wires
and a thin wing flutters.
The medieval city hangs in its stars.

Spider lumbers down the web
and the city stretches with the weight of his walking.
By night we cannot see the flies' faces
and the spider, rocking.

ROBERT HORAN

Spoonerisms

§§›

Winter Eve

Drear fiend: How shall this spay be dent?
I jell you no toque—I do not know.
What can I do but snatch the woe
that falls beyond my pane, and blench
my crows and ted my briny shears?
Now galls another class. I'll sit
and eye the corm that's fought in it.
Maces will I fake, and heart my pare.
Is this that sold elf that once I was
with lapped chips and tolling lung?
I hollow sward and tight my bung
for very shame, and yet no cause—
save that the beery witchery

of Life stows grail. Shall I abroad?
Track up my punks? Oh gray to pod
for him who sanders on the wee!
I'll buff a stag with shiny torts
and soulful hocks, a truthbush too,
perhaps a rook to bead—but no!
my wishes must be dashed. Reports
of danger shake the reaming scare.
Whack against blight! Again that tune,
"A gritty pearl is just like a titty prune"
blows from the fox. I cannot bear
this sweetness. Silence is best. I mat
my mistress and my sleazy lumber.
I'll shake off my toes, for they encumber.
What if I tub my stow? The newt
goes better fakèd to the cot.
I'll hash my wands or shake a tower,
(a rug of slum? a whiskey sour?)
water my pants in all their plots,
slob a male hairy before I seep—
and dropping each Id on heavy lie,
with none to sing me lullaby,
slop off to dreep, slop off to dreep.

ROBERT MORSE

Sunday

Sunday should be different from another day. People may walk,
but not throw stones at birds.

DR. JOHNSON

Swallow, The

It is an owl that has been trained by the Graces. It is a bat that loves the morning light. It is the aerial reflection of a dolphin. It is the tender domestication of a trout.

RUSKIN

Time

Among primitive peoples, the notion that the year has any particular length or duration is generally lacking. The seasons recur, and there may be a word for the cycle of recurring seasons which we can translate as "year," but it cannot be defined as a period of so many moons or days. Nevertheless the counting of moons (lunar months) is quite common, even among primitive peoples. . . .

Any seasonal cycle reckoned in moons must clearly be calibrated by some natural event which, from our point of view, appears to occur at a fixed time in the sidereal year. . . . It is important to realize that such corrections can be made without any awareness of the existence of a solar or sidereal year. . . . The Yami of Botel-Tobago Island near Formosa have an economy greatly influenced by the seasonal arrival of large shoals of flying-fish, which appear in these waters around March. A further seasonal fact is that, from about mid-June, typhoons are so frequent that deep-sea fishing is impracticable in the small craft of the Yami. They reckon time by moons, and all their festivals occur at a particular new or full moon. The check-point for their year is a festival in the dark phase between months nine and ten of their

360 •• A CERTAIN WORLD

cycle; that is, about March. At this festival, the Yami go out to summon the flying-fish with lighted flares. Before this event, flare-fishing is taboo. Provided the flying-fish turn up to the summons, the flare-fishing continues for three moons until the end of the twelfth month, and this is then deemed the end of the yearly cycle. From the beginning of the first month, flare-fishing is taboo again. If no flying-fish turn up to the summons, the Yami do not blame themselves for miscalculating the time—they blame the fish for being late for the appointment. In such years, they extend the flare-fishing season an extra moon, and the year-cycle continues for 13 months instead of 12. In this way, over a period of years the Yami calendar will keep in step with the sidereal year, although the Yami themselves have no notion of such a year and make no astronomical observations.

In ancient centralized states, such as Egypt and Mesopotamia, the common man was still concerned only with the present; his year was a recurring cycle of activities. The official, on the other hand, looked at the past, and was concerned with maintaining precedents and ordering activities into categories. The year and its divisions became instruments of organisation. For the priest, the names and numbers associated with these divisions provided an acrostic which led ultimately to astrology.

In almost all early societies, there were priests or priest-magicians whose status and authority depended upon their secret knowledge. In primitive societies these secrets are techniques of ritual and verbal spells, but, as writing develops, such formulae tend to become associated with geometrical shapes and magic numbers. Arithmetic and number theory may later be developed for their own sake without reference to practical utility. For example, the sexagesimal system of enumeration of ancient Mesopotamia and China was the invention of learned men who must have pursued complexity for the sake of complexity. For the peasant with ten fingers, there is no convenience in having 60 minutes to an hour, 24 hours to a day, and 360 degrees in a circle, but these numbers have exceptionally numerous simple factors, and so have fascination for arithmeticians interested more in magical combinations than in practical calculation. Thus, the administrative official, and the priest, are both interested—for different reasons—in devising time-systems which are neat, symmetrical, and arithmetically attractive. There are two ways of doing this. One is to devise and operate a pure number-system, ignoring the facts of astronomy. The other is to devise a pure number-system, but from time to time to introduce supplementary rules—also of a formal kind—which will gradually bring the number-system into relation with astronomical fact.

The ancient Egyptians, the Chinese, the Maya, and the Greeks each tackled this problem in a slightly different way. The Egyptians produced a number-system which ignored seasons. The Chinese maintained two separate official calendars, one for the peasant, which followed the seasons, and one for the scribe, which was a pure number-system. The Maya devised a pure number-system, and became obsessed by the marvellous intricacy of numbers. They took note of astronomical facts, but only to provide themselves with more and more complex number series which might be built into their magical system. The Greeks pursued a system of magical geometry, and in the process developed a time self-conscious science.

The important dates, from the Maya point of view, were those which completed a cycle, since, in Maya theory, the good or ill fortune of a particular period could be divined from a knowledge of its date of completion. A date which completed several different cycles all at once was correspondingly more important. Thus, by analogy to our system, Saturday would be important as being the last day of a week; a Saturday falling on the 31st day of December would be more important; Saturday, 31st December falling on the last day of a century would be yet more important.

The Maya had 20 basic digits instead of our ten, and they developed positional notation. Thus, a number we should write 861 (i.e., $8 \times 10 \times 10 + 6 \times 10 + 1$) was written by the Maya as 2.3.1 (i.e., $2 \times 20 \times 20 + 3 \times 20 + 1$). Each of the first 13 digits had special magical associations.

There were 20 day-names comparable to our days of the week, following on perpetually in continuous sequence. These days were, however, also numbered in series of 13, likewise in continuous sequence. Thus, each day had both a name and number. If we denote the names by capital letter down to the twentieth letter, which is T, a series might run,

1A; 2B; 3C; 4D; 5E; 6F; 7G; 8H; 9I; 10J; 11K; 12L; 13M;
1N; 2O; 3P; 4Q; 5R; 6S; 7T; 8A; 9B; 10C; 11D; 12E; 13F.

In a period of 260 days, no two days will have both the same name and the same number, but after 260 days the cycle will repeat itself.

E. R. REACH

Dogged morn till bed-time by its dull demands,
The veriest numskull *clock*-cluck understands,
Eked out by solemn gestures of its hands:

A subtler language stirs in whispering sands:

That double ovoid of translucent glass;
The tiny corridor through which they pass,
Shaping a crescent cone where nothing was,

Which mounts in exquisite quiet as the eye
Watches its myriad molecules slip by;
While, not an inch above, as stealthily,

A tiny shallowing on the surface seen
Sinks to a crater where a plane has been.
Could mutability be more serene?

Invert the fragile frame; and yet again
Daydream will rear a castle built in Spain.
'Time' measured thus is dewfall to the brain. . . .

And clepsydra—the clock that Plato knew,
Tolling the varying hours each season through;
Oozing on, drop by drop, in liquid flow,
Its voice scarce audible, bell-like and low
As Juliet's communings with her Romeo.

More silent yet; pure solace to the sight—
The dwindling candle with her pensive light
Metes out the leaden watches of the night.
And, in that service, from herself takes flight.

WALTER DE LA MARE

THE MARSCHALLIN:
Time is a very strange thing.
So long as one takes it for granted, it is nothing at all.
But then, all of a sudden, one is aware of nothing else.
It is all about us, it is within us also,
In our faces it is there, trickling,
In the mirror it is there, trickling,
In my sleep it is there, flowing,
And between me and you,
There, too, it flows, soundless, like an hour-glass.
Oh, Quinquin, sometimes I hear it flowing
Irresistibly on.
Sometimes I get up in the middle of the night
And stop the clocks, all, all of them.
Nevertheless, we are not to shrink from it,
For it, too, is a creature of the Father who created us all.

HUGO VON HOFMANNSTHAL

Tortoise, The

Tortoise Family Connections

On he goes, the little one,
Bud of the universe,
Pediment of life.

Setting off somewhere, apparently.
Whither away, brisk egg?

His mother deposited him on the soil as if he were no more
than droppings,
And now he scuffles tinily past her as if she were an old rusty
tin.

A mere obstacle,
He veers round the slow great mound of her—
Tortoises always foresee obstacles.

It's no use my saying to him in an emotional voice:
"This is your mother, she laid you when you were an egg."

He does not even trouble to answer: "Woman, what have I
to do with thee?"
He wearily looks the other way,
And she even more wearily looks another way still,
Each with the utmost apathy,
Incognisant,
Unaware,
No thing.

As for papa
He snaps when I offer him his offspring,
Just as he snaps when I poke a bit of stick at him,
Because he is irascible this morning, an irascible tortoise
Being touched with love, and devoid of fatherliness.

Father and mother,
And three little brothers,
And all rambling aimless, like little perambulating pebbles
scattered in the garden,
Not knowing each other from bits of earth or old tins.

Except that papa and mama are old acquaintances, of course.
Though family feeling there is none, not even the beginnings.
Fatherless, motherless, brotherless, sisterless
Little tortoise.

Row on then, small pebble,
Over the clods of the autumn, wind-chilled sunshine,
Young gaiety.

Does he look for a companion?

No, no, don't think it.
He doesn't know he is alone;
Isolation is his birthright,
This atom.

To row forward, and reach himself tall on spiney toes,
To travel, to burrow into a little loose earth, afraid of the
    night,
To crop a little substance,
To move, and be quite sure that he is moving:
Basta!
To be a tortoise!
Think of it, in a garden of inert clods,
A brisk, brindled little tortoise, all to himself—
Adam!

In a garden of pebbles and insects
To roam, and feel the slow heart beat
Tortoise-wise, the first bell sounding
From the warm blood, in the dark-creation morning.

Moving, and being himself,
Slow, and unquestioned,
And inordinately there, O stoic!
Wandering in the slow triumph of his own existence,
Ringing the soundless bell of his presence in chaos,
And biting the frail grass arrogantly,
Decidedly arrogantly.

D. H. LAWRENCE

Tradition

Tradition means giving votes to the most obscure of all classes—our ancestors. It is the democracy of the dead. Tradition refuses to submit to the small and arrogant oligarchy of those who merely happen to be walking around.

G. K. CHESTERTON

I should be glad to break free of tradition, and be original right through, but that is a big undertaking and leads to much vexation of spirit. As a genuine earth-native, I should regard it as a supreme point of honor, if I were not so strangely a tradition myself.

GOETHE
(trans. David Luke)

Respect for the past must be pious, but not mad.

V. ROZANOV

What is it sacrilege to destroy? The *metaxu*. No human being should be deprived of his *metaxu*, that is to say, of those relative and mixed blessings (home, country, traditions, culture, etc.,) which warm and nourish the soul and without which, short of sainthood, a *human* life is impossible.

SIMONE WEIL

Translation

To translate means to serve two masters—something nobody can do. Hence, as is true of all things that in theory no one can do—it becomes in practice everybody's job. Everyone must translate and everyone does translate. Whoever speaks is translating his thought for the comprehension he expects from the other, not for an imaginary general "other" but for this particular other in front of him, whose eyes widen with eagerness or close with boredom. . . . The listener translates the words that strike his ear . . . into the language he himself uses. . . . The theoretical impossibility of translating can mean to us only . . . that in the course of the "impossible" and necessary compromises which in their sequence make the stuff of life, this theoretical impossibility will give us the courage of a modesty which will then demand of the translation not anything impossible but simply whatever must be done. Thus, in speaking or listening, the "other" need not have my ears or my mouth—this would render unnecessary not only translation but also speaking and listening. . . . What is needed is neither a translation that is so far from being a translation as to be the original—this would eliminate the listening nation—nor one that is in effect a new original—this would eliminate the speaking nation.

FRANZ ROSENZWEIG

Ever since his own day Tyndale's translation has been blamed for being tendentious. If we are thinking of his violent marginal glosses, this is fair enough; if of his peculiar renderings (*congregation* for *ecclesia*, *senior* or *elder* for *presbuteros*, *favour* for *charis*, and the like), a little explanation seems to be needed. The business of a translator is to write down what he thinks the original meant. And Tyndale sincerely believed that the mighty theocracy with its cardinals, abbeys, pardons, inquisition, and treasury of grace which the word *Church* would undoubtedly have suggested to his readers was in its very essence not only distinct from, but antagonistic to, the thing that St. Paul had in mind whenever he used the word *ecclesia*. You may of course disagree with his premises; but his conclusion (that *Church* is a false rendering of *ecclesia*) follows from it of necessity. Thomas More, on the other hand, believed with equal sincerity that the 'Church' of his own day was in essence the very same mystical body which St. Paul addressed; from his premise it followed of course that *Church* was the only correct translation. Both renderings are

equally tendentious in the sense that each presupposes a belief. In
that sense all translations of scripture are tendentious; translation,
by its very nature, is a continuous implicit commentary. It can
become less tendentious only by becoming less of a translation.

C. S. LEWIS

An interesting example of a "translation," in which the original
is deliberately altered for satirical purposes, is Matthew Prior's
treatment of Boileau Despréaux.

Ode Sur la Prise de Namur, Par les Armes du Roy, L'Année 1692

Contemplez dans la tempeste,
Qui sort de ces Boulevars,
La Plume qui sur sa teste
Attire tous les regards.
A cet Astre redoutable
Toujours un sort favorable
S'attache dans les Combats:
Et toûjours ave la Gloire
Mars amenant la Victoire
Vôle, & le suit à grands pas.

An English Ballad, on the Taking of Namur by the King of Great Britain, 1695

Now let us look for *Louis'* Feather,
  That us'd to shine so like a Star:
The Gen'rals could not get together
  Wanting that Influence, great in War.
O Poet! Thou had'st been discreeter,
  Hanging the Monarch's Hat so high;
If Thou had'st dubbed thy Star, a Meteor,
  That did but blaze, and rove, and die.

Tyranny

Tyranny over a man is not tyranny: it is rebellion, for man is royal.

G. K. CHESTERTON

Tyranny is always better organized than freedom.

CHARLES PÉGUY

Under conditions of tyranny it is far easier to act than to think.

HANNAH ARENDT

It is always observable that the physical and exact sciences are the last to suffer under despotisms.

RICHARD HENRY DANA

How lucky it is for tyrants that one half of mankind doesn't think, and the other half doesn't feel.

J. G. SEUME

Tyrants are always assassinated too late; that is their great excuse.

E. M. CIORAN

Despotism or unlimited sovereignty is the same in a majority of a popular assembly, an aristocratical council, an oligarchical junta, and a single emperor.

J. Q. ADAMS

Every class is unfit to govern.

LORD ACTON

The belief that politics can be scientific must inevitably produce tyrannies. Politics cannot be a science, because in politics theory and practice cannot be separated, and the sciences depend upon their separation. The scientist frames a hypothesis and devises an experiment to test it; if the experiment gives a negative result, he must abandon it. Only when the experiment has confirmed his hypothesis will he begin to consider any practical applications. He can afford to wait for the truth. Since the subjects of his experiments have no will of their own, he does not have to take any subjective factors into consideration. The situation of the politician is utterly different. He cannot try out an hypothesis under laboratory conditions, but must immediately apply it to an historical situation and upon human beings, who not only have wills and opinions of their own but can change them. Consequently, no result at any moment can prove beyond doubt that he is mistaken. I hold the theory, let us say, that farmers will be happier and food production increased if agriculture is collectivized. I collectivize it. The farmers are obviously rebellious and food production drops. Does this prove me mistaken? Not necessarily. I can always argue that the failure is due to the malice and stupidity of the farmers and that, if I continue with the experiment long enough, they will come to see that I am right. Empirical politics must be kept in bounds by democratic institutions, which leave it up to the subjects of the experiment to say whether it shall be tried, and to stop it if they dislike it, because, in politics, there is a distinction, unknown to science, between Truth and Justice.

A Modern Nightmare

When Satan finds a rebel in his realm,
He laces round the head of the poor fool
A frightful mask, a sort of visored helm
That has a lining soaked in vitriol.
The renegade begins to scream with pain.
(The mask is not designed to gag the sound,
Which propagates the terror of his reign.)
The screams come through the visor, but are drowned
By the great shouting of the overlord,
Who, in relaying them, distorts the sense
So that the cringing listeners record

Mere cries of villainy or penitence . . .
Yet Satan has a stronger hold: the fear
That, if his rule is threatened, he will tear
The mask from that pain-crazed automaton
And show his vassals just what he has done.

NORMAN CAMERON

For the entourage of a modern tyrant, life must be pretty much the same as it was for those in attendance on Henry VIII.

Stond who so list upon the Slipper toppe
   Of courtes estates, and lett me heare rejoyce;
And use me quyet without lett or stoppe,
    Unknowen in courte, that hath suche brackishe joyes:
     In hidden place, so lett my dayes forthe passe,
   That when my yeares be done, withouten noyse,
    I may dye aged after the common trace.
For hym death greep' the right hard by the croppe
    That is moche knowen of other; and of him self alas,
  Doth dye unknowen, dazed with dreadfull face.

T. WYATT

Unfavorites and Favorites

✑✑✑

Like everyone else, I have my black list of unfavorite authors and critics, and among intimate friends I sometimes say exactly what I think of them, but I have the feeling that to express my opinions publicly would be in bad taste, that, to people whom one does not know personally, one should speak only of the authors and critics one is fond of.

I find reading savage reviews like reading pornography;

372 👀 A CERTAIN WORLD

though I often enjoy them, I feel a bit ashamed of myself for doing so. Still, I must admit that I find Nietzsche's list of his "impracticals" great fun.

Seneca, or the toreador of virtue.
Schiller, or the moral trumpeter of Sackingen.
Rousseau, or return to nature in *impuris naturabilis.*
Dante, or the hyena *poetizing* among the tombs.
Kant, or cant as an intelligible character.
Victor Hugo, or Pharos in the sea of absurdity.
Liszt, or the school of running after women.
George Sand, or *lactea ubertas;* i.e., the milch-cow with the "fine style."
Michelet, or enthusiasm which strips off the coat.
Carlyle, or pessimism as an undigested dinner.
John Stuart Mill, or offensive transparency.
Les frères de Goncourt, or the two Ajaxes struggling with Homer. Music by Offenbach.
Zola, or "the delight to stink."

To list my own "underbreds," with apt descriptions of the various kennels that sired them—how tempting! But I must stick to my principles and list my "pets" instead. The list is not, of course, exhaustive—there are many, many others I enjoy and admire, and I excluded comic poets because it is impossible to dislike them—but it does name those elder modern poets and modern critics from whom I have learned most.

Arranged in alphabetical order, they run thus:

Poets: Berthold Brecht (the lyric poet), Robert Bridges, Constantine Cavafy, Robert Frost, Robert Graves, Thomas Hardy, David Jones, D. H. Lawrence (of *Birds, Beasts and Flowers*), Walter de la Mare, Marianne Moore, Wilfred Owen, Laura Riding, Edward Thomas, William Carlos Williams (in his last period).

Critics: Erich Auerbach, G. K. Chesterton, T. S. Eliot (the quoter), Rudolf Kassner, W. P. Ker, Karl Kraus, C. S. Lewis, Eugen Rosenstock-Huessy, Leo Spitzer, Paul Valéry, Charles Williams.

Two Plugs:

The greatest long poem written in English in this century: *The Anathemata* by David Jones.

The only first-rate volume of poems specifically about World War II: *Rhymes of a Pfc* by Lincoln Kirstein.

Unitarians

❧§§❧

A Unitarian is a person who believes there is, at most, one God.

A . N . WHITEHEAD

Verse, *Quantitative English*

❧§§❧

When, under the influence of the Humanists, English poets of the sixteenth century tried to write English verse in classical meters, they found themselves in difficulties. Firstly, they ran up against the problem of the relation between vowel length and stress. I certainly don't know myself, and I doubt if the scholars can say with absolute certainty, whether when the Greek and Latin poets recited their verses, long vowels and stresses always coincided, but it is clear that in English they do not. For example, the first syllable of *merry* is short but stressed, the first syllable of *proceed* unstressed but long. Secondly, they found that in a language like English, which has lost most of its inflexional endings, vowels which are in themselves short are constantly becoming long by position, that is to say, followed by more than one consonant. For example, in the line "Of man's first disobedience and the fruit" there is, when scanned quantitatively, only one short syllable, *dis*.

In the following poem, by Campion, the metrical base consists of one spondee, two choriambs and an iambus, but Campion cannot make up his mind as to whether it is more important that the vowel quantities conform to the pattern or that the stresses should. Some lines conform in both respects, some in quantity, some in stress, and some in neither.

Canto Secundo

What faire pompe have I spide of glittering Ladies;
With locks sparckled abroad, and rosie Coronet
On their yvorie browes, trackt to the daintie thies
With roabs like *Amazons*, blew as Violet,
With gold Aiglets adornd, some in a changeable
Pale; with spangs wavering taught to be moveable.

Then those Knights that a farre off with dolorous viewing
Cast their eyes hetherward; loe, in an agonie,
All unbrac'd, crie aloud, their heavie state ruing:
Moyst cheekes with blubbering, painted as *Ebonie*
Blacke; their feltred haire torne with wrathful hand:
And whiles astonied, starke in a maze they stand.

But hearke! what merry sound! what sodaine harmonie!
Looke looke neere the grove where the Ladies doe tread
With their Knights the measures waide by the melodie.
Wantons! whose travesing make men enamoured;
Now they faine an honor, now by the slender wast
He must lift hir aloft, and seale a kisse in hast.

Straight downe under a shadow for weariness they lie
With pleasant daliance, hand knit with arme in arme,
Now close, now set aloof, they gaze with an equall eie,
Changing kisses alike; streight with a false alarme,
Mocking kisses alike, powt with a lovely lip.
Thus drownd with jollities, their merry daies doe slip.

But stay! now I discerne they goe on a Pilgrimage
Towards Loves holy land, faire *Paphos* or *Cyprus*.
Such devotion is meete for a blithesome age;
With sweet youth, it agrees well to be amorous.
Let olde angrie fathers lurke in an Hermitage:
Come, weele associate this jolly Pilgrimage!

In the nineteenth century one or two poets like Tennyson experimented with quantitative verse, but the majority, when they wished to imitate classical poetry, scanned by accent and ignored quantity. The meter they generally chose to imitate was the hexameter. Unfortunately, the English language does not fall naturally into hexameters; in English the meter sounds eccentric. Clough was the first poet to discover that if the accentual hexameter can be used in English at all it is better suited to a low, conversational style than to a high, epic one.

DEAR MISS ROPER,—It seems, George Vernon, before we left
    Rome, said
Something to Mr. Claude about what they call his intentions.
Susan, two nights ago, for the first time, heard this from
    Georgina.
It is *so* disagreeable and *so* annoying to think of!
If it could only be known, though we may never meet him
    again, that
It was all George's doing, and we were entirely unconscious,
It would extremely relieve—Your ever affectionate Mary.

                                    ARTHUR HUGH CLOUGH

So far as I know, Bridges was the first to write quantitative verse in English which ignores stress altogether.

Thus the following extract is written in hexameters, but no ear that listens for stresses will hear them as such.

What was Alexander's subduing of Asia, or that
Sheep-worry of Europe, when pigmy Napoleon enter'd
Her sovereign changers, and her kings with terror eclips'd?
His footsore soldiers inciting across the ravag'd plains,

Thro' bloody fields of death tramping to an ugly disaster?
Shows any crown, set above the promise (so rudely ac-
   complisht)
Of their fair godlike young faces, a glory to compare
With the immortal olive that circles bold Galileo's
Brows, the laurel'd halo of Newton's unwithering fame,
Or what a child's surmise, how trifling a journey Columbus
Adventur'd, to a land like that which he sailed from arriving,
If compar'd to Bessel's magic divination, awarding
Magnificent Sirius his dark and invisible bride.

                                  ROBERT BRIDGES

Voyages

      ᙏᙎ

                                  May 14, 1787

The afternoon passed without our having entered the Gulf of
Naples. On the contrary, we were steadily drawn in a westerly
direction; the boat moved further and further away from Cape
Minerva and nearer and nearer to Capri.

    Everybody was glum and impatient, except Kniep and myself.
Looking at the world with the eyes of painters, we were perfectly content to enjoy the sunset, which was the most magnificent spectacle we had seen during the whole voyage. Cape Minerva and its adjoining ranges lay before us in a display of
brilliant colours. The cliffs stretching to the south had already
taken on a bluish tint. From the Cape to Sorrento the whole coast
was lit up. Above Vesuvius towered an enormous smoke cloud,
from which a long streak trailed away to the east, suggesting that
a violent eruption was in progress. Capri rose abruptly on our left
and, through the haze, we could see the outlines of its precipices.

    The wind had dropped completely, and the glittering sea,
showing scarcely a ripple, lay before us like a limpid pond under
the cloudless sky. Kniep said what a pity it was that no skill with
colours, however great, could reproduce this harmony and that

not even the finest English pencils, wielded by the most practised hand, could draw these contours. I was convinced, on the contrary, that even a much poorer memento than this able artist would produce would be very valuable in the future, and urged him to make an attempt at it. He followed my advice and produced a most accurate drawing which he later coloured, which shows that pictorial representation can achieve the impossible.

With equally rapt attention we watched the transition from evening to night. Ahead of us Capri was now in total darkness. The cloud above Vesuvius and its trail began to glow, and the longer we looked the brighter it grew, till a considerable part of the sky was lit up as if by summer lightning.

We had been so absorbed in enjoying these sights that we had not noticed that we were threatened with a serious disaster; but the commotion among the passengers did not leave us long in doubt. Those who had more experience of happenings at sea than we bitterly blamed the captain and his helmsman, saying that, thanks to their incompetence, they had not only missed the entrance to the straits but were now endangering the lives of the passengers, the cargo and everything else confided to their care. We asked why they were so anxious, for we did not see why there could be any cause to be afraid when the sea was so calm. But it was precisely the calm that worried them: they saw we had already entered the current which encircles Capri and by the peculiar wash of the waves draws everything slowly and irresistibly towards the sheer rock face, where there is no ledge to offer the slightest foothold and no bay to promise safety.

The news appalled us. Though the darkness prevented us from seeing the approaching danger, we could see that the boat, rolling and pitching, was moving nearer to the rocks, which loomed ever darker ahead. A faint afterglow was still spread over the sea. Not the least breath of wind was stirring. Everyone held up handkerchiefs and ribbons, but there was no sign of the longed-for breeze. The tumult among the passengers grew louder and louder. The women and children knelt on the deck or lay huddled together, not in order to pray, but because the deck space was too cramped to let them move about. The men, with their thoughts ever on help and rescue, raved and stormed against the captain. They now attacked him for everything they had silently criticized during the whole voyage—the miserable accommodation, the outrageous charges, the wretched food and his behaviour. Actually, he had not been unkind, but very reserved; he had never explained his actions to anyone and even last night he had maintained a stubborn silence about his manoeuvres. Now they called him and his helmsman mercenary adventurers who knew nothing about navigation, but had got hold of a boat out of sheer greed, and were now by their incompetent bungling about to bring to grief the lives of all those in their care. The captain remained silent and still seemed to be preoccupied with saving the boat. But I, who all my life have hated anarchy worse than death, could keep silent no longer. I stepped forward and addressed the crowd, with almost the same equanimity I had shown in facing the "Birds" of Malcesine. I pointed out to them that, at such a moment, their shouting would only confuse the ears and minds of those upon whom our safety depended, and make it impossible for them to think or communicate with one another. "As for you," I exclaimed, "examine your hearts and then say your prayers to the Mother of God, for she alone can decide whether she will intercede with her Son, that he may do for you what He once did for His apostles on the storm-swept sea of Tiberias. Our Lord was sleeping, the waves were already breaking into the boat, but when the desperate and helpless men woke Him, He immediately commanded the wind to rest, and now, if it should be His will, He can command the wind to stir."

These words had an excellent effect. One woman, with whom I had had some conversation about moral and spiritual matters, exclaimed: "*Ah, il barlamè. Benedetto il barlamè*," and as they were all on their knees anyway, they actually began to say their litanies with more than usual fervour. They could do this with greater peace of mind, because the crew were now trying another expedient, which could at least be seen and understood by all. They lowered the pinnace, which could hold from six to eight men, fastened it to the ship by a long rope, and tried, by rowing hard, to tow the ship after them. But their very efforts seemed to increase the counter-pull of the current. For some reason or other, the pinnace was suddenly dragged backwards towards the ship and the long towing rope described a bow like a whiplash when the driver cracks it. So this hope vanished.

Prayers alternated with lamentations and the situation grew more desperate, when some goatherds on the rocks above us whose fires we had seen for some time shouted with hollow voices that there was a ship below about to founder. Much that they cried was unintelligible, but some passengers, familiar with their dialect, took these cries to mean that they were gleefully looking forward to the booty they would fish out of the sea the next morning. Any consoling doubt as to whether our ship was really dangerously near the rocks was soon banished when we saw the sailors taking up long poles with which, if the worst came to the worst, they could keep fending the ship off the rocks. Of course, if the poles broke, all would be lost. The violence of the surf seemed to be increasing, the ship tossed and rolled more than ever; as a result, my seasickness returned and I had to retire to the cabin below. I lay down half dazed but with a certain feeling of contentment, due, perhaps, to the sea of Tiberias; for in my mind's eye, I saw clearly before me the etching from the Merian Bible. It gave me proof that all impressions of a sensory-moral nature are strongest when a man is thrown completely on his own resources.

How long I had been lying in this kind of half-sleep I could not tell, but I was roused out of it by a tremendous noise over my head. My ears told me that it came from dragging heavy ropes about the deck, and this gave me some hope that the sails were being hoisted. Shortly afterwards Kniep came down in a hurry to tell me we were safe. A very gentle breeze had sprung up; they had just been struggling to hoist the sails, and he himself had not neglected to lend a hand. We had, he said, visibly moved away from the cliff, and, though we were not yet completely out of the current, there was hope now of escaping from it. On deck everything was quiet again. Presently, several other passengers came to tell me about the lucky turn of events and to lie down themselves.

GOETHE

April 9, 1868

The night voyage, though far from pleasant, has not been as bad as might have been anticipated. He is fortunate, who, after ten hours of sea passage can reckon up no worse memories than those of a passive condition of suffering—of that dislocation of mind and body, or inability to think straightforward, so to speak, when the outer man is twisted, and rolled, and jerked, and the movements of thought seem more or less to correspond with those of the body. Wearily go by

> "The slow sad hours that bring us all things ill,"

and vain is the effort to enliven them as every fresh lurch of the vessel tangles practical or pictorial suggestions with untimely scraps of poetry, indistinct regrets and predictions, couplets for a new *Book of Nonsense,* and all kinds of inconsequent imbecilities —after this sort—

Would it not have been better to have remained at Cannes, where I had not yet visited Theoule, the Saut de Loup, and other places?

Had I not said, scores of times, such and such a voyage was the last I would make?

To-morrow, when "morn broadens on the borders of the dark," shall I see Corsica's "snowy mountain-tops fringing the (Eastern) sky"?

Did the sentinels of lordly Volaterra see, as Lord Macaulay says they did, "Sardinia's snowy mountain-tops," and not rather these same Corsican tops, "fringing the southern sky"?

Did they see any tops at all, or if any, which tops?

Will the daybreak ever happen?

Will 2 o'clock ever arrive?

Will the two poodles above stairs ever cease to run about the deck?

Is it not disagreeable to look forward to two or three months of travelling quite alone?

Would it not be delightful to travel, as J.A.S. is about to do, in company with a wife and child?

Does it not, as years advance, become clearer that it is very odious to be alone?

Have not many very distinguished persons, Œnone among others, arrived at this conclusion?

Did she not say, with evident displeasure—

> "And from that time to this I am alone,
> And I shall be alone until I die"?—

Will those poodles ever cease from trotting up and down the deck?

Is it not unpleasant, at fifty-six years of age, to feel that it is increasingly probable that a man can never hope to be otherwise than alone, never, no, never more?

Did not Edgar Poe's raven distinctly say, "Nevermore"?

Will those poodles be quiet? "Quoth the raven, nevermore."

Will there be anything worth seeing in Corsica?

Is there any romance left in that island? is there any sublimity or beauty in its scenery?

Have I taken too much baggage?

Have I not rather taken too little?

Am I not an idiot for coming at all?—

Thus, and in such a groove, did the machinery of thought go on, gradually refusing to move otherwise than by jerky spasms, after the fashion of mechanical Ollendorff exercises, or verb-catechisms of familiar phrases—

Are there not Banditti?

Had there not been Vendetta?

Were there not Corsican brothers?

Should I not carry clothes for all sorts of weather?

Must THOU not have taken a dress coat?

Had HE not many letters of introduction?

Might WE not have taken extra pairs of spectacles?

Could YOU not have provided numerous walking boots? . . .

May THEY not find cream cheeses?

Should there not be innumerable moufflons?

Ought not the cabin lamps and glasses to cease jingling?

Might not the poodles stop worrying?—

thus and thus, till by reason of long hours and monotonous rolling and shaking, a sort of comatose insensibility, miscalled sleep, takes the place of all thought, and so the night passes.

EDWARD LEAR

W*ar*

There have been few more radical changes in the history of Western culture than the change in attitude towards war and the military profession brought about by World War I. Western literature began as the literature of a warrior aristocracy, and until 1914 it took the warrior ethic for granted; it assumed that war was glorious, and the words *hero* and *warrior* were almost synonymous. Conscription and "sophisticated" weapons have changed all that. We may still believe that in certain circumstances a war is just and necessary, but nobody imagines any longer that it will be fun; today we know that war is an atrocious and corrupting business. We can no longer read an epic like the *Iliad* in the same way that even our grandfathers read it; to us, the passages in which Homer describes combat are painful reading, and we turn with relief to the Chinese poets, for whom the soldier was an object of pity, not admiration.

The symbol of the change was the construction after 1918 in all the belligerent countries of monuments to the Unknown Soldier. Previously, monuments had always been erected to known individuals, victorious generals and admirals. About the Unknown Soldier nothing is known whatever except that he lost his life. For all we know, he may, personally, have been a coward. In his monument, that is to say, we pay homage to the warrior, not as a hero but as a martyr.

The story goes that during World War I a Guards officer was on leave. "Do tell us," said his clubmates, "what is war like?" "Awful!" he replied. "The noise! And the *people!*"

Three-quarters of a soldier's life is spent in aimlessly waiting about.

EUGEN ROSENSTOCK-HUESSY

Soldiers who don't know what they are fighting for, know, nevertheless, what they're not fighting for.

KARL KRAUS

I hate war: it ruins conversation.

FONTENELLE

After a lost war one should only write comedies.

NOVALIS

A nation which lives a pastoral and innocent life never decorates the shepherd's staff or the plough-handle; but races who live by depredation and slaughter nearly always bestow exquisite ornaments on the quiver, the helmet and the spear.

You talk of the scythe of Time, and the tooth of Time: I tell you, Time is scytheless and toothless; it is we who gnaw like the worm—we who smite like the scythe. It is ourselves who abolish —ourselves who consume: we are the mildew, and the flame; and the soul of man is to its own work as the moth that frets when it cannot fly, and as the hidden flame that blasts where it cannot illuminate. All these lost treasures of human intellect have been wholly destroyed by human industry of destruction; the marble would have stood its two thousand years as well in the polished statue as in the Parian cliff; but we men have ground it to powder, and mixed it with our own ashes. The walls and the ways would have stood—it is we who have left but one stone upon another, and restored its pathlessness to the desert; the great cathedrals of the old religion would have stood—it is we who have dashed down the carved work with axes and hammers, and bid the mountain-grass bloom upon the pavement, and the sea-winds chant in the galleries.

RUSKIN

All living beings have received their weapons through the same process of evolution that moulded their impulses and inhibitions; for the structural plan of the body and the system of behaviour of a species are parts of the same whole. There is only one being in possession of weapons which do not grow on his body and of whose working plan, therefore, the instincts of his species know nothing and in the usage of which he has no corresponding inhibition.

KONRAD LORENZ

What a country calls its vital economic interests are not the things which enable its citizens to live, but the things which enable it to make war. Gasoline is much more likely than wheat to be a cause of international conflict.

SIMONE WEIL

The Night Watch

Here they stand watch in an ambush of moonshadow
cast by the sloping mountains where night is born

and soars up bearing its stars like bright eagles.

Some rest—those who trust courage—sword-guarded,
mute, safe from fear's grip in their sheltering long shields.

What hour does night's round-shield say it is?
The Big Dipper keeps ladling out stars.

Over there the mercenaries start bragging of luck,
yesterday's, to-morrow's, to hurry the festive day.

Kill legions . . . strip the fat fields, take towns
. . . or a woman, what luck's truer than a woman?

And over there others try to muzzle their gut-gripes:

When will there be a lull in the fighting, when
will hard war end? Our plows, our fields wait.

The sky slowly changes its huge guard of stars.

And there's the young lieutenant, sword buckled
over his heart and his soul on his smooth face:

Soon it's to be life or death . . . either one
means someone's harvest or old age shall ripen.
Live, die, I'm not afraid. Father, fatherland . . .
life-giving earth . . . be safe.

The night marches on, armored in burning stars.

The freedom they shall fight for, may it last forever.

ENNIUS
(Assembled from fragments and trans. by Janet Lembke)

The War-Song of Dinas Vawr

The mountain sheep are sweeter,
But the valley sheep are fatter;
We therefore deemed it meeter
To carry off the latter;
We made an expedition,
We met a host and quelled it;
We forced a strong position,
And killed the men who held it.

On Dyfed's richest valley,
Where herds of kine were browsing,
We made a mighty sally,
To finish our carousing.
Fierce warriors rushed to meet us;
We met them and o'erthrew them:
They struggled hard to beat us;
But we conquered them and slew them.

As we drove our prize at leisure,
The king marched forth to catch us;

His rage surpassed all measure,
But his people could not match us.
He fled to his hall-pillars;
And, ere our force we led off,
Some sacked his house and cellars,
While others cut his head off.

We there, in strife bewild'ring,
Spilt blood enough to swim in:
We orphaned many children,
And widowed many women.
The eagles and the ravens
We glutted with our foemen;
The heroes and the cravens,
The spearmen and the bowmen.

We brought away from battle,
And much their land bemoaned them,
Two thousand head of cattle,
And the head of him who owned them:
Ednyfed, King of Dyfed,
His head was borne before us;
His wine and beasts supplied our feasts,
And his overthrow, our chorus.

                              T. L. PEACOCK

Walcheren

Dumb Show

*A vast army is encamped here, and in the open spaces are infan-
try on parade—skeletoned men, some flushed, some shivering,
who are kept moving because it is dangerous to stay still. Every
now and then one falls down, and is carried away to a hospital
with no roof, where he is laid, bedless, on the ground.*

*In the distance soldiers are digging graves for the funerals
which are to take place after dark, delayed till then that the sight*

of so many may not drive the living melancholy-mad. Faint
noises are heard in the air.

SHADE OF THE EARTH
What storm is this of souls dissolved in sighs,
And what the dingy doom it signifies?

SPIRIT OF THE PITIES
We catch a lamentation shaped thuswise:

CHORUS OF PITIES (*aerial music*)
"We who withstood the blasting blaze of war
When marshalled by the gallant Moore awhile,
Beheld the grazing death-bolt with a smile,
Closed combat edge to edge and bore to bore,
    Now rot upon this Isle!

"The ever wan morass, the dune, the blear
Sandweed, and tepid pool, and putrid smell,
Emaciate purpose to a fractious fear,
Beckon the body to its last low cell—
    A chink no chart will tell.

"O ancient Delta, where the fen-lights flit!
Ignoble sediment of loftier lands,
Thy humour clings about our hearts and hands
And solves us to its softness, till we sit
    As we were part of it.

"Such force as fever leaves is maddened now,
With tidings trickling in from day to day
Of others' differing fortunes, wording how
They yield their lives to baulk a tyrant's sway—
    Yielded not vainly, they!

"In champaigns green and purple, far and near,
In town and thorpe where quiet spire-cocks turn,

Through vales, by rocks, beside the brooding burn
Echoes the aggressor's arrogant career;
　　　And we pent pithless here!

"Here where each creeping day the creeping file
Draws past with shouldered comrades score on score,
Bearing them to their lightless last asile,
Where weary wave-wails from the clammy shore
　　　Will reach their ears no more.

"We might have fought, and had we died, died well,
Even if in dynasts' discords not our own;
Our death-spot some sad haunter might have shown,
Some tongue have asked our sires or sons to tell
　　　The tale of how we fell.

"But such bechanced not. Like the mist we fade,
No lustrous lines engrave in story we,
Our country's chiefs, for their own fames afraid,
Will leave our names and fates by this pale sea
　　　To perish silently!"

Spirit of the Years

Why must ye echo as mechanic mimes
These mortal minions' bootless cadences,
Played on the stops of their anatomy
As is the mewling music on the strings
Of yonder ship-masts by the unweeting wind,
Or the frail tune upon this withering sedge
That holds its papery blades against the gale?
—Men pass to dark corruption, at the best,
Ere I can count five score: these why not now?—
The Immanent Shaper builds Its beings so,
Whether ye sigh their sighs with them or no!

The night fog enwraps the isle and the dying English army.

THOMAS HARDY

Journey to the North

From hump-backed paths I gaze on the temple of Fu;
Valleys and precipices appear and disappear in turn.
Already my path has reached the water's edge.
My serving man is still among the trees.
The horned owl hoots amid yellow mulberries.
The field mice run from their scattered holes.
In the depth of night we cross a battlefield;
A cold moon shines on white bones.
I ponder the fate of a myriad soldiers speedily defeated
In days gone by on the fields of Tung-kuan,
When half the people of the province of Ch'ing
Fell dead, were wounded, were injured and slain.

Chariots Go Forth to War

Chariots rumble and roll; horses whinney and neigh;
Men are marching with bows and arrows at their hips.
Their parents and wives hurry to bid farewell,
Raising clouds of dust over Hsien-yang Bridge.
They pull at the soldiers' clothes, stamp their feet and cry
out.
The sound of their crying soars to the clouds.

Some passers-by speak to the soldiers;
They shake their heads dumbly and say:
"Since the age of fifteen we have defended the northern
rivers.
Till we are forty we shall serve on the western front.
We leave our homes as youths and return as gray-haired men.
Along the frontiers there flows the sea of our blood.
The King hungers for territory—therefore we fight.

"Have you not heard, sir,
How through two hundred countries east of the Tai-yeng
Mountains

Through thousands of villages and tens of thousands of
    hamlets
Thorns and nettles run wild?
Sturdy peasant women swing the hoes and drive the plow,
But neither in the east nor west is anything raised or sown.
The soldiers of Sh'and will fight to the end,
But they cannot be slain like dogs or like hens.

"Oh, sir, it is kind of you to ask me,
But how dare we express our resentment?
Winter has come and the year is passing away;
The war on the western passes is still going on.
The magistrates are pressing us to pay our taxes,
But where shall we get the money?
If only I had known the fate in store for boys,
I would have had my children all girls,
For girls may be married to the neighbors,
But boys are born only to be cut down and buried beneath
    the grass.

"Do you not see, sir,
The long dead ancient bones near the Blue Sea bleached by
    the sun?
And now the lament of those who have just died
Mingles with the voices of those who died long ago,
And darkness falls, and the rain, and the ghostly whimpering
    of voices."

TU FU
(trans. Pu Chiang-hsing)

Bed-Wetting in Barracks

Various writers have observed that enuresis seems to be unduly
common among soldiers. Discounting the not inconsiderable
number of cases of malingering, where bed-wetting is deliberately resorted to in an attempt to obtain a disability discharge or
at least to escape active service, veritable epidemics of real enuresis occur from time to time. If these outbreaks were reported

only among men who are actively engaged in combat or who are training for imminent service, the logical assumption would be that anxiety is here the prime etiological factor. The fact that enuresis may also be recurrent or more or less chronic in barracks during times of prolonged peace suggests a different explanation, namely, that the discipline and arbitrary treatment which form so large a part of military training may reinstate in young men attitudes of hostility and resentment which they felt as children toward parental authority. . . .

O. H. MOWRER

4th Armored

. . . That Colonel Abrams. He sure saved a lotta lives.
Abrams love his ole radio. He git him inta town;
What a lotta bullshit that man throw;
"Now hear this. Now hear this. We have you surrouned."
Surrouned? My ass, but that's Abrams.

"Hear this, you-all.
We have you poor sonsa bitches completely surrouned.
If you-all doan come out an surrener esatly ten minutes,
Our artillery, which have your town already pinpoint,
Will commence."

In esatly ten minute everyone come out. An surrener.
Like usually they do; sometime, not.
One time we lose four tanks in fifteen minute to some of them
Goddam Hitler youth with panzer fists.
They burn our tanks. Flame-throwers. Cooked. We didn
          have
A chance. Them Hitler-youth kids. Was they fierce!

We see one stand up with his girl, her about twelve, maybe
          thirteen,
Both of them with their type bazooka.
Charlie have his Heinie P.38. Wasn use to it then neither.

One hunerd yards, a long shot fera pistol. Hell, long fera
    carbeen.
Hot damn. That kid drop like a hammer hit him.
Later, went over fera look. Charlie plug him jus unner the
    left eye.

He was going to pot sister too. I guess it was his sister.
I say: "Charlie, doan do that."

Then this door. I open up, easy-like. Tavern sorta bar;
They sell beer an santwitches?
Inside?
I'm a son of a bitch if weren twenty-eight Heinie officers,
Two machine-gun tripods, mounted low, on tables—
Swing roun angle one huner eighty degree;
Twenty-eight men, all officers. I count three womin too.
I tell you, mac. I had a lotta things go through my head.

I riz my hand jus like to say:
"Not one peep outa you bastids. You-all jus come on out."
I do this cause I know damn well we have evrythin set up,
    outside.
Atually, this town was very well covered.

Them Krauts come out. They lef their weapons heap on a
    table.
This here P.38, the one Charlie got; he got it here.
Another time, a bluff like this mightn work.
Atually, these Krauts almos didn believe me or somethin
Some silly son of a bitch start to open up.

We had 75's, 88's, 101's, evry fuckin gun you kin think of
In hills back of this town, listenin fer one shot.
They hear this one shot.
Christ: we start to fire, just at roof level:
One, two, three.
Then we hit a leetle lower, a leetle lower—an lower.
Special, we pick out any tall tower, like a church steeple.
One, two, three.

Man, was this cute! Like a typewriter:
One, two,
Three.

LINCOLN KIRSTEIN

A Wartime Baby

Anna's life began in a dugout under a farmer's house in Poland, where her Jewish parents were in hiding to escape extermination by the Germans. Her parents were ill-mated. The mother found the father utterly unattractive and had rejected his courtship for years. Both parents felt they were of opposite temperaments and background. By the time World War II broke out, the father had given up hope of winning the mother, but the invasion of Poland suddenly changed things.

Foreseeing what would happen once Germany had occupied Poland, the father collected a large amount of wool and made arrangements with a gentile peasant friend to staple it in a dugout under his farm-house, together with a loom. When the Germans began to exterminate all Jews, Anna's father took permanent refuge in his small earthen cellar. But first he tried once more to persuade the woman he loved to join him. This proposal she again firmly rejected. She had no use for him, she said, and would sooner be killed by the Germans than be his wife.

Soon things worsened and most of her family was killed. The father, who could no longer leave his hiding place, sent word to her again through his peasant friend, asking her to join him. By this time she was homeless and alone. So very much against her will she took refuge with the father . . . Her condition for accepting was that they would have no sexual relations.

The father managed to support himself and her, and in part also the peasant who hid them during the whole of the German occupation, by weaving in his underground hole. The peasant sold the sweaters that were woven, and by spending what he got for them (clothing being at a premium) he and the couple in hiding were able to live. But the dugout was so small there was not enough space for the parents to so much as stretch out at night unless the loom was taken down. Only then could they bed themselves for the night, using the wool for both cover and bed. . . .

About what then happened, the parents' stories differ. According to the father, they had to tremble for their lives every day, but he at least had his work to keep him going, while his wife was beginning to lose her will to live. In desperation he decided that if she had a child, it would restore her interest in living and might even make her accept him. So he convinced her to have a child, and she agreed to have sex relations for this purpose alone. These were the circumstances in which his wife became pregnant.

According to the mother, the father had never ceased his sexual pursuit. After a year of this, he was no longer willing or able to stand the presence of a woman whom he wanted so much and who rejected him, so he threatened to drive her out of the refuge. Either she slept with him as his wife, or she had to leave—which was tantamount to a death warrant. Under such duress she gave in.

As one can imagine, both before and after Anna was born, there were many fights—the mother screaming how she hated him, couldn't be his wife, had no use for him, and he fighting back in bitterness. To make matters worse, the peasant feared for his life if they should be heard, and threatened to kick them out unless they remained absolutely still and kept the peace. . . .

When Anna, the child of this relation, was born, she did occupy the mother and give her some interest in life, but it made life still more difficult in their narrow confinement. When Anna tried to cry, as infants do, one of the parents had to hold a hand over her mouth since any noise, particularly a baby's crying, would have given them all away. . . .

As long as the mother could nurse Anna, the infant had at least enough food. But her milk gave out before Anna was a year and a half old. Then all the parents could feed her were raw vegetables or such like, since they could not cook in their dugout. Only in 1945, when the Russian occupation had replaced that of the Germans, did things improve a bit. But by that time Anna was unmanageable.

BRUNO BETTELHEIM

Water, Running

᠂ᔆᣛᣛ

Though much a little map unfolds, more still—
Far more—is that which now dissolving mists
The sun confounds and distances deny;
Dumb Wonder speaks by silence, her blind eye
Allows the river, son of that same hill,
        Whose prolix discourse twists
Benevolent to tryannise the plain.
Its borders lined with many an orchard lawn,
If not with flowers stolen from the Dawn,
The stream flows straight while it does not aspire
The heights with its own crystals to attain;
Flees from itself to find itself again,
Is lost, and searching for its wanderings.
Both errors sweet and sweet meanderings
The waters make with their lascivious fire;
And, linking buildings in its silver force.
With bowers crowned, majestically flows
Into abundant branches, there to wind
'Mid isles that green parentheses provide
In the main period of the current's course;
From the high cavern where it first arose,
Until the liquid jasper, there to find
All memory lost and forfeited all pride.

GÓNGORA
(trans. E. M. Wilson)

Springs

There is attraction in every spring or source, but the birthplace
of great rivers, as of great men, is sometimes comparatively unin-
spiring and obscure. Neither Thames Head, near Coberley, nor
the Seven Springs, near Kemble—rival sources of the Thames—is
to-day very impressive, while the bright Test rises in a dull little

Pond by a Hampshire farm, and both Severn and Wye trickle from trifling basins on the boggy slopes of Plinlimmon. Peaty hills and alluvial lowlands alike confuse the sources of their rivers, though they sustain their flow. The fascination of a clear and quivering well-head is redoubled by its comparative rarity among the soft soils and gently moulded hillocks of most English landscapes. Water is the prime necessity of life, and there is a magic in its mysterious upwelling; from the earliest days springs were centres of Nature-worship—natural shrines—and when we play at wishing our wish by the well at Upwey, it is the shadow of an ancient prayer. Their purity is symbolic, and saints and hermits dwelt beside them for their spiritual suggestiveness as well as for the satisfaction of physical need. Beside churches in Wales we can still see the spring, though often sapped and shrunken, that sustained the missionary saint. New settlers clustered thickest where springs were most frequent. Follow the road from Dunstable to Wallingford beneath the Chiltern Hills, or from Helmsley nearly to Scarborough in Yorkshire, and see how closely the villages follow. Often the church, and the mill, and some old cottages, gather close around the spring, forming an unspoilt village picture. The spring called Broadwell, close beside the church at Dursley, in Gloucestershire, preserves in a small town of reviving manufactures the freshness of its older life; and at Swangge the millpond still hangs by the church on the hillside, as if the wateringplace was still a quarrymen's village.

Deep springs welling from a shaft in soft soil rise with unearthly colours. The blueness of complete purity mingles with the faint green of the slightest vegetable contamination into a confusion of wavering lights like the flames over a snapdragon dish. Beneath the blue and the green dance the sand-clouds in a moonlit glimmer. The unearthliness of these colours is heightened by the apparent suspension of the laws of gravity, for the sand seems to rise in defiance of any known principle—so quietly, except for this one sign, gushes the spring. Smaller springs reveal their mechanics more clearly. On the shallow floor we can trace by the small sand-eddies the vents in the angled unworn gravel from which the water is rising. However closely the cresses and blue water-speedwell press upon it, the restlessness of these sand-spirts keeps a clear space of grit and gravel for the issue of the spring. Minnows flick past the spinning sand-towers, like whales between waterspouts; and that broad-headed brookfish, called miller's thumb, or bullhead, lurks, spotted, among the pebbles on the spring's floor. In many of the chalk counties the outlet of the spring has been widened to make a watercress-bed, and is verdant and full of life at all seasons. Wagtails, pied and gold-washed, run and clamber among the cresses to seize small water-snails and wa-ter-flies; as frost seals the crust of the fields, and coats the ponds with ice, the cottage child filling the morning bucket sees a snipe dart from the unfrozen edge where it has fed. Kingfishers perch on the holly boughs stretched from the bank above the spring, and splash in the stillness as they dive for miller's thumb or min-now. Yet fair as are these limpid risings, still more radiant, and in England much rarer, are the fountains which stream from gashes in live rock. They plunge with a flash and babble which has the gaiety of a town fountain in a setting of rustic freshness; and though they half reveal no such mysterious depths as a deep chalk spring, they restore for us, among our own scenes of flag and fern, the pictured charm of Italian spouting marbles, and of the stream which Moses struck from the Rock.

ANTHONY COLLETT

A Mill

Two leaps the water from its race
  Made to the brook below,
The first leap it was curving glass,
  The second bounding snow.

WILLIAM ALLINGHAM

Weather, The

❧

I would give part of my lifetime for the sake of knowing what is the average barometer reading in Paradise.

G. C. LICHTENBERG

No man, I suspect, ever lived long in the country without being bitten by . . . meteorological ambitions. He likes to be hotter and colder, to have been more deeply snowed up, to have more trees and larger blown down than his neighbors.

JAMES RUSSELL LOWELL

Rain

Rain, midnight rain, nothing but the wild rain
On this bleak hut, and solitude, and me
Remembering again that I shall die
And neither hear the rain nor give it thanks
For washing me cleaner than I have been
Since I was born into this solitude.
Blessed are the dead that the rain rains upon:
But here I pray that none whom I once loved
Is dying to-night or lying still awake
Solitary, listening to the rain,
Either in pain or thus in sympathy
Helpless among the living and the dead,
Like a cold water among broken reeds,
Myriads of broken reeds all still and stiff,
Like me who have no love which this wild rain
Has not dissolved except the love of death,
If love it be towards what is perfect and
Cannot, the tempest tells me, disappoint.

EDWARD THOMAS

I look out of the window; there walks long Anthony.

Russian riddle

Clouds

I must here relate something that appears very interesting to me, and something, which, though it must have been seen by every man that has lived in the country, or at least, in any hilly country, has never been particularly mentioned by anybody as far as I can recollect. We frequently talk of clouds coming from dews; and we actually see the heavy fogs become clouds. We see them go up to the tops of hills, and, taking a swim round, actually come, and drop down upon us, and wet us through. But, I am now going to speak of clouds, coming out of the sides of hills in exactly the same manner that you see smoke come out of a tobacco pipe, and, rising up, with a wider and wider head, like the smoke from a tobacco-pipe, go to the top of the hill or over the hill, or very much above it, and then come over the valleys in rain. At about a mile's distance from Mr. Palmer's house at Bollitree, in Herefordshire, there is a large, long beautiful wood, covering the side of a lofty hill, winding round in the form of a crescent, the bend of the crescent being toward Mr. Palmer's house. It was here, that I first observed this mode of forming clouds. The first time I noticed it, I pointed it out to Mr. Palmer. We stood and observed cloud after cloud, come from different parts of the side of the hill, and tower up and go over the hill out of sight. He told me that that was a certain sign that it would rain that day, for that these clouds would come back again, and would fall in rain. It rained sure enough; and I found that the country people, all round about, held this mode of the forming of the clouds as a sign of rain. The hill is called Penyard, and this forming of the clouds, they call Old Penyard's smoking his pipe; and it is a rule that it is sure to rain during the day, if Old Penyard smokes his pipe in the morning. These appearances take place, especially in warm and sultry weather. It was very warm yesterday morning: it had thundered violently the evening before: we felt it hot even while the rain fell upon us at Butser-hill. Petersfield lies in a pretty broad and very beautiful valley. On three sides of it are very lofty hills, partly downs and partly covered with trees: and, as we proceeded on our way from the bottom of Butser-hill to Petersfield, we saw thousands upon thousands of clouds, continually coming puffing out from different parts of these hills and towering up to the top of them. I stopped George several times to make him look at them; to see them come puffing out of the chalk downs as well as out of the woodland hills; and bade him remember to tell his father of it, when he should go home, to convince him that the hills of Hampshire, could smoke their pipes, as well as those of Herefordshire. This is a really curious matter. I have never read, in any book, anything to lead me to suppose that the observation has ever found its ways into print before. Sometimes you will see only one or two clouds during a whole morning, come out of the side of a hill; but we saw thousands upon thousands, bursting out, one after another, in all parts of these immense hills. The first time that I have leisure, when I am in the high countries again, I will have a conversation with some old shepherd about this matter: if he cannot enlighten me upon the subject, I am sure that no philosopher can. . . .

WILLIAM COBBETT

Winter of 1784

The first week in December was very wet, with the barometer very low. On the 7th, with the barometer at 28, five-tenths, came on a vast snow, which continued all that day and the next, and most part of the following night; so that by the morning of the 9th the works of men were quite overwhelmed, the lanes filled so as to be impassable, and the ground covered twelve or fifteen inches without any drifting. In the evening of the 9th, the air began to be so very sharp that we thought it would be curious to attend to the motions of a thermometer: we therefore hung out two; one made by Martin and one by Dolland, which soon began to show us what we were to expect; for, by ten o'clock, they fell to 21, and at eleven to 4, when we went to bed. On the 10th, in the morning, the quicksilver of Dolland's glass was down to half a degree below zero; and that of Martin's, which was absurdly graduated only to four degrees above zero, sunk quite into the brass guard of the ball; so that when the weather became most interesting this was useless. On the 10th, at eleven at night, though the air was perfectly still, Dolland's glass went down to one degree below zero! This strange severity of the weather made me very desirous to know what degree of cold there might be in such an exalted and near situation as Newton. We had therefore, on the morning of the 10th, written to Mr. ——, and entreated him to hang out his thermometer, made by Adams; and to pay some attention to it morning and evening; expecting wonderful phænomena, in so elevated a region, at two hundred feet or more above my house. But, behold! on the 10th, at eleven at night, it was down only to 17, and the next morning at 22, when mine was at 10! . . .

I must not omit to tell you that, during those two Siberian days, my parlour-cat was so electric, that had a person stroked her, and been properly insulated, the shock might have been given to a whole circle of people.

GILBERT WHITE

The Thunderstorm

Suddenly there was a brief glimmer all around us, reddening the rocks. It was the first flash of lightning, but it had been silent, and no thunder followed it.

We walked on. Presently there was more lightning, and as the evening had already darkened appreciably, and the light was diffused by the opaque cloud layer, the limestone turned rose-red before our eyes at every flash.

When we reached the point at which our ways parted, the priest stopped and looked at me. I conceded that the storm was breaking, and said that I would go home with him.

So we took the road leading to the Kar, and walked down the gentle rocky slope into the meadow.

On reaching the presbytery, we sat down for a little on the wooden bench in front of the house. The storm was now in full development and was standing from end to end of the sky like a dark rampart. Presently, against this unbroken darkness, across the foot of the storm wall, we saw long puffed-up streaks of drifting white vapor. So over there the storm had perhaps already begun, although where we were there was still not a leaf or a blade of grass stirring. Those drifting swollen clouds are often bad omens in stormy weather; they always presage violent gales and often hail and flooding. And the flashes of lightning were now being followed by clearly audible thunder.

Finally we went into the house.

The priest said that when there was a storm at night, it was his habit to place a lighted candle on his table and to sit quietly in front of it until the storm was over. During the day, he said, he sat at the table without a candle. He asked me if I had any objection to his observing this custom on the present occasion too. I reminded him of his promise not to put himself out in the slightest degree on my account. So he accompanied me through the entrance hall into the familiar little room, and invited me to take off my things.

I usually carried with me on a leather strap over my shoulder a case containing drawing materials, and also some surveying instruments. Fastened next to the case was a satchel where I kept my cold food, my wine, my drinking glass, and my wine cooler. I took these things off and hung them over the back of a chair in a corner of the room. I stood my long measuring rod against one of the yellow cupboards.

Meanwhile the priest had left the room, and he now entered carrying a candle. It was a tallow candle in a brass candlestick. He placed the candlestick on the table and laid a pair of brass snuffers beside it. Then we both sat down at the table and remained seated, waiting for the storm.

It now seemed imminent. When the priest had brought the candle, the small remnant of daylight that was still coming through the windows had vanished. The windows stood like black panels, and night had fallen completely. The lightning was more vivid, and in spite of the candle each flash lit up every corner of the room. The thunder became more solemn and menacing. Thus things continued for some time. Then at last came the first blast of the storm wind. The tree in front of the house trembled softly for a moment, as if stricken by a fleeting breeze, then it was still again. A little while later there was another tremor, more prolonged and profound. Shortly afterwards came a violent blast, all the leaves rustled, the branches seemed to be shuddering, to judge by the noise we heard from indoors; and now the roar continued unabated. The tree by the house, the hedges surrounding it, and all the bushes and trees of the neighborhood were caught up in one great rushing howl that merely waxed and waned by turns. Through it came the peals of thunder. They grew more and more frequent and penetrating. But the storm had still not reached us. There was still an interval between lightning and thunder, and the lightning, brilliant though it was, came in sheets and not in forked flashes.

At last the first raindrops struck the windows. They hammered singly against the glass but soon there were more of them, and before long, the rain was streaming down in torrents. It increased rapidly, with a hissing, rushing sound, until in the end it was as if whole continuous massive volumes of water were pouring down onto the house, as if the house were throbbing under the weight of it and one could feel the throbbing and groaning from inside. Even the rolling thunder was scarcely audible through the roar of the water; the roaring water became a second thunder. Finally the storm was immediately overhead. The lightning fell like lanyards of fire, the flashes were followed instantly by the hoarse thunderclaps which now triumphed over all the rest of the uproar, and the windowpanes shuddered and rattled under their deep reverberating echoes.

I was glad now that I had followed the priest's advice. I had seldom experienced such a storm. The priest was sitting quietly and simply by the table in his little room, with the light of the tallow candle shining on him.

At last there came a crash of thunder that seemed to try to lift the whole house up out of its foundations and hurl it down, and a second crash followed at once. Then there was a short pause, as often happens in the course of such phenomena; the rain broke off for a moment as if in alarm; even the wind stopped. But soon everything was as before; and yet the main onslaught had been broken, and everything continued more steadily. Little by little the storm abated. The gale fell to no more than a steady wind, the rain weakened, the lightning paled, and the thunder became a dull mutter that seemed to be retreating across-country.

At last, when the rain had died down to a mere continuous drizzle and the lightning to a flicker, the priest stood up and said: "It is over."

ADALBERT STIFTER
(trans. David Luke)

Words, Last

᠊ᖤᖫ᠊

In these days when it has become the medical convention, firstly, to keep the dying in ignorance of their condition and, secondly, to keep them under sedation, how are any of us to utter what could be legitimately called our "last" words? Still, it is fun to imagine what one would like them to be. The best proposed comment I know of is that of my friend Chester Kallman: "I've never done this before."

Among those last words which are reputedly historical, some seem too much in character to be credible as really "last." For instance:

"But the peasants—how do the *peasants* die?"

TOLSTOY

"What's the use? She would only want me to take a message to dear Albert."

DISRAELI
(on hearing that Queen Victoria would like to visit him)

"Let us go in; the fog is rising."

EMILY DICKINSON

For stylishness, it would be difficult to do better than the French eighteenth-century aristocratic lady (whose name I've forgotten):

"*Un instant, Monsieur le Curé; nous partirons ensemble.*"

Work, Labor, and Play

❦§❧

So far as I know, Miss Hannah Arendt was the first person to define the essential difference between work and labor. To be happy, a man must feel, firstly, free and, secondly, important. He cannot be really happy if he is compelled by society to do what he does not enjoy doing, or if what he enjoys doing is ignored by society as of no value or importance. In a society where slavery in the strict sense has been abolished, the sign that what a man does is of social value is that he is paid money to do it, but a laborer today can rightly be called a wage slave. A man is a laborer if the job society offers him is of no interest to himself but he is compelled to take it by the necessity of earning a living and supporting his family.

The antithesis to labor is play. When we play a game, we enjoy what we are doing, otherwise we should not play it, but it is a purely private activity; society could not care less whether we play it or not.

Between labor and play stands work. A man is a worker if he is personally interested in the job which society pays him to do; what from the point of view of society is necessary labor is from his own point of view voluntary play. Whether a job is to be classified as labor or work depends, not on the job itself, but on the tastes of the individual who undertakes it. The difference does not, for example, coincide with the difference between a manual and a mental job; a gardener or a cobbler may be a worker, a bank clerk a laborer. Which a man is can be seen from his attitude towards leisure. To a worker, leisure means simply the hours he needs to relax and rest in order to work efficiently. He is therefore more likely to take too little leisure than too much; workers die of coronaries and forget their wives' birthdays. To the laborer, on the other hand, leisure means freedom from compulsion, so that it is natural for him to imagine that the fewer hours he has to spend laboring, and the more hours he is free to play, the better.

What percentage of the population in a modern technological society are, like myself, in the fortunate position of being workers? At a guess I would say sixteen per cent, and I do not think that figure is likely to get bigger in the future.

Technology and the division of labor have done two things: by eliminating in many fields the need for special strength or skill, they have made a very large number of paid occupations which formerly were enjoyable work into boring labor, and by increasing productivity they have reduced the number of necessary laboring hours. It is already possible to imagine a society in which the majority of the population, that is to say, its laborers, will have almost as much leisure as in earlier times was enjoyed by the aristocracy. When one recalls how aristocracies in the past actually behaved, the prospect is not cheerful. Indeed, the problem of dealing with boredom may be even more difficult for such a future mass society than it was for aristocracies. The latter, for example, ritualized their time; there was a season to shoot grouse, a season to spend in town, etc. The masses are more likely to replace an unchanging ritual by fashion which it will be in the economic interest of certain people to change as often as possible. Again, the masses cannot go in for hunting, for very soon there would be no animals left to hunt. For other aristocratic amusements like gambling, dueling, and warfare, it may be only too easy to find equivalents in dangerous driving, drug-taking, and senseless acts of violence. Workers seldom commit acts of violence, because they can put their aggression into their work, be it physical like the work of a smith, or mental like the work of a scientist or an artist. The role of aggression in mental work is aptly expressed by the phrase "getting one's teeth into a problem."

It may be proved, with much certainty, that God intends no man to live in this world without working: but it seems to me no less evident that He intends every man to be happy in his work. . . . Now in order that people may be happy in their work, these three things are needed: They must be fit for it: they must not do too much of it: and they must have a sense of success in it— not a doubtful sense, such as needs some testimony of others for its confirmation, but a sure sense, or rather knowledge, that so much work has been done well, and fruitfully done, whatever the world may say or think about it. So that in order that a man may be happy, it is necessary that he should not only be capable of his work, but a good judge of his work.

RUSKIN

World, Creation of the

✺§❧

I tell of Giants from times forgotten,
Those who fed me in former days:
Nine worlds I can reckon, nine roots of the Tree,
The wonderful Ash, way under the ground.

When Ymir lived long ago
Was no sand or sea, no surging waves,
Nowhere was there earth nor heaven above,
But a grinning gap and grass nowhere.

The Sons of Bur then built up the lands,
Moulded in magnificence Middle-Earth:
Sun stared from the south on the stones of their hall,
From the ground there sprouted green leeks.

Sun turned from the south, Sister of Moon,
Her right arm rested on the rim of Heaven;

She had no inkling where her hall was,
Nor Moon a notion of what might he had,
The planets knew not where their places were.

The High Gods gathered in council
In their Hall of Judgement, all the rulers:
To Night and to Nightfall their names gave,
The Morning they named and the Mid-Day,
Mid-Winter, Mid-Summer, for the assigning of years.

At Ithervale the Aesir met:
Temple and altar they timbered and raised,
Set up a forge to smithy treasures,
Tongs they fashioned and tools wrought;

Played chess in the court and cheerful were;
Gold they lacked not, the gleaming metal.
Then came Three, the Thurse Maidens,
Rejoicing in their strength, from Gianthome.

The High Gods gathered in council
In their Hall of Judgement: Who of the Dwarves
Should mould man by mastercraft
From Brimir's blood and Blain's limbs?

Motsognir was their mighty ruler,
Greatest of the Dwarves, and Durin after him:
The Dwarves did as Durin directed,
Many man-forms made from the earth. . . .

From *Völuspà*
(trans. P. B. Taylor and W.H.A.)

World, End of the

☙⟨⟩☚

The Fifteen Days of Judgement

"Then there shall be signs in Heaven."—
Thus much in the text is given,
Worthy of the sinner's heeding:
But the other signs preceding
Earth's Last Judgement and destruction,
And its fiery reconstruction,
May be drawn from other channels;
For we read in Hebrew annals
That there shall be altogether
Fifteen Judgement days, but whether
Following or interpolated,
Jerome saith, is nowhere stated.

Day I

On the first day, loud upcrashing,
Shall the shoreless ocean, gnashing
With a dismal anaclysmal
Outrush from its deeps abysmal,
Lifted high by dread supernal
Storm the mountain heights eternal!
Forty cubits of sheer edges,
Wall-like o'er the summit-ridges
Stretching upright forth—a mirror
For the unutterable terror
Of the huddled howling nations,
Smit with sudden desolations,
Rushing hither, thither, drunken,
Half their pleasant realms sea-sunken.

Day II

On the second day, down-pouring,
Shall the watery walls drop roaring

From the ruinous precipices
To the nethermost abysses,
With a horrible waterquaking
In the world-wide cataracts, shaking
Earth's foundations as they thunder.—
Surf-plumed steeds of God Almighty,
Rock and pyramid, forest, city,
Through the flood-rent valleys scourging,
Wide in headlong ebb down-surging,
Down till eye of man scarce reaches
Where, within its sunken beaches,
Hidden from a world's amazement,
Cowers the Deep in self-abasement.

Day III

On the third day, o'er the seething
Of the leprous ocean writhing,
Whale and dragon, orc and kraken,
And leviathan, forsaken
His unfathomable eyrie,
To and fro shall plunge—the dreary
Dumb death-sickness of creation
Startling with their ululation.
Men shall hear the monsters bellow
Forth their burden as they wallow;
But its drift?—Let none demand it!
God alone shall understand it!

Day IV

On the fourth day, blazing redly,
With a reek pitch-black and deadly,
A consuming fire shall quiver
From all seas and every river!
Every brook and beck and torrent
Leaping in fiery current;
All the moats and meres and fountains
Lit, like beacons on the mountains;

Furnace-roar of smolten surges
Scarring earth's extremest verges!

Day V

On the fifth day, Judgement-stricken,
Every green herb, from the lichen
To the cedar of the forest,
Shall sweat blood in anguish sorest!
On the same, all fowls of heaven
Into one wide field, fear-driven,
Shall assemble, cowed and shrinking;
Neither eating aught, nor drinking;
Kind with kind, all ranked by feather,
Doves with doves aghast together,
Swan with swan in downfall regal,
Wren and wren, with eagle, eagle!
Ah! when fowl feel such foreboding,
What shall be the Sinner's goading?

Day VI

On the sixth day, through all nations
Shall be quaking of foundations,
With a horrible hollow rumbling—
All that all men builded crumbling
As the heel of Judgement tramples
Cot and palace, castles, temples,
Hall and minster, thorpe and city;—
All men too aghast for pity
In the crashing and the crushing
Of that stony stream's downrushing!—
And a flame of fiery warning
Forth from sundown until morning
With a lurid coruscation
Shall reveal night's desolation!

Day VII

On the seventh day, self-shattered,
Rifting fourfold, scarred and scattered,

Pounded in the Judgement's mortars,
Every stone shall split in quarters!
Pebble, whinstone, granite sparry,
Rock and boulder—stones of quarry,
Shaped or shapeless, all asunder
Shivering, split athwart and under;
And the splinters, each on other
Shall make war against his brother,
Each one grinding each to powder,
Grinding, gnashing, loud and louder,
Grinding, gnashing on till even,
With a dolorous plea to Heaven.
What the drift?—Let none demand it!
God alone shall understand it!

Day VIII

On the eighth, in dire commotion,
Shall the dry land heave like Ocean,
Puffed in hills and sucked in hollows,
Yawning into steep-down swallows—
Swelling, mountainously lifted
Skyward from the plains uprifted—
With a universal clamour
Rattling, roaring through the tremor;
While, flung headlong, all men living
Grovel in a wild misgiving!
What, O Sinner, shall avail your
Might in solid Earth's own failure?

Day IX

On the ninth day all the mountains
Shall drop bodily, like spent fountains,
All the cloud-capped pride of pristine
Peak and pinnacle amethystine
Toppling, drifting to the level,
Flooding all the dales with gravel;
One consummate moment blasting
All that seems so everlasting—

All men to the caves for shelter
Scurrying through the world-wide welter!

Day X

On the tenth day, hither, thither,
Herding from their holes together,
With a glaring of white faces,
Through the desolate wildernesses
Men shall o'er that mountain ruin
Run as from a Death's pursuing,—
Each one with suspicious scowling,
Shrinking from his fellow's howling—
For all human speech confounded
Shall not sound as once it sounded.
None shall understand his brother—
Mother, child, nor child his mother!

Day XI

On the eleventh day, at dawning,
Every sepulchre wide yawning
At the approach of Earth's Assessor,
Shall upyield its white possessor;—
All the skeletons, close-serried,
O'er the graves where each lay buried,
Mute upstanding, white and bony,
With a dreadful ceremony
Staring from the morn till gloaming
Eastward for the Judge's coming;
Staring on, with sockets eyeless,
Each one motionless and cryless,
Save the dry, dead-leaf-like chattering,
Thorugh that white-branched forest pattering.
What its drift?—Let none demand it!
God alone shall understand it!

Day XII

On the twelfth, the Planets seven
And all stars shall drop from Heaven!

On the same day, scared and trembling,
All four-footed things assembling,
Each after his kind in order—
All the lions in one border,
Sheep with sheep—not needing shepherd—
Stag with stag—with leopard, leopard—
Shall be herded cowed and shrinking,
Neither eating aught nor drinking,
But to Godward bellowing, shrieking,
Howling, barking, roaring, squeaking;—
What the drift? Let none demand it!
God alone shall understand it.

Day XIII

On the thirteenth awful morning
Shall go forth the latest warning,
With a close to all things mortal,
For the Judge is at the portal!
In an agony superhuman,
Every living man and woman,
Child and dotard—every breather—
Shall lie down and die together,
That all flesh in death's subjection
Shall abide the Resurrection!

Day XIV

On the fourteenth, morn to even,
Fire shall feed on Earth and Heaven,
Through the skies and all they cover,
Under earth, and on, and over;
All things ghostly, human, bestial,
In the crucible celestial
Tested by the dread purgation
On that final conflagration;
Till the intolerable whiteness
Dawn, of God's exceeding brightness
Through the furnace-flames erasure
Of yon mortal veil of azure!

Day XV

Last, the fifteenth day shall render
Earth a more than earthly splendor,
Once again shall word be given:
"Let there be new Earth, new Heaven!"
And this fleeting world—this charnel,
Purified, shall wax eternal!—
Then all souls shall Michael gather
At the footstool of the Father,
Summoning from Earth's four corners,
All erst human saints and scorners,
And without revenge or pity
Weigh them in the scales almighty!—
Sinner! Dost thou dread that trial?
Mark yon shadow on the dial!

Ast illi semper modo "cras, cras," umbra docebit.

SEBASTIAN EVANS

Loud howls Garm before Gnipahellir,
Bursting his fetters, Fenris runs:
Further in the future, afar I behold
The Twilight of the Gods who gave victory.

Brother shall strike brother and both fall,
Sisters' sons slay each other,
Evil be on earth, an Age of Whoredom,
Of sharp sword-play and shields' clashing,
A Wind-Age, a Wolf-Age, till the world ruins:
No man to another shall mercy show.

The waters are troubled, the waves surge up:
Announcing now the knell of Fate,
Heimdal winds his horn aloft,
On Hel's Road all men tremble.

Yggdrasil trembles, the towering Ash,
Groans in woe: the Wolf is loose:

Odin speaks with the Head of Mimir
Before he is swallowed by Surt's kin.

From the east drives Hrym, lifts up his shield,
The squamous serpent squirms with rage,
The Great Worm with the waves contending,
The pale-beaked eagle pecks at the dead,
Shouting for joy: the ship Naglfar

Sails out from the east, at its helm Loki,
With the children of darkness, the doom-bringers,
Offspring of monsters, allies of the Wolf,
All who Byleist's Brother follow.

What of the Gods? What of the Elves?
Gianthome groans, the Gods are in council,
The Dwarves grieve before their door of stone,
Masters of walls. *Well, would you know more?*

Surt with the bane of branches comes
From the south, on his sword the sun of Valgods,
Crags topple, the crone falls headlong,
Men tread Hel's Road, the Heavens split open.

A further woe falls upon Hlin
As Odin comes forth to fight the Wolf;
The killer of Beli battles with Surt:
Now shall fall Frigg's beloved.

Now valiant comes Valfather's Son,
Vidar, to vie with Valdyr in battle,
Plunges his sword into the Son of Hvedrung,
Avenging his father with a fell thrust.

Now the Son of Hlodyn and Odin comes
To fight with Fenris; fiercest of warriors,
He mauls in his rage all Middle-Earth;
Men in fear all flee their homesteads;

Nine paces back steps Bur's Son,
Retreats from the Worm, of taunts unafraid.

Now death is the portion of doomed men,
Red with blood the buildings of Gods,
The Sun turns black in the summer after,
Winds whine. *Well, would you know more?*

Earth sinks into the sea, the Sun turns black,
Cast down from Heaven are the hot stars,
Fumes reek, into flames burst,
The sky itself is scorched with fire.

I see Earth rising a second time
Out of the foam, fair and green;
Down from the fells, fish to capture,
Wings the eagle; waters flow.

At Ithervale the Aesir meet:
They remember the Worm of Middle-Earth,
Ponder again the Great Twilight
And the ancient runes of the High God.

Boards shall be found of a beauty to wonder at,
Boards of gold in the grass long after,
The chess-boards they owned in the olden days.

Unsown acres shall harvests bear,
Evil be abolished, Baldur return
And Hropt's Hall with Hoddur rebuild,
Wise Gods. *Well, would you know more?*

Haenir shall wield the wand of prophecy,
The sons of two brothers set up their dwelling
In wide Windhome. *Well, would you know more?*

Fairer than sunlight, I see a hall,
A hall thatched with gold in Gimle:

Kind lords shall live there in delight for ever.

Now rides the Strong One to Rainbow Door,
Powerful from heaven, the All-Ruler:
From the depths below a drake comes flying,
The Dark Dragon from Darkfell,
Bears on his pinions the bodies of men,
Soars overhead. I sink now.

From *Völuspà*
(trans. P. B. Taylor and W.H.A.)

Writing

❦

Literature is the effort of man to indemnify himself for the wrongs
of his condition.

EMERSON

The only end of writing is to enable readers better to enjoy life
or better to endure it.

DR. JOHNSON

When I stop drinking tea and eating bread and butter I say, "I've
had enough." But when I stop reading poems or novels I say,
"No more of that, no more of that."

A. CHEKHOV

There are two kinds of writers, those who are and those who
aren't. With the first, content and form belong together like soul
and body; with the second, they match each other like body and
clothes.

KARL KRAUS

It costs the writer no more effort to write *fortissimo* than *piano*, or *universe* than *garden*.

Cynicism in literary works usually signifies a certain element of disappointed ambition. When one no longer knows what to do in order to astonish and survive, one offers one's *pudenda* to the public gaze. Everyone knows perfectly well what he will see; but it is sufficient to make the gesture.

PAUL VALÉRY

Poetry avoids the last illusion of prose, which so gently sometimes and at others so passionately pretends that things are thus and thus. In poetry they are also thus and thus, but because the arrangement of the lines, the pattern within the whole, will have it so. Exquisitely leaning toward an implied untruth, prose persuades us that we can trust our natures to know things as they are; ostentatiously faithful to its own nature, poetry assures us that we cannot—we know only as we can.

CHARLES WILLIAMS

A man is a poet if the difficulties inherent in his art provide him with ideas; he is not a poet if they deprive him of ideas.

To write regular verses destroys an infinite number of fine possibilities, but at the same time it suggests a multitude of distant and totally unexpected thoughts.

Skilled verse is the art of a profound sceptic.

In poetry everything which *must* be said is almost impossible to say well.

PAUL VALÉRY

[A poem] begins in delight, it inclines to the impulse, it assumes direction with the first line laid down, it runs a course of lucky events, and ends in a clarification of life—not necessarily a great clarification, such as sects and cults are founded on, but in a momentary stay against confusion.

ROBERT FROST

I had towards the poetic art a quite peculiar relation which was only practical after I had cherished in my mind for a long time a subject which possessed me, a model which inspired me, a predecessor who attracted me, until at length, after I had moulded it in silence for years, something resulted which might be regarded as a creation of my own.

GOETHE

Darius

Fernazes the poet on the serious part
Of his epic poem is now at work.
How that the kingdom of the Persians
Was taken over by Darius son of Hystaspes. (From him
Is descended our own glorious monarch
Mithridates, called Dionysos and Eupator.) At this point
Philosophy is called for; he must analyse
The feelings which Darius must have had;
Arrogance perhaps and intoxication? No—rather
A sort of understanding of the vanity of greatness.
Upon this point the poet deeply meditates.

But his servant interrupts him who comes
Running in, and announces the momentous news.
The war with the Romans has begun.
The greater part of our army has crossed the frontiers.

The poet is dumbfounded. What a disaster!
How ever could our glorious monarch now,
Could Mithridates, Dionysos and Eupator,
Give any of his attention to Greek poems?—
To Greek poems, just fancy, in the midst of war!

Fernazes is worried. How unfortunate!
Just as he had it in his grasp with his "Dareios"
Positively to distinguish himself, and his critics,
His envious critics, once and for all to shut them up!
What a putting-off, what a putting-off of all his plans!

And if it were only a hold-up, well and good.
But let us see if we are even safe
Here in Amisos. It isn't a particularly strong town,
The Romans are most frightful enemies.

Can we ever bring it off with them,
We Cappadocians? Can it ever come to pass?
Can we be now a match for the legions?
Great gods, defenders of Asia, help us now.—

None the less in all his trouble and commotion,
Insistently still the poetic notion comes and goes—
Most likely of course arrogance and intoxication;
Arrogance and intoxication must have filled Darius.

C. CAVAFY
(trans. J. Mavrogordato)

Start and Finish

Thursday, September 30, 1926

. . . it is not oneself but something in the universe that one's left
with. It is this that is frightening and exciting in the midst of my
profound gloom, depression, boredom, whatever it is. One sees a
fin passing far out. What image can I reach to convey what I
mean? Really there's none, I think. The interesting thing is that
in all my feeling and thinking I have never come up against this
before. Life is, soberly and accurately, the oddest affair; has in it
the essence of reality. I used to feel this as a child—couldn't step
across a puddle once, I remember, for thinking how strange—
what am I? etc. But by writing I don't reach anything. All I

mean to make is a note of a curious state of mind. I hazard the guess that it may be the impulse behind another book.

Saturday, February 7, 1931

Here in the few minutes that remain, I must record, heaven be praised, the end of *The Waves*. I wrote the words O Death fifteen minutes ago, having reeled across the last ten pages with some moments of such intensity and intoxication that I seemed only to stumble after my own voice, or almost, after some sort of speaker (as when I was mad). I was almost afraid, remembering the voices that used to fly ahead. Anyhow, it is done; and I have been sitting these 15 minutes in a state of glory, and calm, and some tears, thinking of Thoby and if I could write Julian Thoby Stephen 1881–1906 on the first page. I suppose not. How physical the sense of triumph and relief is! Whether good or bad, it's done; and, as I certainly felt at the end, not merely finished, but rounded off, completed, the thing stated—how hastily, how fragmentarily I know; but I mean that I have netted that fin in the waste of water which appeared to me over the marshes out of my window at Rodmell when I was coming to an end of *To the Lighthouse*.

Tuesday, July 14, 1931

. . . my *Waves* account runs, I think, as follows:—

I began it, seriously, about September 10th 1929.

I finished the first version on April 10th 1930.

I began the second version on May 1st 1930.

I finished the second version on February 7th 1931

I began to correct the second version on May 1st 1931, finished 22nd June 1931.

I began to correct the typescript on 25th June 1931.

Shall finish (I hope) 18th July 1931.

Then remain only the proofs.

VIRGINIA WOOLF

In general, I do not draw well with literary men: not that I dislike them, but I never know what to say to them after I have praised their last publication. There are several exceptions, to be sure: but then they have either been men of the world, such as Scott, and Moore, etc., or visionaries out of it, such as Shelley, etc.

LORD BYRON

The business man and the artist are like matter and mind. We can never get either pure and without some alloy of the other.

SAMUEL BUTLER II

A poem is never finished, only abandoned.

PAUL VALÉRY

The artistic temperament is a disease which afflicts amateurs.

G. K. CHESTERTON

The manuscript in the drawer either rots or ripens.

MARIA VON EBNER-ESCHENBACH

On a Day's Stint

And long ere dinner-time I have
  Full eight close pages wrote.
What, Duty, hast thou now to crave?
  Well done, Sir Walter Scott!

WALTER SCOTT

Most of what I know about the writing of poetry, or, at least, the kind I am interested in writing, I discovered long before I took an interest in poetry itself.

Between the ages of six and twelve I spent a great many of my waking hours in the fabrication of a private secondary sacred world, the basic elements of which were (a) a limestone landscape mainly derived from the Pennine Moors in the North of England, and (b) an industry—lead mining.

It is no doubt psychologically significant that my sacred world was autistic, that is to say, I had no wish to share it with others nor could I have done so. However, though constructed for and inhabited by myself alone, I needed the help of others, my parents in particular, in collecting its materials; others had to procure for me the necessary textbooks on geology and machinery, maps, catalogues, guidebooks, and photographs, and, when occasion offered, to take me down real mines, tasks which they performed with unfailing patience and generosity.

From this activity, I learned certain principles which I was later to find applied to all artistic fabrication. Firstly, whatever other elements it may include, the initial impulse to create a secondary world is a feeling of awe aroused by encounters, in the primary world, with sacred beings or events. Though every work of art is a secondary world, such a world cannot be constructed *ex nihilo*, but is a selection and recombination of the contents of the primary world. Even the purest poem, in the French sense, is made of words, which are not the poet's private property but the communal creation of the linguistic group to which he belongs, so that their meaning can be looked up in a dictionary.

Secondly, in constructing my private world, I discovered that, though this was a game, that is to say, something I was free to do or not as I chose, not a necessity like eating or sleeping, no game can be played without rules. A secondary world must be as much a world of law as the primary. One may be free to decide what these laws shall be, but laws there must be.

As regards my particular lead-mining world, I decided, or rather, without conscious decision, I instinctively felt that I must impose two restrictions upon my freedom of fantasy. In choosing what objects were to be included, I was free to select this and reject that, on condition that both were real objects in the primary world, to choose, for example, between two kinds of water turbine, which could be found in a textbook on mining machinery or a manufacturer's catalogue; I was not allowed to invent one. In deciding how my world was to function, I could choose between two practical possibilities—a mine can be drained either by an adit or a pump—but physical impossibilities and magic means were forbidden. When I say forbidden, I mean that I felt, in some obscure way, that they were morally forbidden. Then there came a day when the moral issue became quite conscious. As I was planning my Platonic Idea of a concentrating mill, I ran into difficulties. I had to choose between two types of a certain machine for separating the slimes, called a buddle. One type I found more sacred or "beautiful," but the other type was, as I knew from my reading, the more efficient. At this point I realized that it was my moral duty to sacrifice my aesthetic preference to reality or truth.

When, later, I began to write poetry, I found that, for me at least, the same obligation was binding. That is to say, I cannot accept the doctrine that in poetry there is a "suspension of belief." A poet must never make a statement simply because it sounds poetically exciting; he must also believe it to be true. This does not mean, of course, that one can only appreciate a poet whose beliefs happen to coincide with one's own. It does mean, however, that one must be convinced that the poet really believes what he says, however odd the belief may seem to oneself.

What the poet has to convey is not "self-expression," but a view of a reality common to all, seen from a unique perspective, which it is his duty as well as his pleasure to share with others. To small truths as well as great, St. Augustine's words apply.

"The truth is neither mine nor his nor another's; but belongs to us all whom Thou callest to partake of it, warning us terribly, not to account it private to ourselves, lest we be deprived of it."

Addenda

One day, when I went out to my wood-pile, or rather my pile of stumps, I observed two large ants, the one red, the other much larger and black, fiercely contending with one another, and rolling over on the chips. It was evidently a struggle for life and death which had grown out of a serious feud. Having once got hold, they never let go of each other, but struggled and wrestled and rolled on the chips, each retaining his hold with mastiff-like pertinacity. Looking further, I found to my astonishment that the chips were covered with such combatants, that it was not a *duellum* but a *bellum*, a war between two races of ants, the red always pitted against the black, and frequently two red ones to one black. They covered all the hills and vales of my wood-yard, and, indeed, the ground was already strewn with the dead, both red and black. It was the only war I had ever witnessed, the only battle-field I ever trod while the battle was raging; internecine war; the red republicans and the black despots or imperialists. On every side they were engaged in deadly combat, yet without any noise that I could hear, and never human soldiers fought so resolutely. I watched a couple, in a little sunny valley amid the chips, that were fast locked in each other's embraces, now at noonday prepared to fight till the sun went down. The smaller red champion had fastened himself like a vice to his adversary's front, and through all the tumblings on that field never for an instant ceased to gnaw at one of his feelers near the root, having already caused the other to go by the board, while the stronger black one dashed him from side to side, and, as I saw on looking nearer, had divested him of several of his members. None manifested a disposition to retreat from the combat equal or unequal. It was evident that their battle-cry was conquer or die. They fought like mastiffs or bulldogs, who will not let go though all their legs are cut off. In the meanwhile there came along a single red ant on the side hill of this valley, evidently full of excitement, who either had dispatched his foe or had not yet taken part in the battle; probably the latter, for he had lost none of his limbs. He saw this unequal combat from afar – for the blacks were nearly twice the size of the reds – he drew near with rapid pace till he stood his guard within half an inch of the combatants, then, watching his opportunity, he sprang upon the black warrior and commenced his operations near the root of his right fore-leg, leaving the other to select among his own members, and so there were three united for life until death – as if a new kind of attraction had been invented, which put all other locks and cements to shame. . . .

I took up the chip on which the three I have particularly described were struggling, carried in into my house, and placed it under a tumbler on my window-sill, wishing to see the issue. Holding a microscope to the first-mentioned red ant, I saw that though he was assiduously gnawing at the near fore-leg of his enemy, having severed his remaining feeler, his own breast was all torn away, exposing what vitals he had there to the jaws of the black warrior, whose own breastplate was apparently too thick for him; and the dark carbuncles of his eyes shone with ferocity such as wars only could excite. They struggled for half an hour longer under the tumbler, and when I looked again, the black soldier had severed the heads of his foes from their bodies, and the former were hanging on either side of him still apparently as firmly fastened as ever, and he was endeavouring with feeble struggles, being without feelers and with only one or two legs, and I know not how many other wounds, to divest himself of them; which at length, after half an hour more, he had accomplished. I raised the tumbler, and he went off over the window-sill in that crippled state. Whether he finally survived that combat and had a pension settled on him, I do not know. But I thought that his industry would not be worth much thereafter.

Which part was victorious I never learned, nor the cause of the war. But I felt for the rest of that day as if I had had my feelings harrowed and excited by witnessing the struggle, the ferocity and carnage, of a human battle before my door.

H. D. THOREAU

Death

———————

Madam Life's a piece in bloom
   Death goes dogging everywhere:
She's the tenant of the room
   He's the ruffian on the stair.

You shall see her as a friend,
   You shall bilk him once or twice;
But he'll trap you in the end,
   And he'll stick you for her price.

With his kneebones at your chest,
   And his knuckles in your throat,
You would reason – plead – protest!
   Clutching at her petticoat.

But she's heard it all before,
   Well she knows you've had your fun,
Gingerly she gains the door,
   And your little job is done.

            W E. HENLEY

Death

———————

'Are you in pain, dear mother?'

'I think there's a pain somewhere in the room,' said Mrs. Gradgrind, but I couldn't positively say that I have got it.'

After this strange speech, she lay silent for some time. Louisa holding her hand, could feel no pulse; but kissing it, could see a slight thin shred of life in fluttering motion.

'You very seldom see your sister,' said Mrs. Gradgrind. 'She grows like you. I wish you would look at her. Sissy, bring her here.'

She was brought, and stood with her hand in her sister's. Louisa had observed her with her arm round Sissy's neck, and she felt the difference of this approach.

'Do you see the likeness, Louisa?'

'Yes, mother, I should think her like me. But' –

'Eh? Yes, I always say so,' Mrs. Gradgrind cried, with unexpected quickness, 'and that reminds me. I – I want to speak to you, my dear. Sissy, my good girl, leave us alone a minute.'

Louisa had relinquished the hand: had thought that her sister's was a better and brighter face than hers had ever been: had seen in it, not without a rising feeling of resentment, even in that place and at that time, something of the gentleness of the other face in the room: the sweet face with the trusting eyes, made paler than watching and sympathy made it, by the rich dark hair.

Left alone with her mother, Louisa saw her lying with an awful lull upon her face, like one who was floating away upon some great water, all resistance over, content to be carried down the stream. She put the shadow of a hand to her lips again, and recalled her.

'You were going to speak to me, mother.'

'Eh? Yes, to be sure, my dear. You know your father is almost always away now, and therefore I must write to him about it.'

'About what, mother? Don't be troubled. About what?'

'You must remember, my dear, that whenever I have said anything, on any subject, I have never heard the last of it, and consequently, that I have long left off saying anything.'

'I can hear you, mother.' But, it was only by dint of bending down to her ear, and at the same time attentively watching the lips as they moved, that she could link such faint and broken sounds into any chain of connection.

'You learnt a great deal, Louisa, and so did your brother. Ologies of all kinds, from morning to night, If there is any Ology left, of any description, that has not been worn to rags in this house, all I can say is, I hope I shall never hear its name.'

'I can hear you, mother, when you have strength to go on.' This, to keep her from floating away.

'But there is something – not an Ology at all – that your father has missed, or forgotten, Louisa. I don't know what it is. I have often sat with Sissy near me, and thought about it. I shall never get its name now. But your father may. It makes me restless. I want to write to him, to find out for God's sake, what it is. Give me a pen, give me a pen.'

Even the power of restlessness was gone, except from the poor head, which could just turn from side to side.

She fancied, however, that her request had been complied with, and that the pen she could not have held was in her hand. It matters little what figures of wonderful no-meaning she began to trace upon her wrappers. The hand soon stopped in the midst of them; the light that had always been feeble and dim behind the weak transparency went out; and even Mrs. Gradgrind, emerged from the shadow in which man walketh and disquieteth himself in vain, took upon her the dread solemnity of the sages and patriarchs.

CHARLES DICKENS

Fish

Man's life is warm, glad, sad, 'twixt loves and graves,
    Boundless in hope, honoured with pangs austere,
Heaven-gazing, and his angel-wings he craves: —
    The fish is swift, small-needing, vague yet clear,
A cold, sweet, silver life, wrapped in round waves,
    Quickened with touches of transporting fear.

LEIGH HUNT

Imagination

⟡

I hear that someone is painting a picture "Beethoven writing the Ninth Symphony". I could easily imagine the kind of thing such a picture would show me. But suppose someone wanted to represent what Goethe would have looked like writing the Ninth Symphony? Here I could imagine nothing that would not be embarrassing and ridiculous.

LUDWIG WITTGENSTEIN

Landscape, Industrial

⟡

It was a town of red brick, or of brick that would have been red if the smoke and ashes had allowed it; but, as matters stood, it was a town of machinery and tall chimneys, out of which interminable serpents of smoke trailed themselves for ever and ever, and never got uncoiled. It had a black canal in it, and a river that ran purple with ill-smelling dye, and vast piles of buildings full of windows where there was a rattling and a trembling all day long, and where the piston of the steam-engine worked monotonously up and down, like the head of an elephant in a state of melancholy madness. It contained several large streets all very like one another, and many small streets still more like one another, inhabited by people equally like one another, who all went in and out at the same hours, with the same sound upon the same pavements, to do the same work, and to whom every day was the same as yesterday and tomorrow, and every year the counterpart of the last and the next. . . .

You saw nothing in Coketown but what was severely workful.

If the members of a religious persuasion built a chapel there – as the members of eighteen religious persuasions had done – they made it a pious warehouse of red brick, with sometimes (but this only in highly ornamented examples) a bell in a bird-cage on the top of it. The solitary exception was the New Church; a stuccoed edifice with a square steeple over the door, terminating in four short pinnacles like florid wooden legs. All the public inscriptions in the town were painted alike, in severe characters of black and white. The jail might have been the infirmary, the infirmary might have been the jail, the town-hall might have been either, or both, or anything else, for anything that appeared to the contrary in the graces of their construction. Fact, fact, fact, everywhere in the material aspect of the town; fact, fact, fact, everywhere in the immaterial. The M'Choakum-child school was all fact, and the school of design was all fact, and the relations between master and man were all fact, and everything was fact between the lying-in hospital and the cemetery, and what you couldn't state in figures, or show to be purchaseable in the cheapest market and saleable in the dearest, was not, and never should be, world without end. Amen.

CHARLES DICKENS

Marriage

❧§❧

They went quietly down into the roaring streets, inseparable and blessed; and as they passed along in sunshine and in shade, the noisy and the eager, and the arrogant and the forward and the vain, fretted and chafed, and made their usual uproar.

CHARLES DICKENS

The Meeting of the Waters

There is not in this wide world a valley so sweet
As that vale in whose bosom the bright waters meet;
Oh! the last rays of feeling and life must depart,
Ere the bloom of that valley shall fade from my heart.

Yet it *was* not that Nature had shed o'er the scene
Her purest of crystal and brightest of green;
'Twas *not* her soft magic of streamlet or hill,
Oh! no – it was something more exquisite still.

'Twas that friends, the beloved of my bosom were near,
Who made every scene of enchantment more dear,
And who felt how the best charms of nature improve,
When we see them reflected from looks that we love.

Sweet vale of Avoca! how calm could I rest
In thy bosom of shade, with the friends I love best,
Where the storms that we feel in this cold world should cease,
And our hearts, like thy waters, be mingled in peace.

THOMAS MOORE

Mnemonics

On the chord we are starting,
And once more we're Mozarting.

SIGMUND SPAETH

Names, Proper

"I" is not the name of a person, nor "here" of a place, and "this" is not a name. But they are connected with names. Names are explained by means of them. It is also true that it is characteristic of physics not to use these words.

LUDWIG WITTGENSTEIN

Non-Sequitur, A

Because I am wild about women
I'm mad about the hills.

W. B. YEATS

Parrot, A

I saw it all, Polly, how when you call'd for sop
and your good friend the cook came and fill'd up your pan
you yerk'd it out deftly by beakfuls scattering it
away far as you might upon the sunny lawn
then summon'd with loud cry the little garden birds
to take their feast. Quickly came they flustering around
Ruddock and Merle and Finch squabbling among themselves
nor gave you thanks nor heed while you sat silently
watching, and I beside you in perplexity
lost in the maze of all mystery and all knowledge
felt how deep lieth the fount of man's benevolence
if a bird can share it and take pleasure in it.
    If you, my bird, I thought, had a philosophy
it might be a sounder scheme than what our moralists

propound: because thou, Poll, livest in the darkness
which human Reason searching from outside would pierce,
but, being of so feeble a candle-power, can only
show up to view the cloud that it illuminates.
Thus reason'd I: then marvell'd how you can adapt
your wild bird-mood to endure your tame environment
the domesticities of English household life
and your small brass-wire cabin, who sh'dst live on wing
harrying the tropical branch-flowering wilderness:
Yet Nature gave you a gift of easy mimicry
whereby you have come to win uncanny sympathies
and morsell'd utterance of our Germanic talk
as schoolmasters in Greek will flaunt their hackey'd tags
Φωναντα συνετοισιν and κτημα ξδ αει
ηγλωσσ ομωμαχ, η δε φρην ανωμετοε
tho' you with a better ear copy us more perfectly
nor without connotation as when you call'd for sop
all with that stumpy wooden tongue and vicious beak
that dry whistling shrieking tearing cutting pincer
now eagerly subservient to your cautious claws
exploring all varieties of attitude
in irrepressible blind groping for escape
– a very figure and image of man's soul on earth
the almighty cosmic Will fidgeting in a trap –
in your quenchless unknown desire for the unknown life
of which some homely British sailor robb'd you, alas!
'Tis all that doth your silly thoughts so busy keep
the while you sit moping like Patience on a perch
– *Wie viele Tag' und Nächte bist du geblieben!*
La possa delle gambe posta in tregue –
the impeccable spruceness of your grey-feather'd poll
a model in hairdressing for the dandiest old Duke
enough to qualify you for the House of Lords
or the Athenaeum Club, to poke among the nobs
great intellectual nobs and literary nobs
scientific nobs and Bishops *ex officio*:
nor lack you simulation of profoundest wisdom
such as men's features oft acquire in very old age
by mere cooling of passion and decay of muscle
by faint renunciation even of untold regrets;

who seeing themselves a picture of that which man should be
learn almost what it were to be what they are – not.
But you can never have cherish'd a determined hope
consciously to renounce or lose it, you will live
your three score years and ten idle and puzzle-headed
as any mumping monk in his unfurnish'd cell
in peace that, poor Polly, passeth Understanding –
merely because you lack what we men understand
by Understanding. Well! well! that's the difference
C'est la seule différence, mais c'est important.
Ah! your pale sedentary life! but would you change?
exchange it for one crowded hour of glorious life,
one blind furious tussle with a madden'd monkey
who would throttle you and throw your crude fragments away
shreds unintelligible of an unmeaning act
dans la profonde horreur de l'éternelle nuit?
Why ask? You cannot know. 'Twas by no choice of yours
that you mischanged for monkey's man's society,
'twas that British sailor drove you from Paradise –
Ειθ ωφελ Αργουσ μη διαπταθαι σκαφοε!
I'd hold embargoes on such a ghastly traffic.
I am writing verses to you and grieve that you sh'd be
absolument incapable de les comprendre,
Tu, Polle, nescis ista nec potes scire: –
Alas! Iambic, scazon and alexandrine,
spondee or choriamb, all is alike to you –
my well-continued fanciful experiment
wherein so many strange verses amalgamate
on the secure bedrock of Milton's prosody:
not but that when I speak you will incline an ear
in critical attention lest by chance I might
possibly say something that was worth repeating:
I am adding (do you think?) pages to literature
that gouty excrement of human intellect
accumulating slowly and everlastingly
depositing, like guano on the Peruvian shore,
to be perhaps exhumed in some remotest age
(*piis secunda, vate me, detur fuga*)
to fertilize the scanty dwarf'd intelligence
of a new race of beings the unhallow'd offspring

of them who shall have quite dismember'd and destroy'd
our temple of Christian faith and fair Hellenic art
just as that monkey would, poor Polly, have done for you.

ROBERT BRIDGES

War Song

———————

❦❧❦

In anguish we uplift
   A new unhallowed song:
The race is to the swift,
   The battle to the strong.

Of old it was ordained
   That we in packs like curs,
Some thirty million trained
   And licensed murderers,
In crime should live and act,
   If cunning folk say sooth
Who flay the naked fact
   And carve the heart of truth.

The rulers cry aloud,
   "We cannot cancel war,
The end and bloody shroud
   Of wrongs the worst abhor,
And order's swaddling band:
   Know that relentless strife
Remains by sea and land
   The holiest law of life.
From fear in every guise,
   From sloth, from lust of pelf,
By war's great sacrifice
   The world redeems itself.
War is the source, the theme
   Of art, the goal, the bent
And brilliant academe

Of noble sentiment;
The augury, the dawn
Of golden times of grace;
The true catholicon
And blood-bath of the race."

We thirty million trained
And licensed murderers,
Like zanies rigged, and chained
By drill and scourge and curse
In shackles of despair
We know not how to break –
What do we victims care
For art, what interest take
In things unseen, unheard?
Some diplomat no doubt
Will launch a heedless word,
And lurking war leap out.

We spell-bound armies then,
Huge brutes in dumb distress,
Machines compact of men
Who once had consciences,
Must trample harvests down –
Vineyard and corn and oil;
Dismantle town by town,
Hamlet and homestead spoil
On each appointed path,
Till lust of havoc light
A blood-red blaze of wrath
In every frenzied sight.

In many a mountain pass,
Or meadow green and fresh,
Mass shall encounter mass
Of shuddering human flesh;
Opposing ordnance roar
Across the swathes of slain,
And blood in torrents pour
In vain – always in vain.
For war breeds war again.

The shameful dream is past,
   The subtle maze untrod;
We recognize at last
   That war is not of God.
Wherefore we now uplift
   Our new unhallowed song:
The race is to the swift,
   The battle to the strong.

JOHN DAVIDSON

Windmill, A

. . . At eve thou loomest like a one-eyed giant
   To some poor crazy knight, who pricks along
And sees thee wave in haze thy arms defiant,
   And growl the burden of thy grinding song.

Against thy russet sail-sheet slowly turning,
   The raven beats belated in the blast:
Behind thee ghastly, blood-red Eve is burning,
   Above, rose-feathered drifts are racking fast.

The curlews pipe around their plaintive dirges,
   Thou art a Pharos to the sea-mews hoar,
Set sheer above the tumult of the surges,
   As sea-mark on some spacious ocean floor.

My heart is sick with gazing on thy feature,
   Old blackened sugar-loaf with fourfold wings,
Thou seemest as some monstrous insect creature,
   Some mighty chafer armed with iron stings.

Emblem of man who, after all his moaning,
   And strain of dire immeasurable strife,
Has yet this consolation, all atoning –
   Life, as a windmill grinds the bread of Life.

LORD DE TABLEY

Acknowledgments (*continued from copyright page*)

Acknowledgement is made to the following publishers and authors or their representatives for their permission to use copyright material. Every reasonable effort has been made to clear the use of the material in this volume with the copyright owners. If notified of any omissions the editor and publisher will gladly make the proper corrections in future editions.

George Allen & Unwin Ltd.: "Zero" from *Number: The Language of Science* by Tobias Dantzig. From "Fellowship of the Ring" from *Lord of the Rings* by J. R. R. Tolkien.

Arion: For *The Night Watch* by Ennius, translated by Janet Lembke. *Arion* (6.3) 1967.

John Baker Publishers Ltd.: From *Roman Roads in Britain* by Ivan Margary.

Basic Books, Inc.: From *The Ambidextrous Universe* by Martin Gardner. Copyright © 1964 by Martin Gardner.

Basil Blackwell: From *The Discovery of Mind* translated by Bruno Snell. From *The Klephtic Ballads* translated by John Baggally.

Cambridge University Press, New York: From *Non-Dramatic Literature of the 16th Century* and *The Discarded Image* by C. S. Lewis. From *Góngora* translated by Edward Wilson.

Cambridge University Press, London: From the works of A. N. Whitehead.

Chappell & Co. Ltd.: "Take Him." Words by Lorenz Hart. Copyright © 1952 Chappell & Co. Inc. Reproduced by permission of Chappell & Co. Ltd., London.

The Clarendon Press, Oxford: From *Taliessin through Logres* by Charles Williams, 1938. From *The Heroic Recitations of the Bahima of Ankole* by H. F. Morris, 1964. From *Somali Poetry: An Introduction* by B. W. Andrzejewski and I. M. Lewis, 1964. From *A History of Technology* edited by Charles Singer et al., Vol. 1, 1954 (author, E. R. Reach).

Miss D. E. Collins, representing the author's estate, and A. P. Watt & Son: For extracts from the works of G. K. Chesterton.

Constable & Co. Ltd.: From "The Concept of Cure" by Anthony Storr, from *Psychoanalysis Observed* edited by Charles Rycroft. From *The Desert Fathers* translated by Helen Waddell.

Curtis Brown Ltd., New York: From *Elective Affinities* by Goethe, translated by Elizabeth Mayer and Louise Bogan. Copyright © 1963 by Henry Regnery Company. Reprinted by permission of Curtis Brown Ltd.

The John Day Company: "Journey to the North" and "Chariots Go Forth to War" from *The White Pony* by Tu Fu, translated by Pu Hsiang-hsing, edited by Robert Payne. Copyright 1947 by The John Day Co. Reprinted by permission of the editor.

J. M. Dent & Sons Ltd.: "Samson Agonist̲e̲s̲" from *Family Reunion* by Ogden Nash.

Gerald Duckworth & Co. Ltd.: From *The Flower Beneath the Foot* and *Concerning the Eccentricities of Cardinal Pirelli* by Ronald Firbank.

Encounter: From *On Science and Culture* by J. Robert Oppenheimer, which appeared in the October 1962 issue.

Evans Brothers Ltd.: From *My Memories of Six Reigns* by Princess Marie Louise.

Faber and Faber Ltd.: From Chapter VIII, "Experiments", from *History in English Words* by Owen Barfield. "Buildings as Drawn by Girls and by Boys" from *Identity: Youth and Crisis* by Erik H. Erikson. From *Markings* by Dag Hammarskjöld, translated by W. J. Sjöberg and W. H. Auden. "In the Beginning" from *The Anathemata* by David Jones. "Solvitur Acris Hiems" by Horace, translated by Louis MacNeice, from *The Collected Poems of Louis MacNeice*. "The Gate" from *Collected Poems* by Edwin Muir. "Peter" and an extract from "The Pangolin" from *Complete Poems of Marianne Moore*.

Victor Gollancz Ltd.: From *Crowds and Power* by Elias Cannetti.

Granada Publishing Ltd.: From "Asphodel, That Greeny Flower" from *Pictures from Brueghel* by William Carlos Williams.

Robert Graves and A. P. Watt & Son: "The Climate of Thought" and "Rhea" from *Collected Poems* by Robert Graves.

John Howard Griffin: From *Black Like Me* by John Howard Griffin.

Grune & Stratton, Inc.: From *Strategies of Family Therapy*. Reprinted by permission of Grune & Stratton, Inc. and Jay Haley.

Michael Hamburger: For the translation of "When from the Heavens . . ." and "Tears" by Friedrich Hölderlin.

Hamish Hamilton Ltd.: From *Conversations with Max*. Copyright © 1960 by S. N. Behrman.

Harper & Row, Publishers: From *Through the Valley of the Kwai* by Ernest Gordon. Copyright © 1962 by Ernest Gordon. By permission of Harper & Row, Publishers.

Rupert Hart-Davis: "Park Concert" by James Michie and "The Mole" by Andrew Young.

A. M. Heath & Co. Ltd.: From *August for the People* by Nigel Dennis. By permission of Nigel Dennis.

David Higham Associates Ltd.: From *Odes of Horace* by James Michie, published by The Bodley Head. From *The Descent of the Dove* by Charles Williams, published by Faber and Faber Ltd. From *The Pendulum* by Anthony Rossiter, published by Victor Gollancz Ltd.

Hodder and Stoughton Ltd.: From *The Making of the English Landscape* by W. G. Hoskins.

The Hogarth Press Ltd., Quentin Bell and Angelica Garnett: From *A Writer's Diary* by Virginia Woolf.

The Hogarth Press Ltd. and the Literary Estate of the translator: "Darius" from *Poems* by C. P. Cavafy, translated by J. Mavrogodato.

The Hogarth Press Ltd. and Alan Hodge: "A Modern Nightmare" from *Collected Poems* by Norman Cameron.

The Hutchinson Publishing Group Ltd.: From *Poems* by Ivor Gurney.

John Johnson: "The Thunderstorm" from *Limestone and other stories* by Adalbert Stifter, translated by David Luke.

McIntosh and Otis Inc.: From *My Life with the Eskimo* by Vilhjalmur Stefansson.

Macmillan & Co. Ltd., London: "The Last Signal", "She Revisits Alone the Church of her Marriage", "During Wind and Rain" from the *Collected Poems of Thomas Hardy;* "Walcheren Island: Dumb Show" from *The Dynasts* by Thomas Hardy. By permission of the Trustees of the Hardy Estate and Macmillan & Co. Ltd.

The Macmillan Company, New York: From *The Empty Fortress* by Bruno Bettelheim.

Methuen & Co. Ltd.: From *King Solomon's Ring* by Konrad Lorenz.

John Murray: From *In the Antarctic* by Frank Debenham. From *Earth's Company* by Leslie Reid.

John Murray and The Houghton Mifflin Co.: "False Security" and "I. M. Walter Ramsden" by John Betjeman.

New Directions Publishing Corporation: From *Rhymes and More Rhymes of a PFC* by Lincoln Kirstein. Copyright © 1964, 1966 by Lincoln Kirstein.

The New York Review of Books: Passage on James D. Watson by P. B. Medawar. Copyright © 1968 The New York Review. Reprinted with permission from *The New York Review of Books.*

James Nisbet & Co. Ltd.: From *The Names of the Stars* by C. C. J. Webb, and from *The Changing Face of England* by Anthony Collett.

The Observer: "Dreams" by John Davy. Reprinted from *The Observer* of August 13, 1967.

Oxford University Press, New York: From *Christianity and Classical Culture* by C. N. Cochrane.

Oxford University Press, London: "Hunting a Hare" from *Antiworlds and the Fifth Ace* by Andrei Voznesensky, translated by W. H. Auden.

Penguin Books Ltd.: "Deor" and "Wulf and Edwacer" from *The Earliest English Poems* translated by M. Alexander. "Chamber Music" from *20th Century German Verse* translated by Joseph Weinheber, and passage and poem by Rimbaud, translated by Oliver Bernard. "The Lettuce" and "Cygnet" from *The Penguin Book of Latin Verse* translated by Frederick Brittain.

A. D. Peters & Co.: *Imaginary Book Reviews* by J. B. Norton. Originally printed in the *Daily Express*. Reprinted by permission of A. D. Peters & Company. "Trench Nomenclature" from *Undertones of War* by Edmund Blunden, published by William Collins Sons & Co. Ltd. Reprinted by permission of A. D. Peters & Company.

Laurence Pollinger Ltd. and the Estate of the late Mrs. Frieda Lawrence: "Bibbles", excerpt from "She Goat" and "Tortoise Family Connections" from *The Complete Poems of D. H. Lawrence*, published by William Heinemann Ltd.

Laurence Pollinger Ltd. and Holt, Rinehart & Winston, Inc.: "The Middleness of the Road" and "Were I in Trouble" from *The Complete Poems of Robert Frost*, published by Jonathan Cape Ltd.

Princeton University Press: From *Mimesis: The Representation of Reality in Western Literature* by Erich Auerbach, translated by W. R. Trask (Princeton University Press, 1953; Princeton Paperback, 1968). Reprinted by permission of Princeton University Press.

G. P. Putnam's Sons: From *Across the Arctic America* by Knud Rasmussen. Copyright 1927 by G. P. Putnam's Sons.

The Ronald Press Company: From *Learning Theory and Personality Dynamics* by O. Hobart Mowrer. Copyright 1950 The Ronald Press Company, New York.

Routledge & Kegan Paul Ltd.: From *Gravity and Grace* and *The Notebooks of Simone Weil* by Simone Weil. "Winter Gold" and "Islands of the Earthly Paradise" from *A Celtic Miscellany* by K. H. Jackson.

Russell & Volkening, Inc.: From *An Alphabet for Gourmets* by M. F. K. Fisher, published by Viking Press Inc. Copyright © 1948, 1949 by M. F. K. Fisher.

Schocken Books, Inc.: From *Franz Rosenzweig: His Life and Thought by* Nahum N. Glatzer. Copyright © 1053, 1961 by Schocken Books, Inc. Reprinted by permission of Schocken Books, Inc.

Scientific American, Inc. and W. H. Freeman and Company: From "Leaf Shape" by Eric Ashby. Copyright © 1949 by Scientific American, Inc. All rights reserved.

Scott Meredith Literary Agency, Inc.: From *The Big Love* by Florence Aadland. Copyright © 1961 by Lancer Books, Inc. Reprinted by permission of the author and her agents, Scott Meredith Literary Agency, Inc., 580 Fifth Avenue, New York, N.Y. 10036.

Martin Secker & Warburg Ltd.: From *My Dog Tulip* by J. R. Ackerley. "The Long Cat" from *Creatures Great and Small* by Colette.

Simon & Schuster, Inc.: From *Dictionary of Cuisine* by Dumas, translated by Louis Colman. Reprinted by permission of the translator.

The Society of Authors: "De Profundis" and an extract from "Winged Chariot" by Walter de la Mare. Reprinted by permission of the Literary Trustees of Walter de la Mare and The Society of

Authors as their representative. "When the bells justle in the Tower" by A. E. Housman. Reprinted by permission of The Society of Authors as the literary representative of the Estate of A. E. Housman, and Jonathan Cape Ltd., publishers of A. E. Housman's *Collected Poems*.

The Souvenir Press Ltd.: "The Summit" from *The Mountain of my Fear* by David Roberts.

Sunday Telegraph: "Intercom in Nasakom" by Towyn Mason. Reprinted by permission of the *Sunday Telegraph* and Towyn Mason.

Thames and Hudson Ltd.: From *The Informed Heart* by Bruno Bettelheim.

Myfanwy Thomas: "Home", "Roads" and "Rain" by Edward Thomas.

Helen Thurber: From "Soapland" in *My World—and Welcome to It,* published by Harcourt, Brace & World, New York. Originally printed in *The New Yorker*.

A. P. Watt & Son: From *Lucia's Progress* by E. F. Benson. By permission of The Executors of the late E. F. Benson and William Heinemann Ltd.

Weidenfeld (Publishers) Ltd.: "A Commandant Reminisces" from *Commandant of Auschwitz* by Rudolf Hoess. From *The Intellectual History of Europe* by Friedrich Heer. "Naming Animals" from *The Savage Mind* by Claude Lévi-Strauss.

The World Publishing Company, New York: From *The Face of Violence* by J. Bronowski. Copyright © 1967 by J. Bronowski.

Yale University Press: "Little City" from *A Beginning* by Robert Horan. Copyright © 1948 by Yale University Press. Reprinted by permission of Yale University Press.

Basile Yanovsky: For passage on "Anesthesia". Copyright © 1970 by Basile Yanovsky.

Professor G. E. M. Anscombe: From *Philosophical Investigations* by Ludwig Wittgenstein. Published by Basil Blackwell.

The Clarendon Press, Oxford: "Poor Poll" from *The Poetical Works of Robert Bridges* 1936.

Index of Authors, Translators, and Other Sources